TAKING SIDES

Clashing Views in

Childhood and Society

SIXTH EDITION

TAKING SIDES

Clashing Views in

Childhood and Society

SIXTH EDITION

Selected, Edited, and with Introductions by

Diana S. DelCampo
New Mexico State University

and

Robert L. DelCampo
New Mexico State University

Mc Graw Hill **Contemporary Learning Series**

A Division of The McGraw-Hill Companies

Photo Acknowledgment
Cover image: Geostock/Getty Images

Cover Acknowledgment
Maggie Lytle

Manufactured in the United States of America

Sixth Edition

123456789DOCDOC98765

Library of Congress Cataloging-in-Publication Data
Main entry under title:
Taking sides: clashing views on controversial issues in childhood and society/selected, edited, and
with introductions by Diana S. DelCampo and Robert L. DelCampo.—6th ed.
Includes bibliographical references and index.
1. Children—United States. 2. Child welfare—United States. I. DelCampo, Diana S., comp. II.
DelCampo, Robert L., comp.
                                                            305.23

0-07-319507-3
ISSN: 1094-7558

Printed on Recycled Paper

Preface

Children are society's most valuable resource, and however clichéd that idea may be, there can be no doubt about the urgency of the issues confronting children today and the people who care for them and care about them. Each day we are bombarded with media reports on issues affecting children—complex issues related to child care, schooling, violence, morality, gangs, divorce; the list goes on. In this book we look at 17 of those controversial issues and ask you to think about them, perhaps for the first time, perhaps in ways you may not have previously considered.

For the student who likes to memorize facts and learn *the* right answer, the controversies in this book could be most unsettling! However, a good education should include the nurturing of your ability to think critically and to be an active learner. This book endeavors to put you on the path toward further developing these skills. As you read each side of an issue and grapple with the points made by the authors, you will be moved to consider the merits of each position. In the process, you may adopt the point of view of one side, or the other, or formulate an opinion completely your own on the issue. And when you attend class, you will be exposed to your classmates' and instructor's ideas on the issue as well. This may further challenge you to reconsider and defend your position, which is the essence of critical thinking and a primary purpose of this book.

Plan of the book *Taking Sides: Clashing Views in Childhood and Society,* sixth edition, is designed to be used for courses in child development, human development, or parenting. The issues can be studied consecutively or in any order, as each is designed to be independent of the other. We have included 17 issues encompassing 34 selections from a wide variety of sources and authors. Each part of the book deals with one of four developmental phases of childhood: infancy, early childhood, middle childhood, and adolescence. Within each part are issues related to aspects of child development at that stage. Each issue has an *introduction,* which provides some background about the controversy, briefly describes the authors, and gives a brief summary of the positions reflected in the issue. Each issue concludes with a *postscript,* which contains some final thoughts on the issue and offers a bibliography of related readings should you want to explore the topic further.

A listing of all the *contributors* to this volume is included at the back of the book to give you additional information on the scholars, practitioners, educators, policymakers, and social critics whose views are debated here.

Changes to this edition The sixth edition of *Taking Sides: Clashing Views in Childhood and Society* includes some important changes from the fifth edition. Two completely new issues have been added, and two previous issues have new selections. As a result, there are eight new readings. The new issues are "Is Television Viewing Responsible for the Rise in Childhood Obesity?" (Issue 11) and "Is Gay Adoption and Foster Parenting Healthy for Children?" (Issue 13). Issue 2, "Does Maternal Employment Have Negative Effects on Children's Development?" has been renamed and has two new selections. Issue 5, "Is Spanking Detrimental to Children?" has two new selections.

In addition to changes in topics and selections, the *On the Internet* page that precedes each part opener has been updated. For these pages, several relevant sites on the World Wide Web have been identified and annotated.

A word to the instructor   An *Instructor's Manual With Test Questions* (both multiple-choice and essay) is available through the publisher for the instructor using this volume of *Taking Sides*. A general guidebook, *Using Taking Sides in the Classroom*, which discusses methods and techniques for integrating the pro-con approach into any classroom setting, is also available. An online version of *Using Taking Sides in the Classroom* and a correspondence service for Taking Sides adopters can be found at http://www.mhcls.com/usingts.

Taking Sides: Clashing Views in Childhood and Society is only one title in the Taking Sides series. If you are interested in seeing the table of contents for any of the other titles, please visit the Taking Sides Web site at http://www.mhcls.com/takingsides/.

Acknowledgments   We would like to thank Tara Alderete and Annette Flores for assisting with the sixth edition of the book.

We also want to extend warm thanks to Jill Peter, Senior Developmental Editor, McGraw-Hill Contemporary Learning Series.

We look forward to receiving feedback and comments on this sixth edition of *Taking Sides: Clashing Views in Childhood and Society* from both faculty and students who experience the book. We can be reached via the Internet (ddelcamp@nmsu.edu or rdelcamp@nmsu.edu), or you can write us in care of the Taking Sides series at McGraw-Hill Contemporary Learning Series.

Diana S. DelCampo
New Mexico State University

Robert L. DelCampo
New Mexico State University

Contents In Brief

Contents

Kyla Dunn, a former biotech researcher and now a reporter for PBS and CBS, details the six months that she spent with scientists inside the labs of Advanced Cell Technology (ACT), a group openly pursuing human cloning for medical purposes. Dunn outlines what the group hopes to accomplish through cloning, why the group believes that cloning is the best way to accomplish these goals, and the political and monetary trials that ACT faces. Robert A. Weinberg, a member of the Whitehead Institute for Biomedical Research and a biology professor at MIT, offers his concerns about what he calls the "cloning circus." Weinberg discusses the damage that many cloning groups have been doing to serious research and the impending dangers of reproductive cloning.

Leslie Doty Hollingsworth, assistant professor at the University of Michigan, contends that socialization within an African American family is a unique and distinct experience for children. As a consequence, children not socialized in these families cannot effectively embrace African American definitions of self and family. Rudolph Alexander, Jr. and Carla M. Curtis, both professors at Ohio State University, offer research maintaining that African American children are not psychologically harmed by transracial adoptions.

Columbia University researcher Elizabeth Thompson Gershoff analyzed results from 88 studies and concluded that corporal punishment negatively affected children's behavior. Among the 10 negative outcomes were increased child aggression, decreased quality of the parent-child relationship, and increased risk of abusing a child or spouse in adulthood. Diana Baumrind and Philip A. Cowan, researchers from the University of California-Berkeley, and Robert E. Larzelere, from the Nebraska Medical Center, refuted Gershoff's findings by questioning her definition of corporal punishment and analysis techniques of the 88 studies. They feel mild spankings, when appropriately administered, are useful in shaping children's behavior.

Wade F. Horn, who heads the Marriage Initiative for President George W. Bush, asserts that marriage can remedy the ills of society, including family poverty and poor living standards for children. Stephanie Coontz, author and family advocate, and Nancy Folbre, professor of economics at the University of Massachusetts, contend that improving the living standards of children is a complicated issue, which needs to be approached from many different angles in order to make improvements.

Professor of sociology David Popenoe contends that children from single-parent families and stepfamilies are more likely to have emotional problems and health problems and to do poorly in school than children from intact families with two biological parents. Psychologist Lawrence A. Kurdek maintains that multiple-divorce families, not stepfamilies, differ from two-parent families and that stepfamilies are not inherently problematic for children.

The Henry J. Kaiser Family Foundation, a private non-profit foundation focusing on major health care issues facing the nation, cites research studies that show that the more children watch television; the more likely they will be overweight. They also contend that the rise in childhood obesity can be traced to the increased use of media. The Center for Science in the Public Interest, a consumer advocacy organization on nutrition and health, views the high-calorie, non-nutritious foods found in school vending machines as the culprit in the rise in childhood obesity rates.

Stephen Krashen, professor of education at the University of Southern California, contends that good bilingual education programs provide background knowledge of subject matter and literacy in the child's native language. Then, the program provides English input using English as a second language technique along with sheltered subject matter teaching in English. Krashen argues against assertions that immersion is more successful than bilingual education. Rosalie Pedalino Porter, director for the Institute for Research in English Acquisition and Development (READ), states that bilingual education is a failed endeavor. Porter cites drop-out rates and parental sentiment as evidence as to why bilingual education should be discontinued.

The National Adoption Information Clearinghouse (NAIC) presents facts regarding gay and lesbian adoptive parents. The NAIC gives current information on the background and laws regarding homosexual parenting, and confronts the issues and concerns many people have regarding homosexual adoption, including the idea that children are molested by homosexual parents. Dr. Paul Cameron, of the Family Research Institute, presents his case against allowing homosexuals to become parents—foster parents in particular. He mainly discusses case study information regarding the proclivity for homosexual parents to molest foster children.

Lisa Kolb, a public information specialist, asserts that the family preservation model is the best way to help families in crisis. Family preservation keeps all the family members together in the home while helping the family solve its problems. Freelance writer Mary-Lou Weisman argues that orphanages and out-of-home placements are necessary for children whose parents abuse or neglect them. She maintains that society has an obligation to take children away from parents who are doing serious harm to them and that some children have their only real family experience when living in an institutional setting.

Lisbeth B. Schorr, director of the Harvard University Project on Effective Services, contends that organized intervention programs are working to circumvent social problems such as teen pregnancy, juvenile crime, and school dropout rates. William J. Bennett, former secretary of education and former director of the Office of National Drug Control Policy, sees the decline of the two-parent family and moral confusion as the primary reasons for children's poor living conditions.

Kerby Anderson, president of Probe Ministries International, finds fault with traditional comprehensive sex education. Anderson demonstrates how, in his view, there is a need for abstinence-only sex education by presenting statistics and examples from case studies that support his assertion. Advocates for Youth helps young people make informed and responsible decisions about their reproductive and sexual health. The Sexuality Information and Education Council of the United States (SIECUS) is a national nonprofit organization that promotes comprehensive education about sexuality and advocates the right of individuals to make responsible sexual choices. In this selection, the organizations compare abstinence-only sex education to comprehensive sex education, outline the shortcomings of abstinence-only sex education, and show support for comprehensive sex education.

May Benatar, a clinical social worker, argues that the mass media and contemporary culture question the accuracy and truthfulness of survivors of sexual abuse. By doing this, the long-term effects of these abuses tend to be minimized. Susan P. Robbins, an associate professor of social work, contends that the reason some professionals are skeptical of recovered memories is that there is no research that supports the accuracy of recovered memory. She cautions that the indiscriminate acceptance of recovered memories can lead to a serious backlash of disbelief when legitimate cases of abuse are reported.

Introduction

Children in Society

Diana S. DelCampo
Robert L. DelCampo

Childhood can be a wondrous time when days are filled with play and new discoveries, nights provide rest and security, and dedicated, loving parents nurture their children and meet their needs. Some children do indeed experience the full joy of childhood; however, regretfully, there are other, more sobering scenarios: There are children who do not have nurturing adults to guide them, who go to bed hungry, and some who do not even have homes. Most typically, childhood experiences fall between these two extremes. So there is a wide variety of experiences that can impact the developing child, and larger social forces are at work as well. Ask yourself as you debate the issues in this book the extent to which society must collectively address and resolve them. This a vital function of society because children are society's future.

In order to understand and appreciate children in contemporary society, it may be useful to briefly review how society's views of children have changed over time. Most child development texts review the history of adult perceptions of children in western European society. Would it surprise you to know that in ancient times children were sometimes killed as religious sacrifices and buried in the walls of buildings? People believed that this practice would strengthen a building's structure. Up until the fourth century, parents were legally allowed to kill their newborns if the children were not in good health at birth. They were also permitted to do away with a child if they already had too many children, if the child was female, or if the child was illegitimate. In 374 A.D., the Romans outlawed infanticide, hoping that this would end the killing. Since parents could no longer legally kill their children, unwanted infants began to be abandoned. This practice endured for over 1,000 years. It was not until the 1600s that child abandonment was outlawed throughout most of Europe.

During the seventeenth century, foundling homes were established to provide for the needs of unwanted children. During this period, children were considered to be miniature adults. They were dressed like adults and were expected to act as adults would act. By contemporary standards, parents took a rather casual attitude toward their children. This was probably due to the high child mortality rate at the time. Since parents thought it likely that their children would die in infancy or childhood, they did not get as emotionally close to their young children as parents typically do today. It was not until the end of the century that society began to look upon children as different from adults.

Early in the 1700s European societal attitudes about children underwent further change. Children were no longer considered to be miniature adults, and literature written specifically for children began to emerge. By the end of the century, children who went to school were grouped by age, reflecting an awareness of stages of growth. The eighteenth century also marked the rise of the systematic study of children, which centered around the moral development of children and child-rearing problems.

It was not until the beginning of the twentieth century that three distinct age groupings emerged in the study of human development: infancy through age four or five; childhood to late puberty or early adulthood; and adulthood. This time period also marked the beginnings of the distinct field of child study. Early child study emphasized descriptive accounts of individual children and was mainly concerned with aspects of physical growth. As the century progressed, the term *child study* was changed to *research in child development*. Mothering became an important concept in the study of early child development, and the psychological aspects of development began to be examined more rigorously. Today, in the twenty-first century, research in child development focuses on issues related to family systems and the larger social issues that affect child development.

Nature-Nurture Controversy

There are many things that impact individuals as they progress through the human life cycle. People, places, events, illnesses, education, success, failure—have you ever thought about the number of experiences each of us encounters in our lives? If one were to place all of the variables that influence human development into two general categories, those categories would be heredity and environment. As you may know, your genetic blueprint was determined at the moment of conception with chromosomes contributed by your father and mother. In a sense, for many of us, environment is also determined at the moment of conception. A good portion of the major elements of what makes up one's environment is often determined before a person is born. The society in which one will live, one's cultural and ethnic heritage, and one's family and subsequent socioeconomic status, for example, are usually predetermined for a child.

For this edition of *Taking Sides: Clashing Views in Childhood and Society*, we have selected articles that look at children in general and how they affect or are affected by the issues raised, rather than give you, the reader, clinical case examples of issues related to a certain child or children. For the purposes of this book, we make three assumptions: (1) When we discuss a child's environment, we are usually describing elements of the society in which a child is growing, developing, and otherwise being socialized; (2) all child development occurs within this social context; and (3) children cannot help but affect and be affected by the societal forces that surround them. In most university classes, students derive a certain sense of security in receiving definitions of terms that are used frequently in a given class. We offer the following one for *society,* which we have adapted from Richard J. Gelles's 1995 textbook *Contemporary Families:*

> Society is a collection of people who interact within socially structured relationships. The only way that societies can survive their original members is by replacing them. These "replacements" are the children about whom the issues in this book are concerned.

Determining an appropriate group of societal issues and fitting them into the confines of only one work on children and society is a challenging task. Consider, for example, the diversity of contemporary society. We live in a sea of divergent and unique subcultures and ethnicities. Categorizing and describing the myriad values, customs, and belief systems of these groups could fill many volumes. In America and Canada, for example, there are many ethnic subgroups of citizens who are considered to be of Anglo descent, such as English, Irish, Italians, Polish, Germans, Greeks, Russians, and Scots. There are people of native descent, who are affiliated with scores of different tribes and subtribes. Some Canadian and American citizens trace their heritages to a variety of Asian countries, including China, Japan, Vietnam, Cambodia, Thailand, and the Philippines. Among blacks, there are those who trace their roots to the Caribbean region and those who identify with different regions of Africa.

In light of the above, it may be reasoned that there are really no "typical" children in society! Although there are strong arguments supporting similarities within each of these general groups, there is a wide array of subgroupings and differences in customs and beliefs. As a consequence, when reading a book such as this one, it is important to be mindful of the extent to which differences might exist for those who may be of another race, ethnicity, religion, or socioeconomic status than the target group of children about which a selection focuses. It would also be prudent to consider geographic locale—rural, urban, northeastern, southwestern—when considering the relevance of a given argument to a specific subgroup of children.

Children in Contemporary Society

It is worth understanding children's points of view as they are molded by society. It can be astonishing to take a step back and observe children as they undergo the socialization process in contemporary society. They come into the world totally helpless, unable to feed, care for, or protect themselves. As they grow and develop, children undertake the process of acquiring a sense of identity and learning the rules of the society in which they live. This process of socialization is fostered by many of the subsystems of society that provide prescriptions for behavior in particular areas of life. These subsystems include the family, the peer group, the school system, religion, and the media.

One important consideration is that up to about age five, children are oblivious to most racial, ethnic, religious, or socioeconomic differences. Typically, children can only realize differences in external appearance. One implication of this fact is that children can be much more amenable to learning and embracing a variety of cultural behaviors, attitudes, and even languages when they are young. Only as children move into middle childhood do they begin to recognize and understand other, more subtle differences. It is important to note that although young children may be oblivious to these differences, they are nonetheless impacted by them in the way they are socialized by their parents, families, and the significant others in their lives. This is done through family rituals, traditions, and outings; religious ceremonies; types of food prepared in the home; location where children live; and things that are found in the home, such as books, magazines, music, and so on.

Societal influences on children do not stop within the family system. As children grow, other institutions in society, such as schools, the economy, politics, and religion, expand their life experiences. Controversy arises as to how children react to these experiences. Consider, for example, what happens to children when both parents are employed outside the home. There are factions in our society who adamantly ascribe many of the problems associated with children to the fact that many parents are overly involved with work at the expense of time with their children. They contend that one parent (usually the mother) should stay home with the children, especially when they are young. Children who care for themselves after school and the quality of after-school child care are also hotly contested, related issues.

Few readers of this book will be unfamiliar with the attacks on the mass media for its portrayal of violence in movies, television programming, and video games targeted at children. Again, researchers, clinicians, teachers, policymakers, and others fall on both sides of what should be done to address this.

As children move toward adolescence and become more independent, concerns regarding identity, values, morals, and sexual behavior become issues of controversy. Homosexuality, for example, which often is first evidenced by a person in adolescence, is considered by many to be a learned and abhorrent form of sexual expression. Others believe that there are people who are predisposed to homosexuality for reasons that are as yet unclear.

Events in contemporary society have a direct or indirect impact on children, despite attempts to protect them. Violence, inflation, war, poverty, AIDS, racism, and new technology are just a few of the phenomena that shape the society in which our children are socialized.

Researching Children

In finding answers to controversial topics, policymakers and the public alike often look to research literature for clues. The typical college student might think of researching a topic as going to the library or logging onto the Internet and looking up information on a subject, reading that information, formulating a conclusion or opinion about the topic, and writing a paper that conveys the student's findings. This is not the type of research about which we are referring! The type of research that we refer to here is called empirical research. This means that there is some question or group of interrelated questions to be answered about a topic. Data are then collected relative to the topic, and this typically sheds light on how one goes about answering the question.

Data collection in research on children is undertaken from a variety of approaches. It could entail things like observing children at play in preschool or interacting with their parents at home. This is called observing children in a natural setting. With this method, observers must code behavior in the same way each and every time it is seen. Most of the information we have today on physical growth and developmental stages was acquired through observation by child development pioneers such as Arnold Gessell and Louise Bates Ames. You can imagine how time-consuming this form of study must be.

Another type of data collection is called an experiment. Experimental researchers systematically control how certain things happen in a situation and then observe the results. In this type of research, an experimental group and a control group are chosen. Both groups are examined to determine that they are the same before the experiment begins. The experimental group then receives some kind of treatment, while the control group receives no treatment. Then tests are conducted to see what kind of change, if any, has occurred between the two groups.

Interviewing children with a structured set of questions or giving children a structured questionnaire on a given research topic are other ways of collecting data. Projective techniques, where children might reveal their first thoughts about a picture or word, is also a form of the interview method.

The study of children can be organized in a variety of ways. One is by stages. The parts of this book (infancy, early childhood, middle childhood, and adolescence) are one type of stage organization. Another way to organize research endeavors is by topics. Topics are usually organized within the context of social, emotional, intellectual, physical, creative, and even spiritual aspects of development.

The time frames used to gather data on children also varies. In longitudinal data collection, information is collected from the same subjects over a long period of time. For example, one could examine the effects of preschool education on performance in elementary school by following and testing the same children during the preschool years and all the way through the elementary years. Because this type of research can take years to complete, a shorter method, cross-sectional research, could be used. In the previous example, one group of preschoolers would be compared to a similar group of elementary school children in order to answer the research question.

There are ethical considerations in studying children that some other disciplines may not face. Children should never be manipulated or put in danger in designing an experiment to answer research questions. Similarly, experiments that would not be in a child's best interests should not be conducted. Studies of abuse and neglect, for example, rely on retrospective techniques in which children who have already been abused report what has previously happened to them. No ethical researcher would ever put children at risk in order to observe the effects of abuse on children. Because of these ethical constraints, it can be frustrating for a researcher to fully answer questions raised in a research project. Additionally, it may take years to demonstrate the effectiveness of intervention for a particular social problem. Consequently, research on children and resultant intervention initiatives rarely offer "quick fixes" to the problems of children and society.

Future Directions

The study of children in society can begin to offer solutions to many of the more pressing societal problems. Quality child care, parenting skills education, stress reduction, affordable housing, job training, and humane political policies are a few ideas for solutions to some of the controversies that will be raised in this book.

The imbalance between work and family in the United States has created problems in the economy as well as in the family system. Workers are expected to produce quality goods and services, but they receive little social support in raising their families. Employers must acknowledge the strain that workers feel as they are pulled between work and family responsibilities. Health insurance, family-friendly work policies, flexible work schedules, parental and dependent care leave, exercise facilities, quality child care and sick child care, on-site or nearby one-stop service centers with post offices, grocery stores, and dry cleaners would be ways of providing support for families in the workplace.

Schools contribute to the problems of child-care arrangements by keeping to an antiquated schedule that was first developed to meet the needs of the farm family. Years ago, schools were let out in the early afternoon and all summer so that children could help with the crops, livestock, and other farm-related chores before sunset. However, ours has been a predominantly industrial society for a large part of the twentieth century and into the twenty-first century. As a result, a different type of schedule is required. Many concerned families advocate activities for children after school and schools that are open all year long to match the schedules of workers. The economy has changed and families have changed; why have educational institutions remained static?

The majority of children somehow manage to grow and develop successfully in a variety of family forms, but the stressors on all families are constantly increasing, which may, in turn, decrease the likelihood of continued success. Parents worry that the cost of a college education will be more than they can afford; parents worry about their children and AIDS, violence, and drugs; parents are concerned that in adulthood their children will not be able to live as well as they have lived. Families need emotional support, and parents need opportunities to learn stress management and parenting skills.

Society can promote the optimal growth and development of its children by taking responsibility for them. There is an old saying, "It takes a village to raise a child." Our society can raise its children by establishing policies in schools, workplaces, and other institutions that reflect the importance of nurturing children.

On the Internet . . .

Families and Work Institute

This Web site provides resources from the Families and Work Institue, which conducts policy research on issues related to the changing workforce and operates a national clearinghouse on work and family life.

http://www.familiesandwork.org

Human Cloning Foundation

The Human Cloning Foundation is one of the strongest proponents of human cloning. This Web site includes information on essays, books, reviews, and personalities advocating human cloning.

http://www.humancloning.org

The National Parent Information Network (NPIN)

The National Parent Information Network contains resources related to many of the controversial issues faced by parents raising children in contemporary society. In addition to articles and resources, discussion groups are available.

http://npin.org

Zero to Three: National Center for Infants, Toddlers, and Families

Zero to Three: National Center for Infants, Toddlers, and Families is a national organization dedicated solely to infants, toddlers, and their families. It is headed by recognized experts in the field and provides technical assistance to communities, states, and the federal government. The site provides information that the organization gathers and disseminates through its publications.

http://www.zerotothree.org

The Future of Children

The Future of Children is a publication of The Woodrow Wilson School of Public and International Affairs at Princeton University and The Brookings Institution. The Future of Children Web site provides research and analysis that promotes effective policies and programs for children.

http://www.futureofchildren.org

American Academy of Pediatrics (AAP)

The American Academy of Pediatrics (AAP) and its member pediatricians dedicate their efforts and resources to the health, safety, and well-being of infants, children, adolescents, and young adults.

http://www.aap.org

PART 1

Infancy

*I*nfancy and toddlerhood encompass the time period from birth to age two or three. During this time, the most dramatic growth of a child's life takes place. Traditionally, much of the literature on infancy has dealt with the physical aspects of development; more recently, however, researchers, practitioners, and policymakers have begun to be concerned with the interaction of brain development on later learning and the social and emotional aspects of the infant's development. The issues examined in this section focus on how the family and social institutions influence children's development from the time they are born.

- Is Institutional Child Care Beneficial to Children?

- Does Maternal Employment Have Negative Effects on Children's Development?

- Should Scientists Be Allowed to Clone Children?

- Does Transracial Adoption Harm a Child's Development?

ISSUE 1

Is Institutional Child Care Beneficial to Children?

YES: Greg Parks, from "The High/Scope Perry Preschool Project," *Juvenile Justice Bulletin* (October 2000)

NO: T. Berry Brazelton and Stanley I. Greenspan, from *The Irreducible Needs of Children: What Every Child Must Have to Grow, Learn, and Flourish* (Perseus, 2000)

ISSUE SUMMARY

YES: Greg Parks, an intern program specialist at the Office of Juvenile Justice and Delinquency Prevention, details the results of the Perry Preschool Project. Parks contends that evaluations of the program show significant benefits in adulthood for the children who attended the preschool.

NO: Pediatrician T. Berry Brazelton and Stanley I. Greenspan, clinical professor of psychiatry and pediatrics at George Washington University Medical School, question the practice by many families of placing their children into the institutional settings of child-care centers.

Increasingly, parents are placing their children in some kind of child care during the day so that they are free to work to support the family economically. This is true not only for single parents but also for parents in a two-parent household who must work in order to live even modestly. In the past, the majority of children in child care were cared for in a family setting by a relative or a home day care with a few children. Today, many families have no relatives close by to whom they can turn for help. In addition, mothers used to take as much time as possible after the birth of a baby to stay at home during a large part of the child's infancy. Things have changed; many women return to work within six weeks of giving birth and, when faced with choices for child care, find that they must place their infant in an institutional or chain-type day care facility.

These day care centers usually serve children of varying ages, from infancy to four or five years of age, and often have after-school programs for elementary school children. These centers often have many rooms and are housed in a large building with as many as 20 caregivers. Child-caregivers must meet licensing standards, but because of the low pay and no benefits, the child-care industry is plagued with a high turnover rate. Thus, caregivers might change many times during a child's stay, depending upon the center's pay structure and the administration's philosophy of quality care. These types of centers look somewhat institutional because of their large building size, numerous rooms, and large number of personnel. Many object to the institutional-type child-care centers because they do not have the home-type atmosphere that one usually associates with the care of very young children.

What is a parent to do? Parents must work to support their families, and they must find a safe place to leave their children. Is a large institutional-like setting appropriate for infants and toddlers who need the security of a close, warm environment? Will these young children be harmed by having several caregivers within a week, or is institutional child care the best environment for children? This is the dilemma discussed in the following two selections. T. Berry Brazelton and Stanley I. Greenspan, long respected in the world of child development, voice their concerns about America's youngest children being enrolled in day care at an alarmingly high rate. In contrast, the Perry Preschool Project results, which are detailed by Greg Parks, indicate that child care is beneficial for children. Longitudinal data from the Perry Preschool Project span over 40 years and show the program to have been beneficial for the children who attended the center.

Greg Parks

 YES

The High/Scope Perry Preschool Project

The Office of Juvenile Justice and Delinquency Prevention (OJJDP) recently published *Costs and Benefits of Early Childhood Intervention* (Greenwood, 1999), a Fact Sheet reviewing the benefits of early childhood intervention in the prevention of later delinquency. Among the most notable and longstanding secondary prevention programs considered was the High/Scope Perry Preschool Project of Ypsilanti, MI.[1] This [selection] examines this successful program model, which demonstrates a potential link between early childhood intervention and delinquency prevention.

The High/Scope Perry Preschool Project is a well-established early childhood intervention that has been in operation for almost 40 years. A review of the program's findings is useful at this time in light of the field's growing knowledge of risk factors associated with juvenile delinquency, including early childhood risk factors that may be diminished by secondary prevention programs targeted at high-risk populations. Juvenile justice research has made great strides in identifying risk factors that may be precursors to delinquency. Although the problem of delinquency increases with the number of risk factors, specific risk factors appear to vary according to a child's stage of development and may be reduced with appropriate preventive measures. These developmental differences for risk factors indicate the need for targeted interventions that address specific age-related factors (Wasserman and Miller, 1998). Given this link between early risk factors and later delinquency, it is important for practitioners to plan intervention programs for high-risk youth early in a youth's life so that he or she can develop a strong foundation for later development.

Background

The High/Scope Perry Preschool Project, which began in 1962, is the focus of an ongoing longitudinal study—conducted by the High/Scope Educational Research Foundation—of 123 high-risk African American children.[2] Participants were of low socioeconomic status, had low IQ scores (between 70 and 85, the range for borderline mental impairment) with no organic deficiencies (i.e., biologically based mental impairment), and were at high risk of failing

From Greg Parks, "The High/Scope Perry Preschool Project," *Juvenile Justice Bulletin,* a publication of The Office of Juvenile Justice and Delinquency Prevention (October 2000). References omitted.

school. Fifty-eight of these 3- and 4-year-old children were assigned to the program group, and 65 of these children were assigned to a control group that did not go through the program. The groups were matched according to age, IQ, socioeconomic status, and gender. There were no differences between the groups with regard to father absence, parent education level, family size, household density, or birth order. Researchers collected followup data annually when the children were between ages 4 and 11 and at ages 14, 15, and 19 and collected age 27 data from 1986 to 1991 (Schweinhart, Barnes, and Weikart, 1993; Schweinhart and Weikart, 1995).[3]

The High/Scope Perry Preschool Project's high-quality educational approach is based on an active learning model that emphasizes participants' intellectual and social development. Children attended the preschool Monday through Friday for 2.5 hours per day over a 2-year period. During that same period, a staff-to-child ratio of one adult for every five or six children enabled teachers to visit each child's family in their home for 1.5 hours each week. In addition, parents participated in monthly small group meetings with other parents, facilitated by program staff.

Although it was initiated as an educational intervention, the High/Scope Perry Preschool Project has demonstrated a number of other positive outcomes, including a significantly lower rate of crime and delinquency and lower incidence of teenage pregnancy and welfare dependency. Overall, the program group has demonstrated significantly higher rates of prosocial behavior, academic achievement, employment, income, and family stability as compared with the control group. The success of this and similar programs demonstrates intervention and delinquency prevention in terms of both social outcome and cost-effectiveness and has a number of useful implications for policy, practice, and ongoing research. This Bulletin reviews the program outcomes, describes the early childhood risk factors that can be targeted with intervention, and explores the relationship between program components and risk factors.

Program Outcomes

Outcomes of the High/Scope Perry Preschool longitudinal study can be divided into three major categories: social responsibility, scholastic success, and socioeconomic success (Schweinhart et al., 1985). Social responsibility variables include delinquency, marital status, and pregnancy. Scholastic success is determined by a number of factors including graduation rate, grade point average, and postsecondary education, whereas socioeconomic success is measured in terms of employment, earnings, and welfare assistance. Cost-benefit is included as an additional outcome because of the long-term savings to society as a result of program success.

Social Responsibility

Delinquency   Data collected from police and court records show that juvenile delinquency was significantly lower for the High/Scope Perry Preschool program group as compared with the control group, including fewer arrests and fewer juvenile court petitions (Schweinhart, Barnes, and Weikart, 1993; Schweinhart and Weikart, 1995). Only 31 percent of the program group had ever been arrested, compared with 51 percent of the control group. In addition to police and court records, data collected from respondents at age 19 were used as an overall indicator of delinquency. When study participants were 19 years old, researchers found significant differences between the program and control groups. The program group had fewer arrests overall than the control group (averages of 1.3 versus 2.3 arrests per person), fewer felony arrests (averages of 0.7 versus 2.0 arrests per person), and fewer juvenile court petitions filed (averages of 0.2 versus 0.4 petitions per person).

Like the criminal record data, a misconduct scale based on teacher-report data and self-report data from the 19-year-old respondents demonstrates a significant difference between the program and control groups, as reflected by the following results for the program group:

- Lower overall scores for total misconduct and serious misconduct at ages 15 and 19.
- Lower incidence of fighting and other violent behavior.
- Lower incidence of property damage.
- Fewer police contacts.

Data collected from respondents at age 27 indicate significant differences between the program group and control group for adult arrests: the control group underwent more than twice as many arrests as the program group (averages of 4.0 versus 1.8 arrests per person). Thirty-six percent of the control group accounted for 98 felony arrests between ages 19 and 27, while 27 percent of the program group accounted for 40 felony arrests during the same period. Thirty-five percent of the control group were considered frequent offenders (defined as five or more arrests), compared with only 7 percent of the program group. In addition, 25 percent of the control group had been arrested for drug-related offenses, versus 7 percent of the program group. The control group also averaged more months on probation (6.6 versus 3.2 months) and had more than twice as many of its members placed on probation or parole for longer than 18 months (20 percent versus 9 percent).

Marital status and pregnancy   Marital status among the males was the same for both groups, with 26 percent married at age 27, although program group males, on average, had been married for a longer period (6.2 versus 3.3 years). Marital status among the females differed significantly, with 40 percent of program group females married, compared with 8 percent of the control group females. Although fewer females in the program group were parents (64 percent versus 75 percent), significantly more of them were married, cohabiting parents (28 percent versus 8 percent). Fifty-seven percent of mothers in the program group gave birth out of wedlock, compared with 83 percent of mothers in the control group. In measures related to family stability, the program group scored significantly higher on a measure of closeness to family and friends (66 percent versus 48 percent) and the ability to maintain persistence at tasks (i.e., work or study hard all day) (47 percent versus 33 percent).

Scholastic Success

Participants in the High/Scope Perry Preschool study were characterized by better academic performance than those in the control group, as measured by higher graduation rates, better grades, higher standardized test scores, and fewer instances of placement in special education classes. In addition, the program group spent more time on homework and demonstrated more positive attitudes toward school at ages 15 and 19. More parents of program group members had positive attitudes regarding their children's educational experiences and were hopeful that their children would obtain college degrees. The program group demonstrated significant academic differences in the following areas:

- **Special education for mental impairment.** Only 15 percent of the program group had been placed in special education programs for mental impairment, compared with 34 percent of the control group.
- **Test scores.** Each year from ages 7 to 14, the mean achievement test scores of the program group were noticeably higher than those of the control group (an average difference of 16 percent). The difference in the final achievement test scores of the two groups at age 14 was particularly significant: the program group's scores were 29 percent higher than those of the control group.
- **Grade point average.** The mean high school grade point average of the program group was higher than that of the control group (2.09 versus 1.68).
- **Graduation from high school.** Seventy-one percent of the program group graduated from high school, compared with 54 percent of the control group. The difference was largely accounted for by graduation rates among females (84 percent and 35 percent, respectively).

Socioeconomic Success

Data collected at ages 19 and 27 indicate that the program group has been more successful socioeconomically than the control group. The data for age 19 reveal that significantly more program group members were employed (50 percent versus 32 percent) and self-reporting (45 percent versus 25 percent). These data also reflect that fewer program group members received welfare assistance (18 percent versus 32 percent). The data for age 27 reveal a continuation of significant economic differences characterized by more economic stability among the program group members, as measured by the following indicators:

- **Public assistance.** Fifteen percent of the program group were receiving public assistance, versus 32 percent of the control group.
- **Monthly earnings.** Twenty-nine percent of the program group had monthly earnings of $2,000 or more, versus 7 percent of the control group (36 percent versus 11 percent, respectively, when comparing only employed members in each group).
- **Household earnings.** When the income of the spouses of the study participants was taken into account, 47 percent of the program group

had household income earnings of $3,000 or more per month, versus 17 percent of the control group.

- **Home ownership.** Thirty-six percent of the program group owned a home, versus 13 percent of the control group.
- **Automobile ownership.** Thirty percent of the program group owned a second car, versus 13 percent of the control group.

Cost-Benefit Analysis

A cost-benefit analysis of the High/Scope Perry Preschool study indicates a savings to the public of more than seven times the initial investment per child, with a return of $7.16 for every dollar spent (Barnett, 1983). When adjusted for inflation and a 3-percent discount rate, the investment in early childhood prevention resulted in a taxpayer return of $88,433 per child from the following sources:

- Savings in welfare assistance (prior to welfare reform).
- Savings in special education.
- Savings to the criminal justice system.
- Savings to crime victims.
- Increased tax revenue from higher earnings.

An independent reanalysis is provided in a recent RAND Corporation report (Karoly et al., 1998). This report found that eliminating the largest and least reliable savings category (savings to crime victims) still left a return of more than twice the initial investment. Savings to crime victims make up 65 percent of the total investment return in the earlier analysis (Barnett, 1993). Although victim savings should be considered a significant outcome and societal benefit of early childhood intervention, this factor is also distinct from the other factors that can be estimated based on direct governmental costs and savings. With victim savings factored out of the analysis, the largest savings category is in criminal justice costs (40 percent), followed by increased taxable revenue (26 percent), reduced educational services (25 percent), and reduced welfare costs (9 percent).

Early Childhood Risk Factors for Delinquency

An understanding of early childhood risk factors for delinquency is helpful to interpreting the success of the High/Scope Perry Preschool Project. One factor identified with risk for delinquency is poor language skills. (Stattin and Klackenberg-Larsson, 1993). As a component of overall mental development, language functions as an indicator of later intelligence and is a critical factor in the relationship between intelligence and delinquency. Additional early risk factors include poor attachment to caregivers (Egeland and Farber, 1984; Shaw and Bell, 1993), poor parenting skills (Hawkins et al., 1998; Loeber and Stouthamer-Loeber, 1986), and multiple family stressors (Fergusson and Lynskey, 1996; Shaw et al., 1998). These risk factors may not only directly affect delinquency but may also indirectly influence other factors that interact with delinquency, such as school- and community-related risk factors.

As demonstrated in the Prenatal and Early Childhood Nurse Home Visitation Program supported by OJJDP (Olds, Hill, and Rumsey, 1998), prenatal and early postnatal prevention are shown to reduce risk factors that contribute to the development of antisocial behavior in childhood. Early childhood intervention during the preschool years also offers an opportunity to halt the developmental trajectory toward delinquency and related behavioral disorders. Family support services help develop parenting skills, attachment, and coping mechanisms that have a positive effect on family stressors. A multi-component approach to enhancing child development promotes protective factors and reduces risk factors by addressing the many systems and influences that affect a child's development.

Program Components and Related Risk Factors for Delinquency

The components of the High/Scope Perry Preschool Project affect a number of the early childhood risk factors associated with later delinquency and other behavioral problems. In addition to directly reinforcing early developmental processes in the educational setting, the program strengthens positive parenting skills.

The High/Scope Educational Research Foundation explains the effectiveness of the High/Scope Perry Preschool model in terms of empowerment, which includes developing skills for success by enabling children to be active and independent learners, helping parents to support the development of their children, and providing teachers with effective training and support (Schweinhart and Weikart, 1995).

Because an ongoing home-school relationship enhances socialization, involving parents early in the educational process is critical to the later success of participants in an early childhood intervention such as High/Scope Perry Preschool (Seitz, 1990). Weekly home visits by teachers and regular parent group meetings promote the strengthening of parent-child relationships and increase parent involvement in the educational process. A more recent OJJDP longitudinal study, the Rochester Youth Development Study (Thornberry et al., 1998), confirmed a significant relationship between parents' involvement in their children's lives and reduced delinquency.

In addition to enhancing parent attachment, parent involvement, and parenting skills, early childhood intervention aimed at both parents and children influences a child's attachment to school and later commitment to school success (Thornberry et al., 1998). Findings from the Rochester study confirm earlier research linking poor school attachment, commitment, and achievement to delinquent behavior and drug use (Krohn et al., 1995; Smith et al., 1995). Another OJJDP study, the Seattle Social Development Project (Hill et al., 1999), found that a lack of success in elementary school was linked to later gang membership. Even in the midst of multiple other factors placing youth at high risk for delinquency, school success (as indicated by higher standardized test scores, school commitment, attachment to teachers, college aspirations, and parent expectations) appears to be a protective factor against delinquency (Smith et al., 1995). Academic achievement outcomes of the High/Scope Perry Preschool study indicate that the program group was more successful than the control group in school-related factors that appear to protect against delinquency.

The positive outcomes of the High/Scope Perry Preschool study are the result of a cumulative effect that begins with increased school readiness (Berrueta-Clement et al., 1987; Zigler, Taussig, and Black, 1992). School readiness results in positive reinforcement from teachers in the early grades followed by enhanced academic performance in subsequent grades and an overall stronger commitment to school. A correlational analysis of the High/Scope Perry Preschool data reveals a strong association between school motivation in the early years and literacy scores at age 19 (Schweinhart, Barnes, and Weikart, 1993). School motivation is also higher correlated with the highest year of schooling completed, which is associated with higher monthly earnings in adulthood and fewer lifetime arrests.

Program and Policy Implications

The outcomes of the High/Scope Perry Preschool study demonstrate the value of prevention and early intervention efforts in promoting protective factors that reduce delinquency. The program was developed for high-risk children who stood to benefit the most from such an intervention. The intervention also affected multiple risk factors and was carried out in multiple domains (i.e., home and school). In an extensive review of early childhood interventions, Yoshikawa (1995) concluded that the combination of an early educational component with family support, as exemplified by the High/Scope Perry Preschool Project, is a determining factor in long-term effects on antisocial behavior. Other combination programs that have demonstrated long-term effects on delinquency include the Yale Child Welfare Project (Seitz and Apfel, 1994), Houston Parent Child Development Center (Johnson and Walker, 1987), and Syracuse Family Development Research Program (Lally, Mangione, and Honig, 1988). Single-component models, such as those that address only educational factors, have not been shown to demonstrate significant results.

In addition to the need to target appropriate populations and address multiple risk factors in multiple domains, program quality is essential to success. The High/Scope Perry Preschool model is based on a high-quality educational approach that assumes a low staff-to-child ratio, an active learning curriculum, and a home visitation component that engages parents in the educational process. Furthermore, teachers are well educated, adequately compensated, and well supported in their tasks.

Head Start, perhaps the largest and best-known early childhood intervention program, has recently made efforts to expand and improve its effectiveness by emphasizing family support, staff training, and performance standards (U.S. Department of Health and Human Services, 1999). The 1994 legislation reauthorizing Head Start incorporated a number of recommendations from the Advisory Committee on Head Start Quality and Expansion (1993), including increased parent involvement, a lower staff-to-child ratio, and increased mental health services.[4] Head Start has increased the emphasis on curriculum and child outcomes as a result of this reauthorization and has formed Head Start Quality Research Centers to respond to the need for additional research in the area of early childhood intervention. Further research is clearly needed to build on the limited existing knowledge base and assess the effectiveness of programs across various demographic groups, risk factors, and co-occurring factors that are related to delinquency, such as mental health issues and substance abuse (Yoshikawa, 1995).

Although the High/Scope Perry Preschool study's sample size was small in proportion to its eventual influence, its strong experimental design has contributed to its prominence in the field of early childhood education. Subsequent early childhood research that is carefully controlled and longitudinal in design remains limited. The limited research involving similar models that combine educational and family support components, however, supports the positive outcomes of the High/Scope Perry Preschool model. Subsequent independent evaluations of the programs that have implemented the High/Scope model have rated those programs significantly higher than comparison programs, with 58 percent of High/Scope programs versus 40 percent of comparison programs being rated as high quality (Epstein, 1993). In addition, 72 percent of children in High/Scope programs versus 57 percent of children in comparison programs scored high on measures of emotional, social, cognitive, and motor development.

Some targeted, multicomponent early childhood interventions have been demonstrated to exceed their costs in eventual savings and benefit to the public. However, implementing an effective prevention strategy requires a commitment to provide empirically based quality programming and to invest the up-front resources that will result in long-term savings and positive social change in the lives of children and families. The High/Scope Perry Preschool Project provides one such model for early childhood intervention that has proven successful when executed with quality and commitment to long-term results. The complexity of juvenile delinquency requires multiple strategies that address the problem at various stages of development; early childhood intervention is one promising component in the context of a more comprehensive approach, as recommended in OJJDP's *Comprehensive Strategy for Serious, Violent, and Chronic Juvenile Offenders* (Wilson and Howell, 1993). The High/Scope Perry Preschool model is worthy of consideration as an effective early childhood intervention as communities attempt to implement a comprehensive strategy that includes prevention, intervention, and graduated sanctions (Howell, 1995; Wilson and Howell, 1993).

Notes

1. Unlike primary prevention programs, which are directed at the general population, secondary prevention programs target children at risk for school failure or delinquency.

2. The original Perry Preschool no longer exists, but the High/Scope Educational Research Foundation—founded in 1970 by Perry Preschool researcher David

Weikart—continues to collect followup data from the participants of the 1962 study. The foundation is an independent organization dedicated to nonprofit research, development, training, and public advocacy. Its principal goals are to promote the learning and development of children worldwide from infancy through adolescence and to support and train educators and parents as they help children learn. In a High/Scope program, students should learn through active involvement with materials, events, and ideas. The Foundation disseminates the High/Scope Preschool model worldwide.

3. Researchers are currently collecting followup data from the original program participants. Called the High/Scope Perry Preschool Midlife Study, researchers have already interviewed 30 of the 39- to 41-year-old participants. The interview emphasized health and the performance of the program participants' children. The researchers expect to complete the data collection by the end of 2001. This study is funded by the McCormick Tribune Foundation in Chicago, IL.

4. Head Start Act Amendments of 1994. Pub. L. No. 103–252, tit. 1 § 108, Stat. 624 (1994).

**T. Berry Brazelton and
Stanley I. Greenspan**

The Irreducible Needs of Children

Children who are living with their biological parent or parents and are deprived of the ordinary experiences that would enable them to be warm, loving, and caring are often in families with multiple problems, such as mental illness or severe antisocial patterns in one or both parents. The children aren't provided opportunities for nurturance, interaction, or learning. Here, too, we see chaotic, impulsive, self-absorbed, aimless children with severe language, social, and emotional difficulties.

In reading this, one may sigh with a sense of relief thinking that in your community such patterns of multiple foster care placements or neglect and abuse are very rare. But there is another trend occurring, both in the United States and around the world—a new type of institutional care. This type of care is part of every community. Approximately 50 percent of young children are now reared for significant parts of the day by persons other than their biological parents. Here, we're not talking about after-school programs for school-aged children. We're talking about infants and toddlers in the first three years of life. From the 1970s through the 1990s, there has been a transformation of the attitudes of families towards raising their own children. During this time, there has been a huge increase in the number of families giving up the care of babies, toddlers, and preschoolers to others for 35 or more hours a week. In other words, large numbers of infants, toddlers, and preschoolers are spending the lion's share of their days in nonparental care.

More important than mere numbers are reports regarding the quality of this care. These are not encouraging. The most comprehensive study of the quality of day care reported that the vast majority of center-based care was not of high quality (over 85 percent was not of high quality for preschool children and over 90 percent was not of high quality for infants and toddlers). Similar reports have emerged around other non-parental child care arrangements, such as family day care. In addition, most states in the United States have very weak regulations governing care. New findings regarding daycare options for mothers on welfare are especially alarming. These "Wave 1 Findings" are from the Growing Up in Poverty Project 2000. These findings suggest that day care for such families is of very poor quality (eg. instances of toddlers wandering aimlessly about). The findings about overall lack of care suggest that quality of care is an important contributor to a child's development.

The day care debate gets confused however by focusing only on research reports that maintain it's the quality of care that counts, not whether children are in institutional day care or family day care or cared for by parents. The reports stress that the quality of nurturance, interaction, and sensitivity to the child's cues are what's associated with their development status. It is true, and makes common sense, that quality would be an important variable and certainly, as indicated above, there's no guarantee that biological parents will always provide good quality care. But, what tends to get obscured in these academic discussions is the fact that at present most nonparental care (as revealed in a number of studies, including the study that documented that quality counts) is not of high quality.

We do know that quality child care is essential to the optimal development of small children. In our present setup, as indicated above, only 10% or less of infants and toddlers have access to high quality day care. The rest wind up with care that anyone with real options would not trust. Nor do the parents of these children. When a parent must leave a small child in less than optimal child care, that parent is bound to grieve. The grieving can take many forms: denial, detachment from the child, and anger and/or depression at the workplace that demands the separation. If we want motivated workers we need to offer them optimal child care or flexible hours that permit parental sharing of care.

With over half the nation's children receiving one form or another of nonparental care, the question is whether we want to allow a type of care that is not providing children the needed nurturance and social and intellectual interaction. We have to ask whether this nurturance is possible in settings where caregivers are caring for four or more babies (and later six or more toddlers), are paid minimal wage, and given little training and little incentive to avoid staff turnover (among those who can get better jobs). . . .

Even when children are cared for at home for the first few years, there still are worrisome trends. There has been a shift towards more impersonal, rather than emotionally nurturing types of care–giving for infants, toddlers, preschoolers, and children. A recent report from the Kaiser Foundation revealed that on average, children are spending five to six hours a day in front of the TV or computer screen. During this time, children are not receiving nurturing warmth or age-appropriate social or intellectual interactions.

But this is just one sign of the movement towards impersonal care. Many families are overly scheduled. Both parents are working to make ends meet or to improve the family's economics, leaving little relaxed family time. Education is becoming more impersonal as it is, more technologically oriented, losing the personal touch. Families in their own relationships with one another are also moving towards more impersonal modes of communication. E-mails are replacing lunches together and time in front of the screen is replacing many other forms of personal interaction. Recreation as well as work is taking place in a more impersonal atmosphere, with less interaction among and within families.

One of us (S.I.G.) was recently struck by how pervasive this shift is towards impersonal modes of care. A visit within the same week to two very different settings attempting to provide nurturing care revealed some striking similarities in what might be called "institutional love."

In the first setting, a woman sat in the corner of the room looking at the floor. Around her crawled four babies who seemed to relate only to their own bodies and the objects they can see or touch. One of them got her hand caught in a toy. The woman went to her, pulled her hand free, said, "O.K." and then moved silently back to her chair. Another baby banged on his half-filled bottle of milk. The woman picked him up, put him stiffly on her lap and faced him towards the wall while the baby sucked down the rest of his milk. When the baby was finished, she put him back on the floor without a word. The room was quiet. There were no signs of the familiar gestures, sounds, and expressions that tie people together.

Was this an overwhelmed, economically disadvantaged mother in a worrisome family situation? Or an over-stressed home day care facility in a poor neighborhood? No, in fact this was a scene in an upper-middle class day care center for infants and toddlers. The woman was an aide earning the minimum wage. The director of the private, well-run, fully accredited center said, "She is the norm."

In another room in the same center, a smiling woman animatedly exchanged words, grunts, smiles, laughs, and gestures with five toddlers as they rolled trucks back and forth and giggled at one another. The children pointed at, crawled over, and made sounds at each other and the woman caring for them. Using subtle movements of hand, face, and voice she engaged all five toddlers at once.

"Who is she?" S.I.G. asked.

"Oh, she is the assistant director, substituting for one of the aides who is sick," replied the director.

"Is it possible to have more of the staff that cares directly for the babies show her warmth and interactive skills?" S.I.G. asked.

"Occasionally we have caregivers similar to her, but in general we don't and people with her skills quickly get to higher levels. We can't afford to pay someone like her to spend time with the infants," the director responded.

A few days later, in the second setting, S.I.G. saw similarly unresponsive aides sitting in their chairs. One was telling an elderly woman, "Sit down and stop babbling or you won't get your ice cream." In another room, six other elderly women were sitting and staring silently into space while two more aides sat behind their table looking bored and indifferent. A woman pleaded unsuccessfully for a back rub and later confessed, "I just need some human touch." Another woman brightened up when an aide talked to her and was unnecessarily thankful for the little conversation.

This setting is one of the city's best institutions for the elderly. Here, too, the food, cleanliness and medical care are excellent.

This is "institutional love." It is provided at either end of the lifespan for both the poor and the well-to-do, for those who, because of their age and helplessness, need to depend on others for their care. We all know what this kind of care is like. What we don't want to think about is that this care is what we are providing for those we love.

Surely, one may rationalize, with enough money we can have good services. In fact, in some workplaces parental involvement in on-site day care creates a sense of an extended family. "Cooperative" nursery schools benefit from parent participation. A compassionate head nurse in a home for the elderly may instill a personal touch. But, sadly, these are the exceptions. The irony is that if we as a society keep this up, in 80 years the current infants will be back in these impersonal surroundings and it will feel strangely familiar.

One of us (S.I.G.) has questioned whether we are creating a new view of human nature reflected in our impersonal child care policies and interaction patterns, a concrete, materialistic one. In this view, we are more concerned with the brain than the mind and with biology and genetics than experience. . . .

Ongoing Nurturing Relationships

Day Care

SIG: If parents have options and are able to provide high-quality care themselves, I find it best not to have infants or toddlers (in the first two years) in full-time, 30–40-plus-hour-a-week day care. Current research and my own clinical observations suggest that most day-care centers do not provide high-quality care. The quality of interaction between caregivers and babies is often less than optimal. Also, the current ratios of four babies per caregiver in the first year and six in the second year, coupled with high staff turnover, minimum wages, insufficient training, and the expectable change of caregivers each year, make it difficult to provide high-quality, ongoing, nurturing care in those early years.

The question is, are parents able to shift back to caring for their babies and using day care less?

TBB: I would prefer if day care for babies and toddlers weren't necessary, but I think that there is a large portion of the population right now who can't take the full-time care of their infants.

SIG: Is one reason why parents can't do this a difference in the way people are growing up these days?

TBB: Expectations are changing. It's like what is happening to marriage in a society where the divorce rate is going up to 50 percent. The expectations for marriage have changed. I think the same thing is happening to the way mothers perceive staying at home. In an earlier generation, most mothers were expected to stay at home, and it was easier for them to do so. Now we've changed that expectation entirely, and it's hard to reverse it.

SIG: From the child's point of view, however, let's look at the first year of life in full-time day care—40 or more hours a week. How do you think babies develop relationships in this circumstance?

TBB: Babies can make can make multiple attachments that are meaningful. Certainly I would hope that the parents come first and the baby makes secondary attachments to everybody else. I visited a day–care center recently at a time when all the mothers were there. After a while, only one mother was left and all the children gravitated to her. I turned to the very talented day-care people there and said, "They really seem to desert you, don't they?" They said, "When there's a mother here, we don't even exist." The children were already differentiating among caregivers. It doesn't even have to be their mother; it just has to be a mother.

SIG: That's not so great. In a number of day-care centers, when the children are mobile, I see a lot of emotionally hungry children. Children come up to any new adult and hang on. Some of that reaching out for any mother is simply reaching out to anyone who will give them some attention. It's a little indiscriminate. We see that in institutions such as orphanages where there is emotional deprivation. A minute here and there of reciprocal interaction, sometimes around feeding or diapering, is not enough to provide the needed security and sense of being cared for.

If we are going to give parents flexible options, we need both to improve day care and to reduce the number of hours per week children spend in day-care situations.

TBB: Again, I think it needs to be a case-by-case decision, weighing this or that, rather than simply telling people what to do. Some parents are better parents if there is an outlet for them. But we do need to provide the child with an optimal secondary caregiver.

SIG: When I talk to college students, I often ask them how they see their lives in terms of having children. As they think about a career and getting married, are they taking into account child-rearing, as well as the demands of a profession? Are they engaged to a neurosurgeon or are they going to be neurosurgeons themselves? Are they planning on having several children? Having two neurosurgeons in the family along with four children may be more difficult and demanding than they can possibly imagine. On the other hand, if two people are getting married and both want careers, and one of them is a writer and the other a psychologist, they may have more control of their time. Each one could work two-thirds time or one could work halftime and they could get child care for the limited remaining hours. But a lot of these potential parents haven't thought this out. They want children and a good career and see no problem. What they're being led to believe now is that full-time day care in the first years of life is as good as if not better than what they can provide: "I'll have a baby, take a two month leave of absence, put the baby in day care, and I'll be a lawyer and my spouse will be a lawyer. We'll work until 8:00 at night. We'll pick up the baby, come home, and play for an hour." In families like this I see children not getting their basic needs for nurturing met.

TBB: When I see a family like that I see a lot of grieving. That kind of treatment of the child is ignoring the child's interests to such an extent that there must be a lot of denial. Something is so painful that these parents have to hide behind defenses.

SIG: But do we support this type of denial or help parents out of it? As new parents make their decisions early on, some parents intuitively plan for the flexibility to be home more; sometimes it's the mom and sometimes it's the dad who stays home. The parents who are more ambivalent and tend to use denial often look around for guidance. But they're getting a lot of misinformation. They're told it doesn't make a difference. If parents-to-be knew more about this need for a continuous, close relationship, they might plan more realistically. They would see how hard it is to have such relationships with two full-time jobs and full-time day care. If parents see the options, they could make choices. If they have a caregiver at home and pick well, they have a greater likelihood, if they can afford it, of having the same caregiver being with them for a number of years. In day care, by design, the caregivers change each year. Turnover is so great, though, that there may be another change or two changes even within one year. There may be three changes of caregivers by the time a baby has had a year of day care. Minimum wages, lack of training, and so on contribute to this. The caregiver in a day-care setting is not like a *meta peleth* in a kibbutz in Israel, who is a stable person in a child's life, with him for four or five years. It doesn't have to be the mother. It could be the father or the grandfather or grandmother. The child needs a caregiver in his or her life who's going to be there for the long haul.

TBB: To improve day care, I see three babies per adult as the absolute maximum for the first year of life. But now the norm is four babies per caregiver. Imagine a mother with triplets and how hard it is for her to care for all three babies at the same time.

SIG: Would you recommend, Berry, that a baby should keep the same caregivers for the first three or four years? One group of caregivers, for example, would follow a group of children who started as infants on up through their toddler years.

TBB: This would work as long as the caregiver really liked each baby, but suppose she didn't like one? Couldn't it be moved to another caregiver's group? Caregivers and babies, like parents, could be evaluated for "goodness of fit" between them. Also, when you go up into the second and third years, and taking care of four children becomes possible, a fourth child will be added to the group of three. The fourth baby wouldn't necessarily get the same caregivers.

SIG: The extra children in the group might come from outside, perhaps from home. To make this work, you'd have to have expanding entry into day care at the second and third years, with each class being larger than the last. More children are in day care by age three than in the first two years of life. Then we have to create incentives for the staff of day-care centers to stay on, giving better wages and training.

TBB: We have to increase wages to a decent level, and we need to improve their status. At present, they are thought of as "baby-sitters" with some scorn.

SIG: That's what we need to correct. We need to get across all that's involved in meaningful care of a child: creating ongoing dialogues, reflecting and accepting a variety of emotions. You can sometimes find people who are warm and nourishing and emotionally responsive, even though they haven't been given a chance to educate themselves. Sometimes you can find young people who want to get experience with children and who are naturally sensitive and flexible.

TBB: Day-care staff need constant refueling. It's a demanding job, taking care of somebody else's children. If parents and day–care personnel could handle their natural, inevitable gatekeeping, parents could become peer "fuelers" of the day–care personnel. The team (of parents and child care worker) could share the child's optimal development.

SIG: We need to see all this from the point of view of prevention. It's a public health issue.

TBB: When Congress was talking about that $22 billion for improving child care, I got a chance to go down to Washington, and told them that if they just turn the money over to the states, it will all get eaten up. You'd do better to give the money to states tied to choices based on the quality child care that we know how to produce, and to let them pick their choices. When it came to laying out choices that will work for the child, they said, "Oh, we have to do some research." I told them there was already plenty of research. What we need now is just the will to put the research into practice. They asked if I could tell them what programs work. I said not by myself, but I certainly could gather a bunch of colleagues who could tell you which ones we guarantee would work.

State governments can eat up revenues for child care at the top, if we're not careful. The one sector that could make a real difference and could afford to, and might be motivated to if we were smart enough, would be big business. If we could get them to set up a center in every business site that would contain preventive health care, child care, after-school care, and elder care, then maybe we could begin to reach a lot of people. I don't think we need to use the schools for this, but Ed Zigler at Yale has a model he calls the "School of the 21st Century," in which all these caregiving situations are gathered into school buildings that are not in use and made into centers for families in their communities. In our Touchpoints model, we are recommending that parent centers be established in every community where parents could receive child care, preventive health care, after-school care, and elder care. Parent resource centers, such as Family Support America, could be established for peer resources. Parents could then begin to feel a sense of community around them.

Our Touchpoints model has been developed at Children's Hospital in Boston to train multidisciplinary representatives from communities that are ready for change in an outreach, relational model. We want to improve preventive health care and child care with several goals. At each visit of parents and child, the provider (child care or medical care) identifies the strengths versus the failures of the parent. The child's development is the language between professional and parent. The parent is valued as the expert in the child's development. In this way, the passion of the parent is fostered. The relationship is transactional versus top-down. Each visit becomes an opportunity for sharing the child's new achievements and encouraging the child's development, both physical and psychological. Twenty-five centers have espoused our ideas, and they are changing communities to become parent-friendly. Our goal is to offer preventive outreach for the present 40 percent of underserved. We do know what to do. Can we do it? . . .

Relationships in Day Care

It is also important to consider now how these same principles can be applied to other contexts where children may find themselves such as family day care, makeshift baby-sitting arrangements, as well as institutional day care settings and care by relatives. These same standards for the nurturing care of children growing up in families apply to these other settings. In other words, a child in family day care or day care center should spend most of her time in facilitated activities or direct one-to-one interactions. However, in observations of day-care settings we found it rare that there were long interactive sequences between the caregivers and the babies.

Since it is so hard for caregivers to have long, nurturing interactions when caring for four or more babies (standard in most institutional day care), and because of the staff turnover that is characteristic of most institutional day-care settings, as well as the tendency to have staff change each year as children move from the infant room to the toddler room to the preschool room, we believe that in the first two years of life full-time day care is a difficult context in which to provide the ongoing, nurturing care by one or a few caregivers that the child requires. Part-time day care, on the other hand, may be quite helpful in giving mothers and fathers a chance to do other things and may not compromise either the security of ongoing nurturing care or the types of experiences we have described. But 35-plus hours a week for infants and toddlers makes it very difficult to have the consistency of caregiver and the depth of nurturance required, or the amount of facilitating interaction with the environment or direct interaction that we believe is healthy for infants and toddlers.

Because some families will need full-time day care in the early years, we must work to improve its quality. This means lower child/caregiver ratios, better training and salaries and maintaining the same caregiver from birth to roughly age 3. Although there is general agreement on the need to improve day care, improvements in the last 25 years have been modest. As we pointed out earlier, studies of the quality of available day care are not optimistic. We may be trying to rationalize a system that simply isn't providing the essentials of what children need. It may therefore be best to reconsider our assumptions. The best way these assumptions can be reconsidered is by each and every family having good and accurate information. With awareness we believe most will make a wise and enlightened choice.

Recommendations

In making the recommendations that follow, we are both mindful of the fact that there are many circumstances where nonparental care may be highly desirable or absolutely necessary. Single parents working to put food on the table, even if able to provide high-quality care themselves, may have no choice but to use out-of-home child care for 40-plus hours a week. Here, the goal would be to find the best care available and to work with the child care providers as a team to provide integrated care for that baby or toddler. There may be families where there is emotional stress in individuals or family stress that makes it highly desirable to have 30-plus hours of care provided by others. On balance this will provide a much stronger support system for this particular baby or toddler. Each circumstance has to be weighed individually, and parents have to make wise and enlightened choices regarding their own particular situation.

Continuous Relationships

- In the first three years, every child needs one or two primary caregivers who remain in a steady, intimate relationship with that child.
- During the infancy, toddler, and preschool years, children should always be in the sight of caregivers. There should be no time, other than when they are sleeping, that they are out of sight of caregivers.
- No more than one-third of infants', toddlers', and preschoolers' time should be spent in fully independent activities. The time that is spent in independent activities should be spent for 10 or 15 minutes here and there rather than a longer period in independent activities.
- The other two-thirds or longer time should be spent between two types of activities: those in which the caregiver facilitates interactions with the environment and direct interaction, such as cuddling, holding, shared pretend play, and funny face games. Infants and toddlers need at least four or more 20-minute or longer periods of direct interactive time. Preschoolers need at least three of these direct, interactive play opportunities. In a two-parent family, both parents should be part of these spontaneous, joyful games.
- During the facilitated time, caregivers are available to comment on, respond to, and help in the child's explorations, though also engaged in other activities, such as cooking or putting clothes in the washing machine. Some of this time a small child could be accompanying parents to the supermarket or being a junior chef. During the school years, when we consider available time, we are considering time minus schooltime, after school activities, and peer playtime. Here, too, we recommend that of the available time two-thirds be spent with the caregiver being available for facilitating or directly interacting. The "facilitating" time could be spent helping a child with homework, hobbies, or other activities. The times of direct involvement, which should include at least two 20-minute periods (each parent should participate where possible) might mean imaginative play, games or other activities in which the child can take the lead.
- We recommend that working parents both be available for at least two-thirds of the evening hours, from 5:30 or 6:00 to 9:00, and that, if possible, in addition, one of the parents be available in the late afternoon when the children are home, often playing with peers or siblings, or involved in after-school activities. Also, the parents should be available enough so that they or the children don't have to be measuring each moment of time and the guidelines outlined above can be taken for granted.

Parental Leave

We recommend a leave of most of the first year of life for one parent.

Day Care

- We do not recommend full-time day care, 30 or more hours of care by nonparents, for infants and toddlers *if* the parents are able to provide high-quality care themselves and *if* the parents have reasonable options. We also recommend improving day care considerably by lowering ratios, improving training and wages, and, for children in full-time day care, having the same caregiver remain with the infant she cares for for three to four years. Those families that require day care will then have options for higher-quality day care than is now the case.
- In the first three years, a primary caregiver should be assigned to each child and should remain the same from year to year.
- For the first year there should be no more than three babies to one adult.
- For the second year, there should be no more than four toddlers to one adult.
- For the third and fourth years, there should be no more than five to eight children to one adult.

Group or Institutional Settings

- Various types of institutional arrangements, including children in group situations, need to follow the same guidelines outlined earlier for the family. Ongoing nurturing care with one or a few constant primary caregivers should include direct or "facilitated" interactions for at least two-thirds of the available time. In-service training, growing financial incentives with experience and training, and support structure to facilitate nurturing attitudes are all important components of satisfying this requirement for ongoing nurturing care in group or institutional settings.

POSTSCRIPT

Is Institutional Child Care Beneficial to Children?

The quality of child care appears to be one of the most important issues in the debate over whether or not to send young children to child-care centers. Low adult-child ratios, competent and caring caregivers, and clean and nurturing environments are what contribute to quality child care. Is this type of setting preferable over being at home with a parent who does not want to be there and who does nothing to stimulate a child intellectually or emotionally? Consider another alternative—poor quality child care, with multiple caregivers who have no training and no desire to work with young children in a dirty, nonstimulating environment. Contrast this scenario with a child's being at home with a parent who loves the child and provides educational materials and one-on-one interaction most of the day. These are the extremes to the question of how and where to best care for young children.

Another factor that confounds this argument is how much time and what quality of time parents who use day care spend with their children when they are at home. Mediocre out-of-home care can be mitigated by a stimulating home environment when children and parents are together. On the other hand, a poor, nonnurturing home environment, which could be devastating for a child's development, can be supplemented positively by a quality child-care experience.

An April 2001 release of the results from a longitudinal study by the National Institute of Child Health and Human Development, a federal agency that has been studying children in child-care settings for 10 years, made headlines and caused a furor in the child-care industry. Some conclusions of the study, many say, were taken out of context and sensationalized by the press. It was reported that children who attended day care were found to be more aggressive than their stay-at-home counterparts. In actuality, the level of aggression for day care children was still within the normal range of behavior. These kinds of misinterpretations and partial facts create confusion for parents who are just trying to do the best they can for their children. American society asks parents to work to support their families but then asks them to stay home to take care of their children. This dichotomy of thinking and expectations makes it difficult to feel good about any choice made related to child care.

ISSUE 2

Does Maternal Employment Have Negative Effects on Children's Development?

YES: Wen-Jui Han, Jane Waldfogel, and Jeanne Brooks-Gunn, from "The Effects of Early Maternal Employment on Later Cognitive and Behavioral Outcomes," *Journal of Marriage and Family* (February 2001)

NO: Thomas M. Vander Ven, Francis T. Cullen, Mark A. Carrozza, and John Paul Wright, from "Home Alone: The Impact of Maternal Employment on Delinquency," *Social Problems* (May 2001)

ISSUE SUMMARY

YES: University professors and researchers Wen-Jui Han, Jane Waldfogel, and Jeanne Brooks-Gunn from Columbia University conclude that maternal employment in the first year of a child's life has a significant negative effect on verbal ability at age 3 or 4 and lowered math achievement when children were 7 to 8. When ethnicity was controlled for, these negative effects were found for white children, but not for African-American children.

NO: University professors and researchers Thomas M. Vander Ven, Francis T. Cullen, Mark A. Carrozza, and John Paul Wright found that mother's employment in the first year of the baby's life had no effect on child delinquency when the child got older.

T he numbers of women who combine work and motherhood have risen steadily from 1975 to the present. Fifty-six percent of married mothers with a child under age 1 are employed, and 59 percent of unmarried mothers with a child under 1 are employed. The percentages of women entering the labor force increases as their children get older. Sixty-two percent of married mothers with a child aged 2 are working, and 75 percent of unmarried moms with a child aged 2 are working.

As more women moved into the workforce in the 1960s, research on maternal employment's effects on children became a popular topic of study. For the past 20 years, maternal employment has evolved from being studied as a single factor affecting children's development to being studied as a more complex issue. It was once thought that maternal employment had a direct single influence on children. Now researchers agree that maternal employment is more than a question of whether or not the mother works. The issue needs to be studied within the context of the family, the society, and cultural norms. Study on maternal employment's effects must simultaneously answer these questions. What quality of child care does the child receive? How does the mother feel about working? What societal and family support do the mother and child receive?

Researchers are divided on what variables to study, as well as what methods to use in studying maternal employment effects. For example, some researchers combine several social classes to study the interactive effects of working mothers with child care arrangements, whereas others examine only one social class and how it intersects with the mother's personality traits and type of work and family environment.

The effects of maternal employment on children are determined by many factors such as mother's work satisfaction and morale, amount and control over work, and mother's perception of quality versus quantity time with her children. Depending on which studies one reads, how the data were collected, and which combination of variables was studied, different conclusions are reported. For example, some studies show that working moms spend more quality time with their children than non-working moms, while other studies show exactly the opposite results.

Research on maternal employment continues to become more refined, yet the question still remains: Should moms stay home with their babies? Often women will drop out of the workforce for at least the first few years to stay home and care for their children in order to make a connection. The concept that mother-child attachment in the first few years is critical to the child's later development has been established from years of significant research. Conversely, other research suggests that quality child care providers may be able to meet the same attachment needs that mothers previously met. In addition, research shows that being exposed to a variety of quality caregivers, including other family members, fosters positive personality characteristics and independence in the child later on.

In the following selections, Wen-Jui Han, Jane Waldfogel, and Jeanne Brooks-Gunn argue that maternal employment has negative effects on children. They found that mothers' working was associated with their children's lower scores on verbal ability and lower math achievement scores. Thomas M. Vander Ven, Francis T. Cullen, Mark A. Carrozza, and John Paul Wright assert that maternal employment does not affect children's development. They found that maternal employment during the child's first year of life had no relationship to subsequent child delinquency.

Wen-Jui Han, Jane Waldfogel,
and Jeanne Brooks-Gunn

 YES

The Effects of Early Maternal Employment on Later Cognitive and Behavioral Outcomes

Recent trends in labor force participation have given new urgency to understanding the effects of early maternal employment—employment begun in the child's 1st year of life—on child outcomes. Women with infants have had the fastest growth in labor force participation of any group in the United States. With welfare reform, even more mothers will be working in the labor market before their child's first birthday. These trends are of potential concern given prior research that has found negative effects of early maternal employment on outcomes for children.

Several studies have used data from the 1986 wave of the National Longitudinal Survey of Youth (NLSY) to investigate the effects of maternal employment in the 1st year on children's cognitive and behavioral outcomes as assessed at ages 3 or 4. In this article, we revisit these same children 2 and 4 years later, when they are aged 5 and 6 and aged 7 and 8, to see whether the effects that earlier studies found at ages 3 and 4 would persist. We also wanted to better understand what might cause these effects and how they might be moderated.

With one exception, all the NLSY studies to date have analyzed children at young ages or at one point in time. In a recent study, Harvey analyzed all the children in the NLSY born in 1980 or later. Her study is exceptional in that it assesses some outcomes as late as age 12 and at several different points in time. Unlike our study, however, Harvey's was not longitudinal in design. In our study, we follow one group of children from ages 3 and 4, to ages 5 and 6, and to ages 7 and 8. We are thus able to show whether the effects that many studies have found at a point in time persist over time or whether they attenuate. Another point of difference between our study and Harvey's is that she analyzes White, African American, and Hispanic children together. If there are important differences in the effects of early maternal employment across racial and ethnic groups, as some prior research has found and as we have found here, then analyzing children separately, is likely to yield more accurate estimates.

From *Journal of Marriage and Family*, vol. 63, (February 2001), pp. 336–354. Copyright © 2001 by National Council on Family Relations. Reprinted by permission. References omitted.

Research on maternal employment and child outcomes has been conducted within several theoretical frameworks. The first is attachment theory, which posits that children whose mothers are absent during critical periods of early child development are less likely to develop secure attachments with their mothers. Attachment theory had in mind extended round-the-clock separations due to hospitalizations, illness, incarceration, and so on, and debate continues about whether maternal employment in the 1st year of life constitutes a comparable absence. Early studies conducted in the 1970s and 1980s, for the most part with small samples of primarily middle-class White children, found some evidence that maternal employment in 1st year is associated with insecure attachment, but the effects were small. The most recent research, with a larger and more heterogeneous sample, does not find similar negative results. This discrepancy in findings may reflect in large part the differential selection of mothers into employment in the 1990s as compared with earlier decades when it was less common for mothers of infants to work.

Security of attachment to the mother is not the only child outcome of interest in the debate about maternal employment. Studies informed by child developmental psychology have paid particular attention to socioemotional adjustment (primarily behavior problems) and cognitive outcomes (primarily receptive verbal ability or early achievement test scores). Research on such outcomes has focused on large samples of children, with the bulk of studies analyzing data from the NLSY. These studies have found that maternal employment in the 1st year of life has a different effect on later emotional adjustment than does employment begun thereafter. There is also evidence that employment begun in the 1st year of life may have negative effects on cognitive development for some groups, whereas employment after the 1st year of life seems to have positive effects.

The few studies that have been able to control for childcare quality when examining maternal employment effects find that it plays an important mediating role, as does the type of care. High-quality care, if available to some low-income children, may make a bigger difference in their development than it does in high-income families. It may also matter how many hours the mother works.

Child and family characteristics also can mediate the effects of early maternal employment. The child's age when the mother begins work is obviously a critical mediating factor, but so, too, are factors such as the child's characteristics, family background, and current living situation. Moreover, the effects of early maternal employment may be moderated by family characteristics. For instance, family income is an important variable in its own right; mothers in low-income families may experience greater financial strain and hardship, which are in turn negatively associated with parental psychological functioning and parenting behavior. These effects may be more pronounced in low-income families where mothers are working than in families where they are not. In addition, low-income families may be less able to purchase high-quality and stable child care than more affluent families. Therefore, one might expect greater negative effects of maternal employment in low-income than in middle- or high-income families. Nonetheless, if children from high-income families have more to lose when they are separated from their mothers because their mother are more nurturing or more cognitively skilled, then we might instead expect high-income children to be more vulnerable to the effects of early maternal employment.

Taken together, previous empirical findings and theory generate a rich set of hypotheses as to the likely effects of maternal employment in the 1st year on children's later cognitive and behavioral outcomes, the causes of these effects, and the potential buffers of them. We list the major hypotheses below and indicate which ones we will and will not test in this article. The premise of all these hypotheses is that all development is contextualized; any effects of early maternal employment are likely to vary as a function of context.

> Hypothesis 1: Children of mothers who work in the 1st year of life will have poorer long-term cognitive and behavioral outcomes because the time they would have spent with a cognitively stimulating and nurturing mother is spent instead with a substitute caregiver who is less cognitively stimulating and nurturing (because she or he has lower cognitive skills than the mother, because she or he is less motivated to stimulate and nurture the child, or because she or he is less able to give the child one-on-one attention).

We will test this hypothesis by estimating the effect of 1st-year maternal employment on later child cognitive and behavioral outcomes. We will also test several extensions of this hypothesis.

1. If there are racial or ethnic differences in mother-child interactions in the 1st year and/or in substitute caregiving arrangements in the 1st year, then the effects of maternal employment on child outcomes may differ by racial or ethnic group. We will test this by analyzing non-Hispanic White and African American families separately.
2. If children are more sensitive to maternal absences due to employment early in the 1st year of life than later, then effects of employment should be largest when it occurs earlier in the 1st year. We will test this by examining the quarter of the 1st year in which employment was initiated.
3. If the effects of employment are cumulative, the effects should be largest when mothers work longer hours. We will test this by comparing effects of full-time and part-time employment.
4. If boys are generally more vulnerable in the 1st year of life, then the effects of maternal absence in the 1st year should be larger for boys than for girls. We will test this by comparing the effects of 1st-year employment for boys and girls.
5. If the effects of 1st-year employment are due to the loss of the mothers' cognitive stimulation, then the effects should be more pronounced for children whose mothers have higher cognitive ability themselves. We will test this by comparing the effects of 1st year maternal employment for children whose mothers have differing levels of cognitive ability (as measured by the AFQT).
6. It is unclear a priori how the effects of early maternal employment might vary by family income. If the effects of 1st-year employment are due to the absence of the mother, then the effects might be most

pronounced for children from higher income families in which the mothers might be more stimulating. If the effects of 1st-year employment are due to the low quality of the care in which the child is placed, however, and if income is correlated with quality of child care, the effects might be most pronounced for children from lower income families. We will test these competing hypotheses by comparing the effects of early maternal employment for children from families of differing income levels.

7. If the effects of 1st-year employment are due to the low quality of care in which children are placed, then the effects should be most pronounced for children in the lowest quality care. We cannot test this directly because we lack data on child-care quality. Instead, we will control for child-care type, which may be correlated with quality.

Hypothesis 2: Children of mothers who work in the 1st year of life will have poorer long-term cognitive and behavioral outcomes because during the time the mother is with the child, she is tired and stressed and therefore is less nurturing and stimulating.

We will test this hypothesis by comparing families of different income levels because working mothers in low-income families may face more strain and hardship than those in higher income families. We also would like to test this hypothesis by controlling for the home environment in the 1st year of life, but we have no measures of this (we only have measures of the concurrent home environment starting at age 3).

Hypothesis 3: Children of mothers who work in the 1st year of life may have poorer long-term cognitive or behavioral outcomes because of other omitted factors that are correlated with mothers' employment (e.g., single parenthood, fathers not working, mothers entering and exiting the labor force).

We test this hypothesis by controlling for an extensive set of child and family characteristics, including single parenthood and by comparing the effects of 1st-year maternal employment in families where fathers do or do not work and in families where mothers work continuously compared with families where mothers transition in and out of the labor market.

There are several other hypotheses that we are not able to test with the data at hand. These include hypotheses that focus on child-care characteristics, such as stability and quality; job characteristics, such as low wages, poor working conditions, low satisfaction, and nonstandard working hours; and maternal mental health and role strain.

Implicit in each of our hypotheses is the idea that the effects of early maternal employment on cognitive or behavioral outcomes might be sustained. That is, we might see effects persisting to the latest year when we observe our sample, at ages 7 and 8. This possible persistence of effects raises the question of whether these effects might be moderated by subsequent experiences. Although a full examination of moderating effects is beyond the scope of this study, we do control for subsequent maternal employment, years spent living in a single-mother family, and whether the family was ever poor. We also explicitly examine whether the quality of the home environment starting at age 3 has a moderating effect, given prior evidence on the importance of home environment for child development.

Data and Method

Data

Our main samples are composed of all the White and African American children in the NLSY whom we can follow, with no missing data on any outcome variables, from ages 3 and 4 in 1986 to ages 7 and 8 in 1990. Because there are missing data on PIAT scores for some children and because a number of children (the children of the disadvantaged White oversample) were dropped in 1990, the resulting samples are quite small ($n = 244$ for Whites, $n = 218$ for African Americans). Following Baydar and Brooks-Gunn (1991), we do not analyze Hispanic children because the tests, which were mainly administered in English, may not be reliable for them.

Our sample of children is not a random sample of all children born in 1982 and 1983. Rather, it represents children born in those years to the young women in the NLSY, who ranged in age from 17 to 26 at the time of their child's birth. Consequently, our sample consists of children of relatively young mothers, who will tend to have lower educational levels and lower incomes.

We also conducted supplementary analyses of a somewhat larger sample, the non-Hispanic White children whom we can follow with no missing data from age 3 and 4 in 1986 to age 5 and 6 in 1988; the main difference is that this sample includes children from the White disadvantaged oversample that was dropped in 1990. The results from this larger sample are consistent for the most part with the results for our main sample.

Measures

Maternal employment.   We use the detailed maternal employment information in the NLSY to establish the employment status of a mother during each year of her child's life. The following six measures were constructed: employed during the 1st year of life (coded as 1 if the mother worked any hours at all during the child's 1st year); employed during the 2nd or 3rd year; employed after age 3 up to the year before assessment; currently working; quarter of the 1st year that maternal employment began; and full-time–part-time work in the 1st year, with full-time defined as working 21 or more hours per week. The usual cut-off point of 35 hours for full-time was not used because we assume that very young children are more sensitive to the quantity of time a mother spends with them than are school-aged children. In addition, scholars have found that mothers working more than 20 hours are associated with poorer cognitive outcomes for children.

Parental presence and work status.   Six categories were constructed to represent all possible combinations of the mother's working status and father's presence and working status in the 1st year of a child's life: working mother and no father (7.0%), working mother and nonworking father (2.5%), working mother and working father (43.9%), nonworking mother and no father (7.8%), nonworking mother and nonworking father (0.8%), and nonworking mother and working father (38.0%).

Home environment. The Home Observation for Measurement of the Environment-Short Form was used. This scale, which was scored by either maternal report or interviewer observation, measures the degree to which the child's home environment provided emotional support and cognitive simulation. The earliest information is from 1986 when the children were aged 3 to 4. We use information from the 1986, 1988, and 1990 HOME scores to investigate the effects of contemporary HOME environment on children's achievements. The mean scores for Whites and Blacks were 103 (with *SD* of 13) and 92 (with *SD* of 14), respectively.

Child care. Child-care arrangements during the first 3 years of a child's life were asked of the mothers retrospectively at the time of the 1986 survey. We categorize the primary child-care arrangement during the 1st year of the child's life as follows: parental care (care by mother or father); relative care (care by sibling, grandparent, or other relative); nonrelative care (care by someone other than a relative, whether in home or not); or center care (day-care center, group care center, nursery school, or preschool). As noted earlier, an important limitation of the NLSY data on child care is the absence of information pertaining to the quality of child care. Thus, our child-care results must be interpreted with caution.

Sociodemographic variables. Children and families' sociodemographic characteristics have substantial effects on children's cognitive ability, as evidenced by previous studies. Thus, we also controlled for gender, having older siblings, ever having lived in poverty, and years living in a single-parent family. To compare families at various income levels, three dummy variables were constructed to represent poverty (income-to-needs ratio $\leq$ 1), low income (income-to-needs ratio > 1 and $\leq$ 2), and middle income and higher (income-to-needs ratio > 2) in the 1st year of life. Mother's cognitive ability, as measured by the Armed Forces Qualification Test (AFQT; Bock & Mislevy, 1981) score, was included to not only capture the effect of mother's intelligence on a child's cognitive outcomes, but also to control for its possible effect on selection into the labor force.

Child's achievement and receptive vocabulary outcomes. The Peabody Picture Vocabulary Test-Revised was used to measure children's verbal ability at ages 3 and 4, and the Peabody Individual Achievement Test. Math and Reading Recognition are used to measure math and verbal achievement respectively for children at ages 5 and 6 and at ages 7 and 8. Thus, we are using different tests to compare children's cognitive outcomes at different points in time. Because the PPVT-R correlates significantly with other measures of verbal intelligence and with measures of reading and math achievement, however, these variables should allow us to assess the influence of maternal employment on the cognitive development of a child over time while still using tests that are appropriate to the age of the child. The PPVT-R test assesses vocabulary knowledge in children aged 3 years and older. The PIAT-Math measures achievement in mathematics and the PIAT-Reading Recognition assess the attained reading knowledge of children aged 5 years or older. (We do not use PIAT-Reading Comprehension because many 5- to 6-year-olds have missing values, as their scores were lower than the national PIAT sample. The mean of PPVT-R score for Whites is 96.55 (*SD* 16.40), and it is 73.66 (*SD* 18.47) for Blacks. The mean of PIAT-Math score for Whites is about 102 (*SD* 12), and it is about 95 (*SD* of 12) for Blacks. The mean of PIAT-Reading Recognition for Whites is about 106 (*SD* 13), and it is about 101 (*SD* 11) for Blacks.

Behavioral problems.   The Behavioral Problems Index measures six dimensions of behavior problems (antisocial behavior, anxiousness/depression, headstrongness, hyperactivity, immaturity, and dependency). We use the total BPI score, as well as two subscales (internalizing and externalizing problems). This measure was collected only for children aged four or older. The two subscales used in the analysis have Cronbach's alpha of .70 and .84.

Empirical Strategy

Our statistical procedure is multiple regression, estimated using ordinary least squares. We regress the child's PPVT-R score at ages 3 or 4 and the PIAT-Math and Reading Recognition scores at ages 5 or 6 and at ages 7 or 8 on a set of demographic and socioeconomic family background variables, together with alternative sets of variables describing the mother's employment behavior over the child's early lifetime. We examine not only the impact of early maternal employment per se, but also the impact of the timing and the extent of early maternal employment. We also examine some moderating effects. We then turn to similar models where we estimate the effects of early maternal employment on the BPI and its two subscales.

Empirical Results

Does Early Maternal Employment Affect Cognitive Outcomes, and Do These Effects Vary by Race or Ethnicity?

. . . Consistent with previous studies, maternal employment in the 1st year of life has a significant negative effect on the PPVT-R score at age 3 or 4, reducing the score by 7 points at those ages. The results for the White children at age 5 to 6 and age 7 to 8 indicate that the negative effects of 1st-year maternal employment persist over time. Looking at the PIAT results, having a mother who worked in the 1st year lowers math achievement by 5 points at age 7 to 8 and lowers reading recognition by about 5 points at both age 5 to 6 and age 7 to 8. Subsequent maternal employment, in contrast, is mainly positive; in particular, having a mother who worked in the 2nd or 3rd year largely offsets the effects of 1st-year employment for reading at age 5 to 6 and age 7 to 8.

The results for African Americans . . . are quite different, with no significant effects of maternal employment on cognitive outcomes in any of the models. We also found no significant effects for African Americans in any of the other models that we ran, providing some support for the notion that there are important racial or ethnic differences at work here. Therefore, the rest of our analyses are reported for White children only.

Do the Effects of Early Maternal Employment Vary by When the Employment Began?

The existence of negative effects of 1st-year maternal employment for some children raises the question of whether these effects are more pronounced if they occur during earlier periods within the 1st year. . . . With everything else held constant, timing within the 1st year may matter. The results for PPVT-R at age 3 to 4 suggest that starting employment before the 4th quarter of the year could lower a child's PPVT-R score by 7 points, whereas starting employment in the 4th quarter has no significant effect. The results for other outcomes at other ages further indicate that the strong negative effect for White children of the mother entering the labor force before the 4th quarter persists over time.

Do the Effects of Early Maternal Employment Vary by the Mothers' Hours?

We also examined whether the effects of maternal employment varied by women's full-time versus part-time working status in the 1st year. The results . . . suggest that the effects of working part-time in the 1st year are not significantly different than the effects of working full-time. The analysis was also reestimated using mother's continuous working hours; the results are not significant.

Do the Effects of Early Maternal Employment Vary by the Child's Gender?

We also examined whether the effects of maternal employment varied by the child's gender. . . . We found no significant differences in the effects of maternal employment on cognitive outcomes by gender.

Do the Effects of Early Maternal Employment Vary by Mothers' Cognitive Ability?

To further test the hypothesis that it is the absence of a cognitively stimulating mother that leads to lower outcomes for children whose mothers work in the 1st year and that children of the more highly skilled mothers would be more affected, we use data on mothers' AFQT scores to divide our sample into quartiles of cognitive ability. We use AFQT rather than educational attainment because these scores are strongly associated with children's cognitive scores and are likely to be a better measure of these relatively young mothers' cognitive ability than their educational attainment at the time of the birth.

. . . The results of the F tests . . . indicate that 1st-year maternal employment has statistically significant negative effects in one of five models for children of mothers in the top quartile of AFQT scores, in three of five models for children of mothers in the 2nd quartile, and in two of five for children of mothers in the 3rd quartile; there are no significant effects for children of mothers in the lowest quartile. This pattern of results is consistent with the hypothesis above in that we find some significant effects of early maternal employment for children whose mothers are moderately to highly skilled but no significant effects for children whose mothers are very low skilled (with a mean AFQT of 41).

Do the Effects of Early Maternal Employment on Cognitive Outcomes Vary by Family Income?

As we saw earlier, children from low-income families may be more affected by early maternal employment if their mothers are more stressed or if they are placed in poorer quality child care. At the same time, children from high-income families might be more affected if they have more to lose from the absence of their mother. We tested whether the effects of early maternal employment vary by family income. . . . The F tests . . . indicate that 1st-year maternal employment has statistically significant negative effects in all five models for children of low-income families, compared with in three of five models for middle-income families and two of five for high-income families. Thus, maternal employment has the most significant effects on cognitive outcomes for children in low-income families, as we would expect if income is correlated with child-care quality and if low child-care quality is part of the reason for the adverse effects of early maternal employment, or if mothers who work in low-income families experience greater financial strain and hardship.

Do the Effects of Early Maternal Employment Vary by Child-Care Type?

Given these results, it would be of particular interest to control for child-care quality. As noted earlier, however, we cannot do so with the NLSY. The best we can do is to control for the type of child care the child attended during the 1st year. . . . We find that relative care, nonrelative care, and center care have positive effects on PPVT-R at age 3 to 4 compared with the reference category, parental care, which might suggest that quality child care can compensate to some extent for early maternal employment.

Do Other Factors Such As Fathers' Employment Status, Single Motherhood, or Mothers' Subsequent Employment Patterns Account for the Effects of Early Maternal Employment?

Bearing in mind that these children were born in 1982 or 1983, a time when maternal employment was less typical than it is today and when the United States was undergoing a recession, . . . we tested the hypothesis that mothers' employment might be associated with fathers' employment status and that this might affect child outcomes. . . . [C]hildren from two-parent families whose mothers worked in the 1st year have lower cognitive scores than the reference group (children in two-parent families whose mothers did not work in the 1st year and whose fathers did). . . . [T]he negative effects of 1st-year maternal employment are largest for children whose fathers were present but not working, however, suggesting that there is a connection between mothers' and fathers' work in the 1st year and outcomes for children. . . . [We] compared children in single-mother families where the mother did or did not work in the 1st year. We find no significant differences between these groups (both have lower PPVT-R scores than the reference group at age 3 to 4 and lower PIAT-Math scores at age 7 to 8).

[We] examined the impact of mothers' subsequent employment status by categorizing women according to their employment across the first 3 years of the child's life. The results show that only for those women who worked in the 1st year and then left the labor force is there a significant long-term negative effect of that 1st-year employment; for those who worked in the 1st year and continued working, the effect of 1st-year employment, although still negative, is not significant after the 1st year. . . . [A]lthough White children might have higher cognitive scores at ages 3 to 4 if their mothers delayed entry into the labor force into the 2nd or 3rd year, this difference is no longer significant by the time they are age 5 to 6 and 7 to 8. This result lends some support to the hypothesis that factors other than 1st-year maternal employment (e.g., entry and exits) may account for some of the effects of maternal employment.

Does Contemporary Home Environment Moderate the Effects of Early Maternal Employment?

To test for the moderating effect of the quality of home environment, we added the contemporary HOME score to the model. In results not shown, although the home environment does have a significant positive effect on children's cognitive outcomes, no significant result was found for the interaction between HOME score and early maternal employment, and the addition of HOME scores did not reduce the effect of early maternal employment.

Does Early Maternal Employment Affect Behavioral Outcomes?

In analyses using the total BPI score . . . we find no statistically significant effects of maternal employment on White children's behavioral problems, but timing seems to matter when they are 7 to 8 years old. Specifically, entering the labor force before the 4th quarter of the 1st year has a significant effect on children's behavioral outcomes (the higher the score, the more problems).

. . . [We] compare the difference between internalizing and externalizing problems. The results indicate that 1st-year maternal employment, and entering the labor force early in the 1st year, have a significant effect only on externalizing problems, with effects at age 4 and again at ages 7 to 8.

In results not shown, we interacted gender with maternal employment but found no significant differences in these behavioral problem models; when we interacted family income with early maternal employment, we found that children in high-income families exhibit more externalizing problems at age 4 if their mothers worked in the 1st year.

Discussion and Conclusions

The empirical results in this study indicate that early maternal employment has a significant negative effect on White children's cognitive outcomes at age 3 or 4 and that these effects persist to age 7 or 8 in some instances but not in others. We found no significant effects of early maternal employment on cognitive outcomes for African American children, suggesting that the effects of early maternal employment do vary by racial and ethnic group. We can only speculate as to the reason for this difference, but one possibility is that it reflects the fact that employment of mothers of young children has been traditionally more common in African American families and therefore may be seen as more normative; that is, the context in which early maternal employment occurs may differ for different groups.

Given the small size of our sample, our results are somewhat tentative, but we found evidence that the effects we find among White children may be more pronounced for some children than others. Specifically, we found that the effects may be more pronounced for children whose mothers start work early in their 1st year of life. But we found no significant differences between children whose mothers worked full-time or part-time in the 1st year. We also found no significant differences in the effects of early maternal employment for boys and girls.

With regard to the mother's level of cognitive ability, we found some significant effects of early maternal employment on cognitive outcomes for children of mothers who had moderate to high AFQT scores. We found no significant effects for children of mothers who had very low AFQT scores (in the bottom quartile), however; these children have lower cognitive scores, as expected, but this was the case whether or not their mothers worked. This pattern of results lends some support to the hypothesis that it is the loss of a cognitively stimulating mother that accounts for some of the ill effects of early maternal employment on cognitive outcomes for children.

Comparing children from poverty, low-income, and moderate- and high-income families, we found the most significant effects of early maternal employment for the children from poverty-income families. These stronger effects may be due to the low quality of the child care they attend, to turbulence in their child care arrangements, to the strain and hardship their mothers experience when they are working, or to a combination of these factors. We were not able to assess the impact of child-care quality because of the limitations of the NLSY data.

We found no support for the hypothesis that the effects of early maternal employment might be due to the correlation between employment and single motherhood. We did find, however, that controlling for fathers' employment status and for mothers' subsequent employment status did make a difference. Children whose mothers worked in the 1st year and whose fathers were present but did not work, and children whose mothers worked in the 1st year and then dropped out of the labor market, fared worse in terms of their long-run cognitive outcomes than did other children whose mothers worked in the 1st year of life.

Turning to moderating effects, we found that the effects of early maternal employment may be buffered for children whose families provide a nurturing and stimulating home environment. Whether they might also be buffered for children whose child-care settings are nurturing and stimulating is an important question but one that we are not able to address with the data at hand.

We also found some negative effects of 1st-year maternal employment on behavioral problems for White children, mainly at ages 7 to 8. The effects seem to be concentrated in the area of externalizing problems. We found no significant effects of 1st-year maternal employment on behavioral outcomes for African American children, again suggesting important racial and ethnic differences.

The question remains: Why are there negative effects of 1st-year maternal employment, and why do these effects persist over time for some children but not others? This study included an extensive set of controls. Nonetheless, we were still unable to control for some characteristics that might help explain the persistent effects for some children of maternal employment in the 1st year. For instance, information on the quality of child care, as well as the quality of time mothers spend with their infants, would be helpful, given previous findings on the positive effects of high-quality child care on children's cognitive outcomes.

The significant negative effects of early maternal employment found for some children in this study were not found in Harvey's recent work. The differences between these two sets of results primarily reflect the different approaches used in these two studies. The samples were different: Harvey used a larger sample but did not follow the same children over time, whereas we followed a longitudinal sample that was of necessity smaller. Most important, our study analyzed non-Hispanic White and African American children separately, whereas her study pooled Whites, African Americans, and Hispanics together. When we pooled the three racial and ethnic groups (results not shown), we, too, found much weaker links between 1st-year maternal employment and later outcomes.

The generalizability of our results is limited in that we examined children of relatively young mothers. Analyses of a more representative sample of children should be undertaken. Despite these limitations, however, our study makes a unique contribution by assessing the effects of early maternal employment on children's cognitive and behavioral outcomes over time. Our findings that 1st-year maternal employment has negative effects on cognitive outcomes for White children and that these effects persist in some instances to ages 7 and 8 merit further research, as does the suggestion that there may be some longrun effects on behavioral problems for White children as well. The negative effects we found are fairly small. Nonetheless, if for some children these effects occur in addition to those associated with other risk factors, such as poverty or a non-employed father, the cumulative effects may be of concern.

Proponents of family leave legislation have argued that such laws will improve maternal and child health. Our results suggest that giving parents the right to longer periods of parental leave might improve some children's cognitive and behavioral outcomes as well. In this regard, research on the impact on child outcomes of the recently adopted U.S. Family and Medical Leave Act, and of the more generous family leave legislation in place in other countries, would be welcome. Nonetheless, we are mindful that there is a good deal of variation in preferences and outcomes among families and that the effects of early maternal employment will depend on many contextual factors. Therefore, we also recommend more research on child-care quality and policy initiatives designed to raise the quality of child care provided to infants.

NO ← Thomas M. Vander Ven, Francis T. Cullen, Mark A. Carrozza, and John Paul Wright

Home Alone: The Impact of Maternal Employment on Delinquency

In recent decades, American family life has been transformed dramatically. Family scholars-debate the causes and consequences of these major changes, routinely clashing over whether family forms are changing for the better or whether our most important social institution is experiencing a moral and functional freefall.

One of the most profound changes is the unprecedented number of women who have entered the paid workforce since the 1950s. Census data show that female labor force participation rose from approximately 28 percent in 1940 to close to 60 percent in 1992. This wave of women entering the labor force was accompanied by a large increase in maternal employment. While only 16 percent of all children had working mothers in 1950, close to 70 percent of all mothers with dependent children work today. Recent estimates show that over half of those with children less than one year old are employed outside the home and over 60 percent of those with children younger than six are employed.

While the mass entrance of women and mothers into the labor market might be regarded as a sign of social progress, many Americans are worried about the trend and have been for some time. And in what may be seen as part of the "backlash" to feminist political victories, politicians, social critics, and parenting "experts" have frequently pointed to the working mother as the cause of many of our social problems.

While supporting empirical evidence is scarce, the political Right charges that feminist philosophies damage the American family by encouraging women to choose work and self-fulfillment over family obligations. Additionally, noted psychologists argue that the neglected child of the working mother may suffer from an attachment disorder, which is widely believed to be a major causal factor in the production of extreme child behavior problems. One pediatrician and TV personality warns that mothers should stay home to raise their infants or risk the disruption of the critical mother-child bonding period: "if he doesn't have that through infancy, it's hard to put it in later . . . and these kids that never get it . . . will become difficult in school, they'll never succeed in school,

From *Social Problems* by Thomas M. Vander Ven et al., pp. 236–257. Copyright © 2001 by University of California Press, Journals Division. Reprinted by permission. References and notes omitted.

they'll make everybody angry, they'll become delinquents later and eventually they'll become terrorists."

Although there is no shortage of claims that maternal employment causes negative child outcomes, there is little evidence that this is the case. Recent research shows that the children of working mothers are no less attached than other children and that they experience no deficits in social, emotional, or behavioral functioning. While no work and family issue attracts more scholarly attention than the potential effects of maternal employment on children's development, few researchers have investigated the possible link between working mothers and delinquency.

In this context, we analyze the impact of maternal employment—of kids being left "home alone"—on delinquency using models that include different characteristics of maternal employment (e.g., hours, workplace controls), variations in maternal non-employment (e.g., welfare reliance), and child care arrangements. Our analysis is influenced by the research program of Parcel and Meneghan, who investigated the impact of various dimensions of parental work on a range of social, cognitive, and behavioral outcomes. Similarly, we test models that consider the number of hours usually employed, working conditions, and the timing of work. This more comprehensive measurement of maternal work improves upon past research on maternal employment and delinquency, where mother's work was simply divided into "working mother" and "non-working mother" categories.

Furthermore, in an attempt to isolate the independent effects of maternal work, we simultaneously consider the impact of maternal resources (i.e., maternal cognitive skills, maternal education, family income), child care arrangements, and marital status. By controlling for maternal resources, we are better able to isolate the independent effects of maternal employment.

Maternal Employment and Delinquency

Previous Delinquency Research

Although there is a tremendous body of literature on the effects of maternal employment on child outcomes, studies on the link between maternal work and delinquency are relatively scarce. Early researchers tended to find a small positive effect of maternal employment on delinquency, which they usually assumed was the consequence of low maternal supervision. Most contemporary researchers found little or no connection between maternal work status and delinquency. Other studies suggest that delinquency is less common among the children of regularly employed mothers. In some cases, maternal work actually served as insulation against delinquent risks because working mothers effectively raised the family income, thus improving the living conditions of their children. Maternal employment, then, should be considered as an economic dimension of family life and may be most beneficial for children when the alternative is poverty or welfare dependency.

When examined closely, the extant literature on maternal employment and delinquency suggests that working conditions are an important factor that must be included in analytical models. Glueck and Glueck, for example, found that delinquency was highest among the children of occasionally employed mothers. This finding is provocative because occasional or sporadic work may be indicative of secondary labor market employment. Employment in the secondary labor market is often erratic and coercive due to the vulnerability of the lowskilled, uneducated workers at this level. Such employment may be criminogenic if coercive workplace experiences negatively shape parenting techniques.

In a related vein, Roy found that maternal work was related to delinquency in urban settings, but not in rural areas. This effect, also, may reflect important differences between working conditions in urban vs. rural communities. It may be that maternal work in urban centers and among minority populations is, on average, more likely to be coercive, secondary labor market work. In light of these findings, better measures of maternal employment—including measures for workplace controls and regularity of employment (part-time vs. full-time) are needed.

Maternal Employment and the Pathways to Delinquency

Concerns about the effects of maternal employment suggest that working mothers are less able to supervise, discipline, and nurture their children, which may contribute to misconduct or youth crime. The main pathway between maternal work and delinquency, then, would be a breakdown in parental responsibility. Generally, theories of delinquency divide parental responsibility into two broad categories: control and support. Guided by several strains of criminological thought, we include pathway variables that reflect both parental controls and parental supports in our analysis.

Parental control.   Control theories of delinquency emphasize the importance of both direct controls and indirect controls. Direct parental control is generally measured as the degree to which parents supervise or monitor their children's activities. Lax parental supervision has been identified as a powerful predictor of behavior problems.

The importance of indirect control mechanisms (e.g., attachment to parents) is also a common theme in criminological theory and research. Low parent-child bonding is also a well-documented path to delinquency. Thus, we trace the effects of maternal work on delinquency through both direct (i.e., supervision) and indirect parental controls (i.e., attachment).

The relationship between parental work and parent-child bonds is central to Colvin and Pauly's structural-Marxist theory of delinquency production. The authors argue that coercively controlled workers may be prone to harsh and erratic parenting styles, which include punitive discipline and lax supervision. Children who are socialized on a coercive and erratic schedule are likely to form alienated bonds to parents, which may contribute to behavior problems later on. Thus, we examine the path from workplace controls to modes of parental discipline (i.e., spanking), to supervision, and to attachment.

A breakdown in parental control may also be reflected in a child's association with delinquent peers. That is, if the children of employed mothers spend more time on average in peer interaction and if their peer relationships are less subject to parental review, we might find that delinquent peer association links maternal work to delinquency. As such, we evaluate this potential pathway by including delinquent peer association in our models.

Parental support.   Cullen's social support perspective asserts that, in addition to social control, delinquency is reduced by the receipt by youths of parental social support. Because work commitment and working conditions may influence delinquency indirectly by affecting maternal support, we investigate this potential pathway by including measures of warm and responsive parenting in our models.

Similarly, Sampson and Laub suggest that social relations between individuals—between a parent and child, for example—should be seen as a form of social investment or social capital. According to this view, a parent-child relationship is a social and psychological resource that children "can draw on as they move through life transitions that traverse larger trajectories." While Hirschi depicts the parent-child bond as a psychological constraint or control on deviant impulses, Sampson and Laub describe the parent-child relationship as a matrix for support where children develop cognitive, social, and behavioral skills.

Parental support can result in the cognitive ability and emotional development a child needs to succeed in school and may lead to greater child attachment to school. Thus, if maternal employment prevents mothers from investing in children, it may indirectly result in negative school outcomes. This may be an important link between maternal work and delinquency, because low school attachment is a consistent predictor of delinquent involvement. Accordingly, we examine the indirect effect of maternal work on delinquency through school attachment.

Methodology

Sample

In the 1960s, the United States Department of Labor hired the Center for Human Resource Research at the Ohio State University to gather longitudinal data on the labor market experiences of four representative target groups among the U.S. population. A fifth cohort of men and women between the ages of 14 and 22 was identified in 1979. Known as the National Longitudinal Survey of Youth (NLSY), this project involved a multistaged stratified random sampling that produced 12,686 subjects, 11,404 of whom were interviewed annually about their occupational, educational, familial, and childbearing experiences.

By 1994, 10,042 children of sample mothers were identified to report on their home environment, family relations, and school experiences in addition to taking a number of inventories designed to measure cognitive and socioemotional development. To investigate the relationship between maternal work and delinquency, we conduct our analysis on a sample of 707 adolescents who were between the ages of 12 and 14 in 1994. These children are the offspring of female respondents originally interviewed in 1979. Each of these respondents completed the Child Self-Administered Supplement (CSAS) in 1992 and in 1994. This self-report booklet collects information on a wide range of variables including child-parent interaction, peer relationships, and involvement in various delinquent activities.

Additionally, the children of the NLSY mothers were studied every other year beginning in 1986, so data on various developmental outcomes are available from early childhood up through early and middle adolescence for this sample. To study the effects of both early and current maternal employment on delinquency, we follow this sample from 1994 back to 1986 when study children were between the ages of 2 and 5 years old. We selected 1986 as the study year for early employment effects because it was the first year that NLSY researchers collected extensive data on parent-child interaction and family relations. We take advantage of the longitudinal nature of the NLSY data by controlling for 1994 employment when examining the effects of 1986 employment on 1994 delinquency. By controlling for current employment, it will lend support to any assertions that the effect of early employment is independent of the effect of current employment.

The NLSY data, while presenting great possibilities for research, have their shortcomings. One limitation of these data, for example, is that over 27 percent of the children who were between the ages of 10 and 14 in 1994 were born to mothers who were less than twenty years old when they gave birth to their children. As a result, many of these mothers are less-educated and are more likely to be members of a minority group than one would find in a representative sample where maternal age is normally distributed. Because early childbearers are more prone to having children with developmental deficits, such as low cognitive ability, and are at a greater risk for criminality, these children should be considered to be a high-risk group.

While other researchers use weighted data to correct for the large number of lower socioeconomic and minority women in the sample, we perform our analysis on the unweighted sample. The NLSY guide to Child Data strongly cautions against using weighted data across years because "analyzing data from persons interviewed in multiple years creates problems since the yearly weights are not appropriate to such a universe." Using the weighted data in regression equations that represent longitudinal effects, then, may result in substantial miscalculations of standard errors. Guo argued that bias can be reduced in the unweighted sample by controlling for those characteristics that are overrepresented, such as race, maternal education, and an assessment of mother's cognitive ability. Controls for each of these variables are included in each of our analytical models. As a check on our results, we also performed our main analyses using weighted data. The relationships between variables did not differ substantially when using the unweighted rather than the weighted sample. All reported results, hereafter, reflect the unweighted analysis.

. . . Correlation matrix analysis and tolerance tests did not detect the presence of multicollinearity between any two independent measures. Mean replacement was used to address missing values. The main analysis was also estimated without mean replacement. No substantial differences were found.

Dependent Variable: Delinquency

The 1994 CSAS includes nine highly correlated items that assess involvement in deviant and delinquent acts. Five of the items measure relatively minor to moderate acts of youth deviance: breaking parents' curfew, dishonesty (i.e., lying to a parent), school problems (i.e., parent came to school because of child behavior), truancy, and staying out all night. The other four items involve more serious acts of lawbreaking: alcohol abuse, vandalism (i.e., damaged school property on purpose), store theft, and violence (i.e., hurt someone badly enough to need bandages or a doctor). These nine items are summed to create our scale measuring youth deviance and delinquency (alpha = .78).

The respondents were asked to report on their involvement in each of these behaviors over the last twelve months. If the children reported that they had no involvement in any given act, that variable received a score of 0. If the respondent was involved in that activity over the past year, the variable received a score of 1. Measuring delinquent involvement in this way is common in the delinquency literature. We should note, however, that we also conducted our analyses using the same delinquency scale but with involvement measured by the number of times the respondent committed each act (i.e., the frequency score). The results of this investigation did not differ from results produced by the main analysis.

This measure of delinquency is skewed towards non-offending. Nearly 25 percent of the adolescent sample reported no involvement in any of the nine items used to create the scale. Furthermore, over 75 percent of the sample reported involvement in no more than three of the nine items used to construct the index. This variable is transformed into a new measure equal to the natural logarithm of the delinquency variable in order to increase the explainable variance in delinquency.

Independent Variables

Maternal employment status. A continuous measure of hours usually worked is used in this analysis. In past studies, investigators assigned missing values to work-hour variables for non-employed mothers, who were then excluded from the analysis. Thus, these studies focused on the effects of paid maternal employment among a sub-group of working mothers only. Other studies include non-employed mothers but as a dummy category that is used in equations with other dummy variables capturing increasing levels of time commitment to paid employment (e.g., part-time, full-time, over-time). Measuring maternal work hours via a series of dummy variables is arguably a good strategy for organizing information and for detecting non-linear effects. As Harvey points out, however, this method is problematic because the dummy categories are formed from continuous variables so there are infinite ways one could create categories and arbitrary boundaries between categories are often created. Moreover, using continuous variables does not prevent the detection of nonlinear effects. Based on this rationale, we use a continuous measure of hours worked in our primary analysis.

In order to compare non-working mothers to working mothers on various pathway and delinquency variables, we assign non-working mothers mean values for work hours. As suggested by Menaghan, et al., we run models where dummy variables are employed to capture employment status (i.e., welfare, coercive, technical, and bureaucratic work controls) while substituting mean values for the continuous variable measuring work-role conditions (i.e., hours worked) for non-working mothers. Regression estimates for the continuous hours variable will reflect the effects for working mothers, and coefficients for the occupational class dummy variables will "reflect the contrast between that group and the reference category, evaluated at average conditions on the continuous variables."

One might argue that assigning the mean hours worked to non-employed mothers blurs the analysis since the main objective here is to examine the impact of real differences (e.g., the effects of zero hours of employment vs. the effects of forty hours of employment) in maternal work commitment. To bolster confidence in our measure of work hours, we conducted separate analyses where non-working mothers were assigned zeros for work hours. No substantive differences in the results were found. Furthermore, consistent with Parcel and Menaghan's usual strategy, we also measure work hours with a series of dummy variables capturing part-time, full–time, and overtime work schedules in a separate analysis. Again, our results did not differ from results produced using the continuous measure of work hours. In all analyses, non-working mothers (those who neither worked nor received welfare in the previous year) serve as the reference category.

To identify welfare-reliant mothers, we use a dummy variable, which is coded as 1 if the respondent reported that she did not work during the survey week and if the respondent answered affirmatively to the question, "Did you or your spouse receive income from AFDC in the past calendar year?" In this way, we distinguish between those who draw income primarily from welfare and those who may draw welfare but participate in the workforce as well.

Current employment is measured in 1992. We used the 1992 work variables and controls in the current effects model because the delinquency items ask respondents to report on delinquency involvement over the previous 12 months. Therefore, to approximate the temporal order of our conceptual model, we chose to measure employment status in the year preceding the reported delinquency.

Finally, we construct measures of father's employment to examine the relative effects of father's work as compared to mother's work. Father's work is measured as the paid employment of spouses who are co-residing with the family—biological fathers and stepfathers are counted equally. We assign them work hours values and occupational class classifications drawn from maternal reports in the NLSY data.

Occupational class. We measure occupational class in two ways. First, following Parcel and Menaghan, we construct a 19-item-based occupational complexity scale by matching occupational titles reported by NLSY respondents to job descriptions reported in the Dictionary of Occupational Titles. As stated above, we estimate models using this measure of job complexity along with dummy variables for part-time, full-time and overtime hours. Our primary strategy, however, involves the use of a series of dummy variables capturing workplace controls, as outlined below, along with a continuous measure of work hours. We should note that our results did not differ when substituting the job complexity measure for our workplace control dummy variables.

Our primary measure of workplace conditions is developed based on the work of Mark Colvin. Drawing from Kohn and Edwards, Colvin links the workplace controls experienced by parents to the patterns and styles of control parents exert upon children. Unskilled, non-unionized employees (Fraction I workers) are subjected to "simple control" in the workplace, which is coercive and alienating. Simple control involves exacting worker compliance through the threat of job termination. This type of control is then reproduced in the home through erratic, harsh, and punitive parenting. Children who are raised under these conditions may be likely to form an alienated bond with authority, which frees them to behave in anti-social and delinquent ways.

Skilled laborers and craftspersons (Fraction II workers), who often belong to labor unions, experience greater job security and are controlled via "technical control"—the machine-paced atmosphere of manufacturing and industrial workplaces where workers are motivated to produce by wage increases and job security. Workers who are controlled by "technical control" will be more likely to control their children through extending and suspending rewards and punishments, which results in the formation of calculative bonds to authority in children. Such children are less likely to be involved in serious delinquency than the children of Fraction I workers.

Fraction III workers are those skilled workers, technicians, salaried professionals, and supervisory staff who experience greater self-direction, job complexity, and job security in the workplace. Fraction III workers are controlled in a bureaucratic fashion which relies on the power of normative pressure to control workers. These workers are heavily invested in the rules of the organization due to their favored status and, as a result, tend to be self-regulating employees. Due to high levels of autonomy in the workplace, Fraction III workers are positively bonded to authority, which they reproduce in their children through a steady and consistent style of parenting. Children of Fraction III workers are least likely to deviate from rules and laws due to their strong, normative bond with authority.

Colvin and Pauly's class fraction scheme provides a simple and parsimonious method for linking general job conditions to family life and to delinquency. For that reason, we measure working conditions by assigning each NLSY mother an occupational class value. First, using occupational codes in the NLSY data, we make an initial assessment about class fraction membership based on the presumed skill-level, autonomy, and job stability of each occupation. Fraction I workers are those unskilled, non-union workers found in agricultural labor, small-manufacturing firms, retail and food services, household domestic work, low-level clerical jobs (e.g., stock clerk) and sales (e.g., shoe

sales, retail). All NLSY workers whose occupational titles fit the above description were placed in Fraction I. Those assigned to Fraction II include skilled
blue-collar workers (e.g., welders, plumbers, steelworkers, auto assemblers),
skilled clerical workers (e.g., secretaries), craftsworkers, and low-level supervisors
(e.g., foreman). Fraction III status was assigned to professionals, technicians,
managers, government workers, and proprietors.

Family income.   Total family income is included in all models. By employing
a family income measure, we are able to assess the impact of mother's employment experiences while controlling for the total standard of living of each
family included in the analysis. Controlling for family income helps to isolate
the independent effects of occupational variables in the analysis.

Child care.   Following Parcel and Menaghan, we measure child care with a
series of dummy variables. Dummy variables representing professional daycare
settings, childcare provided by a relative (including fathers), and childcare
provided by a non-relative are included.

Pathway Variables

The NLSY was designed primarily to study labor market experiences across the
life course. Because it was not constructed as a criminological data set, some of
our measures, although reasonable, are not ideal. Further, although scales are
available to measure some variables, for other constructs we used one-item
measures. In these instances, the results should be viewed with appropriate
caution. All pathway variables are measured in 1986 for the early models and
1992 for the current models. All scales are constructed using a simple summing
of the component items.

Supervision.   Criminologists commonly operationalize parental supervision as
the degree to which parents know the whereabouts of children when they are
away from home and who they are with when away from home. We employ a
similar measure of supervision found in the CSAS. The one-item measure is a
four-point scale reflecting the child's report on how often "your mother knows
who you are with when not at home."

Attachment.   Attachment is often measured by items that relate to a child's
feelings of closeness, love, or admiration for a parent. It is difficult to measure
attachment among young children because they are unable to answer standard
survey questions. The NLSY data, however, contain mother-reported items
related to the insecure behaviors exhibited by children. Mothers were asked if
their 2 to 5 year-olds were difficult to soothe or calm, anxious and or worried
when left alone, prone to crying when left alone, or tended to need help with
most things. Attachment in young children is often studied via mother-
reported assessments of child behavior. Our insecure attachment index has
a reliability of .61. To measure attachment in adolescence, we use a one-
item question drawn from the CSAS that asks, "How close do you feel to your
mother?"

Maternal support. In the present analysis, we measure maternal support at two intervals—in 1986 when study children were in their pre-school years and in 1992 in early adolescence. Past researchers using the NLSY data captured expressive maternal support, from mother to children, with a warmth and responsiveness scale. Our warmth and responsiveness scale is an adaptation of the measure used by Menaghan, et al. This five-item index is drawn from interviewer observations of the warmth and responsiveness shown by mothers toward children. Interviewers observed whether or not mothers: spoke simultaneously to their child twice or more, responded verbally to child's speech (excluding scolding), answered child's questions or requests verbally, caressed, kissed, or hugged the child at least once, or conveyed positive feelings about the child. The reliability of the warmth and responsiveness scale is .79.

To examine maternal support in adolescence, we use a five-item index drawn from interviewer observations of maternal treatment of children in the home. This index is similar to the warmth and responsiveness scale used for pre-school children, but the items are tailored for school-age children. The items include whether mothers: encouraged the child to talk, answered child's questions, spoke with child, introduced the child to the interviewer by name, or used a loving voice toward child. The reliability of this scale is .76.

Spanking. Punitive parenting, such as corporal punishment, is associated with negative behavioral outcomes in children. Some scholars argue that the causal relationship between physical discipline and child behavior has yet to be untangled. Child misbehavior and physical punishment, that is, are likely to be related reciprocally. Other researchers claim that early physical discipline is independently related to misbehavior later on. We measure early maternal spanking with an item that asks mothers to report the number of times they spanked their child during the last week. This NLSY item was used by previous researchers interested in the maternal characteristics associated with spanking.

Delinquent peer association. Delinquent peer association is generally captured through survey questions tapping into the number of delinquent friends possessed by the respondent. Johnson, Marcos, and Bahr argue that the differential association process should not be seen simply in terms of the kinds of people one associates with, but should also consider the *situational pressures* that go along with associating with certain types. The process, then, is best evaluated by gaining measures on the amount of pressure to be delinquent exerted by one's friends. The CSAS asked youth to report whether they felt pressure from friends to try cigarettes, drugs, alcohol, skip school, or commit crime or do something violent. We combine these items into a scale ranging from 0 to 5, with 5 being the highest degree of delinquent pressure. The reliability of this scale is .79.

School attachment. Following Wiatrowski, Griswold, and Roberts', we focus on level of satisfaction with school as the measure of school attachment. The response item—drawn from the CSAS—asks respondents to report their satisfaction with their school. The responses range from 1, meaning very dissatisfied, to 4, meaning very satisfied.

Maternal Resources

AFQT. Mother's cognitive skills are estimated by her score on the Armed Forces Qualification Test, administered to all respondents in 1980. An AFQT score can be seen as an individual difference which is likely to influence a mother's life chances and those of her children similarly.

Maternal education. Mother's educational attainment is measured as the highest grade completed by mothers as of 1992. When examining the effects of early maternal employment, education is equal to the highest grade completed as of 1986.

Structural and Family Background Factors

In all models we control for race, sex, and age of study children. Age is an interval measure and race and sex are dummy variables. Race is coded 1 = Black or Hispanic and 0 = White. In separate equations, the Black and Hispanic children were isolated from one another to examine any differences between these groups and between these groups and the white sub-group. No differences were found. Sex is coded 0 = male and 1 = female. Family structure is a measure of the presence of mother's spouse in the home. An "intact" family is a home where the mother is married and presently co-residing with her partner. Thus, biological fathers, stepfathers, and adoptive fathers are all counted equally. Intact Family is coded 0 = no marital partner in the home and 1 = marital partner present.

Neighborhood Disorder

There is a strong relationship between certain neighborhood traits, such as poverty and joblessness, and crime. Those who have unstable, low-paying, or coercively controlled jobs are more likely to live in an economically and socially impoverished community where informal controls on behavior are low. The children of sub-employed or welfare-reliant mothers may be doubly at-risk because of the effects of economic strain and because poverty constrains families to live in socially disorganized settings. Researchers interested in the negative effects of community breakdown focus on the rates of joblessness, poverty, and family breakdown in neighborhoods. Because the NLSY lacks data on the rates of these problems at the community level, we construct a measure of neighborhood disorder from maternal responses to items related to community disorder. Our scale is drawn from responses to questions about whether the neighborhood had a "problem" with crime and violence, lack of parental supervision, and abandoned or run-down buildings (alpha = .85).

Statistical Analysis

The analysis of the data is conducted through the use of ordinary least squares regression (OLS). Our strategy is to examine 1) the direct effects of maternal employment hours and of maternal employment conditions on delinquency and 2) the indirect effects of maternal work on delinquency through the delinquency pathway variables. In this model, non-employed, welfare-reliant, and employed mothers are all included. Because working conditions are captured via a series of dummy variables reflecting the three working class fractions, nonemployed mothers and welfare-reliant mothers are treated as occupational class categories.

The analytic strategy follows a three-equation process. In the first equation, we examine the direct effect of maternal employment on the delinquency pathways. In this equation, each pathway is regressed against the employment/non-employment variables while controlling for maternal resources and child characteristics (age, sex, and race).

The second equation involves regressing the delinquency index against the employment/non-employment variables with mother and child control measures. The results of this equation demonstrate the direct effects of employment on delinquency without taking the delinquency pathways into consideration.

In the third, and final, equation, the delinquency index is regressed against maternal employment and the delinquency pathways. This equation produces estimates for the direct effects of all preceding variables on delinquency. Furthermore, by using this strategy, the third equation produces estimates of the direct effect of maternal employment on delinquency, while controlling for the delinquency pathways.

As a complement to this main strategy, we also perform an Analysis of Moment Structures (AMOS) analysis on the main model. Structural modeling allows us to assess the total, direct, and indirect effects of maternal employment on delinquency and will serve as confirmatory evidence for the findings based on the OLS strategy.

Findings

The Impact of Early Maternal Employment on Early Pathways to Delinquency

. . . [The] results of regression models that examine the effects of early maternal employment status on insecure attachment, maternal warmth and responsiveness, and spanking, controlling for maternal resources, child characteristics, and child care arrangements [show] . . . few significant effects. Child's age is inversely related to insecure attachment, warmth and responsiveness, and mother's use of spanking. Increasing AFQT score is associated with less insecure attachment and increasing warmth and responsiveness. Finally, higher family income is related to less maternal use of spanking. None of the early employment variables are related to the early delinquency risks.

The Impact of Early Maternal Employment on Delinquency

. . . [A] multiple regression equation . . . that examines the impact of early maternal employment status, with controls for mother and child background effects and child care arrangements, on the 1994 delinquency index. Current family income and current hours employed are also controlled to estimate the independent effects of early work.

. . . [C]hild's sex and child's age are both significant predictors of delinquency; females are less involved in delinquency than males, and increasing age is associated with greater involvement in delinquency. As the data show, none of the early employment variables, including welfare reliance, are significant predictors of delinquency in 1994. It should be noted, however, that a near significant effect of coercive maternal work on later delinquency appeared. When mothers were employed under coercive conditions in 1986, their children had greater involvement in delinquency in 1994. This relationship was significant at the .07 level of probability. Finally, current family income is inversely related to delinquency.

The impact of father's early and current employment status and work hours on delinquency was also examined. With professional fathers as the reference category, the effects of father's work were assessed. Controls for maternal resources, child characteristics, family income, and maternal work were included in the model. No significant effects on delinquency for either the early or current measures of paternal work were detected. Furthermore, the inclusion of paternal work measures did not change the relationships between mother's work and delinquency.

Early Maternal Employment, Early Pathways, and Delinquency

. . . [The] effects of early work, maternal resources, child characteristics, childcare, and delinquency pathways on delinquency . . . [show] both child's sex and age remain significantly associated with delinquency. Introducing the pathway variables—spanking, warmth and responsiveness, and insecure attachment—does not diminish the influence of sex and age. Again, we should note that coercive maternal work during the child's early school years remains related to greater delinquency in 1994 at the .07 level. Current family income remains a significant predictor of delinquency.

Furthermore, none of the early pathway variables exhibited a significant influence on delinquent involvement. The addition of these variables did not contribute any additional explained variation over the model that consisted only of maternal resources, child characteristics, and maternal employment. In this sample, spanking, maternal warmth and responsiveness, and insecure attachment cannot be considered "pathways" to delinquency.

Current Maternal Employment and the Pathways to Delinquency

. . . [The] effects of current maternal work on five "pathways" to delinquency—supervision, delinquent peers, warmth and responsiveness, mother-child attachment, and school attachment . . . [show] older children are supervised less by mothers. . . . [Being] female is associated with greater maternal supervision, less delinquent peer association, higher attachment to mothers, and greater school attachment. Greater maternal AFQT and higher family income are linked to more warmth and responsiveness in parenting, while welfare reliance had the opposite effect. Increasing AFQT is also related to a closer mother-child bond in adolescence. Increasing family income positively influences school attachment.

Paid employment appears to share a complex relationship with maternal supervision. Employment hours are positively, but very weakly, related to supervision. This suggests that greater maternal involvement in the paid work-force results in a higher level of maternal supervision of children. On the other hand, being employed in a bureaucratically controlled setting reduces mater-nal supervision. Compared to non-employed mothers, female professionals are less involved in the supervision of their children. Finally, children living in a disorganized neighborhood are prone to more delinquent peer association.

The Impact of Current Maternal Employment and Delinquency

. . . [Only] child's age and child's sex are associated with delinquent involvement. According to the data, being older and being male are associated with greater involvement in delinquency. Consistent with the early employment model, none of the current employment categories exerts influence on delinquency.

The Impact of Current Maternal Employment and Delinquency

Pathways on delinquency. . . . [The] influence of mother's current employment status, delinquency pathways, and control variables on delinquency . . . shows three delinquency pathways exert direct influence on delinquency. Greater maternal supervision, lesser delinquent peer influence, and greater school attachment are associated with less delinquent involvement. That is, control-ling for maternal resources, child characteristics, and mother's work, those children who are supervised more closely, those who have relatively fewer delinquent peer associations, and those more attached to school are less involved in delinquent activities. These pathways exert the most powerful influence on delinquency in the analysis.

The above analysis suggests that maternal employment had no direct effect on delinquency, but did have an indirect impact through its influence on maternal supervision. Specifically, maternal work hours are related to higher supervision, which reduces delinquency. On the other hand, working under bureaucratic controls was related to lower supervision and, thus higher delin-quency. These indirect effects, though small in size, are worth noting. These findings were confirmed by an AMOS structural modeling analysis of the main model: the small effects of maternal hours and bureaucratic workplace controls on delinquency were accounted for entirely by their impact on supervision.

Discussion

Are the children of working mothers more likely to be delinquent than other children? According to past studies and to the results of our analysis, the answer is a qualified "No." The present study demonstrates that regardless of how this issue is examined, having a working mother has only a small and indirect effect on delinquency. This general pattern holds whether we considered maternal employment in a child's pre-school years or maternal work in adolescence. Furthermore, with the lone exception of maternal supervision, maternal employment has little influence on several known pathways to delinquency.

Like Parcel and Menaghan and more recent findings by Harvey, our research suggests that the widespread concern over the fates of working women and their children is largely unsupported. Rather than being a social problem whose untoward effects can be demonstrated empirically, the maternal employment-delinquency connection is better understood as a socially constructed problem. As a perceived social problem, the dark side of maternal employment has a long history in America. Fueled by scientific data on the link between early family processes and delinquency and by cherished popular beliefs in the sanctity of the "first relationship"—the coupling of mother and child—for decades politicians and social commentators have pointed to modern trends in female labor participation to explain social problems such as crime. But if the unprecedented entrance of mothers into the paid workforce is related to delinquency, it must be because working mothers fail their children by depriving them of the support and discipline they need. The current study adds to the growing literature that casts doubt on these assumptions.

Our findings suggest other notable conclusions. First, it is maternal and family resources, rather than the characteristics of maternal work, that most influence some well-known pathways to delinquency in our study. Maternal AFQT score, a measure of intellectual resources, affects both parental support and mother-child bonds in early childhood and in adolescence: mothers who draw from greater cognitive resources are more supportive in parenting and raise more securely attached children.

Although the AFQT measures an individual's intellectual capacity, it reflects the subject's developed abilities rather than a biologically assigned aptitude. The AFQT score varies with family of origin, geographic region, and years of schooling, which implies that, like maternal education, an AFQT score reflects relative social advantage or disadvantage. Our findings should be interpreted as further evidence that social disadvantage is reproduced partly through its effect on parent-child relations. Consistent with this theme, our analysis found that an important family resource, family income, exerts a positive influence on warm and responsive parenting in adolescence, while welfare reliance has the opposite effect. This relationship is consistent with past research that identified economic hardship as a strain on family functioning.

The most powerful predictors of delinquency in our analysis are maternal supervision, delinquent peer association, and school attachment. Adolescents who are supervised more closely, those who have fewer delinquent peers, and those who are more attached to school show less involvement in delinquency. This result supports a large body of research that identifies these factors as important to the production of antisocial behavioral patterns. We reiterate, here, our discovery that maternal employment had relatively little negative impact on these important pathways to delinquency.

In one instance, however, workplace controls had a small indirect effect on delinquency. Specifically, bureaucratic work controls were negatively related to maternal supervision and, thus, had a slightly positive effect on delinquency. One interpretation of this result is that professional mothers may invest more time in their careers than the average mother does which may diminish their ability to monitor children. On the other hand, the negative effect of bureaucratic controls on supervision may not reflect a difference in time spent with children so much as a difference in parenting style. The freedom and autonomy experienced by the professional parent may translate into a parenting style characterized by less overt supervision and greater attempts to equip children with internal normative controls.

Conversely, we found that maternal work hours were indirectly related to lower involvement in delinquency, through their positive effect on supervision. Again, although the effect is small, maternal work hours is actually related to greater supervision in our sample. This may be due to the stabilizing influence of steady employment on family life. As Wilson has argued, a job "constitutes a framework for daily behavior and patterns of interaction because it imposes disciplines and regularities" upon a parent.

Furthermore, while no maternal employment variable is related to delinquent peer association, neighborhood disorder is. This finding is consistent with social disorganization theory: the breakdown of informal neighborhood controls leaves children at a greater risk for being socialized in intimate delinquent peer groups. It is instructive that our analysis points to community breakdown, as it operates through delinquent peer influence, as a cause of delinquency rather than family breakdown related to the absence of a working mother.

Finally, if improving family life is a goal of crime control policy, it would make good sense to aim at addressing the structural factors that limit maternal and family resources and that contribute to community disorder. Our study suggests that policy debates should avoid ideological attacks on working mothers, which portray them as leaving their children "home alone," and concentrate instead on the economic and educational inequalities that weaken families and neighborhoods.

POSTSCRIPT

Does Maternal Employment Have Negative Effects on Children's Development?

Selections in this issue provide an understanding of how some researchers argue the effects of maternal employment. One selection shows a negative effect on cognitive development in children whose mothers join the workforce. The second study opposes the first by asserting that maternal employment has very little effect over children's behavioral outcomes, particularly the development of delinquency. Each selection's authors used valid methods and yet found opposite results. What is the answer to how maternal employment in a child's first year of life affects their children's subsequent development?

It is difficult to control for all characteristics that may affect the outcome of studies on maternal employment. Researchers suggest that more studies be conducted on a larger population so that they might generalize the results for the population as a whole. It is also suggested that the research methods include a larger diversity of ethnic groups and social classes to gain a better understanding of how maternal employment affects a child's development and behavioral outcomes.

Researchers agree that maternal employment's effects on children need to examine the interaction of multiple variables, such as child care quality, control over work situation, and family and societal support systems. They do not agree on which sets of variables combine to give an accurate picture of how a mother's employment affects children's development.

Attitudes toward maternal employment have changed somewhat because of societal changes. It has become more socially acceptable today for moms to work. As more women obtain high-profile jobs in politics and corporations, more workplace assistance programs have been developed. These include on-site child care, flexible work hours, and allowing moms to work from home via computer technology. The realization that it is an economic necessity for single moms as well as both parents in a dual-parent household to work has created more of an acceptance for working mothers. Many families need two incomes to make ends meet.

Time-saving appliances such as self-cleaning ovens, dishwashers, and microwave ovens have given working moms more time to spend with their children. Obtaining food for dinner from the growing number of restaurants offering drive-through or pick-up service has also relieved working moms from the hassle of running home from work to make dinner. Of course, these time-saving means are only available to those who can afford them. Women with lower wages still struggle to balance work and family time. Welfare reform created a predicament for those who believed mothers should stay at home with their infants. With no governmental monetary support, how does a single mom stay at home with her children and still make a living for her family?

Young children want to be with their parents and need their parents to care for them. In an ideal world, most people want babies to be cared for by someone who loves them. In all but extreme abuse cases, this is generally the mom or dad. In our society, those who want to stay home and care for their children should have the opportunity to do so. Yet, the economic environment prevents this from happening. Perhaps another way to look at the issue of maternal employment's effects on children's development is to develop ways to allow moms who want to stay home to raise their children to do so, as well as to give social support to those moms who want to work outside the home.

Related Readings

Barnett, Rosalind Chait. (2004). Women and work: Where are we, where did we come from, and where are we going? *The Journal of Social Issues, 60,* 667–674.

Galinsky, Ellen. (2000). Ask the children: The breakthrough study that reveals how to succeed at work and parenting. Quill Publishers.

Hoogstra, L. (2005). The design of the 500 family study. In *Being together, working apart: Dual-career families and the work-life balance,* edited by B. Schneider and L. Waite. Cambridge University Press.

Schneider, B., & Waite, L.J. (2005). Why study working families? In *Being together, working apart: Dual-career families and the work-life balance,* edited by B. Schneider and L. Waite. Cambridge University Press.

Tiedje, Linda Beth. (2004). Processes of change in work/home incompatibilities: Employed mothers 1986–1999. *The Journal of Social Issues, 60,* 787–800.

Williams, Joan C., & Cooper, Holly Cohen. (2004). The public policy of motherhood. *The Journal of Social Issues, 60,* 849–865.

ISSUE 3

Should Scientists Be Allowed to Clone Children?

YES: Kyla Dunn, from "Cloning Trevor," *The Atlantic Monthly* (June 2002)

NO: Robert A. Weinberg, from "Of Clones and Clowns," *The Atlantic Monthly* (June 2002)

ISSUE SUMMARY

YES: Kyla Dunn, a former biotech researcher and now a reporter for PBS and CBS, details the six months that she spent with scientists inside the labs of Advanced Cell Technology (ACT), a group openly pursuing human cloning for medical purposes. Dunn outlines what the group hopes to accomplish through cloning, why the group believes that cloning is the best way to accomplish these goals, and the political and monetary trials that ACT faces.

NO: Robert A. Weinberg, a member of the Whitehead Institute for Biomedical Research and a biology professor at MIT, offers his concerns about what he calls the "cloning circus." Weinberg discusses the damage that many cloning groups have been doing to serious research and the impending dangers of reproductive cloning.

With several cloning groups, such as the Raelians, claiming to have cloned humans, society's debate over cloning is becoming even more heated. On one side there are conservative politicians, clergymen, scientists, and many members of the American public who believe that cloning is ethically wrong. On the other side are other scientists who have invested their professional lives toward cloning research and people suffering from degenerative diseases whose lives may be saved through therapeutic cloning.

Is cloning morally and ethically wrong? Is there a difference between therapeutic and reproductive cloning? Could cloning possibly be the key to curing many diseases? Is the utilization of embryonic stem cells the only way to proceed with this science, or can adult stem cells be used? These are just a few of the myriad questions being asked about cloning. While some of the questions have definitive answers, the ethical debate over cloning does not have an easy or definite answer.

As you read the following selections, try to suspend the personal attitudes about cloning that you may have developed. Try to learn about the process of cloning, what it truly is intended to do, and what it could possibly accomplish. In addition, consider what could be the consequences of allowing cloning to occur.

In the following selections, Kyla Dunn gives us an inside look into the cloning labs of ACT and the circumstances of a boy whose life could possibly be saved by cloning. The scientists at ACT are trying to make medical breakthroughs that may cure many diseases. However, they must also deal with the pressure of finding adequate funding to continue their work. In addition, they live with the knowledge that on any day, governments around the world might ban their efforts all together. Robert A. Weinberg contends that many cloning groups have made a "circus" out of the scientific research community. He heightens awareness of the problems with animal clones and the far-reaching consequences that these problems may have on human clones.

Can governments worldwide effectively stop the rapidly evolving technology and science of cloning? If human cloning were to be banned worldwide, would scientists throughout the world truly desist in their endeavors? Or, is the "cloning genie out of the bottle" with no possible way to return to the type of science that was practiced before cloning became possible?

YES

Kyla Dunn

Cloning Trevor

At 9:00 in the evening on January 29, just as President George W. Bush was about to begin his first State of the Union address, I gathered with three anxious scientists in a small, windowless laboratory in Worcester, Massachusetts. We were at Advanced Cell Technology—a privately owned biotechnology company that briefly made international headlines last fall by publishing the first scientific account of cloned human embryos. The significance of the achievement was debatable: the company's most successful embryo had reached only six cells before it stopped dividing (one other had reached four cells, another had reached two)—a fact that led to a widespread dismissal, in the media and the scientific community, of ACT's "breakthrough." The work was largely judged to be preliminary, inconsequential, and certainly not worthy of headlines. Many people in political and religious circles, however, had a decidedly different view. They deemed ACT's work an ethical transgression of the highest order and professed shock, indignation, and horror. . . .

Skin cell to embryo—it's one of the most remarkable quick-change scenarios modern biology has to offer. It's also one of the most controversial. Since the announcement, in 1997, of the cloning of Dolly the sheep, attempts to use human cells for cloning have provoked heated debate in the United States, separating those who have faith in the promise of the new technology from those who envision its dark side and unintended consequences.

Crucial to the debate is the fact that human cloning research falls into two distinct categories: reproductive cloning, a widely frowned-on effort that aims to produce a fully formed child; and therapeutic cloning, a scientifically reputable procedure that takes place entirely at the microscopic level and is designed to advance medical therapies and cure human ailments. The two start out the same way—with a new embryo in a petri dish. But the scientists I was observing in the lab had no intention of creating a person. Instead they were embarking on an experiment that, if successful, would be a first step toward creating radical new cures for patients like the donor of the skin cell—Trevor Ross (not his real name), a two-year-old boy afflicted with a rare and devastating genetic disease.

The mood in the lab was tense in part because of the uncertain outcome of the experiment. But it was also tense because of concern over what President Bush might say about cloning in his address to the nation. A radio in one corner of the room was tuned to the broadcast as the scientists began their work, and they were listening carefully: in perhaps no other field of science are researchers as mindful of which way the political winds are blowing. The ACT scientists had good reason to be concerned—what they were doing that night might soon be made illegal.

On July 31 of last year, by a 100-vote margin, the U.S. House of Representatives passed the Human Cloning Prohibition Act of 2001, which would impose a ban on the creation of cloned human embryos for any purpose, whether reproductive or therapeutic. Both forms of cloning would be punishable by up to ten years in prison and a million-dollar fine. The House passed the measure over the objections of a long list of biomedical organizations (including the Association of American Medical Colleges and the American Society for Cell Biology) and patients' advocacy groups. . . .

Politics and religion, it seemed, were trumping science. Therapeutic-cloning research was already ineligible for federal funding in the United States. In 1995 Congress had passed legislation barring the use of federal funds for any experiment in which a human embryo is either created or destroyed, thus making official a de facto ban that had been in existence since 1975. . . . As a result, the burden of moving many areas of important medical research forward has fallen on the private sector, a situation that by many accounts has severely hobbled research into treatments for infertility—and even disorders such as childhood cancer and birth defects. These research areas, like therapeutic-cloning research, demand the kind of long-term study and financial commitment that only the federal government can provide. This past summer human therapeutic cloning already fell squarely under the federal-funding ban, yet Congress was now going further, considering making that research illegal. . . .

Last fall, with the prospect of a Senate vote looming, I decided to take a considered look at cloning research. The time seemed right: it was a unique moment in what could be the development of a major new medical technology, an odd period of legislative limbo in which the first halting steps were being taken toward creating cloned human embryos just as such efforts were in imminent danger of being outlawed. . . .

Progress Measured in Eggs

"That's Trevor's cells," Jose Cibelli told me in the ACT cloning lab on January 23. Cibelli is the vice-president of research at ACT, and the scientist in charge of its therapeutic-cloning attempts. He's a gentle, compact man with dark hair, a trim moustache and goatee, and a vaguely worried expression. A native of Argentina, he speaks quietly and with a thick accent. . . .

The cells had come from a round plug of Trevor's skin, three millimeters across, and had arrived at ACT just five days before. The Rosses' dermatologist had chosen a crease between Trevor's buttock and thigh, where a scar would not be likely to show, and had punched down with a circular razor blade—past the dead cells of the epidermis and into the dermis, where fibroblasts grow and thrive. . . .

Cibelli now had fibroblasts for potential therapeutic-cloning experiments stored away at ACT from five patients: one with a spinal-cord injury, one with diabetes, two with healthy but aging bodies, and Trevor. But skin cells are the easy part—they're plentiful, hardy, easy to obtain and work with. Eggs are much trickier, and Cibelli had thus started measuring the likelihood of progress not in years but in eggs. "When do I think we'll get this to work?" he asked me rhetorically. "About two hundred eggs from now."

"We've gotten a handful of eggs so far," he had earlier explained. "It's a whole different game when you're talking about animal embryology versus human embryology." In the cow-cloning lab next door, for example, ACT receives 1,400 eggs on a typical day. But whereas cow eggs are available in abundance from slaughterhouses, human eggs must be obtained from young women who have undergone two weeks of hormone injections, regular visits to a doctor, and a nontrivial surgical procedure. All told, it costs ACT about $22,000 to take an egg-donation procedure from start to finish. "And the number is so small," Cibelli added. "I mean, you get ten eggs! Instead of working with a hundred embryos, I'm working with one." From July to October of last year, ACT collected a total of seventy-one eggs from seven donors—of which only nineteen were designated for cloning. That didn't leave much room for error, or much chance to tinker with conditions that might improve the chances of success. . . .

At five days of development a human embryo is smaller than a grain of sand. It's a perfectly round ball with a fluid-filled core. The internal architecture of the ball, however, is somewhat lopsided. Huddled against one wall of its interior is a group of cells known as the inner cell mass. The outside of the ball is destined to become the placenta and associated membranes; the inner cell mass is what forms a baby. But after only five days of development no cell's fate has yet been determined—it's impossible to tell which cells will become blood or muscle, skin or brain, gut or liver. All that is present is the simple raw material from which the more than 200 cell types in a human body will eventually be built.

If the inner cell mass of an embryo is removed at this early stage, it can yield cells known as human embryonic stem cells—which retain the ability to form any cell or tissue in the body. In a sense they are immortal, in that they can divide indefinitely in the lab, producing large quantities of cells. With the right coaxing those cells can theoretically be converted into an unlimited supply of tissue for transplant: new heart muscle for heart-attack survivors; insulin-secreting cells for diabetics; neurons to treat those suffering from spinal-cord injuries, the effects of stroke, or Parkinson's disease. Tissue engineers hope someday to build even more complex structures from these stem cells: new blood vessels for bypass surgery, new liver tissue, even new kidneys—all from what began as a loose collection of cells in a lab dish. They dream of a future in which all kinds of organs and tissues can be custom made to replace those ravaged by disease, injury, or a lifetime of hard use. . . .

A Radical Hope

Adrienne and Ben Ross (all names of the family members have been changed) first came to ACT late last October, ten months after their son, Trevor, and two of his cousins had received a diagnosis of X-linked adrenoleukodystrophy (ALD), a relatively rare and underdiagnosed genetic disorder that can abruptly ravage the white matter of the brain, with devastating and often fatal results.

. . . Boys with ALD who are lucky enough to escape childhood cerebral onset are almost certain to suffer a degeneration of the spinal cord in adulthood, which can lead to such symptoms as muscle spasms in the legs, loss of bladder control, and general weakness and stiffness. Although symptoms in adults can vary a great deal in severity, a third of adults with the disease also develop brain involvement and are reduced to a vegetative state or die within three to four years of onset. . . .

Currently, the best treatment for childhood cerebral onset of ALD is a bone-marrow or umbilical-cord-blood transplant from a healthy, well-matched donor. . . . Compatible transplant donors are extraordinarily hard to find, however—and even when suitable donors are found, the transplants don't always take. Sometimes transplants don't work because a patient's immune system rejects the transplanted cells as foreign. In other cases mature immune cells in the transplanted material actually reject and attack their new host, a life-threatening condition known as graft-versus-host disease. . . .

The Rosses had sought out ACT with the radical hope that therapeutic cloning might someday allow doctors to create a transplant that would carry no risk of rejection. The work of a bone-marrow transplant is actually done by hematopoietic stem cells—cells in the marrow that restock our blood and immune systems throughout life, serving as a reservoir of new components as old ones wear out. HSCs are also the cells that have rescued patients with ALD. What the Rosses were exploring with ACT was the idea of coaxing human embryonic stem cells, taken from cloned embryos, into forming HSCs that might someday save Trevor. . . .

❧◈❧

What therapeutic cloning should allow scientists to do, [Michael] West explained, is provide a pure population of genetically modified cells. Use one modified cell for cloning, and the entire cloned embryo will then carry that modification. So will embryonic stem cells derived from it, and any therapeutic tissues they produce. Alternatively, scientists could do the modification in embryonic stem cells after cloning, and then grow a limitless supply of tissue from one properly modified cell. "We can give the patient cells that all have the same precise targeted modification," West said. "One hundred percent. We won't do that with gene therapy in our lifetime."

A therapy for Trevor isn't the only thing at stake. The stem cells derived from cloned embryos bearing an ALD mutation could be powerful research tools. In fact, scientists consider creating cloned embryos that match patients with a genetic predisposition to disease to be one of the most important therapeutic applications of the technology, because, for one thing, it would allow diseased tissues of all kinds to be created and studied in the lab. But such work is rarely discussed in the political debate about cloning.

As she listened to West spin out optimistic future scenarios, Adrienne began to wonder if they would be able to proceed—or if using Trevor's cells for cloning would be pushing the bounds of the law as well as of science. "Can you clarify for me?" she asked, interrupting West. "On the cloning side, if you're not using federal funds, can you do what you want?"

It's understandable that she would wonder. The House's anti-cloning legislation was designed to make everything Mike West and the Rosses were discussing that day illegal. If the Senate were to pass the bill, not only could ACT's scientists be prosecuted for attempting therapeutic cloning for Trevor but Adrienne and Ben could be prosecuted for participating in such an attempt. One provision of the legislation would make it illegal even to "import" a life-saving medical therapy developed elsewhere in the world through cloning.

Adrienne's question was a sore point for West. "Yeah, we're free to do what we want," he answered simply.

"But now they're looking to try to ban that?" Adrienne asked.

West hesitated. "Well, I don't know," he said. "The Senate at some point will take this up, and my honest, best read is, I don't believe the Senate will pass it." Still, he admitted, anything could happen. "We could lose," he said, "and that would be tragic." . . .

A Public-Relations Disaster

A few weeks later ACT took a risk that could have put the company out of business—and, worse, could have closed the door on the budding field of therapeutic-cloning research. On November 9 the company e-mailed a hastily written scientific paper to *e-biomed: The Journal of Regenerative Medicine,* an online publication known for its quick turn-around time. The paper announced dryly that in ACT's lab "three somatic cell-derived embryos developed beyond the pronuclear stage." Robert Lanza, ACT's vice-president of medical and scientific development, called before the report came out to give me a translation. "The news is going to be that we have the world's first cloned human embryos," he said. "I just want to give you a heads-up—because when we make this announcement, it might bump the war [on terrorism] off the front page."

On almost every level the announcement was premature. ACT's original goal had been to publish in a prestigious journal like *Science* or *Nature,* when the company had what it is really after: human embryonic stem cells derived from a cloned embryo. ACT had nothing like that—it had managed only to sustain a cloned embryo to the six-cell stage of development.

At first, ACT's scientists say, they were uncertain whether they should publish such preliminary data. But given that they were working in an ethically fraught area of science, they decided to be as open as possible about their progress.

After Lanza called me about the imminent publication of ACT's cloning paper, I traveled to his house, on an island in a pond in central Massachusetts, to discuss the announcement. . . . He, West, and Cibelli form ACT's core triumvirate. As we sat at his kitchen table, Lanza told me that rumors in the scientific community were starting to make him nervous. Apparently the mavericks of the cloning world—those trying to produce a baby—were possibly on the verge of getting some preliminary results. "If they should come out and make some sort of an announcement first," Lanza said, "it could do severe damage. Because when it breaks, if their goal is reproductive cloning, all of the research will be banned. It will be killed—and it won't matter what we say, because no one's going to listen anymore." Last year, in fact, the outrage surrounding the mavericks' activities had directly contributed to the passage of the House anti-cloning bill.

But ACT itself also bore responsibility. On July 12, just weeks prior to the bill's passage, *The Washington Post* had broken the news that ACT was trying to create cloned human embryos as a source of stem cells—making it the only group in the country to acknowledge such plans publicly. The uproar that followed was still fresh in congressional minds at the time of the vote. Congressman Bart Stupak, of Michigan, one of the bill's co-sponsors, alluded on the day of the vote not only to the renegades but also to ACT. "The need for action is clear," he told his colleagues. "Research firms have announced their intentions to clone embryos for research purposes and then discard what is not needed."

A week before the publication of ACT's paper in *The Journal of Regenerative Medicine,* I called Thomas Okarma, the current chief executive officer of Geron, to get his views on ACT and its reputation. Despite his commitment to stem-cell and therapeutic-cloning research, Okarma was harshly critical of ACT. "They've done more harm to the field than good, I'm afraid," he told me. The most glaring example, he said, was ACT's announcement, just after Mike West joined the company, in the fall of 1998, that it was attempting to fuse human skin cells with cow eggs whose nuclear DNA had been removed. The motivation was sound: ACT was essentially hoping to do therapeutic cloning without the difficulty and expense of using human eggs—reviving experiments Jose Cibelli had started as a graduate student, in 1996, with his own cells. But, in the interest of "transparency" West released details to *The New York Times* and *48 Hours,* and two days after the news broke, President Bill Clinton, "deeply troubled" by the work, asked the head of his National Bioethics Advisory Commission to investigate. By an unfortunate coincidence, one week before the *48 Hours* broadcast, scientists had announced that they had derived human embryonic stem cells for the first time—news that made ACT's announcement seem like me-too publicity.

The cow-human embryos turned out to be "just plain duds," according to West, and ACT has never generated enough data for a significant scientific paper. (Members of the scientific community had predicted this outcome, although researchers in China have recently claimed success using rabbit eggs.) But the damage was done, because the public entirely misinterpreted the experiments. "Religious fundamentalists who, you know, are against reproductive and therapeutic cloning anyway, are using this example," Okarma told me. "'My God,' they say, 'these people are going to make chimeric creatures—mixing cows and humans.' It creates a fantasied negative scenario that casts an umbra on all of us working in the field, and makes it harder for the field to advance. And it's well documented in the scientific literature that fusing cells from two such distantly related species will not work." Okarma was not alone in dismissing ACT: the company's "publication by press release" was widely attacked by other scientists as irresponsible and insubstantial.

He added, "It's not in the same category as the Raëlians"—a religious group, inspired by "revelations" from extraterrestrials, that is working on reproductive cloning—"because there are certainly legitimate scientists at ACT trying to do this work, okay? But from the perspective of the regulatory bodies, they are in the same spaceship." . . .

"An Incredible Gift to Mankind"

. . . The most frequent refrain among political opponents of therapeutic cloning, and of human embryonic-stem-cell research in general, is that adult stem cells are a better choice for the development of medical therapies. Like cells from cloned embryos, adult stem cells are a perfect genetic match for a patient. Unlike embryonic cells, however, they can be found in the tissues of the patient's own body—a fact that prompted Senator [Sam] Brownback [of Kansas], after ACT's announcement, to insist on CNN that adult-stem-cell research is "a much better route to go." Opponents of therapeutic cloning wonder why there's a need to work with embryonic cells at all, since adult stem cells aren't rejected by the immune system, can produce a wide variety of body tissues, and do not require destroying embryos.

A report released by the NIH last July provided some answers, pointing out most adult stem cells are rare, may be difficult or dangerous to harvest from patients, and have a limited capacity to divide in the laboratory, which means that they can't yet be grown in large enough quantities to be of therapeutic value. What's more, adult stem cells have not been found for all types of tissue. . . .

"When there's this ethics debate about adult versus embryonic stem cells and cloning," Mike West told me, "I don't think what's properly weighed in the balance is the amazing breakthrough that this is. I mean, the idea that you can take a person of any age—a hundred and twenty years old—and take a skin cell from them and give them back their own cells that are young! Cells of any kind, with any kind of genetic modification! That's such an incredible gift to mankind! For the U.S. Congress to spend two hours and debate this and say, 'Oh, we'll make all this illegal,' to me is unbelievable. They don't understand." He shook his head. "We've never been able to do anything like this before."

Malcolm Moore's [a specialist in blood-cell development at the Memorial Sloan-Kettering Institute, in Manhattan] main concern is that Congress will shut the door on this research before its full benefits are known—if they indeed exist. "Basically," he told me, "my plea is, don't close down an avenue of research that might be of value in the future in the treatment of human disease. Time, science, and medical practice will be the ultimate proofs of whether these strategies are going to benefit mankind."

Bob Lanza put things more enthusiastically. "I'd stake my life on it," he said. "If this research is allowed to proceed, by the time we grow old, this will be a routine thing." He pounded the table we were sitting at, for emphasis. "You'll just go and get a skin cell removed at the doctor's office, and they'll give you back a new organ or some new tissue—a new liver, a new kidney—and you'll be fixed. And it's not science fiction. This is very, very real."

Breaching the Zona Pellucida

. . . If and when Trevor's skin cell fused with the empty egg, what exactly was going to be created? "You are creating people," Sam Brownback has insisted. "You're creating humans." Opponents of therapeutic cloning believe that embryos deserve governmental protection before they have even divided from one cell into two (although not even the world's major religions agree on when a human life begins).

Positions like Senator Brownback's frustrate Mike West. "I'm just very disappointed," he said to me. "I'm sad, because even the critics admit that millions of human beings and their fate in the hospital may be contingent on this research." As a young man, West was an evangelical Christian and a creationist. He protested outside abortion clinics. But swayed by the scientific evidence for evolution, he eventually abandoned the biblical view of creation. Science now dictates his view of the earliest human embryos as well. "You can be as pro-life as you can get," he told me, "but you can't say that making and destroying a pre-implantation embryo is the destruction of a human. Because it isn't. If it was a human life, I wouldn't touch it. Absolutely not." He went on, "A human individual does not begin at conception. It begins at primitive-streak formation."

The "primitive streak" appears after fourteen days of embryonic development in utero. It's like an arrow drawn on the embryo, one that delineates head and tail, front and back. Until then how many individuals, if any, that tiny ball of tissue will produce is entirely unclear. During the first two weeks of development one embryo can still split into two, a process that produces identical twins. Remarkably, two embryos can also fuse into one, eventually resulting in a single person whose body is a patchwork of two genotypes (with each eye a different color, perhaps, or mottled, two-tone skin). Not until the appearance of the primitive streak are the beginnings of a human individual sketched out. At that point, according to West, "There is no brain, no sensation, no pain, no memory, nothing of that. But it is an individualized human in a very early stage, and I advocate we don't touch that. But before then—they're wrong. It is just cells, it is a kind of raw material for life: the cellular life out of which human life arises."

West's line of thinking is fully consistent with the conclusions laid out by the NIH Human Embryo Research Panel in 1994. "If the President and members of Congress really understood what these little balls of cells were," West went on, "they would have a completely different view."

Adrienne Ross has a blunter assessment. "To me," she told me, "it's like, how dare they tell me that I cannot save my son's life? It's as simple as that.

You know, if you want to practice your religion, practice your religion. But not when it interferes with other people's lives." She continued, "They're telling me, 'Let your child die, because my religious belief is more important than your child's life.' They can make their choices for their own embryos and they can make their choices for their own children. But they have no right to stop me from saving my son's life."

A Shot in the Dark

. . . In the United States the broad consensus in the scientific community is that therapeutic-cloning research merits significant exploration, and that real progress is likely only with government funding and support. "Such research," Harold Varmus, the former NIH director, wrote last year in *The New York Times,* "is vital not just to biotechnology companies and their investors, but to the nation as a whole. By structuring our system so that only those with private funds or a commercial motive do this pioneering work, we curb our full capacity to expand our scientific understanding." To put it another way: as long as a federal-funding ban remains in place, the organizations most likely to move forward with therapeutic-cloning research will be companies like ACT—which, despite generally noble intentions, are bedeviled by the need to raise money, generate buzz, and please investors. . . .

What is clear is that the potential fruits of therapeutic-cloning research will not come soon enough for Trevor Ross. In February, doctors detected the first signs of childhood cerebral onset of ALD. All hopes of developing an experimental cure for Trevor were dashed; time had run out. The Rosses immediately scheduled a more traditional cord-blood transplant, fully aware of the risks and of the odds of failure.

Robert A. Weinberg

 NO

Of Clones and Clowns

Biologists have been rather silent on the subject of human cloning. Some others would accuse us, as they have with predictable regularity in the recent past, of insensitivity to the societal consequences of our research. If not insensitivity, then moral obtuseness, and if not that, then arrogance—an accusation that can never be disproved.

The truth is that most of us have remained quiet for quite another reason. Most of us regard reproductive cloning—a procedure used to produce an entire new organism from one cell of an adult—as a technology riddled with problems. Why should we waste time agonizing about something that is far removed from practical utility, and may forever remain so?

The nature and magnitude of the problems were suggested by the Scottish scientist Ian Wilmut's initial report, five years ago, on the cloning of Dolly the sheep. Dolly represented one success among 277 attempts to produce a viable, healthy newborn. Most attempts at cloning other animal species—to date cloning has succeeded with sheep, mice, cattle, goats, cats, and pigs—have not fared much better.

Even the successes come with problems. The placentas of cloned fetuses are routinely two or three times larger than normal. The offspring are usually larger than normal as well. Several months after birth one group of cloned mice weighed 72 percent more than mice created through normal reproduction. In many species cloned fetuses must be delivered by cesarean section because of their size. This abnormality, the reasons for which no one understands, is so common that it now has its own name—Large Offspring Syndrome. Dolly (who was of normal size at birth) was briefly overweight in her young years and suffers from early-onset arthritis of unknown cause. Two recent reports indicate that cloned mice suffer early-onset obesity and early death.

Arguably the most successful reproductive-cloning experiment was reported last year by Advanced Cell Technology, a small biotech company in Worcester, Massachusetts. Working with cows, ACT produced 496 embryos by injecting nuclei from adult cells into eggs that had been stripped of their own nuclei. Implanting the embryos into the uteruses of cows led to 110 established pregnancies, thirty of which went to term. Five of the newborns died shortly after birth, and a sixth died several months later. The twenty-four surviving calves developed into cows that were healthy by all criteria examined.

But most, if not all, had enlarged placentas, and as newborns some of them suffered from the respiratory distress typical of Large Offspring Syndrome.

The success rate of the procedure, roughly five percent, was much higher than the rates achieved with other mammalian species, and the experiment was considered a great success. Some of the cows have grown up, been artificially inseminated, and given birth to normal offspring. Whether they are affected by any of the symptoms associated with Large Offspring Syndrome later in life is not apparent from the published data. No matter: for $20,000 ACT will clone your favorite cow.

Imagine the application of this technology to human beings. Suppose that 100 adult nuclei are obtained, each of which is injected into a human egg whose own nucleus has been removed. Imagine then that only five of the 100 embryos thus created result in well-formed, viable newborns; the other ninety-five spontaneously abort at various stage of development or, if cloning experiments with mammals other than cows are any guide, yield grossly malformed babies. The five viable babies have a reasonable likelihood of suffering from Large Offspring Syndrome. How they will develop, physically and cognitively, is anyone's guess. It seems unlikely that even the richest and most egomaniacal among us, intent on recreating themselves exactly, will swarm to this technology.

⚜

Biological systems are extraordinarily complex, and there are myriad ways in which experiments can go awry or their results can be misinterpreted. Still, perhaps 95 percent of what biologists read in this year's research journals will be considered valid (if perhaps not very interesting) a century from now. Much of scientists' trust in the existing knowledge base derives from the system constructed over the past century to validate new research findings and the conclusions derived from them. Research journals impose quality controls to ensure that scientific observations and conclusions are solid and credible. They sift the scientific wheat from the chaff.

The system works like this: A biologist sends a manuscript describing his experiment to a journal. The editor of the journal recruits several experts, who remain anonymous to the researcher, to vet the manuscript. A month or two later the researcher receives a thumbs-up, a thumbs-down, or a request for revisions and more data. . . .

We participate in the peer-review process not only to create a sound edifice of ideas and results for ourselves; we do it for the outside world as well— for all those who are unfamiliar with the arcane details of our field. Without the trial-by-fire of peer review, how can journalists and the public possibly know which discoveries are credible, which are nothing more than acts of self-promotion by ambitious researchers, and which smack of the delusional?

The hype about cloning has made a shambles of this system, creating something of a circus. Many of us have the queasy feeling that our carefully constructed world of science is under siege. The clowns—those who think that making money, lots of it, is more important than doing serious science— have invaded our sanctuary.

The cloning circus opened soon after Wilmut, a careful and well-respected scientist, reported his success with Dolly. First in the ring was Richard Seed, an elderly Chicago physicist, who in late 1997 announced his intention of cloning a human being within two years. Soon members of an international religious cult, the Raëlians (followers of Claude Vorilhon, a French-born mystic who says that he was given the name Raël by four-foot-high extraterrestrials, and who preaches that human beings were originally created by these aliens), revealed an even more grandiose vision of human cloning. To the Raëlians, biomedical science is a sacrament to be used for achieving immortality: their ultimate goal is to use cloning to create empty shells into which people's souls can be transferred. As a sideline, the Raëlian-affiliated company Clonaid hopes to offer its services to couples who would like to create a child through reproductive cloning, for $200,000 per child.

Neither Seed nor the Raëlians made any pretense of subjecting their plans to review by knowledgeable scientists; they went straight to the popular press. Still, this wasn't so bad. Few science journalists took them seriously (although they did oblige them with extensive coverage). Biologists were also unmoved. Wasn't it obvious that Seed and the Raëlians were unqualified to undertake even the beginnings of the series of technical steps required for reproductive cloning? Why dignify them with a response?

The next wave of would-be cloners likewise went straight to the mainstream press—but they were not so easily dismissed. In March of last year, at a widely covered press conference in Rome, an Italian and a U.S. physician announced plans to undertake human reproductive cloning outside the United States. The Italian member of the team was Severino Antinori, a gynecologist notorious for having used donor eggs and *in vitro* fertilization to make a sixty-two-year-old woman pregnant in 1994. Now he was moving on. Why, he asked, did the desires of infertile couples (he claimed to have 600 on a waiting list) not outweigh the concerns about human cloning? He repeatedly shouted down reporters and visiting researchers who had the temerity to voice questions about the biological and ethical problems associated with reproductive cloning.

The American member of the team was Panayiotis Zavos, a reproductive physiologist and an *in vitro* fertilization expert at the Andrology Institute of America, in Lexington, Kentucky. "The genie is out of the bottle," he told reporters. "Dolly is here, and we are next." Antinori and Zavos announced their intention of starting a human cloning project in an undisclosed Mediterranean country. Next up was Avi Ben-Abraham, an Israeli-American biotechnologist with thwarted political ambitions (he ran unsuccessfully for the Knesset) and no reputable scientific credentials, who attempted to attach himself to the project. Ben-Abraham hinted that the work would be done either in Israel or in an Arab country, because "the climate is more [receptive to human cloning research] within Judaism and Islam." He told the German magazine *Der Spiegel*, "We were all created by the Almighty, but now we will become the creators."

Both Antinori and Zavos glossed over the large gap between expertise with established infertility procedures and the technical skills required for reproductive cloning. Confronted with the prospect of high rates of aborted or malformed cloned embryos, they claimed to be able to weed out any defective embryos at an early stage of gestation. "We have a great deal of knowledge," Zavos announced to the press. "We can grade embryos. We can do genetic screening. We can do [genetic] quality control." This was possible, he said, because of highly sensitive diagnostic tests that can determine whether or not development is proceeding normally.

The fact is that no such tests exist; they have eluded even the most expert biologists in the field, and there is no hope that they will be devised anytime soon—if ever. No one knows how to determine with precision whether the repertoire of genes expressed at various stages of embryonic development is being "read" properly in each cell type within an embryo. Without such information, no one can know whether the developmental program is proceeding normally in the womb. (The prenatal tests currently done for Down syndrome and several other genetic disorders can detect only a few of the thousands of things that can go wrong during embryonic development.)

Rudolf Jaenisch, a colleague of mine with extensive experience in mouse reproductive cloning, was sufficiently exercised to say to a reporter at the *Chicago Tribune*, "[Zavos and Antinori] will produce clones, and most of these will die in utero . . . Those will be the lucky ones. Many of those that survive will have [obvious or more subtle] abnormalities." The rest of us biologists remained quiet. To us, Antinori, Zavos, and Ben-Abraham were so clearly inept that comment seemed gratuitous. In this instance we have, as on other occasions, misjudged the situation: many people seem to take these three and their plans very seriously indeed. And, in fact, this past April, Antinori claimed, somewhat dubiously, that a woman under his care was eight weeks pregnant with a cloned embryo.

⋘⦿⋙

In the meantime, the biotechnology industry, led by ACT, has been moving ahead aggressively with human cloning, but of a different sort. The young companies in this sector have sensed, probably correctly, the enormous potential of therapeutic (rather than reproductive) cloning as a strategy for treating a host of common human degenerative diseases.

The initial steps of therapeutic cloning are identical to those of reproductive cloning: cells are prepared from an adult tissue, their nuclei are extracted, and each nucleus is introduced into a human egg, which is allowed to develop. However, in therapeutic cloning embryonic development is halted at a very early stage—when the embryo is a blastocyst, consisting of perhaps 150 cells—and the inner cells are harvested and cultured. These cells, often termed embryonic stem cells, are still very primitive and thus have retained the ability to develop into any type of cell in the body (except those of the placenta). . . .

Therapeutic cloning has the potential to revolutionize the treatment of a number of currently untreatable degenerative diseases, but it is only a potential. Considerable research will be required to determine the technology's possibilities and limitations for treating human patients.

Some worry that therapeutic-cloning research will never get off the ground in this country. Its proponents—and there are many among the community of biomedical researchers—fear that the two very different kinds of cloning, therapeutic and reproductive, have merged in the public's mind. Three leaders of the community wrote a broadside early this year in *Science*, titled "Please Don't Call It Cloning!" Call therapeutic cloning anything else— call it "nuclear transplantation," or "stem cell research." The scientific community has finally awakened to the damage that the clowns have done.

This is where the newest acts of the circus begin. President George Bush and many pro-life activists are in one ring. A number of disease-specific advocacy groups that view therapeutic cloning as the only real prospect for treating long-resistant maladies are in another. In a third ring are several biotech companies that are flogging their wares, often in ways that make many biologists shudder.

Yielding to pressure from religious conservatives, Bush announced last August that no new human embryonic stem cells could be produced from early human embryos that had been created during the course of research sponsored by the federal government; any research on the potential applications of human embryonic stem cells, he said, would have to be conducted with the existing repertoire of sixty-odd lines. The number of available, usable cell lines actually appears to be closer to a dozen or two. And like all biological reagents, these cells tend to deteriorate with time in culture; new ones will have to be derived if research is to continue. What if experiments with the existing embryonic-stem-cell lines show enormous promise? Such an outcome would produce an almost irresistible pressure to move ahead with the derivation of new embryonic stem cells and to rapidly expand this avenue of research.

How will we learn whether human embryonic stem cells are truly useful for new types of therapy? This question brings us directly to another pitfall: much of the research on human embryonic stem cells is already being conducted by biotech companies, rather than in universities. Bush's edict will only exacerbate this situation. (In the 1970s a federal decision effectively banning government funding of *in vitro* fertilization had a similar effect, driving such research into private clinics.)

Evaluating the science coming from the labs of the biotech industry is often tricky. Those who run these companies are generally motivated more by a need to please stock analysts and venture capitalists than to convince scientific peers. For many biotech companies the peer-review process conducted by scientific journals is simply an inconvenient, time-wasting impediment. So some of the companies routinely bypass peer review and go straight to the mainstream press. Science journalists, always eager for scoops, don't necessarily feel compelled to consult experts about the credibility of industry press releases. And when experts are consulted about the contents of a press release, they are often hampered by spotty descriptions of the claimed breakthrough and thus limited to mumbling platitudes.

ACT, the company that conducted the successful cow-cloning experiment and has now taken the lead in researching human therapeutic cloning, has danced back and forth between publishing in respectable peer-reviewed journals and going directly to the popular press—and recently tried to find a middle ground. . . . Last fall, with vast ambitions, ACT reported that it had conducted the first successful human-cloning experiment. In truth, however, embryonic development went only as far as six cells—far short of the 150-cell blastocyst that represents the first essential step of therapeutic cloning. Wishing to cloak its work in scientific respectability, ACT reported these results in a fledgling electronic research journal named *e-biomed: The Journal of Regenerative Medicine.* Perhaps ACT felt especially welcome in a journal that, according to its editor in chief, William A. Haseltine, a widely known biotech tycoon, "is prepared to publish work of a more preliminary nature." It may also have been encouraged by Haseltine's stance toward cloning, as revealed in his remarks when the journal was founded. "As we understand the body's repair process at the genetic level, we will be able to advance the goal of maintaining our bodies in normal function, perhaps perpetually," he said.

Electronic publishing is still in its infancy, and the publication of ACT's research report will do little to enhance its reputation. By the usual standards of scientific achievement, the experiments ACT published would be considered abject failures. Knowledgeable readers of the report were unable to tell whether the clump of six cells represented the beginning of a human embryo or simply an unformed aggregate of dying cells. . . .

⋅◈⋅

No one yet knows precisely how to make therapeutic cloning work, or which of its many claimed potential applications will pan out and which will not. And an obstacle other than experimental problems confronts those pushing therapeutic cloning. In the wake of the cloning revolution a second revolution has taken place—quieter but no less consequential. It, too, concerns tissue-specific stem cells—but ones found in the tissues of adults. These adult stem cells may one day prove to be at least as useful as those generated by therapeutic cloning. . . .

Until two years ago the dogma among biologists was that stem cells in the bone marrow spawned only blood, those in the liver spawned only hepatocytes, and those in the brain spawned only neurons—in other words, each of our tissues had only its own cadre of stem cells for upkeep. Once again we appear to have been wrong. There is mounting evidence that the body contains some rather unspecialized stem cells, which wander around ready to help many sorts of tissue regenerate their worker cells.

Whether these newly discovered, multi-talented adult stem cells present a viable alternative to therapeutic cloning remains to be proved. Many of the claims about their capabilities have yet to be subjected to rigorous testing. Perhaps not surprisingly, some of these claims have also reached the public without careful vetting by peers. Senator Sam Brownback, of Kansas, an ardent foe of all kinds of cloning, has based much of his case in favor of adult stem cells (and against therapeutic cloning) on these essentially unsubstantiated scientific claims. Adult stem cells provide a convenient escape hatch for Brownback. Their use placates religious conservatives, who are against all cloning, while throwing a bone to groups lobbying for new stem-cell-based therapies to treat degenerative diseases.

Brownback would have biologists shut down therapeutic-cloning research and focus their energies exclusively on adult stem-cell research. But no one can know at present which of those two strategies is more likely to work. . . .

Precisely this issue was debated recently by advisory committees in the United States and Germany. The U.S. committee was convened by Bruce Alberts, the president of the National Academy of Sciences and a highly accomplished cell biologist and scientific educator. Quite naturally, it included a number of experts who are actively involved in exploring the advantages and disadvantages of stem-cell therapies. The committee, which announced its findings in January, concluded that therapeutic cloning should be explored in parallel with alternative strategies.

For their trouble, the scientists were accused of financial self-interest by Steven Milloy of Fox News, who said, "Enron and Arthur Andersen have nothing over the National Academy of Sciences when it comes to deceiving the public . . . Enter Bruce Alberts, the Wizard of Oz–like president of the NAS . . . On his own initiative, Alberts put together a special panel, stacked with embryonic-stem-cell research proponents and researchers already on the taxpayer dole . . . Breast-feeding off taxpayers is as natural to the NAS panel members as breathing." . . .

President Bush, apparently anticipating the NAS panel's conclusion, has appointed an advisory committee all but guaranteed to produce a report much more to his liking. Its chairman, Leon Kass, has gone on record as being against all forms of cloning. (Earlier in his career Kass helped to launch an attack on *in vitro* fertilization.)

Meanwhile, a coalition of a hundred people and organizations recently sent a letter to Congress expressing their opposition to therapeutic cloning— among them Friends of the Earth, Greenpeace, the Sierra Club, the head of the National Latina Health Organization, and the perennial naysayer Jeremy Rifkin. "The problem with therapeutic cloning," Rifkin has said, "is that it introduces commercial eugenics from the get-go." Powerful words indeed. Few of those galvanized by Rifkin would know that therapeutic cloning has nothing whatsoever to do with eugenics.

Usually progress in biology is held back by experimental difficulties, inadequate instruments, poorly planned research protocols, inadequate funding, or plain sloppiness. But in this case the future of research may have little connection with these factors or with the scientific pros and cons being debated earnestly by members of the research community. The other, more public debates will surely be the decisive ones.

The clashes about human therapeutic cloning that have taken place in the media and in Congress are invariably built around weighty moral and ethical principles. But none of us needs a degree in bioethics to find the bottom line in the arguments. They all ultimately converge on a single question: When does human life begin? Some say it is when sperm and egg meet, others when the embryo implants in the womb, others when the fetus quickens, and yet others when the fetus can survive outside the womb. This is a question that we scientists are neither more nor less equipped to decide than the average man or woman in the street, than a senator from Kansas or a cardinal in Cologne. (Because Dolly and the other cloned animals show that a complete embryo can be produced from a single adult cell, some biologists have proposed, tongue in cheek, that a human life exists in each one of our cells.) Take your pick of the possible answers and erect your own moral scaffolding above your choice.

POSTSCRIPT

Should Scientists Be Allowed to Clone Children?

Both selections discuss the distinction between therapeutic and reproductive cloning. Is one type of cloning "more ethical" than the other? One type of cloning would be used to heal people, but at the same time it would be destroying a human embryo. The other type of cloning would let the embryo live, but it could possibly tamper with the very essence of the propagation of the human race.

Is a human life present in the group of indeterminable cells used for embryonic stem cell research? Would we be better off if the federal government decided to fund cloning research? Would we be better off if cloning was banned completely and totally? Is there truly a difference between the ethical dilemmas involved with therapeutic cloning and those involved with reproductive cloning? After a debate on cloning, it seems as if we are left with more questions than answers. The future will ultimately tell us whether we will make a mistake by either allowing cloning and tampering with the natural order of things or by dismissing cloning as science fiction and consequently watching many people die whose lives could have been saved.

Suggested Readings

Burne, J., & Gurdon, J. (2002). Commentary on human cloning; http://www.reproductivecloning.net/cloning.pdf.

Coghlan, A. (2002). Race is on to stop human cloning. *New Scientist, 175,* 11.

Kaebnick, G. (2003). All clones are not the same: The difference between reproductive and therapeutic cloning. *The New York Times*, Jan. 2, 2003, 29.

Lewis, Ricki. (2002). Mike West: Cloning for human therapeutics. *The Scientist, 16,* 60–61.

President's Council on Bioethics. (2002). Human Cloning and human dignity: An ethical inquiry; http://www.bioethics.gov/reports/cloningreport/index.html.

ISSUE 4

Does Transracial Adoption Harm a Child's Development?

YES: Leslie Doty Hollingsworth, from "Symbolic Interaction-ism, African American Families, and the Transracial Adoption Con-troversy," *Social Work* (September 1999)

NO: Rudolph Alexander, Jr. and Carla M. Curtis, from "A Review of Empirical Research Involving the Transracial Adoption of African American Children," *Journal of Black Psychology* (May 1996)

ISSUE SUMMARY

YES: Leslie Doty Hollingsworth, assistant professor at the University of Michigan, contends that socialization within an African American family is a unique and distinct experience for children. As a conse-quence, children not socialized in these families cannot effectively embrace African American definitions of self and family.

NO: Rudolph Alexander, Jr. and Carla M. Curtis, both professors at Ohio State University, offer research maintaining that African American children are not psychologically harmed by transracial adoptions.

$\mathbf{A}$merican society has long embraced the notion that children do much bet-ter by being adopted into loving homes rather than being placed in institutions or orphanages. The family unit not only socializes a child but can provide a child with nurturance, a sense of security, and unconditional love. Unfortu-nately, there are hundreds of thousands of children in U.S. society who, for various reasons, are not with their biological families. They, like all children, are in need of and entitled to loving families, but they cannot get them. These are mostly nonwhite children. The question thus arises: Should these children be adopted, transracially, by white families, especially if the alternative is a succession of foster homes or institutionalization?

Transracial adoption typically refers to a family in which a minority child (e.g. Asian American, Native American, African American, or Latino) or a child with a mixed racial background is adopted by an Anglo-American couple.

Transracial adoptions account for about 15 percent of all adoptions in the United States annually. This type of adoption became more commonplace in the United States in the late 1940s. Children with mixed racial backgrounds came from Europe and Asia after World War II, Korean American children came from the Korean War, and refugee Chinese children in Hong Kong were adopted by Anglo-American couples in the United States. Finding adoptive homes for Native American children followed. The movement to place African American children with Anglo-American families is the most recent evolution of transracial adoption.

A common opinion among adoption professionals today is that eligible children should be placed in an adoptive home without delay. However, whenever possible, children should be raised by people of their own culture and heritage. The Multi-Ethnic Placement Act of 1994 forbade using race as the sole factor in deciding whether or not a family can adopt a given child. Race is to be used as one of several factors in the decision. The National Association of Black Social Workers (NABSW) has argued vociferously against transracial adoption. Its position is that the practice is destructive to minority families and communities. The sentiment of the members of this group is so strong that they have even suggested that the placement of African American children with Anglo-American families could be conceived as a form of cultural genocide. Leora Neal, executive director of the National Association of Black Social Workers Child Adoption, Counseling, and Referral Service outlines several problems incurred by transracial adoptees:

- They may feel unaccepted by both the Anglo-American and minority community from which they came.
- In a racist society, children need to learn coping skills. Since white parents have never had to deal with racism, they are often ill equipped to help their children understand and deal with it effectively.
- Children lose contact with the fullness of their culture of origin.
- Adopting family members do not always realize that they are now part of a mixed-race family. As a result, they must acknowledge and accept this fact.

As you read the following two selections, consider the issue from both the adoptive parents' point of view and the child's. What are the critical issues that come to your mind that might cause you to support the point of view of the NABSW? Which issues might cause you to support prospective parents and children who are involved in a transracial adoption?

YES

Leslie Doty Hollingsworth

Symbolic Interactionism, African American Families, and the Transracial Adoption Controversy

Historical Background

Transracial adoption is the legal adoption of children of one race or ethnic group by a family of a different race or ethnic group. In the United States transracial adoption almost without exception has involved the adoption by white parents of children of racial or ethnic minority groups from the United States or other countries. In cases in which African American children were involved, the practice began to increase during the 1950s (Simon & Alstein, 1977), precipitated by a decrease in healthy white infants available for adoption and an increase in white parents desiring to adopt (McRoy, 1989). Between 1967 and 1972 approximately 10,000 African American children were transracially adopted, with about 2,500 placements occurring in 1971 (McRoy, 1989). Advocacy groups were established to promote and facilitate transracial adoptions (Simon & Alstein, 1992). Standards-setting groups, such as the Child Welfare League of America (1968), reversed their race- and religion-matching standards, and adoption research began to be directed at examining the motivation for transracial adoption (Hollingsworth, 1998).

In November 1972 the National Association of Black Social Workers (NABSW) (cited in McRoy, 1989, and Simon & Alstein, 1977) passed a resolution opposing the transracial adoption of African American children. The resolution read in part:

> Black children should be placed only with Black families, whether in foster care or adoption. Black children belong physically, and psychologically and culturally in black families in order that they receive the total sense of themselves and develop a sound projection of their future. Human beings are products of their environment and develop their sense of values, attitudes, and self-concepts within their own family structure. Black children in white homes are cut off from the healthy development of themselves as black people (cited in Simon & Alstein, 1977, p. 50).

Although the wording of the actual resolution became a source of controversy, much of the controversy was about some of the supporting language:

Our position is based on:

1. the necessity of self-determination from birth to death of all Black people.
2. the need of our young ones to begin at birth to identify with Black people in a Black community.
3. the philosophy that we need our own to build a strong nation (p. 50). . . .

This resolution was not put forward arbitrarily. The experience of African American children in the United States formed the context within which the resolution was introduced. Chestang (1972) was among the first to call social workers' attention to the cultural concerns that transracial adoption presented. He identified three conditions in the United States that characterized the experience of African American people: *societal inconsistency,* which he defined as being put in a position of having to maintain a sense of competence while coping with discrimination and prejudice; *social injustice*—that is, being confronted with inequities in employment, housing, and education on the basis of race; and *personal impotence*—the sense of shame, inadequacy, and diminished self-worth that is associated with being powerless to affect the oppressive situation. Chestang pointed out that African American people are faced with these conditions from birth to death. He called attention to what life under these conditions would be like for African American children who were transracially adopted and for their adoptive families. Finally, he reminded social workers that the situation in which the child welfare system found itself—that is, a large number of African American children in the foster care and institutional systems—was the result of discrimination and other barriers to adoption by African American families and not their unwillingness to adopt. . . .

The rise in opposition to same-race adoption policies, beginning in the early 1980s, has been documented (Hollingsworth, 1998). Opponents were concerned about possible discrimination, about the overresponsibility on the part of children of color for the good of the group, and about the lack of empirical support for same-race policies (Bartholet, 1991). Several highly publicized lawsuits were filed (McRoy, 1989), and transracial adoptions increased once more.

Meanwhile, the NABSW called attention to three circumstances that negatively affected the status of African American children in the child welfare system. First, experience with the child welfare system did not demonstrate a commitment to the preservation of African American families. Children frequently were removed from their families because of neglect. Although neglect has been shown to be associated with poverty, the economic condition of these families that may have given rise to the neglect of children seldom was addressed. In addition, barriers existed that impeded the children's placement with relatives. Second, efforts to reunite children with their biological families were insufficient. The NABSW called attention to the fact that African American children tended to remain in foster care or the institutional system after having been removed from their families and that the child welfare and judicial systems lacked the capacity to reunite these children with their families in a timely manner. Moreover, biological parents frequently did not have the financial resources necessary to correct the circumstances that led to their children's removal. However, substantial resources were directed to foster parents and institutions, leading the NABSW to question whether institutions were retaining children to acquire more funds for their care. Third, the NABSW continued to object to the implication that African Americans do not adopt in large enough numbers to resolve the crisis of African American children in the foster care system. The organization called attention to the fact that the majority of children in the foster care system were hard-to-place white children with special needs and that only 1 percent or fewer white families who were willing to adopt African American children requested those with special needs (special needs typically are defined as being over eight years old, in sibling groups, and with emotional and physical disabilities). Adoption alone was considered insufficient to address the foster care crisis.

The Omnibus Budget Reconciliation Act of 1993 (P.L. 103–66) eventually was passed. This legislation provided funding for the expansion of community-based family support programs and family preservation programs. The NABSW ("Preserving," 1994) subsequently modified its position on transracial adoption. In its current position, it places priority on family preservation and reunification with birth families, alternative care by biological relatives, and adoption by same-race nonrelatives, recognizing the importance of providing permanent homes for all children. Transracial adoption is seen as a last resort. Children should not be removed from their birth families when economic resource limitations or institutional barriers are the sources of the problem ("Preserving," 1994).

The Interethnic Adoption Section of the Small Business Job Protection Act of 1996 (P.L. 104–188) lacked language that had allowed the best interests of the child to be considered in decisions to use race or ethnicity in adoptive placements. Penalties were established for federally funded agencies that delayed or denied placement based on these considerations. The Adoption and Safe Families Act of 1997 (P.L. 105–89) was passed. Although the law is credited with better protecting children from maltreatment, it makes it easier to terminate the rights of biological parents. It occurs in a legislative environment of diminishing economic resources to poor families whose children are at greatest risk of maltreatment. . . .

Symbolic Interactionist Explanation

. . . [T]he African American community consists of people and institutions similar in their African heritage (Nobles, 1974) and in their experience with racism and oppression (Baldwin, 1981). Thus, the African American community is central in the socialization of African American children.

Symbolic interactionism has framed a number of studies of African American life. These include studies that demonstrate the lower rate of work-family conflicts among African American women who were socialized to balance both roles (Myers, 1989), the appropriateness of group work for intervention with African American youths from low-income families who present school behavior problems (Brown, 1984), the meaning of leisure among older African American women (Chin-Sang & Allen, 1991), and common experiences of African Americans with AIDS (Hudson & Morris, 1994). Baldwin's (1981) African self-consciousness theory derives from assumptions that are consistent with symbolic interactionism. A preference for the adoption and socialization of African American children by same-race parents can be understood from this perspective.

. . . [T]he objection to transracial adoption may be understood in terms of the meaning that Africans and African Americans attach to children. According to the African scholar Mbiti (1969), it is desirable in traditional African societies to have many children because the dead are believed to remain among the living as long as there is someone who remembers them and can refer to them personally by name. Traditional Africans think of their children as divine gifts (Erny, 1973), as is evident in the Ashanti proverb that "children are the reward of life" (Willis, 1996). It is possible that children also have a special meaning in contemporary African American communities that causes these communities to want to hold on to them. The acceptance of children born outside of marriage (the idea that "there are no illegitimate children") and the active role of grandparents in their care (Flaherty, Facteau, & Garver, 1995) exemplifies this position.

The relationship between meaning and behavior is also apparent in NABSW's definition of its constituency as being the black individual, the black family, and the black community. Its mission is directed toward their welfare and toward a commitment to action for the improvement of social conditions over personal interests. Considered within this framework, that the organization opposes transracial adoption is fully comprehensible. . . .

As a method of survival on arriving in a foreign land, African slaves established plantation communities (James, 1992). The process by which slave children learned to call non-blood-related adults "uncle" and "aunt" is believed to have socialized them into the slave community. The community, then, became the family of the child whose parents had been sold or were required to work and live away from the child. After the Civil War, U.S. officials, preparing to arrange the care of what they believed were thousands of orphaned black children who were freed but whose parents had already been sold, were surprised that the children had already been taken into the families of former friends and neighbors (Gutman, 1976).

In its code of ethics, the National Association of Black Social Workers recognizes the concept of a black extended family, with all black people considered as kin, and with no distinction made between the destiny of other black people and [one's] own destiny. It seems clear, therefore, that the meaning of such concepts as the family is influenced by the interaction of African and African American people in the life of the ethnic group.

"Meanings are handled in and modified through an interpretive process used by the person in dealing with things he or she encounters" (LaRossa & Reitzes, 1994, p. 143). Among Africans and African Americans, adoption traditionally seems to have been interpreted as a natural and informal process arising in response to a need rather than a formal one involving legal ownership and individual rights. Thus, the results of Hill's (1977) survey of the informal adoption patterns of African Americans from 1969 to 1976 showed that 90 percent of children who were born "out-of-wedlock" were kept by the extended family—the majority (57 percent) by grandparents and great-grandparents and the next largest number (26 percent) by aunts and uncles.

As a result of such knowledge development as that provided by Hill (1977), professionals who were involved in adoption services and policy making began to attach a different meaning to the resistance to transracial adoption. Agency policies and practices were modified to reflect an emphasis on same-race adoptions. In some instances separate agencies or programs were established that specialized in the recruitment of same-race adopters. The success of these programs has been described elsewhere (Gant, 1984; Gilles & Kroll, 1991; Hairston & Williams, 1989; Jackson-White, Dozier, Oliver, & Gardner, 1997; McRoy, Oglesby, & Grape, 1997).

A surge has been noted in kinship foster care arrangements, especially among African Americans. Because adoption has been interpreted by African Americans as an informal process, many African Americans are resistant to formally adopting the kin who are in their care (Hollingsworth, 1998). Although these arrangements are often permanent, relatives cite the fact that the children are already family and that they do not want to create dissension with the child's birth parents whom they consider family also (Thornton, 1991). Some associate the practice of paying fees to adopt children with slave trading (Gilles & Kroll, 1991). The differences in interpretation, however, do not change the outcome of the process—that is, that permanent homes and families are provided to children who need them.

. . . The NABSW (cited in Simon & Alstein, 1977) indicated that African American children could "receive [a] total sense of themselves and develop a sound projection of their future" only in African American families (p. 50). The organization also asserted that because "human beings are products of their environment and develop their sense of values, attitudes, and self-concepts within their own family structure, . . . black children in white homes [would be] cut off from the healthy development of themselves as black people" (p. 50). According to symbolic interactionism, it is through contact with others in the social group that children learn a sense of "I," "my," and "mine," as well as a concept of "we" (LaRossa & Reitzes, 1994). If the individual is to develop an African American self-identity, it is necessary that it be acquired in a family in which African Americans are present.

The African American "self" is considered a collective rather than an individual one. Mbiti (1969) wrote of traditional Africans: "In traditional life, the individual does not and cannot exist alone except corporately. He owes his existence to other people, including those of past generations and his contemporaries. He is simply part of the whole. The community must therefore make, create, or produce the individual; for the individual depends on the corporate group" (p. 108).

According to Mbiti (1969), traditional Africans live according to the tenet, "I am, because we are, and since we are therefore I am" (pp. 108–109). Nobles (1974) also discussed the African extended self, whereby individual identity and purpose evolve from an identification with the collective. The position taken by the NABSW (cited in McRoy, 1989, and Simon & Alstein, 1977) therefore can be considered a lived example of a collective identity and as clarifying the group identity that Africa-descended people require.

"Self-concepts, once developed, provide an important motive for behavior" (p. 144). If the identity of African Americans is a collective one, actions that are perceived as a threat to the survival of the group can be expected to motivate individuals to act to resist the threat. The NABSW concern about genocide (cited in McRoy, 1989, and Simon & Alstein, 1977) or in this case, concern about the elimination of the African American group through the widespread transracial adoption of African American children can be understood within this context. Abdullah (1996) called attention to the original wording of the United Nations' 1948 position on genocide: "Genocide . . . is the committing of certain acts with the intent to destroy—wholly or in part—a national, ethnic, racial or religious group as such, including measures to prevent birth and forcibly transferring children of one group to another" (United Nations, 1991, as cited in Abdullah, 1996, p. 260). . . . Assertions often are found in the public media and in some professional literature that African American children are languishing in the foster care system while potential parents wait to adopt them. The implication is that the alternative to transracial adoption for African American children is life in a foster home or institution. Other realities are seldom mentioned, such as the small number of white families who want to adopt transracially, the willingness of relatives to provide care and of nonrelative African American families to become foster parents and adoptive parents, and the relationship of insufficient economic and social support to child maltreatment in many families (Hollingsworth, 1998). Also, the dual cultural adaptation that is required of African Americans and members of other ethnic groups in the United States (Chestang, 1972; DuBois, 1903; Norton, 1978) may increase the potential for influences from the larger society. . . .

Implications for Research, Practice, and Policy Advocacy

. . . Based on the symbolic interactionist conceptualization that has been presented here, I make four recommendations. First, social work scholars should continue to examine scientifically the questions that have been set forth regarding transracial adoption (Alexander & Curtis, 1996; Bartholet, 1991). Theory building and empirical falsification continue to be the standards that are used by scholars to examine research questions. This work should be conducted from an African-centered ideological perspective (Allen, 1978). It also should be phenomenological, so that the lived experiences of African American children in families may be examined.

Second, social workers should become familiar with theories that have already been advanced about African American life and culture and with research that has been conducted with regard to questions of racial identity and self-esteem effects of transracial adoption. Baldwin's (1981) theory of African self-consciousness and Nobles' (1978) concept of Africanity are examples, as are studies by Andujo (1988); Hollingsworth (1997); Baker (1992); Black (1985); Feigelman and Silverman (1983); Grow and Shapiro (1974); McRoy and Zurcher (1983); Shireman (1988); Shireman and Johnson (1975; 1980); Johnson, Shireman, and Watson (1987); Simon and Alstein (1977, 1981, 1987, 1992); Simon, Alstein, and Melli (1994); Vroegh (1997), and Womack (1981). Reviews by Alexander and Curtis (1996), Curtis (1996), Hollingsworth (1997), and Silverman (1993) are useful. Many of these can be used to advance the critical analysis and dialogue suggested by Doherty et al. (1994) within the context of African-centered values and culture. However, social work critics should examine the validity and reliability of the studies and the perspectives that have been used in interpreting their results.

Third, social workers should be familiar with the realities faced by African American children and families in the child welfare system. The relationship of poverty and single-female parenthood to child maltreatment has been documented consistently (Johnson, 1997; Pelton, 1978; 1988; Sedlak & Broadhurst, 1996). Child maltreatment and especially child neglect are frequent reasons for the removal of children from their birth families and for their placement in foster care or adoptive homes. African American families are represented disproportionately in the rates of poverty and the statistics of single-female parenthood (Hollingsworth, 1998). It is therefore simplistic to limit examination to the results rather than the causes of the phenomena that bring African American children into the foster care system.

Finally, social workers should advocate for public policies and agency practices that recognize the African American family as a unique cultural group, offering a valuable socialization experience for African American children. Such policies and practices are necessary to ensure that the legitimate identity and the psychosocial health of African Americans are protected.

In conclusion, I have used symbolic interactionism to conceptually frame objections to the transracial adoption of African American children, taking the position that the community of people of African descent (that is, the African diaspora) forms the group within which their children are socialized. Because meaning and development of the self are dependent on the group, African American children necessarily require the African American family for socialization into the group. From a symbolic interactionist perspective, becoming a part of the larger group structure is a natural outcome for its members. Thus, rather than being discriminatory or self-serving, the early objection to transracial adoption by the National Association of Black Social Workers and the expressed support for ethnic consistency in adoption by groups such as the North American Council on Adoptable Children (Gilles & Kroll, 1991) are in the service of the healthy development of African American children. Research, theory development, analysis of existing research and theory, and policy advocacy are important to this process.

References

Adoption and Safe Families Act of 1997, P.L. 105–89, 111 Stat. 21150.

Abdullah, S. B. (1996). Transracial adoption is not the solution to America's problems of child welfare. *Journal of Black Psychology, 22,* 254–261.

Alexander, R., Jr., & Curtis, C. M. (1996). A review of empirical research involving the transracial adoption of African American children. *Journal of Black Psychology, 22,* 223–35.

Allen, W. (1978). The search for applicable theories of black family life. *Journal of Marriage and the Family, 40,* 117–29.

Andujo, E. (1988). Ethnic identity of transethnically-adopted Hispanic adolescents. *Social Work, 33,* 531–535.

Baker, M. E. (1992). *Psychological adjustment of adopted minority children.* Unpublished master's thesis, University of North Carolina at Chapel Hill.

Baldwin, J. (1981). Notes on an Africentric theory of black personality. *Western Journal of Black Studies, 5,* 172–179.

Bartholet, E. (1991). Where do black children belong? The politics of race matching in adoption. *University of Pennsylvania Law Review, 139,* 1163–1256.

Black, S.E.C. (1985). *The perception of racial identity in transracial and inracial adoptees.* Unpublished master's thesis, University of Houston.

Brown, J. A. (1984). Group work with low-income black youths. *Social Work with Groups, 7,* 111–124.

Chestang, L. (1972). The dilemma of biracial adoption. *Social Work, 17,* 100–105.

Child Welfare League of America. (1968). *Standards for adoption service.* Washington, DC: Author.

Child Welfare League of America. (1973). *Standards for adoption service.* Washington, DC: Author.

Chin-Sang, V., & Allen, K. R. (1991). Leisure and the older black woman. *Journal of Gerontological Nursing, 17,* 30–34.

Curtis, C. M. (1996). The adoption of African American children by whites: A renewed conflict. *Families in Society, 77,* 156–165.

Doherty, W. J., Boss, P. G., LaRossa, R., Schumm, W. R., & Steinmetz, S. K. (1994). Family theories and methods: A contextual approach. In P. G. Boss, W. J. Doherty, R. LaRossa, W. R. Schumm, & S. K. Steinmetz (Eds.), *Sourcebook of family theories and methods: A contextual approach* (pp. 3–30). New York: Plenum Press.

DuBois, W.E.B. (1903). *The souls of black folk.* Chicago: A. C. McClurg.

Erny, P. (1973). *Childhood and cosmos.* New York: Black Orpheus Press.

Feigelman, W., & Silverman, A. (1983). *Chosen children: New patterns of adoptive relationships.* New York: Praeger.

Flaherty, M. J., Sr., Facteau, L., & Garver, P. (1995). Grandmother functions in multigenerational families: An exploratory study of Black adolescent mothers and their infants. In R. Staples (Ed.), *The Black family: Essays and studies* (pp. 195–203). Belmont, CA: Wadsworth.

Foster, H. J. (1983). African patterns in the Afro-American family. *Journal of Black Studies, 14,* 201–232.

Gant, L. M. (1984). *Black adoption programs: Pacesetters in practice.* Ann Arbor, MI: National Child Welfare Training Center.

Gilles, T., & Kroll, J. (1991). *Barriers to same race placement.* St. Paul, MN: North American Council on Adoptable Children.

Goddard, L. L. (1996). Transracial adoption: Unanswered theoretical and conceptual issues. *Journal of Black Psychology, 22,* 273–281.

Grow, L. J., & Shapiro, D. (1974). *Black children—white parents: A study of transracial adoption.* New York: Child Welfare League of America.

Gutman, H. G. (1976). *The black family in slavery and freedom: 1970–1925.* New York: Random House.

Hairston, C. F., & Williams, V. G. (1989). Black adoptive parents: How they view agency adoptive practices. *Social Casework, 70,* 534–538.

Herzog, E., Sudia, C., Harwood, J., & Newcomb, C. (1971). *Families for black children: The search for adoptive parents.* Washington, DC: U.S. Government Printing Office.

Hill, R. D. (1977). *Informal adoption among black families.* Washington, DC: National Urban League.

Hollingsworth, L. D. (1997). Effect of transracial/transethnic adoption on children's racial and ethnic identity and self-esteem: A meta-analytic review. *Marriage & Family Review, 25,* 99–130. Co-published simultaneously in H. E. Gross & M. B. Sussman (Eds.), Families and adoption (pp. 99–130). Binghampton, NY: Haworth Press.

Hollingsworth, L. D. (1998). Promoting same-race adoption for children of color. *Social Work, 43,* 104–116.

Howard, A., Royse, D. D., & Skerl, J. A. (1977). Transracial adoption: The black community perspective. *Social Work, 22,* 184–189.

Hudson, A. L., & Morris, R. I. (1994). Perceptions of social support of African Americans with acquired immunodeficiency syndrome. *Journal of National Black Nurses' Association, 7,* 36–49.

Indian Child Welfare Act of 1978, P.L. 95–608, 92 Stat. 3069.

Jackson-White, G., Dozier, C. D, Oliver, J. T, & Gardner, L. B. (1997). Why African American adoption agencies succeed: A new perspective on self-help. *Child Welfare, 76,* 239–254.

James, C.L.R. (1992). The Atlantic slave trade and slavery: Some interpretations of their significance in the development of the United States and the Western World. In F. W. Hayes, II (Ed.), *A turbulent voyage: Readings in African American studies* (pp. 213–236). San Diego: Collegiate Press.

Johnson, P. R., Shireman, J. F., & Watson, K. W. (1987). Transracial adoption and the development of black identity at age eight. *Child Welfare, 66,* 45–55.

Johnson, S. (1997) *Child welfare: Challenges and opportunities* [The 1997 Fedele F. and Iris M. Fauri Lecture]. Ann Arbor: University of Michigan.

LaRossa, R., & Reitzes, D.C. (1994). Symbolic interactionism and family studies. In P. G. Boss, W. J. Doherty, R. LaRossa, W. R. Schumm, & S. K. Steinmetz (Eds.), *Sourcebook of family theories and methods: A contextual approach* (pp. 135–163). New York: Plenum Press.

Mbiti, J. S. (1969). *African religions and philosophy.* New York: Praeger.

McRoy, R. G. (1989). An organizational dilemma: The case of transracial adoptions. *Journal of Applied Behavior Science, 25,* 145–160.

McRoy, R. G., & Zurcher, L. A. (1983). *Transracial and inracial adoptees: The adolescent years.* Springfield, IL: Charles C Thomas.

McRoy, R. G., Oglesby, Z., & Grape, H. (1997). Achieving same-race adoptive placements for African American children: Culturally sensitive practice approaches. *Child Welfare, 76,* 85–104.

Multiethnic Placement Act of 1994, P.L. 103–382, 108 Stat. 4057.

Myers, L. W. (1989). Early gender role socialization among black women: Affective or consequential? *Western Journal of Black Studies, 13,* 173–178.

Nobles, W. W. (1974). Africanity: Its role in black families. *Black Scholar, 5,* 10–17.

Norton, D. G. (1978). *The dual perspective: Inclusion of ethnic minority content in the social work curriculum.* New York: Council on Social Work Education.

Omnibus Budget Reconciliation Act of 1993, P.L. 103–66, 107 Stat. 312.

Pelton, L. H. (1978). Child abuse and neglect: The myth of classlessness. *American Journal of Orthopsychiatry, 48,* 608–617.

Pelton, L. H. (1988). The institution of adoption: Its sources and perpetuation. In D. Valentine (Ed.), *Infertility and adoption* (pp. 87–117). Binghampton, NY: Haworth Press.

Penn, M. L., & Coverdale, C. (1996). Transracial adoption: A human rights perspective. *Journal of Black Psychology, 22,* 240–245.

Preserving African American families: Position statement. (1994). Detroit: National Association of Black Social Workers.

Sedlak, A. J., & Broadhurst, M.L.A. (1996). *Executive summary of the third national incidence study of child abuse and neglect.* [Online]. Available: http://www.casanet.org/library/abuse/stabuse/htm.

Shireman, J. F. (1988). *Family life project: A longitudinal adoption study—Growing up adopted: An examination of major issues* (Phase IV). Chicago: Chicago Child Care Society.

Shireman, J. F., & Johnson, P. R. (1975). *Adoption: Three alternatives* (Phase I). Chicago: Chicago Child Care Society.

Shireman, J. F., & Johnson, P. R. (1980). *Adoption: Three alternatives* (Phase II). Chicago: Chicago Child Care Society.

Shireman, J. F., & Johnson, P. R (1986). A longitudinal study of black adoptions: Single parent, transracial, and traditional (Phase III). *Social Work, 31,* 172–177.

Simon, R. J. (1978). Black attitudes toward transracial adoption. *Phylon, 39,* 135–142.

Simon, R. J., & Alstein, H. (1977). *Transracial adoption.* New York: John Wiley & Sons.

Simon, R. J., & Alstein, H. (1981). *Transracial adoption: A follow-up.* Lexington, MA: Praeger.

Simon, R. J., & Alstein, H. (1987). *Transracial adoptees and their families: A study of identity and commitment.* New York: Praeger.

Simon, R. J., & Alstein, H. (1992). *Adoption, race and identity: From infancy through adolescence.* New York: Praeger.

Simon, R. J., Alstein, H., & Melli, M. S. (1994). *The case for transracial adoption.* Washington, DC: American University Press.

Silverman, A. R. (1993). Outcomes of transracial adoption. *Future of Children: Adoption, 3,* 104–118.

Small Business Job Protection Act of 1996, P.L. 104–188, 110 Stat. 17550.

Thornton, J. L. (1991). Permanency planning for children in kinship homes. *Child Welfare, 70,* 593–601.

Vroegh, K. S. (1997). Transracial adoptees: Developmental status after 17 years. *American Journal of Orthopsychiatry, 67,* 568–575.

Willis, M. G. (1996). The real issues in transracial adoption: A response. *Journal of Black Psychology, 22,* 246–253.

Womack, W. M., & Fulton, W. (1981). Transracial adoption and the black preschool child. *Journal of the American Academy of Child Psychiatry, 20,* 712–724.

Rudolph Alexander, Jr. and
Carla M. Curtis

A Review of Empirical Research Involving the Transracial Adoption of African American Children

In 1972, the National Association of Black Social Workers (NABSW) strongly advocated same-race adoption of African American children, thwarting a growing policy of placing African American children with White families (Adamec & Pierce, 1991). The position of NABSW was that the placement of African American children with White families constituted cultural genocide (Adamec & Pierce, 1991; Bartholet, 1991, 1993) and was unnecessary (Aigner, 1986; G. K. Smith, personal communication, September 4, 1992; National Association of Black Social Workers, 1992). Furthermore, some African American professionals contended that these children had been psychologically harmed by these placements (Hermann, 1993). Other mental health professionals speculated that transracial adoption was more stressful to African American children than in racial adoptions involving Whites (Helwig & Ruthven, 1990). For these reasons, a national policy of same-race adoption was pursued for more than a decade, and transracial adoptions dropped precipitously (Hayes, 1993).

However, this policy has been abruptly reversed. First, in recent years social scientists retrieved previous research, pointing to the benefits of transracial adoptions and presenting more recent findings (Silverman, 1993; Simon & Altstein, 1981, 1987, 1992; Simon, Altstein, & Melli, 1994). Second, the courts got involved, repeatedly ruling in favor of White parents wanting to adopt African American children (*McLaughin v. Pernsley*, 1988; *Reisman v. State Dept. of Human Servs.*, 1993). Third, legislators began decrying the perceived crisis in foster care and adoption. Estimates were that 500,000 children were in foster care—where many children wait to be adopted—and African American children constituted the largest group, or 40% (Davis, 1995). In New Jersey, Maryland, and Louisiana, more than 50% of the children in foster care were African American (McRoy, 1995). Concerned about this situation, Senator Howard Metzenbaum introduced legislation in 1994 that forbade discrimination in adoption and foster care placement. This legislation, known as the Multiethnic Placement Act, was passed by the 104th Congress and was signed by President Clinton weeks later.

From Rudolph Alexander, Jr. and Carla M. Curtis, "A Review of Empirical Research Involving the Transracial Adoption of African American Children," *Journal of Black Psychology*, vol. 22, no. 2 (May 1996). Copyright © 1996 by The Association of Black Psychologists. Reprinted by permission of Sage Publications, Inc.

These recent events in the courts and in Congress seem to dismiss NABSW's position that African American children have been harmed by their adoption in White families. Typically, commentaries about studies that have supported transracial adoptions have universally accepted the findings of these studies without critically evaluating the research methodology (e.g., see Silverman, 1993). A critical evaluation may or may not lead to similar conclusions; however, such scrutiny is needed given the importance of the issue. For this reason, we critically review the empirical literature to discern the impact of parenting by White families upon African American children's mental health. . . .

Adjustment Studies

Descriptive Cross-Sectional Studies

In an early study, Grow and Shapiro (1974) studied 125 transracial families to learn the extent to which the families experienced a successful adoption. In effect, adjustment was operationalized to be successful adoption. The researchers chose not to employ a comparison group, conceding that same-race was preferable. Hence this study was descriptive. They administered two personality tests to the children and obtained parents' assessments of their children in several areas. Based on this conceptualization, they concluded that 77% of the children had adjusted successfully following their adoption by White families. In another descriptive study, Johnson, Shireman, and Watson (1987), using the Clark Doll Test [in which children identify a doll as having a "race" similar to their own], found that 73% of African American children adopted by White parents identified themselves as African Americans compared to 80% of African American children adopted by African American parents. These researchers concluded that 73% of the transracial adoptees were doing well, compared to 80% of the inracial adoptees.

The two studies discussed above were descriptive and did not use inferential statistics to test relationships between and among variables. Accordingly, these studies did not provide much information. However, a number of studies employed comparison groups consisting of either White adoptive children or African American children adopted by African American parents. Studies that used comparison groups provide more knowledge about the relationship between the type of family and the extent of adjustment.

Cross-Sectional Comparison Studies

McRoy, Zurcher, Lauderdale, and Anderson (1982) compared African American children who had been adopted by White and African American families. These researchers, indicating that their study was exploratory, were interested in possible differences in the children's level of self-esteem and extent of racial identity. Using cross-tabulation, they studied 60 families and found no differences in the children's level of self-esteem. However, they found differences in the extent of racial identity. The researchers concluded that White families might be able to provide a loving home for children, but these families may not be able to instill a sense of positiveness about identity. However, they stopped short of recommending against transracial adoption. Instead, they stated that when a transracial adoption was completed, an independent assessment needed to be made of the total ecological environment.

Brenner (1993) studied how transracial adoption affected children's identity formation and other adolescent developmental tasks. In addition, the researcher studied racial identity and the extent to which children engaged in search behaviors (i.e., the practice of looking for birth parents). Of the children, 11 were Asian, 8 were White, and 5 were African American. All the parents were White. Brenner found that African American children did not manage their emotions and frustrations. They also had more uneasiness with their physical appearance than White and Asian adoptees. All the African American children engaged in search behaviors, whereas a majority of White and Asian children did not. Brenner concluded that, all in all, no significant difference existed between transracial and inracial children, and the status of the children was unrelated to issues regarding adjustment and identity formation (Brenner, 1993).

Multivariate Analysis

Indirectly looking at adjustment, several researchers compared the amount of disruption in White and African American adoptions. They employed a multiple discriminant analysis to learn which of 23 variables predicted a stable or unstable adoption. One of the 23 variables was the extent of matching— whether an African American child was matched with an African American or White family. Six variables were related to the dependent variable: the child's age, the child's sex, the number of problems experienced by children, whether there was a previous adoption placement, whether the adoption was by a foster parent, and the mother's education level. Because matching was not significant, the researchers concluded that transracial adoptions were no more likely to be unstable than inracial adoption (Barth, Berry, Yoshikami, Goodfield, & Carlson, 1988).

Specifically examining the quality of the children's experiences, Rosenthal, Groze, and Curiel (1990) surveyed 1,328 families who adopted transracially and inracially and received 799 returned questionnaires. Of this total, 22% of the families were transracial. Using multiple regression, they found some differences between the two groups of children. Particularly, the transracial group had more history of sexual abuse, group home experience, and psychiatric placement. Controlling for these variables, however, they concluded that as a group, transracial adoptees were doing reasonably well.

In a somewhat related study about the difficulties of African American children adopted by White families, Silverman and Feigelman (1981a) examined questionnaires of 97 White families who adopted African American children and 56 families who adopted White children. They found that African American children exhibited more maladjustment and were more likely to experience hostility in their environments preceding their adoption than White children. African American children were more likely also to be older than White children at adoption. The researchers concluded that the age of the child at adoption had more of an impact on adjustment than transracial adoption (Silverman & Feigelman, 1981a).

Revealing more of their study, Silverman and Feigelman (1981b) mailed 1,121 surveys and received 713 returned questionnaires. They used factor analysis to create a measure of maladjustment based on parental responses to four questions, which later was reduced to three. The resulting index had a range of 1 to 12 (1 = *no maladjustment,* 12 = *extreme maladjustment*). No child received a score of more than 8. They used cross tabulation and found significant relationships between the extent of maladjustment and the race of the child, the degree of family opposition to the adoption, age of the child at adoption, and age of the child at the time of the study. African American children in particular were found to be more maladjusted. The researchers then put these significant variables into a regression equation and found that only age at adoption and the degree of family opposition predicted the extent of maladjustment among the children (Silverman & Feigelman, 1981b).

The studies discussed above were primarily cross-sectional designs that used surveys. In a cross-sectional design, a researcher examines a phenomenon, such as transracial adoption, at one point in time. It is referred to as a snapshot of a problem. Longitudinal designs, however, allow the examination of a phenomenon over a long period of time and thus permit observations of changes in the phenomenon (Rubin & Babbie, 1993). Some transracial adoption researchers have conducted surveys, but a few researchers have studied the issue of transracial longitudinally.

Longitudinal Studies

Shireman and Johnson (1986) compared African American children adopted by single parents, White families, and African American families. The children were studied at 4, 8, 12, 16, and 20 years of age. Using the Clark Doll Test, Shireman and Johnson found that African American children in White homes had a more positive racial identity at age 4 than African American children in African American families. By age 8, the two groups were similar. In subsequent years, the children's adjustment was studied. Adjustment was measured by the number and severity of problems as reported by the parents, direct observations using projective testing, and standardized test materials. The researchers concluded that overall adjustment was excellent (Shireman & Johnson, 1986).

In another longitudinal study, Feigelman and Silverman (1984) compared White, Korean, Colombian, and African American children adopted by White families. Their primary measure was the extent of maladjustment and differences among the groups of children. They found, using multiple regression, that African American children had poorer adjustment than the other three groups of adoptees. However, this difference disappeared when age of the children was examined.

Building upon Feigelman and Silverman's work and tying his findings to American studies, Bagley (1993) studied 27 Afro-Caribbean and mixed-race children adopted by White families in Britain. Bagley's measures were the extent of psychoneurosis, depression, free floating anxiety, self-esteem, identity, ego identity, and self-image. Originally, the children were studied in 1979 and 12 years later. Bagley found no differences between the children on any variable.

The most active researchers in transracial adoption have been Simon and Altstein, who have followed a group of African American children for about 20 years. Their research began in 1972 when they received the names of families who had adopted transracially in five Midwest cities. Their primary hypothesis was that the "atypical environment in which children were being reared would affect their responses in such a manner as to mute the typical White preferences and reduce differences in responses about awareness and identity that are attributed to race" (Simon & Altstein, 1992, p. 127). They were initially able to interview 204 families and 366 children. Of the children, 120 were African American and the remainder were White and Native American. The researchers' primary variables of interest were the extent of racial identity, awareness, and attitudes. Over a 20-year period, they have regularly reported that African American children adopted by White families fared no worse than other children (Simon & Altstein, 1992; Simon et al., 1994).

All of the previously discussed studies focused primarily upon adjustment and racial identity, and the consensus of these studies has been that African American children have had adequate adjustment and racial identity. A few researchers, however, have focused on how African American children's intelligence was affected when adopted by White families. The extent of a child's intelligence is tangentially related to mental health because teachers have been found to respond more favorably to perceived high-intelligent children than perceived low-intelligent children. The effect of this differential treatment is that perceived low-intelligent children are led to feel inferior (Winston, 1987).

Transracial Adoption and Intelligence

Weinberg, Scarr, and Waldman (1992) studied school achievement and the intelligence quotient (IQ) of 101 transracially adopted children. This was the second study of a longitudinal research project that was conducted 10 years earlier. In the first study, the purpose was to examine the relationship between cross-fostering and IQ performance of African American and biracial (i.e., one African American and one White parent) children (Scarr & Weinberg, 1976). These researchers hypothesized that social environment played a critical role in IQ development. They found that their subsequent data supported their earlier study. Particularly, they originally hypothesized that African American children adopted by White families would perform well on IQ tests because these children were being socialized within the culture (e.g., home and school) that produced the test. That is to say, Whites developed IQ tests based on their culture. So children, regardless of race, reared in the White culture would perform better on IQ tests than children not reared in that culture (Weinberg et al., 1992).

Also, Moore (1986), reporting the validity and reliability of all measures, compared African American and biracial children who had been adopted by White and African American families. All children were placed by two adoption agencies. Twenty-three children were placed with African American parents, and of this number, six were biracial. Likewise, 23 children were placed with White families, and 14 of their children were biracial. The adoption worker indicated that African American families had expressed an interest in children who had African American biological parents. This preference was the reason that fewer biracial children were placed with African American families. All the children were placed with the families before the age of 2, and all the families were classified as middle class. The researcher administered the IQ test to children between the ages of 7 and 10 and found that the children adopted by White families scored higher on the IQ tests. Also, children adopted by White parents were found to be more assertive. The researcher concluded that the ethnicity of the rearing environment was more important than social class or the mother's educational level (Moore, 1986).

Methodological Issues

A neglected aspect of most social research is that researchers favor statistical significance. They also are interested in whether a majority or minority of a group of research participants is better or worse on some social or psychological measure. As an example, one researcher reported that about 75% of transracially adopted children were doing well. Unstated was that 25% of transracially adopted children were not doing well in their White families. At first glance, the 25% may cause some African American professionals to become alarmed and conclude that transracial adoptions are harmful. However, a more thoughtful examination would force professionals to look at the percentage of inracially adopted families that were assessed to be doing well. This percentage was 80%. So, 20% of these families were not doing well. Race could not be used to explain this situation. Further, only a 5% difference existed between the transracial and inracial groups.

Although the tendency to overlook the lesser percentage in social and psychological research is regrettable when children are involved, lessons may be drawn from medical research. In medical research, a newly developed medication may be shown to help 75% of patients with a serious illness. This discovery would be considered to be significant, and this new medication likely would receive quick approval to be used. Then, the goal of the medical researcher would be to find out why the other 25% did not receive the same benefits and what medications may be needed for them. Social research has not followed medical research in this respect. So, statistical significance and percentages continue to be highlighted.

These shortcomings aside, certainly, the weight of the research evidence favors proponents of transracial adoption, albeit all the evidence was not produced by the strongest research methodology. For instance, a random probability sample of *all* families who have adopted transracially was not conducted. Although researchers used samples that were available, they failed to note the limitations and weaknesses of their sampling methods. Instead, they confidently extrapolated their findings to the entire country.

The most active researchers in this area were Simon and Altstein, who published several books on their study and whose work has been cited by several courts. Methodologically, a number of research limitations are apparent in their work that they did not acknowledge. These limitations should have caused them to temper their conclusions. For instance, Simon and Altstein's primary data analysis methods were descriptive statistics and cross-tabulations. Firm conclusions from correlational studies cannot be made because these studies tend to have low internal validity and rival hypotheses always exist. Typically, researchers control for these alternative explanations by use of control and comparison groups. When these cannot be utilized, multivariate analysis, which provides statistical control, is employed. Either experimental studies or multivariate analyses lend themselves to stronger conclusions based on the findings. Other methods, such as use of correlation and cross-tabulation, should force researchers to temper their conclusions.

Another issue is the sampling method used by Simon and Altstein, who conducted longitudinal research on families in the Midwest who were members of two organizations. Little was written about whether these two organizations were representative of White families who have adopted African American children. Further, in subsequent studies based on their original sample, they lost a significant number of their families. Because their final sample was significantly smaller, they failed to state that their ultimate findings might be suspect because they did not know how the families they could not find might differ. These unresearched families might have had significantly adverse problems that skewed Simon and Altstein's ultimately favorable conclusions. Their failure to acknowledge this possibility and temper their conclusions is a substantial weakness in their methodology.

Related to the issue of sampling is the external validity of their findings. According to Rubin and Babbie (1993), a study may have sound internal validity but lack external validity. External validity refers to the extent to which a study's conditions, setting, and population may be generalized to other locations. Although a study does not have to be representative of all characteristics of a community to have good external validity, it should address the extent to which the study's findings may be generalized. Simon and Altstein suggested that their study has strong external validity and supported a national policy of transracial adoption. Although these issues were apparent in Simon and Altstein's work, as well as in many researchers' works, their studies provided little support for them to make definitive conclusions about transracial adoption.

On the other hand, opponents of transracial adoption, such as NABSW and other African American professionals, had no empirical support for their positions. They stated that African Americans encountered significant mental health problems by their placement in White families, but could not produce any empirical studies supporting their position. In sum, African American professionals have failed to research transracial adoptions to support their contention of psychological damage to African American children. Because no empirical research existed to support this contention, courts have been forced to accept the findings of proponents of transracial adoptions.

Conclusion

The foremost criticism is aimed at African American professionals and researchers who allowed this area to go virtually unresearched. Obviously, African American researchers could have sought grants to study this issue themselves. If they believed that psychological harm had been and was being done to African American children, their research studies should support the conclusion. If the measures used to operationalize psychological variables are inadequate or biased, African American researchers bear the responsibility of creating unbiased instruments. African American faculty can do some of this research themselves. They can also encourage African American graduate students to develop culturally sensitive scales for their theses and dissertations. A research project can have as its end the development of a valid and reliable scale. Of course, the research that produces these scales and subsequent studies that assert that African American children are psychologically harmed by transracial adoption must be scrutinized as other research is scrutinized.

Undoubtedly, the weight of empirical evidence supports the placement of African American children with White families for both foster care and adoption. No empirical evidence exists to demonstrate that such placements are harmful to the mental health of African American children. However, the conclusion drawn from the literature that African American children are not harmed by transracial adoption should not convey that African American children should be placed with White families as a first choice. Most professionals and legislators have acknowledged that same-race adoptions are desirable and preferable for children. Race may be a factor, as the Multiethnic Placement Act permits, but cannot be the sole factor. This acknowledgment provides options for the African American community.

African American professionals—such as members from NABSW and other organizations—who oppose transracial adoption can further enhance efforts to work with adoption and child protection agencies to recruit more African American families as potential adoptive parents. Throughout the United States, many child welfare agencies have initiated special programs and projects. They have encouraged the support of African American churches, civic organizations, and fraternal societies to recruit more African American adoptive parents.

Once prospective adoptive parents are identified, they must be evaluated to determine if placement is appropriate. The African American community can monitor this process to ensure that African American families are not indiscriminately denied the opportunity to adopt based on family assessments (Day, 1979; Hill, 1977; Howard, 1984). In some locations, African American social workers are working hard to see that African American families are not discriminated against when they seek to adopt. For instance, an African American social worker, who ironically refused to join NABSW because of its racial views, zealously enforced Massachusetts state policy that allowed any African American family that passed a criminal history check to be eligible to adopt (Rabin, 1995).

For localities that prefer a more formal assessment, a different standard should be used in assessing African American families. One such model is the

Afrocentric model for family assessment and child development. This model is empirically based and standardized and helps to identify qualified African American parents (T. Oliver, personal communication, September 6, 1994).

Another option is for the African American community to work to alleviate the stresses that influence family disruption and dissolution. This effort would reduce the need for foster placement, and in many cases, the relinquishment of parental rights. Effectively addressing such problems as drugs, crime, poverty, and teen pregnancy prevents the breakdown of the family unit that makes placement and adoption necessary. In sum, effectively addressing some of the social problems in the African American community would lead to fewer African American children needing homes. But when the need to place an African American child in a foster or adoptive home exists, an African American family could be easily found. Then, there would be no need to declare without scientifically accepted evidence that African American children's mental health is harmed by transracial adoption.

References

Adamec, C., & Pierce, W. L. (1991). *The encyclopedia of adoption*. New York: Facts on File.

Aigner, H. (1986). *Adoption in America coming of age*. Greenbrae, CA: Paradigm.

Bagley, C. (1993). Transracial adoption in Britain; A follow-up study with policy consideration. *Child Welfare, 72*, 285–299.

Barth, R. P., Berry, M., Yoshikami, R., Goodfield, R. K., & Carlson, M. L. (1988). Predicting adoption disruption. *Social Work, 33*, 227–233.

Bartholet, E. (1991). Where do Black children belong? The politics of race matching in adoption. *University of Pennsylvania Law Review, 139*, 1163–1256.

Bartholet, E. (1993). *Family bonds: Adoption and the politics of parenting*. Boston: Houghton Mifflin.

Brenner, E. M. (1993). Identity formation in the transracially-adopted adolescent (Ph.D. dissertation, California School of Professional Psychology). *Dissertation Abstracts International, 15*, 3871.

Davis, R. (1995, April 13). Suits back interracial adoptions: Minority kids wait longer, groups say. *USA Today*, p. 3A.

Day, D. (1979). *The adoption of Black children*. Lexington, MA: Lexington Books.

Feigelman, W., & Silverman, A. R. (1984). The long-term effects of transracial adoption. *Social Service Review, 58*, 589–602.

Grow, L. J., & Shapiro, D. (1974). *Black children. White parents: A study of transracial adoption*. New York: Child Welfare League of America.

Hayes, P. (1993). Transracial adoption: Politics and ideology. *Child Welfare, 72*, 301–310.

Helwig, A. A., & Ruthven, D. H. (1990). Psychological ramifications of adoption and implications for counseling. *Journal of Mental Health Counseling, 12*, 24–37.

Hermann, V. P. (1993). Transracial adoption: Child-saving or child-snatching. *National Black Law Journal, 13*, 147–164.

Hill, R. B. (1977). *Informal adoption among Black families*. Washington, DC: National Urban League.

Howard, M. (1984). Transracial adoption: Analysis of the best interests standard. *Notre Dame Law Review, 59*, 503–555.

Johnson, P., Shireman, J., & Watson, K. (1987). Transracial adoption and the development of Black identity at age eight. *Child Welfare, 66*, 45–56.

McLaughlin v. Pernsley, 693 F. Supp. 318 (E.D. Pa. 1988).

McRoy, R. G. (1995, June 5). Questions: Should Congress facilitate transracial adoptions; No: Lower barriers to Black adoptive families. *Washington Times,* p. 19.

McRoy, R. G., Zurcher, L. A., Lauderdale, M. L., & Anderson, R. N. (1982). Self-esteem and racial identity in transracial adoption. *Social Work, 27,* 522–526.

Moore, E. G. J. (1986). Family socialization and the IQ test performance of traditionally and transracially adopted Black children. *Developmental Psychology, 22,* 317–326.

National Association of Black Social Workers (NABSW). (1992, Fall). *National Association of Black Social Workers* [Newsletter]. Detroit, MI.

Rabin, R. (1995, July 10). Can Black children raised by White parents develop a positive sense of self and a strong racial identity? *Newsday,* p. B04.

Reisman v. State Dept. of Human Servs., 843 F. Supp. 356 (W. D. Tenn., 1993).

Rosenthal, J. A., Groze, V., & Curiel, H. (1990). Race, social class, and special needs adoption. *Social Work, 35,* 532–539.

Rubin, A., & Babbie, E. (1993). *Research methods for social work* (2nd ed.). Pacific Grove, CA: Brooks/Cole.

Scarr, S., & Weinberg, R. A. (1976). IQ test performance of Black children adopted by White families. *American Psychology, 31,* 726–739.

Shireman, J. F., & Johnson, P. R. (1986). A longitudinal study of Black adoptions: Single parent, transracial, and traditional. *Social Work, 31,* 172–176.

Silverman, A. R. (1993). Outcomes of transracial adoption. *The Future of Children, 3,* 104–118.

Silverman, A. R., & Feigelman, W. (1981a). *The adjustment of Black children adopted by White families.* Paper presented at the Annual Meeting of the American Sociological Association. Toronto, Ontario.

Silverman, A. R., & Feigelman, W. (1981b). The adjustment of Black children adopted by White families. *Social Casework, 62,* 529–536.

Simon, R. J., & Altstein, H. (1981). *Transracial adoption: A follow-up.* Lexington, MA: D. C. Heath.

Simon, R. J., & Altstein, H. (1987). *Transracial adoptees and their families: A study of identity and commitment.* New York: Praeger.

Simon, R. J., & Altstein, H. (1992). *Adoption, race, and identity: From infancy through adolescence.* New York: Praeger.

Simon, R. J., Altstein, H., & Melli, M. S. (1994). *The case for transracial adoption.* Washington, DC: American University Press.

Weinberg, R. A., Scarr, S., & Waldman, I. D. (1992). The Minnesota transracial adoption study: A follow-up IQ test performance at adolescence. *Intelligence, 16,* 117–135.

Winston, J. A. (1987). Fulfilling Brown's promise: The second generation fight for educational opportunity. *Lawyers' Committee for Civil Rights Under Law Committee Report, 1*(3)1, 18–19.

POSTSCRIPT

Does Transracial Adoption Harm a Child's Development?

There are many more minority children in need of adoptive homes than can be accommodated intraracially. Is there a place for transracial adoption, which can be effective for children yet satisfy the concerns of those opposed to it? Perhaps if the prospective family was screened to ascertain sensitivity to some of the problems enumerated in the Introduction to this issue and outlined by Hollingsworth and Alexander and Curtis, the family could experience some success in maximizing the child's ethnic and psychological development.

From the parental perspective, consider the plight of suitable white adoptive parents. Many of them feel that the system is unjust in that they might wait years for a child, regardless of race, while suitable black adoptive parents, for example, rarely wait as long. Is this not a form of discrimination? Often these frustrated white parents look toward foreign adoptions. This does nothing to help address the problem of the need for adoptive parents for American children waiting to be adopted. How could this be a benefit to society?

Transracial adoption continues to be intensely debated. However, there may be some common ground upon which those on both sides of the issue can agree: (1) There could be increased efforts in the area of family planning, which would help diminish the growing numbers of children in need of adoption; (2) American society must be creative in developing interventions that strengthen all types of families in order to reduce the number of children who might be removed from their families of origin.

Suggested Readings

Hayes, P. (1993) Transracial adoption: Politics and ideology. *Child Welfare, 72,* 301–310.

National Association of Black Social Workers (April, 1994). Position Statement: Preserving African-American Families. Detroit, MI: National Association of Black Social Workers.

Silverman, A. R. (1993). Outcomes of transracial adoption. *The Future of Children, 3,* 104–118.

Simon, R. J., Alstein, H., & Melli, M. S. (1994). *The Case for Transracial Adoption.* Washington, DC: American University Press.

http://www.transracialadoption.com provides a wealth of statistics and information in support of parents who adopt transracially.

Kids Count

This Kids Count section of the Annie E. Casey Foundation Web site posts data on national and state indicators of child well-being, referred to as state report cards. The Annie E. Casey Foundation is an organization that is dedicated to building a better future for disadvantaged children in the United States.

http://www.aecf.org/kidscount/

Children's Defense Fund

The Children's Defense Fund site includes data from every state on issues related to child care.

http://www.cdfactioncouncil.org

National Network for Child Care (NNCC)

This Web site from the National Network for Child Care (NNCC) provides resources for raising children. Included are links to sites designed especially for children, as well as sites that offer activities for children, nutrition information, and information on parent involvement issues.

http://www.nncc.org

Educational Resources Information Center (ERIC)

This Educational Resources Information Center (ERIC) Web site, sponsored by the U.S. Department of Education, leads to numerous documents related to elementary and early childhood education as well as to other curriculum topics and issues.

http://www.ed.gov

Just in Time Parenting Information

The Just in Time Parenting Information Web site includes newsletters that are designed to provide information relating to a child's specific age. These newsletters were developed by the Cooperative Extension Service in several different states. The timely information helps parents to understand how their children are developing.

http://www.parentinginfo.org

PART 2

Early Childhood

*T*he period of early childhood is sometimes referred to as the preschool years. It generally encompasses ages two or three through four or five. This is a time when children become much more adept at taking part in physical activities, satisfying curiosities, and learning from experience. Preschoolers play more frequently with other children, become increasingly skilled in daily tasks, and are much more responsive to people and things in their environment. Many children begin school during their preschool years, an experience that gives them their first extended contacts with a social institution other than the family. Changing attitudes about discipline, family size, divorce, and the mass media all have implications for a child's development. This section examines some of the choices families make in rearing their preschool children.

- Is Spanking Detrimental to Children?

- Are Fathers Really Necessary?

- Does Divorce Create Long-Term Negative Effects for Children?

- Is Television Violence Viewing Harmful for Children?

ISSUE 5

Is Spanking Detrimental to Children?

YES: Elizabeth Thompson Gershoff, from "Corporal Punishment by Parents and Associated Child Behaviors and Experiences: A
Meta-Analytic and Theoretical Review," *Psychological Bulletin* (vol. 128,
no. 4, 2002)

**NO: Diana Baumrind, Philip A. Cowan, and Robert E.
Larzelere,** from "Ordinary Physical Punishment: Is It Harmful? Comment on Gershoff (2002)," *Psychological Bulletin* (vol. 128, no. 4, 2002)

ISSUE SUMMARY

YES: Columbia University researcher Elizabeth Thompson Gershoff
analyzed results from 88 studies and concluded that corporal punishment negatively affected children's behavior. Among the 10 negative outcomes were increased child aggression, decreased quality of
the parent-child relationship, and increased risk of abusing a child or
spouse in adulthood.

NO: Diana Baumrind and Philip A. Cowan, researchers from the
University of California–Berkeley, and Robert E. Larzelere, from the
Nebraska Medical Center, refuted Gershoff's findings by questioning
her definition of corporal punishment and analysis techniques of the
88 studies. They feel mild spankings, when appropriately administered, are useful in shaping children's behavior.

The topic of spanking, also known as corporal punishment, provokes highly
emotional responses from family practitioners, parents, researchers, and children.
There seems to be no one who is neutral about the subject, especially children. It
would be interesting to ask children about their feeling toward spanking. Were
you spanked as a child? What was used to spank you? Bare hand? hairbrush?
ruler? switch? The list could go on and on. Do you think the spankings negatively affected you, or did they teach you how to act appropriately? The following quotes are often used in relationship to spanking: "Spare the rod and spoil
the child. I was spanked and I turned out OK. Kids need to be spanked to show
them who's boss."

If you were not spanked, what was used to correct your misbehavior? Was the misbehavior explained? Was your correct behavior rewarded and your misbehavior punished? What about children who were not spanked or corrected in any way? Are they considered spoiled or out of control? Perhaps verbal abuse or a slap to the face was used to correct your behavior, or maybe you were ignored altogether. These techniques are considered similar to spanking in that they can become abusive or neglectful.

Ninety-four percent of American parents report spanking their children by the time their children are 3 years old. Although spanking is a popular form of discipline in the United State, several countries have outlawed spanking and the physical punishment of children: Austria, Croatia, Cyprus, Germany, Israel, Italy, Latvia, Norway, Denmark, Sweden, and Finland. Proponents of spanking point out that these countries' rates of child abuse have not declined as a result of banning spanking.

Spanking is associated with family violence and child abuse. These are the stories often found in the media about parents injuring or even killing their children as a result of physical punishment. While the media exploits these situations and makes the public feel outraged that children are treated this way, one must remember these are extreme cases. Most families feel they use spanking judiciously and do not consider it abusive.

Ultimately, spanking is used as a teaching tool and a way to solve problems. Parents see children misbehave, look for a way to gain the children's attention immediately, and spank them. Parents believe that by inflicting pain, they are changing children's behavior and solving the problem of misbehavior. Opponents of spanking ask the question of how children will change misbehavior if they are not taught what *to do* versus what *not to do*. In addition, the message is sent that I am bigger than you so I can solve this problem by hitting you.

In the following selections, Elizabeth Thompson Gershoff argues that spanking harms children by decreasing moral internalization, increasing aggression as a child and adult, increasing child delinquency and antisocial behavior, decreasing the quality of the parent-child interaction, decreasing the quality of mental health in childhood and adulthood, increasing the risk of being physically abused in adulthood, and increasing the risk of abusing a child or spouse in adulthood. Diana Baumrind, Philip A. Cowan, and Robert E. Larzelere refute Gershoff's claims by showing flaws in her definition of corporal punishment and her method of analyzing the 88 studies she used for her research study. They feel that Gershoff did not address the real issue of whether or not mild spanking is harmful.

Elizabeth Thompson Gershoff

 YES

Corporal Punishment by Parents and Associated Child Behaviors and Experiences: A Meta-Analytic and Theoretical Review

Corporal punishment has been an integral part of how parents discipline their children throughout the history of the United States and has been a focus of psychological research for decades. Although a growing number of countries have adopted policies or laws that prohibit parents from using corporal punishment as a means of discipline (Austria, Croatia, Cyprus, Denmark, Finland, Germany, Israel, Italy, Latvia, Norway, and Sweden), both support for and use of corporal punishment remain strong in the United States, with 94% of American parents spanking their children by the time they are 3 or 4 years old.

Psychologists and other professionals are divided on the question of whether the benefits of corporal punishment might outweigh any potential hazards; some have concluded that corporal punishment is both effective and desirable, whereas others have concluded that corporal punishment is ineffective at best and harmful at worst. This controversy over corporal punishment has inspired a series of recent debates among psychological, sociological, and legal scholars about what corporal punishment does and does not do for children.

Despite this controversy and the hundreds of scientific studies invoked on either side of the debate, understanding of the child behaviors and experiences associated with parental corporal punishment has been limited to narrative reviews and "vote count" summaries of the number of positive and negative effects that accrue from corporal punishment. Crucial questions remain unanswered, such as what range of child behaviors and experiences are empirically associated with parental corporal punishment, as well as why, how, and for whom corporal punishment might have such effects. This article provides preliminary answers to these questions by synthesizing the current empirical evidence of, and theoretical explanations for, associations between parental corporal punishment and 11 child behaviors and experiences. . . .

From *Psychological Bulletin*, vol. 128, no. 4, 2002, pp. 539–544. Copyright © 2002 by American Psychological Association. Reprinted by permission. References omitted.

Meta-Analyses of Parental Corporal Punishment and Associated Child Behaviors and Experiences

The first step in understanding whether and how parental corporal punishment affects children is to establish to what degree corporal punishment is associated with the child constructs of interest. Toward this end, I present in this section the results of separate meta-analyses of the associations between parental corporal punishment and 11 frequently identified child constructs. Despite the inability of meta-analyses to yield definitive causal conclusions, they do constitute an effective means of establishing whether the associations of interest are present and thus pave the way for further research into causal mechanisms. To underscore the inability of meta-analyses to support causal conclusions, I refer to child "behaviors and experiences" or "constructs" associated with parental corporal punishment rather than to child "outcomes" in the context of the meta-analyses.

Distinguishing Corporal Punishment from Physical Abuse

Before examining the associations between corporal punishment and child constructs, it is important to establish what is meant by the term *corporal punishment*. Regarding legal definitions, 48 states and the District of Columbia specify what constitutes corporal punishment in their legal statutes defining child abuse; 29 states assert that corporal punishment encompasses the use of "reasonable" force with some adding qualifiers that it must also be "appropriate" (AL, AK, AZ, CA, CO), "moderate" (AR, DE, SC, SD), or "necessary" (MT, NH, NY, OR, TX, WI). Three states see the need to clarify that corporal punishment is limited to "nondeadly force" (AK, NY, TX). The present article adopts the definition of corporal punishment offered by Straus. "Corporal punishment is the use of physical force with the intention of causing a child to experience pain but not injury for the purposes of correction or control of the child's behavior."

A frequent criticism of research on corporal punishment is that nonabusive corporal punishment is often confounded with harmful and abusive behaviors, thus preventing conclusions about the effects of everyday spanking. This apparent confound has arisen because the majority of child abuse researchers view corporal punishment and potentially abusive techniques as points on a continuum of physical acts toward children. However, a consensus on where to draw the line between acceptable corporal punishment and dangerous physical abuse is noticeably absent in the United States. State laws defining what constitutes physical abuse often specifically include corporal punishment. Davidson reviewed the state definitions of *child maltreatment* and found that 12 states (DC, FL, IL, MT, NE, NJ, NY, ND, OH, RI, SC, WV) included the phrase "excessive corporal punishment" in their definitions of child maltreatment; an additional 10 states qualified corporal punishment as constituting abuse when characterized as "cruel" (CT, CO, NE, NM, OH, SD), "unlawful" (CA), "excessive or unreasonable" (WY), "severe" (NJ), "cruel and inhuman" (KS), or "extreme" (ME).

For the purposes of this article, I consider physical abuse to be a potential outcome of corporal punishment. Herein, corporal punishment will be operationally distinguished from physical abuse according to the definition of physical abuse provided by the National Clearinghouse on Child Abuse and Neglect Information, namely:

> Physical abuse is characterized by the infliction of physical injury as a result of punching, beating, kicking, biting, burning, shaking or otherwise harming a child. The parent or caretaker may not have intended to hurt the child, rather the injury may have resulted from over-discipline or physical punishment. (What Are the Main Types of Maltreatment? section, para. 2)

Behaviors that do not result in significant physical injury (e.g., spank, slap) are considered corporal punishment, whereas behaviors that risk injury (e.g., punching, kicking, burning) are considered physical abuse. The studies included in the meta-analyses discussed below explicitly targeted parental corporal punishment, rather than parental physical abuse, as potential predictors of child behaviors and experiences. As I describe in detail below, studies that included potentially abusive techniques in their definitions of corporal punishment were excluded from the analyses.

Methodological Concerns in the Measurement of Corporal Punishment

It is important to acknowledge at the outset that the majority of studies examining links between parental corporal punishment and child behaviors and experiences measure both constructs at the same point in time, thus preventing any conclusions about causality. As I discuss below, even measuring parental corporal punishment at one time point and a child behavior at a future time point may not be sufficient to infer causal direction. True detection of causality may require controlling for the child's rate of the behavior of interest at the first time point as well to account for autocontingency of behavior over time. With these points in mind, the meta-analyses described here do not afford causal conclusions but allow understanding only of whether corporal punishment and child constructs are associated.

In addition, because corporal punishment is used primarily with children younger than 5 years of age, because corporal punishment is used rarely by parents (1–2 times per month), and because assigning parents to spank or no-spank experimental conditions is untenable, researchers must rely on parent reports of corporal punishment rather than on observations. Although some methods of having parents report their use of corporal punishment, such as nightly phone calls or detailed daily discipline diaries, do have high validity, the majority of information on corporal punishment comes from parents' or adolescent and adult children's recollections of frequency of corporal punishment.

Child Behaviors and Experiences Associated with Parental Corporal Punishment

The goal of most research on parenting is to identify which practices promote positive and adaptive behaviors in children. However, in the study of parents' use of corporal punishment, much research has been biased toward finding negative child outcomes associated with corporal punishment. The meta-analyses below specifically include a balance of potentially desirable child constructs (immediate compliance, moral internalization, quality of relationship with parent, and mental health) as well as undesirable child constructs (aggression, criminal and antisocial behavior, abuse of own child or spouse, and victim of abuse by own parent). Discussion of why corporal punishment should be associated with such behaviors and experiences is presented briefly here; the hypothesized processes linking the experience of corporal punishment with these constructs are detailed in the process–context model in the second section of the article.

Immediate Compliance

The primary goal most parents have in administering corporal punishment is to stop children from misbehaving immediately. Laboratory research on learning has confirmed that corporal punishment is indeed effective in securing short-term compliance. Although there are many studies that purport to examine relations between corporal punishment and compliance, most of these studies do not involve observations of whether children comply immediately after corporal punishment is administered. Rather, such studies ask parents how often they typically use corporal punishment and correlate this frequency with parents' reports of how compliant their children are to all forms of discipline. To assess corporal punishment's effect on short- and long-term compliance separately, the subsequent meta-analysis of immediate compliance only includes studies that measured children's compliance to corporal punishment. Compliance that occurs at a point in time removed from an instance of corporal punishment is considered evidence of internalization.

Moral Internalization

Although immediate compliance may be a salient goal when parents initiate discipline, promoting the development of children's internal controls is more important to long-term socialization than immediate compliance. *Moral internalization* is defined by Grusec and Goodnow as "taking over the values and attitudes of society as one's own so that socially acceptable behavior is motivated not by anticipation of external consequences but by intrinsic or internal factors," and it is thought to underlie the development of children's social and emotional competence. Children's internalization of morals is thought to be enhanced by parental discipline strategies that use minimal parental power, promote choice and autonomy, and provide explanations for desirable behaviors. Attribution theorists emphasize that power-assertive methods such as corporal punishment promote children's external attributions for their behavior and minimize their attributions to internal motivations. Additionally, corporal punishment may not facilitate moral internalization because it does not teach children the reasons for behaving correctly, does not involve communication of the effects of children's behaviors on others, and may teach children the desirability of not getting caught.

Aggression

The association between corporal punishment and children's aggression is one of the most studied and debated findings in the child-rearing literature. Over the years, several reviews of the literature have concluded that corporal punishment is associated with increases in children's aggressive behaviors. Corporal punishment has been hypothesized to predict increases in children's aggression because it models aggression; promotes hostile attributions, which predict violent behavior; and initiates coercive cycles of aversive behaviors between parent and child. Early experiences with corporal punishment may model and legitimize many types of violence throughout an individual's life, particularly violence in romantic relationships. Indeed, in one longitudinal study, parents' use of corporal punishment in childhood was the strongest predictor of adolescents' aggression 8 years later, whereas permissive parenting was not a significant predictor. It was my expectation that corporal punishment would be associated in the meta-analyses with aggression in childhood as well as in adulthood.

Although aggression is often combined with antisocial behavior to constitute what are typically referred to as externalizing behavior problems, antisocial behaviors such as stealing are nonviolent and may be related to corporal punishment in different ways than aggression. In the present meta-analyses, the extent to which children engage in delinquent or illegal behaviors are separated from the extent of their aggressive behaviors.

Delinquent, Criminal, and Antisocial Behavior

Across decades of research, corporal punishment has been implicated in the etiology of criminal and antisocial behaviors by both children and adults. Attribution theory posits that associations between corporal punishment and child delinquent or antisocial behavior result from an inability of corporal punishment to facilitate children's internalization of morals and values. Social control theory suggests that parental corporal punishment erodes the parent–child relationship and in turn decreases children's motivation to internalize parents' values and those of the society, which in turn results in low self-control. These same processes may explain the relation between corporal punishment and adult criminality. In Glueck and Glueck's longitudinal study of delinquency, whether boys experienced a harsh parental disciplinary style predicted their arrest rates at ages 17 through 45. J. McCord also found in her longitudinal study that the extent to which parents were aggressively punitive predicted their children's criminal behavior as adults. The connection between criminal and antisocial behavior in childhood and adulthood is examined here in separate meta-analyses.

Quality of the Parent–Child Relationship

The potential for parental corporal punishment to disrupt the parent–child relationship is thought to be a main disadvantage of its use. The painful nature of corporal punishment can evoke feelings of fear, anxiety, and anger in children; if these emotions are generalized to the parent, they can interfere with a positive parent–child relationship by inciting children to be fearful of and to avoid the parent. If corporal punishment does lead children to avoid their parents, such avoidance may in turn erode bonds of trust and closeness between parents and children.

Mental Health

Although little theoretical work has been done to identify the processes by which corporal punishment would lead to mental health problems, harsh punishment (including corporal punishment) has been associated significantly with adolescents' depressive symptomatology and distress, even after controlling for age, gender, family socioeconomic status (SES), and history of physical abuse. Coercive techniques have been associated with decreases in children's feelings of confidence and assertiveness and with increases in feelings of humiliation and helplessness. If corporal punishment does have indelible effects on children's mental health, an association between corporal punishment and adult mental health also might be expected. In the meta-analyses I present below, the constructs of child mental health and adult mental health are analyzed separately and include varied indices of poor mental health, including depression, alcoholism, suicidal tendency, and low self-esteem.

Adult Abuse of Own Child or Spouse

If corporal punishment is associated with a general aggressive tendency in adulthood, this aggression also may manifest in relationships with family members, particularly with a child or spouse. The same processes hypothesized to account for an association between corporal punishment and general aggression also are expected to account for a tendency toward violence against family members. Specifically, if parental corporal punishment leads individuals to view aggression or violence as legitimate, make external attributions for their behavior, and attribute hostile intent to the behaviors of others, they may be more likely to resort to aggression and violence during conflicts with their children and spouses. A tendency toward intergenerational transmission of aggression in close relationships is evident in a strong tendency for parents who were corporally punished to continue the practice with their own children. Similarly, experience with both average (e.g., spanking) and extreme (e.g., kicking, biting, burning, and beating up) forms of corporal punishment by parents are associated with increases in an individual's likelihood of acting violently with an adult romantic partner.

Becoming a Victim of Physical Abuse

As stated above, child abuse researchers tend to see corporal punishment and physical abuse on a continuum, such that if corporal punishment is administered too severely or too frequently, the outcome can be physical abuse. The notion of a corporal punishment–physical abuse continuum is corroborated in part by physically abusive parents themselves: Parents who had abused their children revealed that as many as two thirds of their abusive incidents began as attempts to change children's behavior or to "teach them a lesson." Unfortunately, use of severe and potentially abusive physical techniques may be more common than has been realized. In a recent study, 16% of incidents reported by mothers and 21% of those reported by fathers were rated by independent coders as severe (e.g., use of spoons, sticks, or belts). The potential for the widely used practice of corporal punishment to be associated with a risk for injury to children behooves further research into this connection.

Method

Sample of Studies

I used three main sources to identify all articles that examined the associations between parental corporal punishment and child behaviors and experiences and were available through June 2001. The first source was the reference lists of relevant reviews, namely by Becker, Larzelere, Steinmetz, and Straus. Second, I conducted a computer-based literature search of *Psychological Abstracts* Psy-cINFO, *Educational Resources Information Center, Social Sciences Index*, and *Dissertation Abstracts International*. Key words used to identify relevant articles were *corporal punishment, physical punishment,* and *spank.* The third and final search involved the "ancestry approach" applied to the reference sections of all retrieved articles, book chapters, and dissertations. In the interest of being exhaustive, qualification for inclusion was not restricted to peer-reviewed journals; I made every attempt to include all relevant and accessible journal articles, book chapters, and dissertations so as to avoid publication biases.

The abstracts and often the full text of over 300 relevant works, including 63 dissertations, were studied for inclusion in the present meta-analyses. Half of these works did not include data, as they were instead focused on the debate about corporal punishment ($n = 69$), the prevalence of corporal punishment in the United States or abroad ($n = 42$), the antecedents to parents' use of corporal punishment ($n = 40$), attitudes about corporal punishment ($n = 21$), or other issues such as the history of corporal punishment and theories about how it affects children ($n = 27$). Of the 189 studies that did present data on potential effects of corporal punishment, 101 were excluded according to the following criteria: (a) 27% combined corporal punishment with abusive techniques or only examined abusive behaviors; (b) 22% predicted dependent variables that have not been considered consistently in the literature on corporal punishment (e.g., intelligence); (c) 22% did not provide sufficient statistics for calculation of an effect size (e.g., only included betas from regression with other variables); (d) 17% combined corporal punishment with other types of discipline (e.g., corporal punishment was grouped with verbal punishment); and (e) 12% did not study corporal punishment administered by parents, used exceptional populations, or were unavailable through interlibrary loan.

A sample of 88 studies, including 8 dissertations, met the above criteria and were included in the analyses. (Multiple articles from the same study were represented in the analyses by the effect size from only one article.) Of the studies included, 67 provided an effect size for a single metaanalysis, 15 provided effect sizes for two meta-analyses, 4 provided three effects sizes, and 2 provided four effect sizes, for a total of 117 effect sizes across the 11 analyses conducted. The total number of participants was 36,309 (studies contributing more than one effect size only counted once), with an average of 413 participants per study and a range of 14 to 4,529 participants per study. The earliest study was from 1938; 5% of the studies were from 1950–1959, 10% from 1960–1969, 10% from 1970–1979, 25% from 1980–1989, 47% from 1990–1999, and 2% from 2000. The range of studies incorporated in the meta-analyses included 26 nonsignificant effect sizes. . . .

Results

Meta-Analyses

. . . All of the composite effect sizes were significant (none of the confidence intervals include zero) and thus parental corporal punishment was associated significantly with each of the 11 child behaviors and experiences. According to J. Cohen's criteria for judging effect sizes, three of the composite mean weighted effect sizes are small (–0.09, 0.13, –0.33), four are small to medium (0.36, 0.42, 0.42, –0.49), two are medium (0.57, –0.58), one is medium to large (0.69), and one is large (1.13, immediate compliance).

Ten of the 11 meta-analyses indicate parental corporal punishment is associated with the following undesirable behaviors and experiences: decreased moral internalization, increased child aggression, increased child delinquent and antisocial behavior, decreased quality of relationship between parent and child, decreased child mental health, increased risk of being a victim of physical abuse, increased adult aggression, increased adult criminal and antisocial behavior, decreased adult mental health, and increased risk of abusing own child or spouse. Corporal punishment was associated with only one desirable behavior, namely, increased immediate compliance. . . .

Diana Baumrind, Philip A. Cowan, and Robert E. Larzelere

 NO

Ordinary Physical Punishment: Is It Harmful? Comment on Gershoff (2002)

In . . . her comprehensive article, Gershoff (2002) used meta-analyses of 88 studies to provide what she offered as a conclusive answer to the question of whether corporal punishment (CP) is significantly associated with 11 frequently identified aspects of children's behavior. She found that except for an association with immediate compliance to parental demands, CP is associated with negative or undesirable behaviors (e.g., aggression, lower levels of moral internalization and mental health). . . .

Measurement Issues: Corporal Punishment, Spanking, and Abuse

Disputes about the potential impact of corporal punishment are occurring in the social context of a vigorous debate about the impact of spanking. There is an international movement by lay organizations such as EPOCH-Worldwide to criminalize corporal punishment or to discourage its use. The advocates of a blanket injunction against spanking have cited associations between physical punishment and detrimental child outcomes, such as those presented in Gershoff's meta-analyses, to support their position. Such direct application of correlational research to social policy decisions presupposes a causal link between physical punishment and the detrimental child behaviors with which it is associated. Before we deal with the issues of causal inference, it is necessary to examine what Gershoff meant by *corporal punishment* to be clear about how it is being defined and measured.

There is a sense in which participants in the current debate about the effects of corporal punishment are talking past each other. One issue to which some attention has been given is the need to make a distinction between legal abuse and corporal punishment. A second issue, which has not been given the attention it deserves, is the distinction between harsh and punitive but not legally designated abusive punishment and the more moderate application of

From *Psychological Bulletin*, vol. 128, no. 4, 2002, pp. 580–584, 586. Copyright © 2002 by American Psychological Association. Reprinted by permission. References and notes omitted.

normative spanking within the context of a generally supportive parent–child relationship. Although Gershoff cited Baumrind and Larzelere as concluding "that corporal punishment is both effective and desirable," it would be more correct to say they concluded only that a blanket injunction against disciplinary spanking is not warranted by the data.

An important scientific consensus conference on corporal punishment defined *spanking* as that subset of the broader category of corporal punishment that is "a) physically non-injurious; b) intended to modify behavior; and c) administered with an opened hand to the extremities or buttocks." Conferees, including Baumrind and Larzelere, agreed that the important debate was not about overly severe forms of corporal punishment but only about parental spanking, which inflicts a minor, temporary level of physical pain, if that. Conferees agreed that abusive corporal punishment should be criminalized and corporal punishment that exceeds mild to moderate spanking or is used with children younger than 18 months or after puberty should be strongly discouraged. Conferees also agreed that a mild spank as a "back-up" to other disciplinary tactics (e.g., reasoning, time-out) could increase the effectiveness of these alternative disciplinary tactics in preschoolers with behavior problems. There was agreement that by itself spanking cannot accomplish the longer term objective of parents—to promote children's competence, moral character, and mental health—and that frequent or severe punishment of any kind signals the presence of a problem in the family dynamics. The issue that was and remains controversial is whether mild to moderate disciplinary spanking (in the years between 18 months and puberty) has been shown to be harmful.

Gershoff's meta-analyses, however, do not address that issue because her conceptual and operational definitions of *corporal punishment* included punishment that was often too severe and was thus a proxy for the harsh, punitive discipline that is acknowledged by all experts to be detrimental to children's well-being and ethically unacceptable. In the fifth moderator variable in the note to her Table 3 (indexing how researchers operationalized corporal punishment), Gershoff included "severity" as Category 2 and "frequency and severity" as Category 3, indicating that severity (as well as frequency) contributed to the CP measure in those studies so categorized. But her other categories, such as "frequency" (Category 1), did not exclude overly severe forms of CP when the specific question asked of the respondent was about their frequency. This meant that slapping in the face or beating with a stick or hitting, pushing, grabbing, or shoving were not coded as severe when the studies asked about their frequency.

Straus claimed that the physical abuse or Severe Violence items in the Conflict Tactics Scale can be used "to partial out physical abuse in a statistical analysis or to remove abused children from the sample in order to avoid confounding corporal punishment with physical abuse." Although Straus's own studies rarely did that, he clearly agreed with us that it is proper to do so. However, Gershoff indicated in her Table 1 that 16% of the 88 studies in her review operationalized CP as "hit with an object," which Straus included in his index of abuse or Severe Violence on the Conflicts Tactics Scale. Thus, some of Gershoff's CP measures included behaviors that are part of Straus's abuse construct.

To determine the influence of overly severe CP on the results of Gershoff's meta-analyses, Larzelere coded the severity of CP for 64 primary studies, including 52 of the 54 studies in the aggression composite (i.e., studies measuring aggression or antisocial behavior in children or aggression, criminal behavior, or physical abuse in adults). Baumrind also coded 41% of the studies for reliability, which yielded good interrater agreement (κ = .91) for severe versus not overly severe CP. Almost two thirds (65.4%) of the 52 aggression composite studies used overly severe CP. Variables were categorized as overly severe if there was direct evidence of severity, such as a CP measure based only on hitting with a belt or stick (30.8% of the 52 studies in Gershoff's aggression composite); if severity was part of the definition of the highest CP score (28.8%); or if severity was inferred from the label, such as *punitive discipline* (5.8%). That left only 34.6% of the 52 effect sizes in the aggression composite for which the CP measure was not influenced directly by overly severe CP.

This problem of overly severe (and overly broad) CP can best be illustrated with quotes from Gershoff's primary studies. The following descriptions were used to describe at least part of their definition of CP: "slapped on face, head, and ears" and "shook"; "severity of punishment for aggression to parents"; "throwing something at the child" and "severe, strict, often physical" as contrasted with "nonrestrictive, mostly positive guidance," usage of "switch, belt, razor strap, paddle, buggy whip, boxing ears"; and "hit with belt, stick." In all of these five studies, an effect size could have been based on a CP measure that did not include such overly severe components of CP. For example, Mahoney et al. presented separate data for six tactics included in the revised Conflict Tactics Scale's CP measure. The corresponding effect sizes (*d*) ranged from 0.08 for "spanked bottom with bare hand" to 0.58 for "slapped on face, head, and ears."

In other studies, effect sizes could only be based on CP measures contaminated by overly severe components. Examples include "slaps in the face" and "beating with a stick, a belt, etc."; "slap him in the face" and "wash out his mouth with soap"; "How often were you beaten by your mother (father)?"; "kicked, bit, or hit you with a fist," causing "bruises or cuts," and six more violent items; "rough handling, shaking"; "mom (dad) was a violent or physically abusive person"; and "severe punishment, parents very angry or hostile, beatings, . . . 'Punished him so he wouldn't forget it.'"

In at least one other primary study in the meta-analyses, a large majority of those who were physically punished were also physically abused. In Lester's study of inmate records, 49% of those who had attempted suicide had been physically punished by their fathers, but almost as many (44%) had been physically abused. Therefore, it would appear that only 5% of the inmates were physically punished without being abused.

We thus conclude that the meta-analyses included studies of overly severe CP to a far greater extent than a casual reading of the selection criteria would indicate. To address the current debate about mild to moderate spanking, Gershoff would have had to exclude CP that is excessive, extreme, or cruel. But Gershoff only excluded CP that "knowingly would cause severe injury to the child," although (according to Gershoff) corporal punishment constitutes abuse in definitions of 22 states not merely when it is intended to result in "significant" physical injury but when it is "excessive," "cruel," "extreme," or "severe."

Beyond the question of measurement of CP, there is an important question of meaning. In her review, Gershoff stated that many studies ask parents about their use of CP but do not define what the researchers mean and do not ascertain what the participants mean. The question is whether it makes sense to aggregate all these studies in a meta-analysis when the definition of the key variable measuring CP is so varied and ambiguous.

Threats to the Validity of the Meta-Analyses

With the exception of the links between CP and immediate compliance or physical abuse, Gershoff disavowed causal implications of the meta-analyses she presented. However, it is primarily within a causal context that meta-analysis is judged to be superior to a conventional review for theory development and application to social policy. The very term *effect size* implies a causal relationship. If, for example, an equally plausible argument can be made that child aggression is a contributing cause of CP as can be made that CP is a contributing cause of child aggression, then it is arbitrary to treat CP as though it is the independent variable and child aggression as the dependent variable, and certainly without first establishing temporal order. Yet antispanking advocates frequently draw causal implications from the associations between CP and child behaviors. For example, on the basis of similar associations, Straus projected that a reduction in CP would "result in fewer people who are alienated, depressed or suicidal, and in fewer violent marriages" and "include lower crime rates . . . and less money spent on controlling or treating crime and mental illness."

Methodologists in epidemiology and behavioral science have emphasized the importance of empirically establishing the causal status of a correlate by first showing that it is a risk factor and then that it is a causal risk factor. A *risk factor* (causal or not) must be shown to precede the outcome and to be associated with an increase in the outcome compared with its population baserate. An experimental or prospective longitudinal design is a prerequisite for establishing a temporal sequence by showing that the outcome has not occurred prior to, or simultaneously with, the presumed risk factor. Although, as Greenland stated, "No meta-analysis can compensate for the inherent limits of non-experimental data for making inferences about causal effects," non-experimental studies differ greatly in their research quality and thus in their relevance to a causal argument.

We next consider threats to the validity first of the primary studies in Gershoff's analyses and then of the synthesis itself that may have systematically inflated the effect size estimates or compromised the generalizability of the results.

Threats to the Validity of the Primary Studies

Although experimental studies are the gold standard in separating causal from noncausal explanations, correlational studies can contribute to a causal explanation to the extent that they meet certain criteria, the most important of which are temporality and control of third variables that could plausibly account for an association. Other threats include the use of retrospective reports or shared method variance in assessing parenting behavior and children's outcomes.

Establishing temporal sequences between risks and outcomes. A cross-sectional design cannot show that an association is a risk factor because it cannot establish temporal order. Fifty-eight percent of all the effect size estimates in Gershoff's meta-analyses came from cross-sectional analyses, and only 17% came from either experimental or prospective longitudinal studies. Thus, most of the primary studies did not provide adequate information for identifying a risk factor, much less a causal risk factor. A *causal risk factor* for an outcome is a risk factor believed to be a generative cause of that outcome—that is, to have produced that outcome. Experimental designs or systematic attempts to rule out plausible confounds in quasi-experimental and prospective longitudinal designs are necessary to establish a risk factor as causal.

Prospective longitudinal studies, unlike cross-sectional studies, can establish temporality and have more potential for controlling third variables adequately. They can provide evidence of causal direction from parents' use of CP to subsequent child behaviors by controlling for baseline child behaviors that provoke punishment and for the autocorrelation of behavior over time. We should note that Gershoff cited a paper by Cowan, Powell, and Cowan to the effect that correlational and follow-back studies are not sufficient to establish causality. Although they have some design advantages that we have highlighted in this section, it is still important to note that longitudinal models are necessary but not sufficient to establish the order of events. Parenting behavior assessed at Time 1 may predict child behavior at Time 2, but it is also possible that the parent may be reacting to child behavior that occurred before the study began.

Controlling for third variables. In their seminal discussion of the use of meta-analytic synthesis for theory development, Miller and Pollock stated "Assessing evidence that a relationship exists and that it is nonartifactual is a first step in assessing its validity." In correlational studies this requires controlling for plausible third variables. For a relationship not to be spurious, it must persist in the form of a nonzero partial correlation between the supposed independent variable and the dependent variable with plausible third variables held constant (for example, baseline child misbehavior or parental rejection). Quasi-experimental studies are designed to exclude spurious variables from the group of causal influences affecting the results being observed. However, Gershoff used DSTAT, whose manual explicitly prohibits basing effect sizes on coefficients from multiple regression. If only the zero-order correlations can be used to calculate effect size, the methodological advantage of most quasi-experimental studies is lost, which makes the meta-analytic conclusions less relevant for determining whether CP is a causal risk factor for the detrimental child outcomes with which it is associated.

The use of retrospective recall. As Gershoff pointed out, reliance on retrospective recall in all but three of the studies linking CP in childhood to adult aggression, criminality, mental health, and physical abuse is a severe method-ological inadequacy of those studies. Typically, retrospective recall is biased by the current status of the reporter. For example, adult reporters asked to report on their own depression and their parents' disciplinary practices may try to explain their current mental state by their parents' mistreatment.

Shared method variance. Problems associated with the fact that raters are not independent and thus that information about parenting and child out-comes is filtered through the same source constitute a critical limitation of half of the primary studies in the review. Shared method variance results in spuriously high correlations among constructs. The largest proportion of inde-pendent data sources occurred in compliance studies (four of five), whereas the smallest proportion of independent data sources were in adulthood stud-ies of abuse (one of five) and aggression (one of four). The bias introduced by shared method variance is well illustrated in the analyses by Yarrow et al. They grouped their results in tables to demonstrate how a "contaminated design" artifactually increases an association. Mothers' reports on "severity of punish-ment for aggression to parents" correlated at .40 with their reports on the child's aggression toward adults in the home (which the authors refer to as the *contaminated design*), compared with a .13 correlation with teacher-reported aggression. Gershoff chose to base her effect size on the correlation of .40 from the contaminated design rather than the .13 correlation in the uncontami-nated design.

Threats to the Validity of the Synthesis

In addition to the problems caused by an overinclusive definition of CP, which could inflate effect sizes, Gershoff also based effect size estimates partly on cross-sectional correlations when longitudinal correlations were available. An alternative strategy would have been to base effect sizes on the most valid associations available in a study or the ones most relevant to the debate about mild or moderate corporal punishment. Gershoff did not state the rules she used to include or exclude effect sizes when several options were available in a study. A rule that seems reasonable in selecting among relevant effect sizes within a study is to choose the one most likely to both exclude severe CP and to minimize shared method variance. To do otherwise would systematically increase the estimate of effect size with contaminated designs and with parents who use CP too severely.

The Yarrow et al. study illustrates the somewhat arbitrary nature of the myriad of decisions the synthesist must make in selecting which statistic should represent a study. Two tables summarized correlations of four punish-ment measures with three aggression measures. Gershoff based her effect size estimate on the largest of these 12 correlations. Furthermore, that correlation seems to be the poorest choice in terms of CP severity and validity threats. It was a correlation of .40 of "severity of punishment for aggression to parents" and aggression to adults at home, both based on the maternal interview. The most valid correlation was –.19 between maternal-reported physical punish-ment (overall) and teacher-reported aggression 2 months later. It was more valid because it was based on physical punishment overall, not severity of punishment in general, and because the CP and aggression measures were collected at different occasions from independent sources. Thus, the basis of an effect size between CP and child's aggression varies from –.19 in an uncontaminated design to .40 in a design contaminated by shared method variance, cross-sectional data, and overly severe punishment.

Furthermore, following the DSTAT manual's proscription against basing effect sizes on regression coefficients, even when controlling for third variables thought to be plausible confounds, Gershoff's effect sizes never reflected the most causally relevant statistics in longitudinal designs. Other metaanalytic experts recommend controlling for plausible confounds whenever possible, and some provide equations for calculating effect sizes from regression coefficients.

Reanalysis of the Data to Correct for Flaws in the Included Aggression Composite Studies

There are different views about whether poorly designed studies should be included in a meta-analysis. Mansfield and Busse recommended, and we concur, that all studies with severe methodological inadequacies should be eliminated from consideration and the remainder divided into two categories: those that have significant but not severe methodological limitations (e.g., retrospective longitudinal studies for which the likelihood of biased recall may be small) and those that are well designed in that they do not suffer from shared method variance, do use a prospective longitudinal or experimental design, and explicitly rule out severe corporal punishment. Unfortunately, as we show, that would leave too few studies for a meta-analytic review of the link between CP and most child behaviors (a situation in which one could conclude that a meta-analysis is premature).

Alternatively, methodological qualities of the studies can be coded and then used to see whether effect sizes from poorly designed studies are significantly different from those from the best-designed studies. Gershoff did attempt such analyses with her aggression composite variables, but these analyses were limited in two ways. First, almost all the studies had major methodological problems. More than half of the studies in the aggression composite used overly severe CP measures, more than half used cross-sectional or retrospective designs, and half had shared method variance. These problems were confounded with each other in unknown ways, making it difficult to sort out the differences those problems made by themselves or in combination. Second, Gershoff's analysis of study characteristics used a very conservative criterion for significance, especially considering the large number of categorical predictors (21) and small number of studies (22). This explains the unusual result of accounting for 86% of the variance in effect sizes without any of the categorical predictors being significant according to her conservative Bonferroni correction.

In contrast, we implemented more realistic analyses of whether effect sizes varied by CP severity, research design, or independence of data sources. We analyzed Gershoff's effect sizes in her aggression composite using the chi-square analyses of weighted effect sizes recommended by Hedges. Our analyses differ from Gershoff's analyses in the following ways: We treated each effect size as a separate case rather than combining effect sizes into one per study; we analyzed each methodological issue as a main effect rather than incorporating all predictors into one combined analysis; and finally, we used our codes for overly severe CP and corrected the design code for six cases.

As expected, effect sizes varied significantly by CP severity, by research design, and by independence of data sources. We found significantly higher effect sizes for overly severe than for nonsevere CP measures (mean weighted effect sizes, $d_+ = 0.46$ vs. 0.30, respectively, $\chi^2[1, N = 12,244] = 74.5, p < .001$). Effect sizes were also higher for cross-sectional than for longitudinal studies ($d_+ = 0.46$ vs. 0.37, $\chi^2[1, N = 7,807] = 16.1, p < .001$). Finally, effect sizes were higher for studies based partly or entirely on shared data sources than for independent sources of data ($d_+ = 0.35$ vs. 0.29, $\chi^2[1, N = 13,591] = 8.44, p < .01$). Only 3 of 54 studies in the aggression composite were methodologically sound on all three study characteristics. Their mean weighted effect size was 0.12, significantly less than the other 51 effect sizes in the aggression composite ($d_+ = 0.33, \chi^2[1, N = 13,591] = 5.99, p < .05$). This effect size is smaller than what Cohen labeled as small ($d = 0.20$).

Gershoff's analyses were limited in investigating important substantive distinctions as well. For example, there have been some discussions recently about whether the associations of CP differ by ethnicity. Gershoff could not investigate ethnic differences because none of her primary studies investigated ethnic minorities alone. Nonetheless, two of her primary studies included separate statistics for African American subsamples. In both studies, the mean effect sizes were negative, such that CP predicted less aggression subsequently at school in the African American subsample. Furthermore, Gunnoe and Mariner went beyond a longitudinal correlation by controlling statistically for baseline aggression, which resulted in stronger causal evidence that CP reduces subsequent school aggression in African American children ($\beta = -.30$). At least two other studies have also found that the association of CP with antisocial behavior differs significantly for African American and European American children.

Similarly, it is not clear that mild to moderate CP increases subsequent aggression and antisocial behavior at ages when parents are most likely to use CP (18 months to 6 years of age). Only one effect size in Gershoff's aggression construct was based on longitudinal and independent data on the use of nonsevere CP in this age range, and it was one of the smallest effect sizes ($d = 0.06$). Other primary studies had tiny effect sizes or ones for which CP predicted reductions in aggression for this age range when focusing on a young subsample and using data uncontaminated by the above three methodological problems. Furthermore, Gunnoe and Mariner showed that CP predicted significantly less fighting in 4- to 7-year-olds after controlling for baseline antisocial behavior. . . .

Conclusion

Gershoff acknowledged the necessity to distinguish between the harsh, punitive parental discipline that all experts would regard as both harmful and unethical (including such advocates of spanking as Dobson and Rosemond) and the more normative parental actions that involve the infliction of mild physical pain but not injury. In this response to Gershoff's article, we reanalyzed portions of Gershoff's meta-analyses to show that this separation was not in fact made in many primary studies. Because her measure included many instances of extreme and excessive physical punishment, her analyses are not relevant to the current political debate about whether normative spanking (a specific form of CP) is harmful for children.

Punishment by definition is aversive and therefore must be used sparingly and efficaciously to be acceptable. As Larzelere stated, "There may be more potential in identifying more vs. less effective ways to use each disciplinary tactic. The effect of any tactic may depend on the overall disciplinary style and the parent– child, family, and cultural contexts." Larzelere suggested a conditional sequence model as optimal in which parents begin with the mildest disciplinary tactic they think will be effective, such as reasoning, and resort to firmer tactics only if the child is defiant about a nonnegotiable request. If used efficaciously as a back-up at ages 2 to 6, both physical and nonphysical punishment are less likely to be needed as children learn to attain a reasonable level of behavioral compliance to mild disciplinary tactics such as reasoning.

Larzelere's conditional sequence model and Gershoff's process–context model should be tested with well-designed studies from culturally diverse populations. Even though randomized clinical trials are probably not practical, intervention studies are possible that would add to the knowledge base. To determine if normative physical punishment has any unique effect on 2- to 6-year-olds over and above that of otherwise optimal parenting, parents could be trained in techniques of authoritative discipline, which would include efficacious use of punishments of their choice. Some parents would choose to include spanking in their disciplinary repertoire, providing the opportunity for researchers to assess the child outcomes associated with disciplinary spanking when used efficaciously by comparing them with child outcomes associated with the alternative disciplinary tactics used by parents who choose to never spank. With a large and diverse enough sample, it should be possible to evaluate the moderating effects of third variables that would not be controlled, such as child and parent temperament and social stressors, in such quasi-experimental intervention studies. . . .

POSTSCRIPT

Is Spanking Detrimental to Children?

Both selections on corporal punishment addressed the issue of the need to define corporal punishment and to have researchers agree on the definition before they begin research on the subject. Gershoff found a relationship between children being spanked and 10 negative behavioral outcomes in childhood, some of which also extended into adulthood. Although spanking was associated with short-term compliance from the child, the 10 negative outcomes far outweighed the one short-term positive result.

Authors of the opposing selection showed that there was no support for a causal relationship between corporal punishment and detrimental child behaviors. The authors concede that no one feels abusive physical punishment is appropriate, but that mild spanking after 18 months of age and before puberty is OK. They feel spanking within the context of other discipline methods is useful.

Although these selections are more concerned with definitions and methodology than with resolving the spanking controversy, there is a real debate over what mild spanking is, and how it fits into the overall parenting discipline technique. Child development experts agree that reasoning, talking, and listening to children teaches them right from wrong and preserves their positive self-image. They admit this approach takes more time and effort but that in the long run, it is more effective and leads children to a better adjusted adulthood.

There are authorities in child development who believe spankings, when properly administered, and within the context of a loving home are effective in shaping children's behavior. Most agree to spank from about 2 years of age up until puberty and to only use an open hand and never use objects to hit children. They urge parents to explain to their children why they are being spanked.

Are spankings useful and justified, or is there a fine line between spanking and child abuse? Is it likely that parents who spank will cross that line to abuse in the heat of the moment? Is it really possible to spank with appropriate force and with logical thought? Can studies on the effects of spanking be designed to answer these questions? With all the studies already conducted, methodology and definitions are still being debated. It appears that there are many critical variables that need to be quantified before conducting research on the subject. In the meantime, parents are presented with the dilemma of how best to guide and discipline their children from childhood to becoming responsible adults.

Related Readings

Campbell, S. (September/October 2002). Spare the rod to spare the child? *Psychology Today, 35*, 26.

Davis, P.W., Chandler, J.L., & LaRossa, R. (December 2004). I've tried the switch but he laughs through the tears: The use and conceptualization of corporal punishment during the Machine Age, 1924–1939. *Child Abuse & Neglect, 28*, 1291–310.

Deater-Deckard, K., Pettit, G.S., & Lansford, J.E. (September 2003). The development of attitudes about physical punishment: An 8-year longitudinal study. *Journal of Family Psychology, 17*, 351–60.

Giles-Sims, J. & Lockhart, C. (March 2005). Culturally shaped patterns of disciplining children. *Journal of Family Issues, 26*, 196–218.

Walsh, W. (2002). Spankers and nonspankers: Where they get information on spanking. *Family Relations, 51*, 81–88.

ISSUE 6

Are Fathers Really Necessary?

YES: W. J. Doherty, Edward F. Kouneski, and Martha F. Erickson, from "Responsible Fathering: An Overview and Conceptual Framework," *Journal of Marriage and the Family* (May 1998)

NO: Alexis J. Walker and Lori A. McGraw, from "Who Is Responsible for Responsible Fathering?" *Journal of Marriage and the Family* (May 2000)

ISSUE SUMMARY

YES: Professor of family social science W. J. Doherty, psychologist Edward F. Kouneski, and Martha F. Erickson, director of the University of Minnesota's Children, Youth and Family Consortium, explore the contextual influences on fathering and conclude that a quality marriage in the optimal context promotes responsible fathering.

NO: Professor of human development and family sciences Alexis J. Walker and Lori A. McGraw, 4-H program coordinator at Oregon State University, contend that there is no empirical evidence that children need active fathers in their lives.

There has been a dramatic rise in single-parent homes headed by men. Since the 1990 census, households headed by single fathers have risen from about 1.3 million homes in 1990 to over 2.1 million in 2000. As a consequence of this increase, an issue that has confronted researchers revolves around the necessity of two-parent families. One specific issue that has been hotly debated is whether or not fathers are necessary in raising children. Children need nurturing, guidance, and economic security, but must they receive these things from *both* father and mother? Some scholars argue that children need active, involved fathers throughout their childhood and adolescence. If this does not occur, the children may be more prone to involvement in crime, premature sexuality, out-of-wedlock childbirth, lower educational achievements, depression, substance abuse, and poverty.

Other scientists question whether or not the ability to meet children's needs is gender-specific. While few would argue that it is more challenging to raise a child in a single-parent home, well-socialized and successful children have come from single-parent homes. The vast majority of these homes are female-headed. In fact, there are over 7.5 million single mothers raising children in the United States today. Another consideration is that there has been an increase in adoption by gay and lesbian parents in two-parent homes. While these children may face challenges in dealing with the prejudice associated with being raised in such households, one might ask why children would be permitted to be adopted into these homes if there was evidence that children needed both a male and a female parent. Many scientists argue that there is little, if any scientific evidence that suggests children must be raised by both a male and a female.

As you read the following selections, consider the type of family in which you were raised. Was your upbringing an optimal situation? Did the role that your father played have a positive or a negative effect on your life? W. J. Doherty, Edward F. Kouneski, and Martha F. Erickson contend that children need and deserve fathers who are actively involved with their children throughout childhood and adolescence. To achieve this, they promote responsible fathering as a way to help meet the needs of children. Alexis J. Walker and Lori A. McGraw believe that while there may be an ideological basis for the assumption that children need and deserve active and involved fathers, empirical support for this ideal is lacking.

YES W. J. Doherty, Edward F. Kouneski, and Martha F. Erickson

Responsible Fathering: An Overview and Conceptual Framework

Responsible Fathering

The use of the term "responsible fathering," which was the original language used by the U.S. Department of Health and Human Services in commissioning our work, reflects a recent shift by academics and professionals away from value-free language and toward a more explicit value-advocacy approach. "Responsible" suggests an "ought," a set of desired norms for evaluating fathers' behavior. The term also conveys a moral meaning (right and wrong) because it suggests that some fathering could be judged "irresponsible." The willingness to use explicitly moral terms reflects a change in the social climate among academics, professionals, and policymakers, who until recently embraced the traditional notion that social science, social policy, and social programs could be value free. In the late twentieth century, there is more appreciation of the inevitability of value-laden and moral positions being part of social science and social interventions and a greater willingness to be explicit about values so that they can be debated openly and their influence on social science and policy can be made clear, rather than being covert (Doherty, 1995a; Doherty et al., 1993; Wolfe, 1989). Indeed, there has always been a strong but implicit undercurrent of value advocacy in fathering research, much of it conducted by men and women interested in promoting more committed and nurturing involvement by men in their children's lives. Similarly, there has always been a moral undertone to the focus on fathers' deficits that has characterized much of the literature on absent, "deadbeat," and emotionally uninvolved fathers (Doherty, 1990). The term "responsible fathering," as we use it, applies to fathers across all social classes and racial groups, not narrowly to men in lower social classes or minority groups. Now that value advocacy has become more explicit in the fathering area (Dollahite, Hawkins, & Brotherson, 1997), responsible fathering needs to be clearly defined. James Levine and Edward Pitt (1995) have made an important start in their delineation of responsible fathering. They write:

From W. J. Doherty, Edward F. Kouneski, and Martha F. Erickson, "Responsible Fathering: An Overview and Conceptual Framework," *Journal of Marriage and the Family*, vol. 60 (May 1998). Copyright © 1998 by The National Council on Family Relations, 3989 Central Avenue, NE, Suite 550, Minneapolis, MN 55421. Reprinted by permission.

A man who behaves responsibly towards his child does the following:

- He waits to make a baby until he is prepared emotionally and financially to support his child.
- He establishes his legal paternity if and when he does make a baby.
- He actively shares with the child's mother in the continuing emotional and physical care of their child, from pregnancy onwards.
- He shares with the child's mother in the continuing financial support of their child, from pregnancy onwards. (pp. 5–6)

Levine and Pitt's elements of responsible fathering have the advantage of referring to both resident and nonresident fathers, a reflection of the diversity of fathers' situations. The authors also assert that commitment to this ethic of responsible fatherhood extends beyond the father to the mother, to professionals who work with families, and to social institutions entrusted with the support of families. We employ Levine and Pitt's definition in this [selection], but we narrow our scope to men who are already fathers; we do not address the issue of postponing fatherhood.

The developmental backdrop for the discussion of fathering reflects children's needs for predictability, nurturance, and appropriate limit setting from fathers and mothers, as well as for economic security and a cooperative, preferably loving relationship between their parents (Hetherington & Parke, 1993). Furthermore, the specific needs of children vary by their developmental stage. Parents are required to provide higher levels of physical caregiving when their children are infants and greater levels of conflict management when their children become adolescents. Although we do not review the literature on the effects of active fathering on children, an assumption behind this [selection]— and our value stance—is that children need and deserve active, involved fathers throughout their childhood and adolescence. The prime justification for promoting responsible fathering is the needs of children. . . .

Influences on Fathering: A Conceptual Model

The fathering literature has been long on empirical studies and short on theory. Researchers mostly have adapted concepts from social sciences to fit their particular area, but work is beginning on overarching conceptual frameworks to guide research and program development. In his review of theory in fathering research, Marsiglio (1995) mentions life course theory (which emphasizes how men's experience of fatherhood changes with life transitions), social scripting theory (which emphasizes the cultural messages that fathers internalize about their role), and social identity theory (which focuses on how men take on the identity of a father in relation to their other social roles). Hawkins, Christiansen, Sargent, and Hill (1995), Hawkins and Dollahite (1997), and Snarey (1993) have used Erik Erikson's developmental theory in their work on how fathering can promote generativity among adult men. Other scholars have explored the utility of economic theories to understand fathers' decisions to invest in, or withdraw from, their children (Becker, 1991).

The most specific conceptual model frequently used in the fatherhood literature is Lamb's and Pleck's four-factor model of father involvement, which is not explicitly grounded in a broader theory such as Erikson's theory or social identity theory. (See Lamb et al., 1985.) Lamb and Pleck proposed that father involvement is determined by motivation, skills and self-confidence, social support, and institutional practices. These factors may be viewed as additive, building on one another, and as interactive, with some factors being necessary prior to others. For example, motivation may be necessary for the development of skills. Ihinger-Tallman, Pasley, and Buehler (1995) proposed an eight-factor model of mediators between father identity and actual involvement after divorce: mother's preferences and beliefs, father's perception of mother's parenting, father's emotional stability, mother's emotional stability, sex of child, coparental relationship, father's economic well-being, father's economic security, and encouragement from others. Recently, Park (1996) articulated a systems model of residential father involvement that includes individual, family, extrafamilial, and cultural influences.

Based on the research literature, prior theoretical work on fathering, and the systemic ecological orientation described earlier, we present a conceptual model of influences on responsible fathering. (See Figure 1.) Unlike prior work, the model is intended to include fathering inside or outside marriage and regardless of coresidence with the child. The focus is on the factors that help create and maintain a father-child bond. The model attempts to transcend the dyadic focus of much traditional child development theory by emphasizing first the child-father-mother triad and then larger systems' influences.

The model highlights individual factors of the father, mother, and child; mother-father relationship factors; and larger contextual factors in the environment. Within each of these domains, the model outlines a number of specific factors that can be supported by the research literature. The center of the model is the interacting unit of child, father, and mother, each formulating meanings and enacting behaviors that influence the others. The three are embedded in a broader social context that affects them as individuals and affects the quality of their relationships.

We are particularly interested in highlighting factors that pertain to fathers because one of the goals of this [selection] is to guide father-specific research, program development, and public policy. All of the factors in the model affect the mother-child relationship, as well, because they are generic to parenting (see Belsky, 1984), but many of them have particular twists for fathers. Because theory and research on parenting so often have been derived from work on mothers, it seems particularly important to illuminate the distinctive influences on fathering. The arrows point to the father-child relationship, in particular to the four domains of responsible fathering covered in this review—paternity, presence, economic support, and involvement. Although the model can depict fathers' indirect influence on their children through their support for the mother, the focus here is on direct father-child interaction. And although the influences depicted in the model also can be viewed as influencing the father directly, we prefer to focus on the effects on father-child relations because enhancing those relations and, therefore, the well-being of children is the ultimate goal of programs for fathers.

Figure 1

Influences on Responsible Fathering: A Conceptual Model

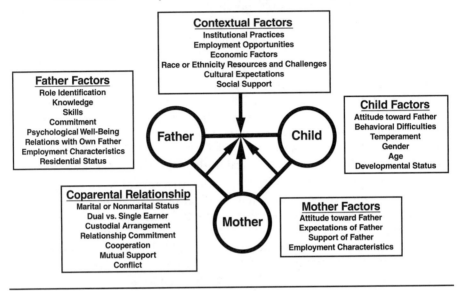

The research reviewed for this [selection] supports the notion that father-child relations are more strongly influenced than mother-child relations by three of the dimensions of the model: the coparental relationship, factors in the other parent, and larger contextual factors.

Coparental Relationship

A number of studies have shown that the quality of father-child relations both inside and outside marriage is more highly correlated with the quality of the coparental relationship than is true for the mother-child relationship (Belsky & Volling, 1987; Cox, Owen, Lewis, & Henderson, 1989; Feldman, Nash, & Aschenbrenner, 1983; Levy-Shiff & Israelashvili, 1988). Fathers appear to withdraw from their child when they are not getting along with the mother, whereas mothers do not show a similar level of withdrawal. This is one way to understand the tendency of fathers to remove themselves from their children's lives after a breakup with the mother, especially if they have a negative relationship with the mother (Ahrons & Miller, 1993). As Furstenberg and Cherlin (1991) have asserted, for many men, marriage and parenthood are a "package deal." Or one might say that in American culture, a woman is a mother all of her life, but a man is a father if he has a wife. Furthermore, if he has a wife but does not get along with her, he may be present as a father, but the quality of his relationship with his children is apt to suffer.

One reason that fathering is particularly sensitive to the marital or coparental relationship is that standards and expectations for fathering appear to be more variable than those for mothering. There is more negotiation in families over what fathers will do than over what mothers will do and hence more dependence among fathers on the quality and outcome of those negotiations (Backett, 1987). As Lewis and O'Brien (1987) state, men have a less clear "job description" as fathers than women do as mothers. Therefore, fathers' behavior is strongly influenced by the meanings and expectations of fathers themselves, as well as mothers, children, extended family, and broader cultural institutions.

One of the most sensitive areas of research on fathering is the importance of fathers being married to the children's mothers. Because many fathers are not married to the mother, it can seem prejudicial to these men and their children—and perhaps to single-parent mothers—to emphasize the importance of marriage. On the other hand, an implication of our review of the research and our conceptual framework is that, for most American heterosexual fathers, the family environment most supportive of fathering is a caring, committed, and collaborative marriage. This kind of marriage means that the father lives with his children and has a good partnership with their mother. These are the two principal intrafamilial determinants of responsible fathering.

Some of the controversy over the role of marriage in responsible fathering can be circumvented by specifying the quality of the marriage, as we have done. It is the quality of the marital process, rather than the legal or coresidential status, that most affects fathering. One might argue, then, that being married is not important because cohabiting couples could have the same qualities of relationship. Although, in principle, this is true, the best national research on cohabitation indicates that cohabitation is a temporary arrangement for most heterosexual couples; they eventually either marry or break up (Bumpass et al., 1991). We conclude that, in practice, the kind of mother-father relationship most conducive to responsible fathering in contemporary U.S. society is a caring, committed, collaborative marriage. Outside of this arrangement, substantial barriers stand in the way of active, involved fathering.

Mother Factors

Among external influences on fathering, the role of the mother has particular salience because mothers serve as partners and sometimes as gatekeepers in the father-child relationship, both inside and outside marriage (De Luccie, 1995). Mother factors in the conceptual model, of course, interact with the coparental relationship because the mother's personal feelings about the father influence the coparental relationship. But there is also evidence that, even within satisfactory marital relationships, a father's involvement with his children, especially young children, is often contingent on the mother's attitudes toward, expectations of, and support for the father, as well as the extent of her involvement in the labor force (De Luccie, 1995; Simons, Whitbeck, Conger, & Melby, 1990). Marsiglio (1991), using the National Survey of Families and Households data set, found that mothers' characteristics were more strongly correlated with fathers' involvement than fathers' own characteristics were. Indeed, studies have shown that many mothers, both inside and outside marriage, are ambivalent about the fathers' active involvement with their children

(Baruch & Barnett, 1986; Cowan & Cowan, 1987). Given the powerful cultural forces that expect absorption by women in their mothering role, it is not surprising that active paternal involvement would threaten some women's identity and sense of control over this central domain of their lives. The evolution of a social consensus on responsible fathering, therefore, will necessarily involve a consensus that responsible mothering means supporting the father-child bond.

Contextual Factors

Research demonstrates the particular vulnerability of fathering to contextual and institutional practices—from the establishment of legal paternity to the greater impact of unemployment on fathering than on mothering. Lack of income and poor occupational opportunities appear to have a particularly negative effect on fathering (Thomson, Hanson, & McLanahan, 1994). The prevalence of the abandonment of economic and psychological responsibilities among poor, unemployed men and among other men who undergo financial and employment crises is partly a function of the unique vulnerability of fathering to perceived success in the external environment (Jones, 1991; McLoyd, 1989). This analysis suggests that fathering is especially sensitive to changes in economic forces in the work force and marketplace and to shifts in public policy. It also suggests that fathering suffers disproportionately from negative social forces, such as racism, that inhibit opportunities in the environment. McLoyd (1990), in a review and conceptual analysis of economic hardship in African American families, describes how poverty and racism combine to create psychological distress, which is, in turn, associated with more negative parenting styles and more difficulty in the coparental relationship.

Our conceptual model also depicts the positive contribution of ethnic and cultural factors to fathering. One aspect of responsible fathering, that of economic support, is nearly universally expected of fathers by their cultures (Lamb, 1987b). LaRossa (1997), in his historical analysis, has demonstrated how changing cultural expectations in the first part of the twentieth century led to more nurturing father involvement in the U.S. Allen and Connor (1997) have examined how role flexibility and concern for children in the African American community create opportunities for men to become involved in surrogate father relationships with children who lack day-to-day contact with their biological fathers. Unfortunately, there has not been much empirical research that examines fathering in its cultural context, using representative samples of fathers to explore how cultural meanings and practices influence fathers' beliefs and behaviors.

The final contextual factor in the model is social support, which Belsky (1984) emphasized in his theoretical model of parenting and which McLoyd (1990) documented as a crucial factor in diminishing the negative effects of poverty on parenting behavior. However, most of the research on social support specifically for fathers has focused on mothers as sources of social support. Pleck (1997) reviewed the limited research on extrafamilial social support for fathering and found the studies skimpy and inconsistent, except for the pattern that highly involved fathers tend to encounter negative attitudes from acquaintances, relatives, and fellow workers. Clearly, there is a need for studies that examine the sources and influences of social support on fathering, particularly the role of other fathers.

From the perspective of both the contextual factors and the mother factors discussed thus far, fathering can be conceptualized as a more contextually sensitive process than mothering is. Not that mothering is not also contextually sensitive, but the cultural norms are stricter on the centrality and endurance of the mother-child dyad, regardless of what is happening outside that relationship. Father-child relations, on the other hand, are culturally defined as less dyadic and more multilateral, requiring a threshold of support from inside the family and from the larger environment. Undermining from the mother or from a social institution or system may induce many fathers to retreat from responsible fathering unless their own individual level of commitment to fathering is quite strong.

This point about the ecological sensitivity of fathering is a principal conclusion of this [selection]. It suggests that fathering programs and policy initiatives that focus only on fathers will benefit mainly fathers who already have a supportive social and economic environment. Fathers whose context is less supportive—for example, fathers who do not live with their children, who have strained relationships with the mother, or who are experiencing economic stress—will need more extensive and multilateral efforts to support their fathering.

Child Factors

Individual child factors are included in the model for completeness, but the child factors studied in the research literature do not appear to be as important as the other dimensions in influencing fathering. Fathers do appear to find it easier to be more involved with their sons, especially older sons, presumably because they identify with them and are more comfortable communicating with them (Marsiglio, 1991). Most of the other child factors, such as age, appear to influence mothers as much as fathers, although Larson (1993) and Larson and Richards (1994) have documented how fathers withdraw more from parent-adolescent conflict than mothers do. More research is needed on the influence of the child's temperament and developmental status on relations with nonresidential fathers. Similarly, research is needed on how the child's beliefs about father involvement influence fathers' and mothers' expectations and behavior.

Mother-Child Relationship Factors

We include this domain for theoretical completeness, but we could find no research directly examining how the father-child relationship is affected by the mother-child relationship. Such effects may be tapped indirectly through other dimensions in the model, such as the mother's attitudes toward the father's involvement with the child. For example, a close mother-child bond, combined with an ambivalent maternal attitude toward paternal involvement, might lead to less closeness of the father than a situation in which a mother had the same attitude but, herself, was less close to the child.

Father Factors

Fathers' role identification, skills, and commitment are important influences on fathering (Baruch & Barnett, 1986; Ihinger-Tallman et al., 1995; Pleck, 1997). These three appear to fluctuate from low to high levels along with a number of interpersonal and contextual factors, such as the mother's expectations and the father's residential status with his children (Marsiglio, 1995; Ihinger-Tallman et al., 1995). In American culture, fathers are given more latitude for commitment to, identification with, and competence in their parental role. This latitude brings with it the price of confusion for many fathers about how to exercise their roles (Daly, 1995).

The variability of the individual father factors suggests two important implications of our conceptual model: that the positive support from mothers and the larger context can move men in the direction of more responsible parenting even in the face of modest personal investment, and that strong father commitment, knowledge, and skills are likely to be necessary to overcome negative maternal, coparental, and contextual influences. This latter point is similar to Lamb's (1987a) hypothesis that high levels of father motivation can override institutional barriers and the lack of social support.

As for the father's experience in his own family of origin, some research suggests that the father's relationship with his own father may be a factor—either through identifying with his father or compensating for his father's lapses—in contributing to his own role identification, sense of commitment, and self-efficacy (Cowan & Cowan, 1987; Daly, 1995). Snarey (1993), in a longitudinal study, documented the role of multigenerational connections between fathers.

The final father factors, psychological well-being and employment characteristics, have been studied extensively. Research examining psychological adjustment and parenting quality consistently shows a positive relationship between fathers' (and mothers') psychological well-being and their parenting attitudes and skills (Cox et al., 1989; Levy-Shiff & Israelashvili, 1988; Pleck, 1997). The research on job loss and economic distress generally has examined declines in psychological well-being as mediating factors leading to poorer fathering (Elder et al., 1984; Elder et al., 1985; Jones, 1991). And fathers' work situations have been shown to have mixed relationships with involvement with children. Specific work schedules are not strongly related to involvement, but greater flex time and other profamily practices are associated with more father involvement (Pleck, 1997). Indeed, consistent with other research on fathering, mothers' employment characteristics are more strongly associated with fathers' involvement than fathers' employment characteristics. When mothers are employed, fathers' proportionate share of parenting is greater, although studies are inconsistent about the absolute level of father involvement (Pleck, 1997).

Conceptual Overview

The conceptual model outlines multiple factors that influence fathering, from individual and relational to contextual. The factors can be viewed as additive. For example, low identification with the parental role, combined with low expectations from the mother, would be strongly associated with low involvement of the father in both residential and nonresidential contexts. High identification with the parental role, combined with high expectations from the mother, would lead to greater father involvement in any residential context.

The factors in the model also can be viewed as interactive. For example, high role identification and good employment and income might be sufficient to offset low expectations from the mother. Similarly, not living with the child could be offset by the father's strong commitment to his children and the support of the mother. And strong institutional support through public policies could mitigate unmarried fathers' and mothers' reluctance to declare paternity.

Although the conceptual framework is intended to apply to the four domains of responsible fathering (paternity, presence, economic support, and involvement), most of the research has focused on one or another of these areas. Indeed, the bulk of the empirical research has been on father involvement. Researchers have tended to assume that economic factors uniquely influence economic support and that father factors uniquely influence father involvement. Putting a range of factors into one model challenges researchers to examine how all the factors might influence all the domains of responsible fathering. We acknowledge that some components of the model are likely to influence some aspects of fathering more than others.

Finally, the model should be seen as depicting a dynamic set of processes, rather than a set of linear, deterministic influences. Systemic, ecological models run the risk of reducing the target behavior—in this case, responsible fathering—to a contextually determined phenomenon stripped of individual initiative and self-determination. We want to emphasize the pivotal role of fathers, themselves, in appropriating or discarding cultural and contextual messages, in formulating a fathering identity and developing fathering skills with their own children, in working out their feelings about their own fathers, and in dealing collaboratively with their children's mother. The social construction of fatherhood is an evolving creation of all stakeholders in the lives of children, and contemporary fathers have a central role in this creation. The active construction of fathering by fathers, themselves, is not a prominent theme in the research literature, although it is crucial to programs that work with fathers. More qualitative research is needed to explore the kinds of identity development and social negotiation that constitute the experience of fathering.

Conclusion

This [selection] delineates a conceptual model of influences on fathering that can serve as a stimulus for future research, programming, and policy development. The main premise, supported by a variety of studies, is that fathering is uniquely sensitive to contextual influences, both interpersonal and environmental. Fathering is a multilateral relationship, in addition to a one-to-one relationship. A range of influences—including mothers' expectations and behaviors, the quality of the coparental relationship, economic factors, institutional practices, and employment opportunities—all have potentially powerful effects on fathering. These contextual factors shape the major domains of responsible fathering discussed here: acknowledgment of paternity, willingness to be present and provide economic support, and level of involvement with one's children. When these influences are not supportive of the father-child bond, a man may need a high level identification with the father role, strong commitment, and good parenting skills to remain a responsible father to his children, especially if he does not live with them.

This review and conceptual model deal with factors that promote active, involved fathering, not with the effects of that kind of fathering on children. (See review by Pleck, 1997.) Nor do we take a position on whether there are essential characteristics of fathering versus mothering or whether having parents of two genders is necessary for the well-being of children. The growing literature on gay and lesbian parenting suggests that these kinds of questions are more complex than many scholars assumed in the past (Patterson, 1992; Patterson & Chan, 1997). However, it is not necessary to resolve these issues in order to address the factors that enhance and inhibit the parenting of men in the role of father in the late twentieth century.

A potentially controversial conclusion of this [selection] is that a high quality marriage is the optimal context for promoting responsible fatherhood. This position moves opposite the trend in contemporary family studies to disaggregate marriage and parenting. We do not suggest that men cannot parent adequately outside this context or that children must be raised in a married household in order to grow up well adjusted. However, we believe that the research strongly indicates that substantial barriers exist for most men's fathering outside a caring, committed, collaborative marriage and that the promotion of these kinds of enduring marital partnerships may be the most important contribution to responsible fathering in our society.

An encouraging implication of this systemic, ecological analysis is that there are many pathways to enhancing the quality of father-child relationships. Fathering can be enhanced through programs and policies that help fathers relate to their coparent, that foster employment and economic opportunities if needed, that change institutional expectations and practices to better support fathers, and that encourage fathers' personal commitment to their children.

References

Ahrons, C. R., & Miller, R. B. (1993). The effect of the postdivorce relationship on paternal involvement: A longitudinal analysis. *American Journal of Orthopsychiatry, 63,* 441–450.

Allen, W. D., & Connor, M. (1997). An African American perspective on generative fathering. In A. J. Hawkins & D. C. Dollahite (Eds.), *Generative fathering: Beyond deficit perspectives.* Newbury Park, CA: Sage.

Backett, K. (1987). The negotiation of fatherhood. In C. Lewis & M. O'Brien (Eds.), *Reassessing fatherhood: New observations on fathers and the modern family*. Newbury Park, CA: Sage.

Baruch, G. K., & Barnett, R. C. (1986). Consequences of fathers' participation in family work: Parent's role strain and well-being. *Journal of Personality and Social Psychology, 51*, 983–992.

Becker, G. S. (1991). *A treatise on the family*. Cambridge, MA: Harvard University Press.

Belsky, J. (1984). The determinants of parenting: A process model. *Child Development, 55*, 83–96.

Belsky, J., & Volling, B. L. (1987). Mothering, fathering, and marital interaction in the family triad during infancy. In P. W. Berman & F. A. Pedersen (Eds.), *Men's transitions to parenthood: Longitudinal studies of early family experience* (pp. 37–63). Hillsdale, NJ: Erlbaum.

Bumpass, L. L., Sweet, J. A., & Cherlin, A. (1991). The role of cohabitation in declining rates of marriage. *Journal of Marriage and the Family, 53*, 913–927.

Cowan, C. P., & Cowan, P. A. (1987). Men's involvement in parenthood: Identifying the antecedents and understanding the barriers. In P. W. Berman & F. A. Pedersen (Eds.), *Men's transitions to parenthood: Longitudinal studies of early family experience* (pp. 145–174). Hillsdale, NJ: Erlbaum.

Cox, M. J., Owen, M. T., Lewis, J. M., & Henderson, V. K. (1989). Marriage, adult adjustment, and early parenting. *Child Development, 60*, 1015–1024.

Daly, K. J. (1995). Reshaping fatherhood: Finding the models. In W. Marsiglio (Ed.), *Fatherhood: Contemporary theory, research, and social policy* (pp. 21–40). Thousand Oaks, CA: Sage.

De Luccie, M. F. (1995). Mothers as gatekeepers: A model of maternal mediators of father involvement. *The Journal of Genetic Psychology, 156*, 115–131.

Doherty, W. J. (1990). Beyond reactivity and the deficit model of manhood: A commentary on articles by Napier, Pittman, and Gottman. *Journal of Marital and Family Therapy, 17*, 29–32.

Doherty, W. J. (1995a). *Soul searching: Why psychotherapy must promote moral responsibility*. New York: Basic Books.

Doherty, W. J., Boss, P. G., LaRossa, R., Schumm, W. R., & Steinmetz, S. K. (1993). Family theories and methods: A contextual approach. In P. G. Boss, W. J. Doherty, R. LaRossa, W. R. Schumm, & S. K. Steinmetz (Eds.), *Family theories and methods: A contextual approach*. New York: Plenum Press.

Dollahite, D. C., Hawkins, A. J., & Brotherson, S. E. (1997). Fatherwork: A conceptual ethic of fathering as generative work. In A. J. Hawkins & D. C. Dollahite (Eds.), *Generative fathering: Beyond deficit perspective*. Newbury Park, CA: Sage.

Elder, G., Liker, J., & Cross, C. (1984). Parent-child behavior in the Great Depression: Life course and intergenerational influences. In P. Baltes & O. Brim (Eds.), *Life span development and behavior* (Vol. 6, pp. 109–158). Orlando, FL: Academic Press.

Elder, G., Van Nguyen, T., & Caspi, A. (1985). Linking family hardship to children's lives. *Child Development, 56*, 1628–1636.

Feldman, S. S., Nash, S. C., & Aschenbrenner, B. G. (1983). Antecedents of fathering. *Child Development, 54*, 1628–1636.

Furstenberg, F. S., & Cherlin, A. J. (1991). *Divided families: What happens to children when parents part*. Cambridge, MA: Harvard University Press.

Hawkins, A. J., Christiansen, S. L., Sargent, K. P., & Hill, E. J. (1995). Rethinking fathers' involvement in child care. In W. Marsiglio (Ed.), *Fatherhood: Contemporary theory, research, and social policy* (pp. 41–56). Thousand Oaks, CA: Sage.

Hawkins, A. J., & Dollahite, D. C. (1997). Generative fathering: Beyond deficit perspectives. Thousand Oaks, CA: Sage.

Hetherington, E. M., & Parke, R. D. (1993). *Child psychology: A contemporary view*. New York: McGraw-Hill.

Ihinger-Tallman, M., Pasley, K., & Buehler, C. (1995). Developing a middle-range theory of father involvement postdivorce. In W. Marsiglio (Ed.), *Fatherhood:*

Contemporary theory, research, and social policy (pp. 57–77). Thousand Oaks, CA: Sage.

Jones, L. (1991). Unemployed fathers and their children: Implications for policy and practice. *Child and Adolescent Social Work Journal, 8,* 101–116.

Lamb, M. E. (1987a). Introduction: The emergent American father. In M. E. Lamb (Ed.), *The father's role: Cross-cultural perspectives* (pp. 3–25). Hillsdale, NJ: Erlbaum.

Lamb, M. E. (Ed.). (1987b). *The father's role: Cross-cultural perspectives.* Hillsdale: NJ: Erlbaum.

Lamb, M. E., Pleck, J., Charnov, E. L., & Levine, J. A. (1985). Paternal behavior in humans. *American Zoologist, 25,* 883–894.

LaRossa, R. (1997). *The modernization of fatherhood: A social and political history.* Chicago: University of Chicago Press.

Larson, R. W. (1993). Finding time for fatherhood: The emotional ecology of adolescent-father interactions. In S. Shulman & W. A. Collins (Eds.), *Father-adolescent relationships* (pp. 7–25). San Francisco: Jossey-Bass.

Larson, R. W., & Richards, M. H. (1994). *Divergent realities: The emotional lives of mothers, fathers, and adolescents.* New York: Basic Books.

Levine, J. A., & Pitt, E. W. (1995). *New expectations: Community strategies for responsible fatherhood.* New York: Families and Work Institute.

Levy-Shiff, R., & Israelashvili, R. (1988). Antecedents of fathering: Some further exploration. *Developmental Psychology, 24,* 434–440.

Lewis, C., & O'Brien, M. (1987). Constraints on fathers: Research, theory and clinical practice. In C. Lewis, & M. O'Brien (Eds.), *Reassessing fatherhood: New observations on fathers and the modern family* (pp. 1–19). Newbury Park, CA: Sage.

Marsiglio, W. (1991). Paternal engagement activities with minor children. *Journal of Marriage and the Family, 53,* 973–986.

Marsiglio, W. (1995). Fathers' diverse life course patterns and roles: Theory and social interventions. In W. Marsiglio (Ed.), *Fatherhood: Contemporary theory, research, and social policy* (pp. 78–101). Thousand Oaks, CA: Sage.

McLoyd, V. C. (1989). Socialization and development in a changing economy: The effects of paternal job loss and income loss on children. *American Psychologist, 44,* 293–302.

McLoyd, V. C. (1990). The impact of economic hardship on Black families and children: Psychological distress, parenting, and socioemotional development. *Child Development, 61,* 311–346.

Park, R. D. (1996). *Fatherhood.* Cambridge, MA: Harvard University Press.

Patterson, C. J. (1992). Children of lesbian and gay parents. *Child Development, 63,* 1025–1042.

Patterson, C. J., & Chan, R. W. (1997). Gay fathers. In M. E. Lamb (Ed.), *The role of the father in child development* (3rd ed.). New York: Wiley.

Pleck, J. H. (1997). Paternal involvement: Levels, sources, and consequences. In M. E. Lamb (Ed.), *The role of the father in child development* (3rd ed.). New York: Wiley.

Simons, R., Whitbeck, L., Conger, R., & Melby, J. (1990). Husband and wife differences in determinants of parenting: A social learning and exchange model of parental behavior. *Journal of Marriage and the Family, 52,* 375–392.

Snarey, J. (1993). *How fathers care for the next generation: A four-decade study.* Cambridge, MA: Harvard University Press.

Thomson, E., Hanson, T., & McLanahan, S. S. (1994). Family structure and child well-being: Economic resources versus parent socialization. *Social Forces, 73,* 221–242.

U.S. Department of Health and Human Services (1995). *Report to Congress on out-of-wedlock childbearing* (Pub. No. PHS 95-1257-1). Washington, DC: U.S. Government Printing Office.

Wolfe, A. (1989). *Whose keeper? Social science and moral obligation.* Berkeley: University of California Press.

NO Alexis J. Walker and Lori A. McGraw

Who Is Responsible for Responsible Fathering?

William Doherty, Edward Kouneski, and Martha Erickson proposed a conceptual framework on "Responsible Fathering." For both empirical and theoretical reasons, we found their essay to be problematic. The proposed model excludes key features of fatherhood and of motherhood, and researchers who attempt to operationalize it or practitioners who attempt to develop programs from it are destined to be misguided.

We are not concerned that the authors wrote from a position of advocacy. We agree that the new research on fatherhood primarily reflects a position valuing involved fathers and that discussions about absent fathers sometimes have a moral overtone. This is particularly evident in policy arenas. Congress, in fact, titled a 1998 child support bill, The Deadbeat Parents Punishment Act. As demonstrated by the plethora of empirical studies blaming mothers for their children's behavioral, psychological, and social problems (Caplan & Hall-McCorquodale, 1985), discussions about motherhood have moral overtones as well. Arguments grounded solely in ideology are inherent in the nature of public discourse. What is important for researchers who advocate a specific policy position in our journals is to adhere to principles and practices agreed upon within a scientific community, regardless of ideology (Furstenberg, 1999).

We appreciate the authors' willingness to make their underlying assumptions explicit. We draw attention to the empirical literature the authors neglected, however, and raise questions about their explicit and implicit reasoning. We take issue with their assumptions and their conclusions, and we critique their model by highlighting the sociohistorical context of fatherhood, childhood, and motherhood.

What Do Children Need?

A key, explicit assumption of the authors is "that children *need* [italics added] and deserve active, involved fathers throughout their childhood and adolescence" (p. 279). Although there might be an ideological basis for this assumption, it lacks

From Alexis J. Walker and Lori A. McGraw, "Who Is Responsible for Responsible Fathering?" *Journal of Marriage and the Family,* vol. 62 (May 2000). Copyright © 2000 by The National Council on Family Relations, 3989 Central Avenue, NE, Suite 550, Minneapolis, MN 55421. Reprinted by permission.

empirical support. Members of the scientific community may agree on what children need—broadly defined—for biological, physical, emotional, psychological, and social well-being. There is not agreement, however, that these needs must be met by a parent of a certain gender. In their study of children from single-parent households, Downey, Ainsworth-Darnell, and Dufur (1998) asked: "Do women and men play unique roles in shaping children's well-being?" (p. 878). They concluded that "the challenge for family researchers is to distinguish between familial characteristics that are necessarily important for creating positive family environments for children and those, such as sex of parent, that are not" (p. 892). We have no objection to children having actively involved fathers, but research has demonstrated that children's needs can be met within the full range of fathers' involvement, from no involvement to fathers raising children on their own (Acock & Demo, 1994; Risman, 1987).

Which Fathers Matter?

Doherty et al. focused on heterosexual, biological fathers "to delimit the review" (p. 279). Except for marital status, nothing in the authors' conceptual model accounts for their emphasis on biological fathers. Furthermore, there is no empirical evidence that biology predisposes fathers to be responsible and involved (Cooksey & Fondell, 1996). The authors deliberately excluded adoptive, gay, step, fictive kin, and other father surrogates, many of whom are involved, responsible fathers. They suggested that nonbiological and gay fathers deserve empirical and programmatic focus, but they saw such focus as beyond the scope of their paper. Given the authors' concerns about children's needs and the variety of ways through which men function as fathers in contemporary society (e.g., Hawkins & Eggebeen, 1991), we are at a loss to understand their decision. Because there are involved and engaged fathers who are meeting their children's needs in all of the excluded groups, a contextual model of responsible fathers would and should include them.

Mothers' "Gatekeeping," Fathers' Resistance

Doherty et al. exaggerated the problematic behavior of mothers and minimized the role fathers play in their own involvement with their children. They found three studies, two of them focused on young fathers, providing evidence that mothers and grandmothers act as gatekeepers between their husbands and their children. They also cited larger scale studies (e.g., Marsiglio, 1991), demonstrating that father involvement is tied more closely to mothers' than to fathers' characteristics. They relied on this research to argue that mothers control fathers' involvement. The authors concluded that "*many* [emphasis added] mothers are ambivalent about fathers' active involvement with their children" (p. 287). Because their essay was published, an additional study of mothers' gatekeeping has been reported (Allen & Hawkins, 1999).

Gatekeeping by mothers is an idea that has emerged to explain the relatively low levels of involvement of fathers with their children. It has been conceptualized in a variety of ways, most recently as a mother's cognitive schema that includes (a) high standards for housework and child care and enjoying control over family work; (b) an identity that is dependent on others' views of how well-groomed one's children are and how clean one's home is; and (c) a conventional attitude that women enjoy housework and find it easier to do housework and child care than men do (Allen & Hawkins, 1999). Note that interaction with children, other than through housework or child care, was neither part of this conceptualization nor measured as an outcome of gate-keeping. Allen and Hawkins did not include in gatekeeping the idea that fathers may play a direct or indirect role in setting standards for housework and childcare or in influencing the division of labor in other ways. Although they attempted to include mothers' sense of responsibility for family work (these items were eliminated because of poor measurement properties), they did not consider fathers' sense of responsibility. Furthermore, neither mothers' desires nor their deliberate attempts to exclude fathers from interacting with their children were included. Even accepting this limited conceptualization, however, only one fifth of their sample of married mothers could be described as "gatekeepers."

In contrast to the idea that mothers keep fathers from their children, evidence suggests that women generally value and actively promote relationships between children and fathers (e.g., Haavind, 1984; Marsiglio, 1991; Pleck, 1985; Thompson, 1991). Even stepmothers function in this way. Consider recent evidence from the wives of remarried men over 60 in the Normative Study of Aging. Vinick and Lanspery (1998) described stepmothers as "'carpenters' of damaged family relationships" (p. 4) who worked to establish friendly contact with adult children who were hostile toward their fathers. Stepmothers encouraged their husbands to keep in touch with their children, reminding them to make phone calls, issuing invitations, or communicating with the stepchildren themselves. In separate interviews, their husbands spontaneously supported these findings. Vinick and Lanspery concluded:

> Stepmothers often fulfilled pivotal roles in stepfamilies as rebuilders and nurturers of associations with the younger generation. Relationships with stepchildren, as well as husbands' relations with their own biological children, had frequently improved due, in large measure, to women's efforts, acting on their own behalf, and that of their husbands and their stepchildren. (p. 5)

To emphasize women who are ambivalent about or act as gatekeepers of fathers' involvement does a disservice to mothers. We do not deny that some mothers make it difficult for fathers to connect with their children, but any instance of gatekeeping must be viewed in the larger context of mothers' facilitation and of men's authority in families. This empirical question has yet to be addressed: To what extent are mothers able to limit coresidential fathers' involvement when fathers have a strong interest in building connections with their children?

Doherty et al. wrote about mothers' gatekeeping but not about men's resistance. Fathers play a role in their limited involvement with children by resisting mothers' attempts to facilitate interaction. Arendell (1992, 1995) described how fathers' resistance to cooperating with mothers may become stronger after divorce. As husbands and fathers, men have legitimate control and authority in families. They expect, desire, and believe they have certain "rights to their parenthood" (1992, p. 569), and they see these rights as challenged after divorce. Similarly, Bertoia and Drakich (1993) demonstrated that, rather than involvement with and responsibility for children after divorce, noncustodial fathers felt they "deserved" access, information, and decision-making authority equal to that of custodial mothers. A focus on legitimacy and authority works against fathers' involvement with their children. As Arendell (1992) concluded, uninvolved nonresidential fathers do not see fathering "as an array of activities, interactional processes, and particular kinds of social relations" (p. 582). Instead, they focus on fatherhood as a status concomitant with certain rights. In part, then, men's conceptualization of fatherhood forecasts their involvement with their children.

Fathers and Financial Support

Doherty et al.'s model and discussion of responsible fathering minimized children's dependence on fathers' financial resources. There is ample and compelling empirical support that the most important activity fathers can do for their children's well-being is to support them financially (e.g., Crockett, Eggebeen, & Hawkins, 1993; King, 1994; McLanahan & Sandefur, 1994). Regardless of family structure, fathers who provide economic resources improve their children's developmental outcomes (Acock & Demo, 1994). In our society, men have greater access to resources than women do, and men are defined, in part, through their ability to be good providers (Bernard, 1981). Doherty et al. pay insufficient attention to this aspect of father involvement.

We intend neither to reduce men to their ability to provide money, nor to minimize the role mothers increasingly play in generating income for family members. Instead, we take issue with Doherty et al.'s decision to ignore the social context in which men's participation as fathers is grounded. There is simply no getting around the fact that men's financial contributions matter for both residential and nonresidential children, and that currently, these contributions have a greater impact on children than any other aspect of fathers' involvement.

That the social context creates differing financial imperatives and opportunities for women and men also makes it problematic to compare nonresidential mothers to nonresidential fathers. Doherty et al. minimized problems with noncustodial fathers' financial support by comparing it to that of noncustodial mothers. The causes and consequences of noncustodial motherhood are not the same as those for noncustodial fatherhood (e.g., Arditti & Madden-Derdich, 1993; Cancun & Meyer, 1998). At a minimum, being a noncustodial mother is far more nonnormative than being a noncustodial father. Furthermore, the reasons for noncustodial mothers' noncompliance with child support have yet to be determined. One cannot conclude, as Doherty et al. did, that "there is something in the structure of nonresidential parenting, rather than in the culture of fatherhood, that is the principal inhibitor of economic support for children outside of marriage" (p. 282).

The authors attributed fathers' noncompliance, in part, to mothers' role in "misusing the funds and . . . withholding the children from the father" (Doherty et al., p. 282). What fathers describe as misusing funds, mothers describe as meeting children's needs. What fathers see as withholding children from them, mothers see as a strategy to gain fathers' compliance with child support orders. Stephens (1996) reported county data from Texas in which 14,000 complaints were registered for noncompliance compared with 700 complaints regarding visitation. Most noncustodial fathers were satisfied with the frequency and duration of their visits with children, and fathers' complaints were unrelated to compliance (Stephens). Again, Arendell's (1992, 1995) research is relevant here. Some noncustodial fathers view child support payments as a loss of control over their income rather than as a way to enhance and support their children. This is lamentable because the problems caused by noncompliance are significant, particularly given the effect of such support on children's well-being.

Marriage and Father Involvement

The authors identified marriage as the best context for involved fathers. To support their position, they noted the problems fathers have interacting with and relating to their children, highlighting these problems for never-married and divorced fathers and minimizing the same problems for married fathers. For example, they cited research by Zill, Morrison, and Coiro (1993) showing that 65% of children aged 18 to 22 whose parents divorced reported poor relationships with their fathers. This same study found that nearly 1 in 3 (29%) children in the same age group with *married* parents also reported poor relationships with their fathers. Although the proportion is higher for divorced fathers, the proportion in stable families is alarmingly high. In contrast, mothers' relationships with their children, both inside and outside of marriage, are generally positive (Aquilino, 1994; Rossi & Rossi, 1990; Silverstein & Bengtson, 1997).

Doherty et al. also overstated the role of marriage in father involvement in other ways. For example, they exaggerated fathers' involvement when wives are employed. They reported that fathers with employed wives perform a greater proportion of parenting activities than do fathers with nonemployed wives. They did not explain that the proportion is greater primarily because employed wives do less than nonemployed wives. They stated that "fathers are a significant source of primary care when mothers work" (p. 284). Careful attention to this literature demonstrates that fathers serve as primary care providers in response to their wives' paid work schedules (e.g., Brayfield, 1995; Presser, 1988). Care-giving fathers of younger children typically work for pay during daytime hours, and their wives typically work for pay during evening and nighttime hours. Most of the time during which fathers are responsible for young children is when their children are asleep. In contrast, fathers provide daytime, after-school care for older children who have less demanding needs for care.

By not attending to the context in which fathers are fully responsible for their children, Doherty and his colleagues risk exaggerating fathers' involvement, as well as fathers' interest in being involved. We agree that fathers are capable of caring involvement with their children. It is not necessary to exaggerate what fathers do to support this view. That some serve as primary child care givers provides hope that fathers indeed may be more involved in the future.

Doherty and his colleagues argued that "a caring, committed, collaborative marriage" (p. 290) fosters responsible fatherhood. Unstated is the fact that husbands' behavior is a major contributor to this type of marriage (e.g. Gottman, 1998). Husbands who are responsive to and appreciative of their wives and who facilitate their wives' sense of partnership and equality have better quality marriages (Hochschild, 1989; Schwartz, 1994; Thompson, 1991). Coltrane (1989) found that fathers who participate in child care from infancy also have more egalitarian partnerships with their wives. The connection between a collaborative marriage and an involved father may reflect something other than marital quality. The type of man who helps to develop a cooperative marriage may be the type of man who will be an involved father.

Collaborative marriages are not inevitable. Furthermore, prescribing marriage as a solution to the lack of father involvement is not without risk. Marriages characterized by conflict have a negative influence on children (e.g., Buehler et al., 1998; Gottman, 1998). An emphasis on marriage or other aspects of family structure absent of consideration of family process is misguided (e.g., Cooksey & Fondell, 1996; King, 1994; Miller, Forehand, & Kotchick, 1999). Indeed, Demo (1992) concluded that family structure has far less influence on child outcomes than is assumed. Data on fathering demonstrate that marriage is neither a sufficient nor a necessary context for responsible fathering. In considering her findings and those of others, King concluded that relationship quality, an important precursor to marital stability, is not changed easily by intervention or by social policy.

Toward the end of their article, Doherty et al. stated that "a high quality marriage is the optimal context for promoting responsible fatherhood" (p. 290), suggesting that "the promotion of these kinds of enduring marital partnerships may be the most important contribution to responsible fathering in our society." They were concerned that their conclusion would be "potentially controversial" because it is opposite of a "trend in contemporary family studies to disaggregate marriage and parenting" (p. 290). It is inappropriate and unfair to take practitioners of the discipline to task in this way. The disaggregation of marriage and parenting is not a trend in the study of families. It is, instead, a trend in the lived experience of individuals in the United States and in other industrialized nations that is well documented by researchers in the field (e.g., Adler, 1997).

Father Involvement

The literature in family science has attended increasingly to fathers, highlighting their importance to their children, and arguing that their contributions have been minimized. Although the authors reviewed a chapter by Pleck (1997) concluding that heterosexual, married, biological fathers are significantly more involved now than they were 20 years ago, empirical evidence suggests otherwise (e.g., Perkins & DeMeis, 1996; Press & Townsley, 1998; Sanchez & Thomson, 1997). In 1988, Ralph LaRossa highlighted the disjunction between the culture and the conduct of fatherhood. All evidence suggests that this disjunction continues to exist. Doherty et al. stated their intention to avoid between-gender comparisons but pointed out that fathers' involvement remains well below that of mothers. Our point is that fathers' involvement is well below that of the cultural standard for fathers.

Studies using nationally representative data sets show little change in residential and nonresidential father involvement over time, and no influence or weak influence on child outcomes when fathers are involved (e.g., Cooksey & Fondell, 1996; Harris, Furstenberg, & Mariner, 1998; Stephens, 1996). For example, despite public and scholarly discourse to the contrary, except during the 1990–1991 economic recession, there was virtually no change from the mid-1960s to 1993 in the proportion of preschoolers cared for by fathers when mothers are employed (Casper & O'Connell, 1998). King's (1994) research is illustrative of the literature on the involvement of nonresidential fathers. Using the National Longitudinal Survey of Youth, she reported "that there is only limited evidence to support the hypothesis that nonresident father involvement has positive benefits for children" (p. 970). Other researchers (Mott, Kowaleski-Jones, & Menaghan, 1997) have found no significant long-term effects of father absence on children's behavior. (See also Argys, Peters, Brooks-Gunn, & Smith, 1998.) This does not mean that all fathers are uninvolved with their children or that fathers who are highly involved have no influence. It does mean that, on average, the level of fathers' involvement continues to be minimal and that there is insufficient variance in father involvement for it to have strong and significant associations with child outcomes.

One consistent and key predictor of father involvement is education (e.g., Amato & Booth, 1997; Cooksey & Craig, 1998; Cooney, Pedersen, Indelicato, & Palkovitz, 1993; King, 1994; Stephens, 1996). Highly educated men appear to have adopted a cultural standard for fathers that is at odds with fatherhood as practiced by the vast majority of men, most of whom have far less education. Given that education is so important in predicting fathers' involvement, policies and programs should stress greater access to and support for education for all men so as to encourage responsible fatherhood.

Fatherhood, Motherhood, and Social Location

Doherty and his colleagues suggested that, in comparison with mothers, fathers suffer disproportionately from negative social forces, such as racism, that inhibit them from being involved with their children. Fathers of color do suffer from racism, but so do mothers and children (e.g., Hill Collins, 1992). Oppression based on social location is a system of interacting influences: racism, classism, sexism, heterosexism, and ageism. Some individuals are affected by more of these influences than are others.

Additionally, fathers have greater access to economic resources than mothers do, and this fact shapes both fathering and mothering (Gerson, 1993; LaRossa, 1988). There are fewer deterrents to fathers' than to mothers' participation in paid labor, a highly valued activity, and fathers have greater discretion than mothers to participate in child care, a less valued activity. Fathers lose status when they participate in labor defined as "women's work" (Gerson, 1993; Hochschild, 1989). Thus, not all fathers choose to be involved. For fathers to become more responsible for child care and more involved with their children would require a restructuring of paid and unpaid work. This restructuring would necessitate fathers giving up paternal privilege (Goode, 1982).

Who Is Responsible for Responsible Fathers?

We do not agree that Doherty et al.'s model is a contextual, social constructionist one. Any such model would attend to a number of features absent from their analysis. We note, for example, their failure to attend to a key feature of the needs of children: that they are socially constructed. Children's "needs" have evolved over time to shape and control the behaviors of mothers as much as they have been about promoting children's development (Ambert, 1994; Ehrenreich & English, 1978; Gerson, 1985). Fatherhood, motherhood, and childhood are *all* social constructions. A fully contextual model cannot ignore this key fact, nor the patriarchal context in which this social construction occurs.

Another context the authors ignored is the gendered nature of mothering and fathering in the United States. Their model disproportionately placed responsibility for fathers' involvement with their children on women. Instead of identifying things mothers can do to "move men in the direction of more responsible fathering" (p. 288)—activities destined to be described as nagging— we ask what responsibility *men* have for being responsible fathers?

We share the authors' inclusive and flexible definition of who can nurture, discipline, and provide for children. In an ideal world, parenting—the activities of nurturing, disciplining, and providing for children—would be work taken up by women *and* by men according to their individual proclivities and within a climate of economic justice and an ethic of care at all levels of society (Okin, 1989). We do not live in such a society, however. In our society, women and men do not have access to the same level of economic resources, nor are they held equally accountable for the undervalued activity of caring for dependent people. Any definition of responsible fathering must reflect the real world, even if it aims for a better world in the future.

References

Acock, A. C., & Demo, D. H. (1994). *Family diversity and well-being*. Newbury Park, CA: Sage.

Adler, M. A. (1997). Social change and declines in marriage and fertility in Eastern Germany. *Journal of Marriage and the Family, 59*, 37–49.

Allen, S. M., & Hawkins, A. J. (1999). Maternal gatekeeping: Mothers' beliefs and behaviors that inhibit greater father involvement in family work. *Journal of Marriage and the Family, 61*, 199–212.

Amato, P R., & Booth, A. (1997). *A generation at risk: Growing up in an era of family upheaval.* Cambridge, MA: Harvard University Press.

Ambert, A. (1994). An international perspective on parenting: Social change and social constructs. *Journal of Marriage and the Family, 56,* 529–543.

Aquilino, W S. (1994). Impact of childhood family disruption on young adults' relationships with parents. *Journal of Marriage and the Family, 56,* 295–313.

Arditti, J. A., & Madden-Derdich, D. A. (1993). Noncustodial mothers: Developing strategies of support. *Family Relations, 42,* 305–314.

Arendell, T (1992). After divorce: Investigations into father absence. *Gender & Society, 6,* 562–586.

Arendell, T (1995). *Fathers and divorce.* Thousand Oaks, CA: Sage.

Argys, L. M., Peters, H. E., Brooks-Gunn, J., & Smith, J. (1998). The impact of child support on cognitive outcomes of young children. *Demography, 35,* 159–173.

Bernard, J. (1981). The good provider role: Its rise and fall. *American Psychologist, 36,* 1–12.

Bertoia, C., & Drakich, J. (1993). The fathers' rights movement: Contradictions in rhetoric and practice. *Journal of Family Issues, 14,* 592–615.

Brayfield, A. (1995). Juggling jobs and kids: The impact of employment schedules on fathers' caring for children. *Journal of Marriage and the Family, 57,* 321–332.

Buehler, C., Krishnakumar, A., Stone, G., Anthony, C., Pemberton, S., Gerard, J., & Barber, B. K. (1998). Interparental conflict styles and youth problem behaviors: A two-sample replication study. *Journal of Marriage and the Family, 60,* 119–132.

Cancun, M., & Meyer, D. R. (1998). Who gets custody? *Demography, 35,* 147–157.

Caplan, P J., & Hall-McCorquodale, I. (1985). The scapegoating of mothers: A call for change. *American Journal of Orthopsychiatry, 55,* 610–613.

Casper, L. M., & O'Connell, M. (1998). Work, income, the economy, and married fathers as child-care providers. *Demography, 35,* 243–250.

Coltrane, S. (1989). Household labor and the routine production of gender. *Social Problems, 36,* 473–490.

Cooksey, E. C., & Fondell, M. M. (1996). Spending time with his kids: Effects of family structure on fathers' and children's lives. *Journal of Marriage and the Family, 58,* 693–707.

Cooksey, E. C., & Craig, P H. (1998). Parenting from a distance: The effects of paternal characteristics on contact between nonresidential fathers and their children. *Demography, 35,* 187–200.

Cooney, T M., Pedersen, E A., Indelicato, S., & Palkovitz, R. (1993). Timing of fatherhood: Is "on-time" optimal? *Journal of Marriage and the Family, 55,* 205–215.

Crockett, L. J., Eggebeen, D. J., & Hawkins, A. J. (1993). Father presence and young children's behavioral and cognitive adjustment. *Journal of Family Issues, 14,* 355–377.

Demo, D. H. (1992). Parent-child relations: Assessing recent changes. *Journal of Marriage and the Family, 54,* 104–117.

Doherty, W. J., Kouneski, E. E, & Erickson, M. F. (1998). Responsible fathering: An overview and conceptual framework. *Journal of Marriage and the Family, 60,* 277–292.

Downey, D. B., Ainsworth-Darnell, J. W., & Dufur, M. J. (1998). Sex of parent and children's well-being in single-parent households. *Journal of Marriage and the Family, 60,* 878–893.

Ehrenreich, B., & English, D. (1978). *For her own good: 50 years of the experts' advice to women.* Garden City, NY: Anchor Press.

Furstenberg, E E, Jr. (1999). Children and family change: Discourse between social scientists and the media. *Contemporary Sociology: A Journal of Reviews, 28,* 10–17.

Gerson, K. (1993). *No man's land: Men's changing commitments to family and work.* New York: Basic Books.

Gerson, K. (1985). *Hard choices: How women decide about work, career, and motherhood.* Berkeley, CA: University of California Press.

Goode, W. J. (1982). Why men resist. In B. Thorne & M. Yalom (Eds.), *Rethinking the family: Some feminist questions* (pp. 131–147). New York: Longman.

Gottman, J. M. (1998). Toward a process model of men in marriages and families. In A. Booth & A. C. Crouter (Eds.), *Men in families: When do they get involved? What difference does it make?* (pp. 149–192): Mahwah, NJ: Erlbaum.

Haavind, H. (1984). Love and power in marriage. In H. Holter (Ed.), *Patriarchy in a welfare state* (pp. 136–167). Oslo, Sweden: Universitetsforlaget.

Harris, K. M., Furstenberg, F. F., Jr., & Marmer, J. K. (1998). Paternal involvement with adolescents in intact families: The influence of fathers over the life course. *Demography, 35,* 201–216.

Hawkins, A. J., & Eggebeen, D. J. (1991). Are fathers fungible? Patterns of coresident adult men in maritally disrupted families and young children's well-being. *Journal of Marriage and the Family, 53,* 958–972.

Hill Collins, P. (1992). Black women and motherhood. In B. Thorne & M. Yalom (Eds.), *Rethinking the family: Some feminist questions* (2nd ed., pp. 215–245). Boston: Northeastern University Press.

Hochschild, A., with Machung, A. (1989). *The second shift: Working parents and the revolution at home.* New York: Viking.

King, V. (1994). Variation in the consequence of nonresident father involvement for children's well-being. *Journal of Marriage and the Family, 56,* 963–972.

LaRossa, R. (1988). Fatherhood and social change. *Family Relations, 37,* 451–457.

Marsiglio, A. (1991). Paternal engagement activities with minor children. *Journal of Marriage and the Family, 53,* 973–986.

McLanahan, S., & Sandefur, G. (1994). *Growing up with a single parent: What hurts, what helps.* Cambridge, MA: Harvard University Press.

Miller, K. S., Forehand, R., & Kotchick, B. A. (1999). Adolescent sexual behavior in two ethnic minority samples: The role of family variables. *Journal of Marriage and the Family, 61,* 85–98.

Mott, E. L., Kowaleski-Jones, L., & Menaghan, E. G. (1997). Paternal absence and child behavior: Does a child's gender make a difference? *Journal of Marriage and the Family, 59,* 103–118.

Okin, S. M. (1989). *Justice, gender, and the family.* New York: Basic Books.

Perkins, H. W., & DeMeis, D. K. (1996). Gender and family effects on the "second-shift" domestic activity of college-educated young adults. *Gender & Society, 10,* 78–93.

Pleck, J. H. (1985). *Working wives/working husbands.* Beverly Hills, CA: Sage.

Pleck, J. H. (1997). Paternal involvement: Levels, sources, and consequences. In M. E. Lamb (Ed.), *The role of the father in child development* (3rd ed., pp. 66–103). New York: Wiley.

Press, J. E., & Townsley, E. (1998). Wives' and husbands' housework reporting: Gender, class, and social desirability. *Gender and Society, 12,* 188–218.

Presser, H. B. (1988). Shift work and child care among young dual-earner American parents. *Journal of Marriage and the Family, 50,* 133–148.

Risman, B. J. (1987). Intimate relationships from a microstructural perspective: Men who mother. *Gender and Society, 1,* 6–32.

Rossi, A. S., & Rossi, P H. (1990). *Of human bonding: Parent-child relations across the life course.* New York: Aldine de Gruyter.

Sanchez, L., & Thompson, E. (1997). Becoming mothers and fathers: Parenthood, gender, and the division of labor. *Gender and Society, 11,* 747–772.

Schwartz, P. (1994). *Peer marriage: How love between equals really works.* New York: Free Press.

Silverstein, M., & Bengtson, V. L. (1997). Intergenerational solidarity and the structure of adult child-parent relationships in American families. *American Journal of Sociology, 103,* 429–460.

Stephens, L. S. (1996). Will Johnny see Daddy this week? An empirical test of three theoretical perspectives of postdivorce contact. *Journal of Family Issues, 17,* 466–494.

Thompson, L. (1991). Women's sense of fairness. *Journal of Family Issues, 12,* 181–196.

Vinick, B. H., & Lanspery, S. (1998, March). *Cinderella's sequel: Stepmothers' long-term relationships with adult stepchildren.* Paper presented at the annual meeting of the American Society on Aging, San Francisco.

Zill, N., Morrison, D. R., & Coiro, M. J. (1993). Long-term effects of parental divorce on parent-child relationships, adjustment, and achievement in young adulthood. *Journal of Family Psychology, 7,* 91–103.

POSTSCRIPT

Are Fathers Really Necessary?

What role does a father play in the development of a child? Is it the role of dad and what society says he "should" be that becomes important to the child rather than how he treats his child? Or, is it that is important? If the former is true, then anyone, regardless of how they treat the child, will be important to the child. We often see evidence of this phenomenon in dealing with abused children. No matter what the abuse, most children in this situation want to stay at home with abusive fathers rather than be placed in foster care. When confronted with "telling on" their fathers, children often will not say what abuse has occurred for fear of losing their father's love and being separated from them.

If the latter is true, the quality of interaction and events that children share with their fathers becomes key to their development. Then why couldn't women play that role? Women can interact with children in nearly all of the same ways that men can. Women can just as easily accompany children to baseball games, act as the soccer coach, or go to the school play as can men. Thus the question might not be "are fathers really necessary?" but might be "are men really necessary for the positive development of children?" To many, this would not only mean an assault on the role of fatherhood but also would constitute an attack on men in general.

As with most issues, extremes on either side make less sense than the middle ground. Child development experts would probably agree that the more adults, both male and female, involved in a child's life, the better. Having a variety of people in one's life brings a variety of experiences and an extensive social support network that can benefit children throughout their lives.

Significant research on fathering is becoming more prolific. Perhaps within the next few years scientists will be able to make more definitive statements with regard to the roles for both mother and father in a child's life. One could conclude that we are all responsible for fathering and mothering. This is especially true for families who do not have the choice of raising children in a two-parent system due to divorce or death of a spouse. We must continue to strive to find ways to support all families so that children will experience optimal need gratification as they grow and develop.

Suggested Readings

Amneus, D. (1995). The father's role in society; http://www.menweb
.org/throop/nofather/articles/amneus.html.

Coley, R. L. (1990). Children's socialization experiences and functioning in single-mother households: The importance of fathers and other men. *Child Development, 69,* 219–230.

Popenoe, D. (2000). Life without father; `http://www.themens-center.com`.

Sanchez, L., & Thompson, E. (1997). Becoming mothers and fathers: Parenthood, gender, and the division of labor. *Gender and Society, 11,* 747–772.

Stapleton, M. (2000). The unnecessary tragedy of fatherless children. *Policy and Practice of Public Human Services, 58,* 43–48.

Stephens, L. S. (1996). Will Johnny see Daddy this week? An empirical test of three theoretical perspectives of post-divorce contact. *Journal of Family Issues, 17,* 466–494.

ISSUE 7

Does Divorce Create Long-Term Negative Effects for Children?

YES: Karl Zinsmeister, from "Divorce's Toll on Children," *The American Enterprise* (May/June 1996)

NO: David Gately and Andrew I. Schwebel, from "Favorable Outcomes in Children After Parental Divorce," *Journal of Divorce and Remarriage* (vol. 18, nos. 3–4, 1992)

ISSUE SUMMARY

YES: Karl Zinsmeister, editor in chief of *The American Enterprise*, argues that divorce causes damage from which children never recover and that the conflict within a marriage will not cause the same amount of problems for children that the breakup of a marriage creates.

NO: Educators David Gately and Andrew I. Schwebel contend that children of divorce are not doomed to failure; they often display positive characteristics, such as enhanced levels of maturity, self-esteem, empathy, and adaptability.

According to some reports, children from divorced homes are more likely to become divorced themselves. Conversely, other studies indicate that the quality of the postdivorce home is more responsible for subsequent development in children than the divorce itself. Is society setting children up for failed marriages by condoning divorce? Or is divorce simply a way to solve the problem of choosing the wrong marriage partner, giving individuals and families a way to correct that mistake? Does the event of divorce spell disaster for children as they grow into adulthood, or are there other explanations for the problems that children from divorced homes exhibit?

The 1990s saw a movement to do away with no-fault divorce, which has spawned a renewed interest in divorce's effects on children. As the divorce debate evolved from the 1960s to the 1980s, many professionals began viewing divorce as an acceptable alternative to living in an unhappy home. Now family scientists, therapists, and researchers are questioning the belief that children can eventually adjust to the effects of divorce and that it is better for children to live in a divorced home than in an unhappy, intact home.

How does divorce affect children? Do children perceive it as positive or negative? How would their lives differ if their parents work out their problems and stay together? How do the children from divorced families compare with those who grow up in an unhappy, intact family? Do both groups have similar characteristics, or are they different? These are some of the questions related to the study of divorce's effects on children.

There are many studies of divorce's effects on children. Some of these studies show that children benefit from a family's divorce, whereas others show it as the worst thing that ever happens to children. On the positive side, children from divorced families can reap benefits as a consequence of their divorce experience, particularly if the parents model responsible coping skills. Some children do better in a home without the constant tension and fighting that an unhappy, intact home exhibits. These children appear more mature, are more realistic about life, and are more flexible.

On the other hand, problems for children in divorced families are well documented. These children are caught in a situation that they cannot control. Their parents split legally but not emotionally. Such families might ride an emotional roller coaster for years after the initial divorce decree. One parent pitted against the other with the children in the middle is not uncommon. This family turmoil may result in children doing poorly in school, beginning to have sex at an early age, and displaying delinquent behavior. Children are not consulted in the decision to divorce but must live through the instability and confusion that the breakup causes.

In the following selections, arguments are made about the negative and positive effects of divorce on children. Karl Zinsmeister uses studies of children and divorce to argue against the contention made by many parents that it is better to divorce than to rear children in a marriage with conflict. He maintains that children's sense of stability and family structure supersedes parental needs. David Gately and Andrew I. Schwebel analyze a different set of studies of divorce and children; their interpretations of the results and methods of those studies are quite different from those of Zinsmeister.

Karl Zinsmeister **YES**

Divorce's Toll on Children

Originally, notes family historian John Sommerville, marriage arose to create "security for the children to be expected from the union." Yet nowadays "the child's interest in the permanence of marriage is almost ignored." During the divorce boom that began in the mid-1960s, divorces affecting children went up even faster than divorces generally, and today *most* crack-ups involve kids. Since 1972, more than a million youngsters have been involved in a divorce *each year.*

The result is that at some time before reaching adulthood, around half of today's children will go through a marital rupture. Most of these youngsters will live in a single-parent home for at least five years. A small majority of those who experience a divorce eventually end up in a step-family, but well over a third of them will endure the extra trauma of seeing that second marriage break up.

The typical divorce brings what researcher Frank Furstenberg describes as "either a complete cessation of contact between the non-residential parent and child, or a relationship that is tantamount to a ritual form of parenthood." In nine cases out of ten the custodial parent is the mother, and fully half of all divorce-children living with their mom have had no contact with their father for at least a full year. Only one child in 10 sees his non-custodial parent as often as once a week. Overall, only about one youngster in five is able to maintain a close relationship with both parents.

Joint child custody receives a lot of publicity (it is now allowed in about half the states), but it remains unusual. In California, where it is much more common than anywhere else, only 18 percent of divorced couples have joint physical custody. Most divorced children still live solely with their mothers.

"For most men," sociologist Andrew Cherlin notes, "children and marriage are part of a package deal. Their ties to their children depend on their ties to their wives." Studies show that remarriage makes fathers particularly likely to reduce involvement with the children from their previous marriage.

Even when divorced parents do maintain regular contact with their children, truly cooperative child rearing is very rare. Most often, research shows, the estranged parents have no communication or mutual reinforcement. As a result, mother and father frequently undercut each other, intentionally or not, and parent-child relations are often unhealthy.

A series of interviews with children of divorce conducted by author/ photographer Jill Krementz illustrates this phenomenon. "My relationship with my parents has changed because now my mother does all the disciplining," says 14-year-old Meredith, "and sometimes she resents it—especially when we tell her how much fun we have with Dad. It's as if it's all fun and games with him because we're with him so little." Ari, also 14, confides, "I really look forward to the weekends because it's kind of like a break—it's like going to Disneyland because there's no set schedule, no 'Be home by 5:30' kind of stuff. It's open. It's free. And my father is always buying me presents." Zach, age 13, reports "whenever I want to see my other parent I can, and if I have a fight with one of them, instead of having to take off . . . I can just go eat at my Mom's house or my Dad's."

Other youngsters feel torn in two after a divorce, particularly in cases of joint custody where they must physically bounce back and forth between two houses. "It's hello, goodbye, hello, goodbye all the time," says one father. Gary Skoloff, chairman of the American Bar Association's family law section, explains that "joint custody was going to be a great panacea, the ultimate solution. . . . But it turned out to be the world's worst situation." The lack of a stable home has proved so harmful to children that several states, including California where the practice was pioneered, have recently revoked statutes favoring joint custody.

Fear and Loathing of Divorce Among the Young

Children's view of divorce is unambiguous: it's a disaster. In 1988, professor Jeanne Dise-Lewis surveyed almost 700 junior high school students, asking them to rate a number of life events in terms of stressfulness. The only thing students ranked as more stressful than parental divorce was death of a parent or close family member. Parental divorce received a higher rating than the death of a friend, being "physically hit" by a parent, feeling that no one liked them or being seriously injured.

The "fairy tale" believed by adults, says University of Michigan psychologist and divorce expert Neil Kalter, is that if they simply present new family setups to their children in a calm, firm way, the children will accept them. Actually, he says, that "is seen by the kids as a lot of baloney." Among the hundreds of children he's worked with in setting up coping-with-divorce programs for schools, "there are very few who have anything good to say about divorce." "Children are generally more traditional than adults," agrees Judith Wallerstein. "Children want both parents. They want family." If children had the vote, she says, there would be no such thing as divorce.

Indeed, Gallup youth surveys in the early 1990s show that three out of four teenagers age 13 to 17 think "it is too easy for people in this country to get divorced." Go into a typical high school today and ask some students what their most important wish for the future is and a surprising number will answer "that there wouldn't be so many divorces." Young Arizonan Cynthia Coan has lots of company when she says, "as a child of divorce, I cannot help but hope that the next generation of children will be spared what mine went through."

You'll sometimes hear the claim that divorce doesn't hurt children as much as conflict in a marriage. This is not supported by the evidence. "For kids," reports Kalter, "the misery in an unhappy marriage is usually less significant than the changes" after a divorce. "They'd rather their parents keep fighting and not get divorced." Even five years later, few of the youngsters in Wallerstein's study agreed with their parents' decision to separate. Only ten percent were more content after the split than before.

Contrary to popular perceptions, the alternative to most divorces is not life in a war zone. Though more than 50 percent of all marriages currently end in divorce, experts tell us that only about 15 percent of all unions involve high levels of conflict. In the vast number of divorces, then, there is no gross strife or violence that could warp a youngster's childhood. The majority of marital break-ups are driven by a quest for greener grass—and in these cases the children will almost always be worse off.

Many mothers and fathers badly underestimate how damaging household dissolution will be to their children. A 1985 British study that quizzed both parents and children found that the children reported being far more seriously upset by their parents' separation than the parents assumed. Despite the common perception that the best thing parents can do for their children is to make themselves happy, the truth is that children have their own needs that exist quite apart from those of their parents. One may argue that a parent should be allowed to rank his own needs above those of his children (though this is not the traditional understanding of how families should work). But one ought not cloak that decision with the false justification that one is thereby serving the children's best interests.

Wade Horn, former commissioner of the U.S. Administration for Children, Youth, and Families, illustrates how parents can be deluded in this way:

> Families used to come to me when I was practicing psychology, seeking advice about how to divorce. They would say, "We want a divorce because we really don't get along very well any more, and we understand that our child will be better off after we divorce than if we stay together." Rarely, if ever, did I hear a family say, "We're having conflict, but we have decided to work as hard as we can at solving our problems because we know that children of divorce are more disturbed than children of intact families."

A major reason parents are making this mistake is because that is what some authorities and many ideologues in the cause of family "liberation" have been telling them. "For years experts said, 'Once the initial trauma wears off, kids make adjustments,'" complains psychologist John Guidubaldi, past president of the National Association of School Psychologists. While it's true that kids make adjustments, Guidubaldi notes in the *Washington Post*, "so do people in prisons and mental institutions. The pertinent question is: Are those adjustments healthy? And the weight of the evidence has become overwhelming on the side that they aren't."

Short- and Long-Term Effects of Divorce on Children

The longer-term effects of divorce on children are something we've learned a lot about over the last decade. Guidubaldi, who orchestrated one of the large studies documenting these effects, concludes from his work that "the old argument of staying together for the sake of the kids is still the best argument. . . . People simply aren't putting enough effort into saving their marriages." Family scholar Nicholas Zill points out that "if you looked at the kind of long-term risk factors that divorce creates for kids and translated them to, say, heart disease, people would be startled."

In the early months after divorce, young children are often less imaginative and more repetitive. Many become passive watchers. They tend to be more dependent, demanding, unaffectionate, and disobedient than their counterparts from intact families. They are more afraid of abandonment, loss of love, and bodily harm. A significant number—in some studies a quarter—say they blame themselves for their parents' smash-up.

A small study conducted some years ago by University of Hawaii psychiatrist John McDermott sorted pre-schoolers who had been involved in a divorce a few months earlier into three categories. Three out of 16 children were judged to have weathered the initial storm essentially unchanged. Two of 16 became what he called "severely disorganized" and developed gross behavior problems. The rest, more than two-thirds, he categorized as "the sad, angry children." They displayed resentment, depression, and grief, were restless, noisy, possessive and physically aggressive.

In Judith Wallerstein's landmark study, almost half of the pre-schoolers still displayed heightened anxiety and aggression a full year after their parents' divorce. Forty-four percent "were found to be in significantly deteriorated psychological condition." All of the two- and three-year-olds showed acute regression in toilet training. They displayed unusual hunger for attention from strangers. Older pre-schoolers had become more whiny, irritable, and aggressive, and had problems with play.

Wallerstein's study also returned to its subjects five and 10 years later, and the collected results were quite staggering. In overview they look like this: initially, two-thirds of all the children showed symptoms of stress, and half thought their life had been destroyed by the divorce. Five years down the road, over a third were still seriously disturbed (even more disturbed than they had been initially, in fact), and another third were having psychological difficulties. A surprisingly large number remained angry at their parents.

After a decade, 45 percent of the children were doing well, 14 percent were succeeding in some areas but failing in others, and 41 percent were still doing quite poorly. This last group "were entering adulthood as worried, underachieving, self-deprecating, and sometimes angry young men and women." In addition to their emotional problems and depression, many felt sorrow over their childhoods and fear about their own marriage and child-rearing prospects. About a third of the group had little or no ambition at the 10-year mark. Many expressed a sense of powerlessness, neediness, and vulnerability. Most of the ones who had reached adult age regarded their parents' divorce as a continuing major influence in their lives.

It should be noted that the 131 children in the study experienced divorce in what Wallerstein and associates call the "best of circumstances." Most of their parents were college educated, and at the beginning these children were achievers in school. None of the participants was initially being treated for psychiatric disorder. Most of the families were white and middle class; half regularly attended church or synagogue.

Even in families with all these advantages, divorce wreaks havoc among the young. Summarizing her findings on the offspring of broken marriages, Wallerstein has written that "it would be hard to find any other group of children—except, perhaps, the victims of a natural disaster—who suffered such a rate of sudden serious psychological problems." Other long-term studies teach similar conclusions. "Divorce," says psychiatrist McDermott, "is now the single largest cause of childhood depression." Marital disruption, quite clearly, can wound children for years.

A Catalogue of Behavioral Changes

Let's look more specifically at some of the changes in behavior that affect children of divorce. John Guidubaldi and Joseph Perry found in their survey of 700 youngsters that children of divorced parents performed worse than children of intact families on 9 of 30 mental health measures, showing, among other things, more withdrawal, dependency, inattention, and unhappiness, plus less work effort. Divorced students were more likely to abuse drugs, to commit violent acts, to take their own life, and to bear children out of wedlock.

A University of Pittsburgh study in the late 1980s found that there were 30 percent more duodenal ulcers and 70 percent more suicide attempts—both symptoms of serious psychological stress—among children who had lost a parent. In Wallerstein's middle-class sample, one-third of the girls with divorced parents became pregnant out of wedlock, and 8 percent had at least two abortions. Two-thirds of the girls had a history of delinquency, and almost 30 percent of the boys had been arrested more than once.

The National Survey of Children showed that more than 30 percent of the individuals whose parents separated or divorced before they were eight years old had received therapy by the time they were teenagers. Divorce-children are two to four times as numerous in psychiatric care populations as they are in society at large. In fact, more than 80 percent of the adolescents in mental hospitals, and 60 percent of the children in psychiatric clinics, have been through a divorce. And what is being treated in most cases is much more than just a short-term reaction: the average treatment takes place five years after their parents' marital breakup. At the fully adult age of 23, middle-class women whose mother and father had divorced were three times likelier to have a psychological problem than counterparts from intact families, according to a massive multi-year British study.

Schooling is another problem area. Children exposed to divorce are twice as likely to repeat a grade, and five times likelier to be expelled or suspended.

(Fully 15 percent of all teenagers living with divorced mothers have been booted from school at least temporarily, according to the National Survey of Children.) Even in Wallerstein's middle-class sample, 13 percent of the youngsters had dropped out of school altogether. Barely half of Wallerstein's subjects went on to college, far less than the 85 percent average for students in their high schools. Wallerstein concludes that 60 percent of the divorce-children in her study will fail to match the educational achievements of their fathers.

Children of divorce also frequently have problems with sexual identity. In most studies, boys seem to be harder hit than girls. Pre-school boys tend to be unpopular with male peers, to have difficulty gaining access to play groups, to spend more time with younger compatriots and females, and to engage in more activities traditionally considered to be feminine. Young boys tend to be more vehemently opposed to the divorce, to long more for their father, to feel rejected by him, and to feel uncertain about their masculinity. They are more likely than girls to become depressed and angry. Many later have problems developing intimacy, and build lifestyles of solitary interests and habits.

For girls there is a "sleeper effect"—beginning at adolescence, seemingly well-adjusted individuals often develop serious problems with sexuality, self-control, and intimacy. Kalter found higher rates of substance abuse, running away, and sexual activity among girls who had been through divorce, particularly when the father had departed early on. Wallerstein found that a "significant minority" of girls expressed insecurity, anger, or lack of self-respect in promiscuity, some gravitating to older men or a series of aimless sexual relationships. "I'm prepared for anything. I don't expect a lot," said one 20-year-old. "Love is a strange idea to me. Life is a chess game. I've always been a pawn."

Mavis Hetherington of the University of Virginia has found that girls have special problems when their divorced mothers remarry. She has also shown that the pattern of low self-respect and sexual precocity among girls with a divorced mother does *not* hold true among girls living with a solo mother due to death of the father—apparently it is active alienation from the father, more than his simple absence, that causes the disturbance. This fits well with psychologist Erik Erikson's view that it is less deprivation *per se* that is psychologically destructive than deprivation without redeeming significance.

Wallerstein points out that teenage girls often view their absent fathers with a combination of idealization and distrust.

> The idealized father that the young adolescent girl imagines is the exact opposite of the image that later becomes prominent in her mind as she grows older—namely, the father as betrayer. . . . Because daughters of divorce often have a hard time finding out what their fathers are really like, they often experience great difficulty in establishing a realistic view of men in general, in developing realistic expectations, and in exercising good judgment in their choice of partner.

Researcher Conrad Schwarz has hypothesized that children who are allied only with their same-sex parent (as a girl growing up with a divorced mother would be) tend to hold a chauvinistic and alienated view of the opposite sex. Conversely, he suggests, children growing up with only opposite-sex parents (like boys living with divorced mothers) tend to have problems with gender identity and self-esteem. One study that fits this hypothesis found that college-age women who had experienced divorce in childhood were more prone to see men as unfeeling and weak than counterparts from intact families.

Female children of divorced parents are more likely to choose "inadequate husbands" and to have marital problems of their own. They are substantially likelier to have extensive premarital sexual experience and twice as likely to cohabit before marriage. They are more frequently pregnant at their weddings.

And both male and female children of divorce see their own marriages dissolve at significantly higher rates than counterparts who grew up in intact families. Partly this is attitudinal: One eight-year study of 1,300 men and women found that people who had watched their own parents divorce were much more tolerant of the idea of divorce, and that this tolerance translated into increased marital breakup.

The other thing that childhood divorce encourages, of course, is the avoidance of marriage. "My mom got remarried and divorced again, so I've gone through two divorces so far. And my father's also gotten remarried—to someone I don't get along with all that well. It's all made me feel that people shouldn't get married," 14-year-old Ari explained to Jill Krementz.

Divorces involving children thus set a whole train of losses into motion, transporting unhappy effects not only over the years but even across generations. And not even children fortunate enough to live in stable homes are wholly insulated from the turmoil. As writer Susan Cohen observes:

> Although I am not divorced and live in a conventional nuclear family with a husband and two children . . . divorce has been part of my daughter Sarah's life since she was two or three. Divorce is in her books, on her television programs, in her lessons at school, in her conversations with her friends, and in her questions to me.

Indeed, divorce is in the very air our children breathe—with lasting significance for their later views of love, families, and life.

NO

**David Gately and
Andrew I. Schwebel**

Favorable Outcomes in Children After Parental Divorce

SUMMARY. The present paper is based on a review of the literature that considers the short- and long-term effects parental divorce has on children. Most studies in this literature have identified unfavorable outcomes that develop in many areas of children's lives as they struggle to cope with their changed family situations. However, as children adjust to the challenges they face before, during, and after parental divorce, neutral and favorable outcomes are also possible in one or more areas of their lives. In fact, the literature review indicated that many investigators have identified certain strengths in children who had experienced parental divorce. In particular they have observed that following the divorce of their parents some children, in comparison to peers or their own pre-divorce development, have shown enhanced levels of functioning in four areas: maturity, self-esteem, empathy, and androgyny.

Over ten million divorces were granted in the United States during the 1980s (U.S. Bureau of the Census, 1990). The great number of people affected by divorce in the second half of the 20th century stimulated scholarly interest in this area. One topic that received considerable attention is the effects of parental divorce on children, a group affected at a rate of about one million per year since the mid 1970s (U.S. Bureau of Census, 1990).

Findings consistently show that children experience distress during the process of parental separation and divorce and that it is associated with a variety of short- and long-term negative outcomes (see reviews by Anthony, 1974; Fry & Addington, 1985; Kelly, 1988; Kurdek, 1981; Long & Forehand, 1987; Lopez, 1987; Santrock, 1987). Wallerstein and Blackeslee (1989) stated, "Almost all children of divorce regard their childhood and adolescence as having taken place in the shadow of divorce. . . . Almost half of the children entered adulthood as worried, underachieving, self-deprecating, and sometimes angry young men and women" (pp. 298–299).

In fact, studies indicate that children may experience difficulties in interpersonal relationships, school behavior, academic achievement, self-esteem, in future life outlook, etc. Besides delineating the wide range of unfavorable outcomes that

From David Gately and Andrew I. Schwebel, "Favorable Outcomes in Children After Parental Divorce," *Journal of Divorce and Remarriage,* vol. 18, nos. 3–4 (1992), pp. 57–63, 66–78. Copyright © 1992 by The Haworth Press, Inc. Reprinted by permission.

can develop in children before, during, and after the divorce, the literature also identifies factors that can moderate and exacerbate the problems children face.

Although much of the literature discusses children's struggle to cope with parental divorce and the unfavorable outcomes they may experience in one or more aspects of their lives, some children in adjusting to their changed circumstances before, during, and after parental divorce may also become strengthened in one or more areas. These individuals develop competencies or grow psychologically because of what they learn while undertaking the divorce-related challenges they face and/or because of the changes they experience in self-view as a result of successfully meeting the challenges.

Decades ago Bernstein and Robey (1962) suggested that successful coping with the demands presented by parental divorce can spur emotional and personality growth in children. Since then a number of investigators have found these favorable outcomes in youngsters relative either to their pre-divorce status or to matched peers from intact family backgrounds. (These include: Grossman, Shea, & Adams, 1980; Hetherington, 1989; Kelly & Wallerstein, 1976; Kurdek & Siesky, 1979, 1980a, 1980b, 1980c; MacKinnon, Stoneman & Brody, 1984; Reinhard, 1977; Richmond-Abbott, 1984; Rosen, 1977; Santrock & Warshak, 1979; Slater, Stewart, & Linn, 1983; Springer & Wallerstein, 1983; Wallerstein, 1984, 1985a, 1987; Wallerstein & Kelly, 1974, 1976, 1980b; Warshak & Santrock, 1983; Weiss, 1979.)

The present paper is based on a comprehensive review of the literature that investigated post-divorce outcomes in children. The review included literature generated from computer searches of the Psychological Abstracts and Family Resources and Educational Resources Information Center data bases. Manual searches of the Psychological Abstracts, The Inventory of Marriage and Family Literature, and the Social Sciences Index bases were conducted to supplement the computer searches. Finally, empirical and theoretical contributions published in books, chapters, and Dissertation Abstracts were reviewed. Following a brief assessment of this body of literature, the present paper focuses on those studies that reported favorable outcomes in children following parental divorce.

Most of the earliest investigations used a pathogenic model that viewed the divorced family as a deviation from the traditional 2-parent family, and attempted to link this "inferior" family structure to negative effects on children's adjustment and psychosocial development (Levitin, 1979). The picture of the effects of parental divorce on children were further colored in a negative way because these projects typically employed clinical samples and studied the crisis period immediately following divorce (Bernstein & Robey, 1962; Kalter, 1977; McDermott, 1968; Westman, 1972).

Later studies employing non-clinical samples showed that, although divorce is associated with an initial crisis reaction in most children, long-term consequences are variable (Hetherington, Cox, & Cox, 1982; Hetherington, 1989). While longitudinal studies demonstrated that parental divorce may have long-term negative effects on the social, emotional, and cognitive functioning of children (Guidubaldi & Cleminshaw, 1985; Hetherington, Cox, & Cox, 1985), they also showed that children may escape long-term negative outcomes if the crisis of divorce is not compounded by multiple stressors and continued adversity (Hetherington, 1979, 1989; Hetherington et al., 1982, 1985).

The finding that divorce does not necessarily result in long-term dysfunction led to a search for individual, family, and environmental factors that moderate children's adjustment. Researchers found the quality of adjustment related to: the child's gender and age at the time of separation/divorce (Guidubaldi & Perry, 1985; Hetherington et al., 1982, 1985; Kalter & Rembar, 1981; Wallerstein & Kelly, 1980a); the child's temperament, locus of control, interpersonal knowledge, and level of coping resources (Ankerbrandt, 1986; Hetherington, 1989; Kurdek & Berg, 1983; Kurdek, Blisk, & Siesky, 1981; Kurdek & Siesky, 1980a); the amount of interparental conflict prior to, during, and following separation/divorce (Emery, 1982; Hetherington et al., 1982; Jacobson, 1978; Wallerstein & Kelly, 1980b); the quality of parent-child relationships (Hess & Camara, 1979; Hetherington, Cox, & Cox, 1982; Wallerstein & Kelly, 1980a); the parents' mental and physical health (Guidubaldi & Cleminshaw, 1985; Guidubaldi & Perry, 1985); the type of custody arrangement (Ambert, 1984; Lowery & Settle, 1985; Santrock & Warshak, 1979; Santrock, Warshak, & Elliot, 1982; Warshak & Santrock, 1983; Wolchik, Braver, & Sandler, 1985); parental remarriage (Clingempeel & Segal, 1986; Hetherington et al., 1982; Santrock, Warshak, Lindbergh & Meadows, 1982); the number of major life changes experienced following divorce (Hetherington et al., 1985; Stolberg, Camplair, Currier, & Wells, 1987), including the amount of financial decline experienced by the post-divorce family (Desimone-Luis, O'Mahoney, & Hunt, 1979); and the social support available to both the parents and children (Isaacs & Leon, 1986).

Drawing upon the concept of stress, Wallerstein (1983a) and Peterson, Leigh, & Day (1984) developed models that could account for the absence of negative outcomes in children. For example, Wallerstein conceived of divorce as an acute social stressor that had consequences and made unique demands on children (differing from those associated with stressors like the death of a parent). Although families experiencing divorce and the loss of a parent pass through similar transitional stages (Schwebel, Fine, Moreland, & Prindle, 1988), studies comparing the short- and long-term effects on children of separation/divorce and death of a parent support Wallerstein's contention (Boyd & Parish, 1983; Felner, Stolberg, & Cowen, 1975; Hetherington, 1972; Mueller & Cooper, 1986; Rozendal, 1983).

Wallerstein (1983a, 1983b) described the sequence of adjustments a child must make: (1) acknowledge the marital disruption, (2) regain a sense of direction and freedom to pursue customary activities, (3) deal with loss and feelings of rejection, (4) forgive the parents, (5) accept the permanence of divorce and relinquish longings for the restoration of the pre-divorce family, and (6) come to feel comfortable and confident in relationships. The successful completion of these tasks, which allows the child to stay on course developmentally, depends on the child's coping resources and the degree of support available to help in dealing with the stressors. Of course, the divorce process also may include pre-separation distress, family conflict, and compromised parenting which both place children at risk and call for them to make adjustments well before the time when the legal divorce is granted (Block, Block, & Gjerde, 1986).

Reports describing protective factors that could mitigate negative outcomes for children following parental divorce complemented findings being described in stress research. More specifically, several authors (Garmezy, 1981; Rutter, 1987; Werner, 1989; Werner & Smith, 1982) found that some children, although exposed to multiple stressors that put them at risk, did not experience negative outcomes. Protective factors diminished the impact of these stressors. Although these investigators studied different stressors, their findings were remarkably similar and suggested that the factors which produce "resilience" in children-at-risk fit into three categories: (1) positive personality dispositions (e.g., active, affectionate, socially responsive, autonomous, flexible, intelligent; possessing self-esteem, an internal locus of control, self-control, and a positive mood); (2) a supportive family environment that encourages coping efforts; and (3) a supportive social environment that reinforces coping efforts and provides positive role models (Garmezy, 1981).

These protective factors reduce the likelihood of negative outcomes by means such as: decreasing exposure to or involvement with risk factors; opening of opportunities for successful task accomplishment and growth; and promoting self-esteem and self-efficacy through secure, supportive personal relationships (Rutter, 1987). Besides helping children avoid short-term harm, these resiliency-building factors strengthen children so they will cope more effectively with and master the stressful life events they will encounter in the future. This "steeling" effect is a favorable outcome that develops after an exposure to stressors of a type and degree that is manageable in the context of the child's capacities and social situation (Rutter, 1987).

The number of studies that identify favorable outcomes of any type of children following parental divorce is small in contrast to the number of studies that have reported unfavorable outcomes. To state the obvious, this difference in the volume of research reports primarily reflects the reality of what children face before, during, and after their parents' divorce. However, a small yet significant part of the difference may be due to the way science has addressed the question of children's outcomes. Specifically, the content of the literature has certainly been shaped, in part, by the fact that neither the pathological nor the stress models heuristically guide researchers to search for favorable outcomes (Kanoy & Cunningham, 1984; McKenry & Price, 1984, 1988; Scanzoni, Polonko, Teachman, & Thompson, 1988) and the fact that the research methods which have been typically employed are more likely to detect negative consequences than positive ones (Blechman, 1982; Kanoy & Cunningham, 1984). For instance, the wide use of measures that identify weaknesses (Blechman, 1982; Kanoy & Cunningham, 1984) and of subjects drawn from clinical samples, who are more maladjusted than their peers (Isaacs, Leon, & Donohue, 1987), makes the likelihood of detecting favorable outcomes unlikely (Kanoy & Cunningham, 1984).

A similar issue is presented by the tendency among researchers to neglect children as a source of data while, at the same time electing to use informants (e.g., parents, teachers, clinicians) aware of children's family status (Kanoy &

Cunningham, 1984). Although parents' ratings of their elementary school children's adjustment is not related to the children's assessment of the emotional support they are receiving, the children's self-ratings of their adjustment are significant (Cowen, Pedro-Carroll & Alpert-Gillis, 1990). Teachers hold more negative expectations for children from divorced families than for their counterparts from intact families (Ball, Newman, & Scheuren, 1984) while parents and clinicians, in contrast to the children, tend to overestimate the negative effects of the divorce (Forehand, Brody, Long, Slotkin, & Fauber, 1986; Wolchik, Sandler, Braver, & Fogas, 1985). In fact, correlations between children's ratings of their own post-divorce adjustment and their parent's ratings are typically low (Kurdek & Siesky, 1980b), a finding consistent with correlations found between children's self-ratings and the ratings of adult informants in other areas of the literature (Achenbach, McConaughy, & Howell, 1987). . . .

The review of . . . the divorce-adjustment literature suggested four areas, in particular, in which children may experience favorable outcomes following their parents' divorce: in maturity, self-esteem, empathy, and androgyny. Each is discussed below.

Maturity

Intact families have an "echelon structure" in which parents form the executive unit. In the single-parent home this structure is replaced by a parent-child partnership that encourages children to assume more self and family responsibility and to participate more fully in important family decisions (Weiss, 1979). Such involvement fosters maturity which is evidenced by increased levels of responsibility, independence, and awareness of adult values and concerns.

Studies employing nonclinical samples have supported Weiss's conclusions. Kurdek and Siesky (1980a) reported that about 80% of the 132 5–19 year-old children they sampled (four years post-separation) believed they had assumed increased responsibilities after the divorce and learned to rely on themselves more. Their parents agreed, with about 75% of the 74 parents sampled rating their children as more mature and independent (Kurdek & Siesky, 1980b). Similar findings were reported by Rosen (1977), who assessed children 6–10 years after parental divorce, and by Reinhard (1977), who surveyed 46 adolescents three years post-divorce.

Children from single-parent families spend more time working in the home and taking care of siblings (Amato, 1987; Bohannon & Erikson, 1978; Hetherington, 1989; Zakariya, 1982). These chores can foster maturity in children, if they are age-appropriate and if the children receive adequate support. The maturity may exhibit itself in the form of an increased level of independence, realism, or identity development (Grossman et al., 1980). Single-parents further foster maturity when they (1) involve children in appropriate decision making and in a healthy range of other responsibilities in the post-divorce family (Bohannon & Erickson, 1978; Devall, Stoneman, & Brody, 1986; Hetherington, 1989; Kurdek & Siesky, 1979, 1980a; Reinhard, 1977; Wallerstein, 1985a; Weiss, 1979; Zakariya, 1982), and (2) allow children appropriate access to feelings that they, the adult caretakers, have as vulnerable individuals who may not always be able to meet the children's needs (Springer & Wallerstein, 1983; Wallerstein & Kelly, 1974).

Finally, a distinction is needed between pseudomaturity, a precocious adoption of adult roles and responsibilities, and maturity, an adaptive development that helps individuals cope more effectively. Pseudomaturity is seen in females from divorced families who display flirtatious and attention-seeking behavior with male interviewers (Hetherington, 1972), who engage in earlier and more frequent sexual activity (Boss, 1987; Hetherington, 1972; Kinnaird & Gerard, 1986) and who possess a greater likelihood of premarital pregnancy (Boss, 1987) than counterparts from intact families. Pseudomaturity is also found in both males and females from divorced families who engage in earlier and more frequent dating activity (Booth, Brinkerhoff, & White, 1984; Hetherington, 1972) and marry earlier (Boss, 1987; Glenn & Kramer, 1987) than peers from intact families.

Self-Esteem

Children may experience increased self-esteem in the aftermath of parental divorce because they cope effectively with changed circumstances, are asked to assume new responsibilities, successfully perform new duties, and so forth. Santrock and Warshak (1979) studied 6–11 year-old children, three years after their parents' divorce, and matched youngsters from intact, mother-custody and father-custody families. Father-custody boys demonstrated higher levels of self-esteem and lower levels of anxiety than intact family boys, while the opposite was true for girls. Slater et al. (1983) studied matched adolescents and found that boys from divorced family backgrounds possessed significantly higher levels of self-esteem than boys from intact and girls from both intact and divorced family backgrounds. Girls from divorced family backgrounds had lower levels of self-esteem than their counterparts from intact families. These results are consistent with Wallerstein and Kelly's (1980a).

One circumstance that appears to foster boys' increased self-esteem in post-divorce families is that they may be more heavily relied upon by custodial parents (most of whom are women) than girls, and as a result may gain a new position of increased responsibility and status. A study of children raised during the Great Depression indicated that older children were strengthened by assuming domestic responsibilities and part-time work (Elder, 1974).

Besides developing as a result of an individual's accomplishments, feelings of self-efficacy may also evolve from vicarious experience, verbal persuasion, and a reduction in the level of fear associated with performing particular behaviors (Bandura, Adams, & Beyer, 1977). Concretely, this suggests that divorcing parents benefit their children by modeling adaptive coping behavior (Kaslow & Hyatt, 1982) and by persuading children to be less fearful and to cope more effectively. Children are most likely to develop hardiness in facing post-divorce challenges if the demands upon them are moderate, if their parents support their efforts to perform new responsibilities, and if family members hold a positive view of divorce-related changes (Maddi & Kobasa, 1984).

Empathy

Some children in divorced and single-parent families show increased concern for the welfare of family members (Kurdek & Siesky, 1980b; Reinhard, 1977; Weiss, 1979). For example, Hetherington (1989) found older girls in divorced families, in contrast to peers, are more often involved in supportive and nurturing teaching, play, and caretaking activities with younger sisters and tend to help and share more frequently. Likewise, about 25% of Rosen's (1977) South African children sample reported they had gained a greater understanding of human emotions as a result of their parent's divorce 6 to 10 years earlier.

Although Wallerstein (1985b) suggested that children's increase in empathy does not extend beyond the parent-child relationship, Hetherington (1989) believes the increased empathy and sensitivity may reflect a more general orientation. The conditions prevalent during children's adjustment may determine the extent to which empathy develops and generalizes. If children are encouraged to provide age-appropriate emotional and practical support to family members, they may be able to extend themselves, gaining an understanding of others' feelings and, in this way, practice and refine their role- and perspective-taking skills. Hetherington and Parke (1979) suggested that more advanced role-taking skills are related to increased altruism, prosocial behavior, communication skills, moral standards, and empathetic understanding.

Androgyny

Necessity, encouragement from others, and the observation of models are among the factors that can lead children to shift away from stereotypical sex-role thinking and behavior and toward androgyny. This shift, in turn, can result in increased cognitive and behavioral flexibility (Bem, 1975; Bem & Lenney, 1976; Bem, Martyna, & Watson, 1976).

MacKinnon et al. (1984) investigated the effects of marital status and maternal employment on sex-role orientations in matched groups of mothers and children between 3 and 6 years old. While employment influenced mother's sex-role views, divorce appeared related to children's sex-role views. These authors suggested that the more androgynous sex-role views of the children in the post-divorce homes may stem from the mothers modeling more generalized sex-role behavior, or from the children assuming more nontraditional responsibilities.

Kurdek & Siesky (1980c) investigated the sex-role self-concepts of divorced single parents and their 10 to 19 year-old children, approximately four years post-separation. They found that custodial and noncustodial parents and their children possessed higher levels of self-reported androgyny, when compared to published norms, and that the boys and girls possessed more androgynous sex-role self-concepts than a comparison group of children from intact family backgrounds.

Richmond-Abbott (1984) found that the sex-role attitudes of children, ages 8 to 14, tended to reflect the liberal ones of their divorced, single-parent mothers. However, although the mothers stated that they wanted their children to behave in nontraditional ways, children were encouraged to pursue and tended to prefer sex-stereotyped chores and activities. This fits with the failure of others to find an effect of divorce on preadolescent female's sex-role orientation (Kalter, Riemer, Brickman, & Chen, 1985; Hetherington, 1972). Another finding, that the girls in the sample did foresee themselves engaging in nontraditional behaviors and occupations in the future, supports a conclusion that clear post-divorce increases in androgynous attitudes and behaviors may not emerge until children cope with adolescent identity issues.

Stevenson and Black (1988) conducted a meta-analysis of 67 studies that compared the sex-role development of children in father-present and father-absent homes. The applicability of their findings to the present issue is limited, however, by the fact that father absence because of divorce was not treated separately from father absence because of death or other reasons. Nonetheless, some conclusions they drew fit well with points made above. Specifically, father-absent female adolescents and young adults were slightly but consistently less feminine than their father-present peers in measures of traditionally feminine characteristics such as nurturance and expressiveness. Similarly, father-absent preschool boys, compared to their father-present peers, made fewer stereotypically sex-typed choices in picking toys and activities. However, older father-absent boys were more stereotypical than their father-present peers in their overt behavior, particularly in the expression of aggression. This latter difference could be reflecting the fact that in a mother-headed household an older boy may be asked to assume "man-of-the-house" duties.

In conclusion, the literature suggests that increased androgyny in children may develop following divorce if parents model nontraditional attitudes and behaviors or if children, by necessity and/or with parental encouragement, engage in nontraditional activities following divorce. While children in adolescence may struggle with androgynous thoughts, feelings, and behaviors, by their late teens and early twenties many will have worked through the issues. For example, two studies used by Stevenson and Black (1988) showed that college men who had experienced father absence reported fewer stereotypical vocational preferences. Finally, methodology has affected findings: While data collected from parents and teachers suggest that father-absent boys' behavior is more stereotypical than father-present boys', self-report measures indicate the opposite. In this connection, teachers' assessments have differed depending on whether they thought they were rating a child from a divorced or an intact home (Ball et al., 1984; Santrock & Tracy, 1978).

Research and Treatment Implications

Research is needed to identify a full list of favorable outcomes that can emerge following children's adjustment to parental divorce. Longitudinal studies would be desirable, especially those using matched comparison groups of intact family children while controlling for possible confounding variables, including parental conflict and family SES.

Hurley, Vincent, Ingram, and Riley (1984) categorize interventions designed to cope with unfavorable consequences in children following parental divorce as either therapeutic or preventative. The therapeutic approaches, which include psychodynamic and family systems interventions, focus on treating psychopathology, while the preventative approaches help healthy children avoid significant dysfunction by coping effectively with the normal post-divorce crisis reaction. Preventative interventions take the form of school-based support groups for children (Cantor, 1977; Gwynn & Brantley, 1987; Moore & Sumner, 1985; Pedro-Carroll & Cowen, 1985) or school and community-based support groups for parents (Davidoff & Schiller, 1983; Omizo & Omizo, 1987) and families (Magid, 1977; Stolberg & Cullen, 1983). Outcome studies show that parents, children, and group leaders believe support groups decrease distress and dysfunction in children (Cantor, 1977; Freeman, 1984; Gwynn & Brantly, 1987; Magid, 1977; Omizo & Omizo, 1987; Pedro-Carroll & Cowen, 1985). At this point, mental health workers could draw from the literature and design a third type of intervention: ones aimed at promoting favorable outcomes in children who must adjust to their parents' divorce.

References

Achenbach, T. M., McConaughy, S. H., & Howell, C. T. (1987). Child/adolescent behavioral and emotional problems: Implications of cross-informant correlations for situational specificity. *Psychological Bulletin, 101,* 213–232.

Amato, P. R. (1987). Family processes in one-parent, stepparent, and intact families: The child's point of view. *Journal of Marriage and the Family, 49,* 327–337.

Ambert, A. M. (1984). Longitudinal changes in children's behavior toward custodial parents. *Journal of Marriage and the Family,* (May), 463–467.

Ankenbrandt, M. J. (1986). Learned resourcefulness and other cognitive variables related to divorce adjustment in children. *Dissertation Abstracts International, 47* B, DA8628750, 5045.

Anthony, E. J. (1974). Children at risk from divorce: A review. In E. J. Anthony & C. Koupernik (Eds.), *The child in his family: Children at psychiatric risk* (Vol. 3), 461–478. N.Y.: John Wiley & Sons.

Ball, D. W., Newman, J. M., Scheuren, W. J. (1984). Teachers' generalized expectations of children of divorce. *Psychological Reports, 54,* 347–352.

Bandura, A., Adams, N. E., & Beyer, J. (1977). Cognitive processes mediating behavioral changes. *Journal of Personality and Social Psychology, 35,* 125–139.

Bem, S. L. (1975). Sex-role adaptability: One consequence of psychological androgyny. *Journal of Personality and Social Psychology, 31,* 634–643.

Bem, S. L. & Lenney, E. (1976). Sex typing and the avoidance of cross-sex behavior. *Journal of Personality and Social Psychology, 33,* 48–54.

Bem, S. L., Martyna, W., & Watson, C. (1976). Sex typing and androgyny: Further explorations of the expressive domain. *Journal of Personality and Social Psychology, 34,* 1016–1023.

Bernstein, N. & Robey, J. (1962). The detection and management of pediatric difficulties created by divorce. *Pediatrics, 16,* 950–956.

Blechman, E. A. (1982). Are children with one parent at psychiatric risk? A methodological review. *Journal of Marriage and the Family, 44,* 179–195.

Block, J. H., Block, J., & Gjerde, P. F. (1986). The personality of children prior to divorce: A prospective study. *Child Development, 57,* 827–840.

Bohannon, P. & Erickson, R. (1978, Jan.) Stepping in. *Psychology Today, 11,* 53–59.

Booth, A., Brinkerhoff, D. B., White, L. K. (1984). The impact of parental divorce on courtship. *Journal of Marriage and the Family, 46,* 85–94.

Boss, E. R. (1987). The demographic characteristics of children of divorce. *Dissertation Abstracts International, 48 1026A, DA8714900.*

Boyd, D. A. & Parish, T. (1983). An investigation of father loss and college students' androgyny scores. *The Journal of Genetic Psychology, 145,* 279–280.

Cantor, D. W. (1977). School based groups for children of divorce. *Journal of Divorce, 1,* 183–187.

Clingempeel, W. G. & Segal, S. (1986). Stepparent-stepchild relationships and the psychological adjustment of children in stepmother and stepfather families. *Child Development, 57,* 474–484.

Cowen, E., Pedro-Carroll, J., & Alpert-Gillis, L. (1990). Relationships between support and adjustment among children of divorce. *Journal of Child Psychology and Psychiatry, 31,* 727–735.

Davidoff, I. F. & Schiller, M. S. (1983). The divorce workshop as crisis intervention: A practical model. *Journal of Divorce, 6,* 25–35.

Desimone-Luis, J., O'Mahoney, K., & Hunt, D. (1979). Children of separation and divorce: Factors influencing adjustment. *Journal of Divorce, 3,* 37–41.

Devall, E., Stoneman, Z., & Brody, G. (1986). The impact of divorce and maternal employment on pre-adolescent children. *Family Relations, 35,* 153–159.

Elder, G. H. (1974). *Children of the great depression.* Chicago: University of Chicago Press.

Emery, R. E. (1982). Interparental conflict and the children of discord and divorce. *Psychological Bulletin, 92,* 310–330.

Felner, R. D., Stolberg, A., & Cowen, E. L. (1975). Crisis events and school mental health referral patterns of young children. *Journal of Consulting and Clinical Psychology, 3,* 305–310.

Forehand, R., Brody, G., Long, N., Slotkin, J., & Fauber, R. (1986). Divorce/divorce potential and interparental conflict: The relationship to early adolescent social and cognitive functioning. *Journal of Adolescent Research, 1,* 389–397.

Freeman, R. (1984). Children in families experiencing separation and divorce: An investigation of the effects of brief intervention. Family Service Association of Metropolitan Toronto (Ontario).

Fry, P. S. & Addington, J. (1985). Perceptions of parent and child adjustment in divorced families. *Clinical Psychology Review, 5,* 141–157.

Garmezy, N. (1981). Children under stress: Perspective on antecedents and correlates of vulnerability and resistance to psychopathology. In A. I. Rabin, J. Arnoff, A. N. Barclay, & R. A. Zucker (Eds.), *Further explorations in personality* (pp. 196–269). N.Y.: Wiley.

Glenn, N. D. & Kramer, K. B. (1987). The marriage and divorce of children of divorce. *Journal of Marriage and the Family, 49,* 811–825.

Grossman, S. M., Shea, J. A., & Adams, G. R. (1980). Effects of parental divorce during early childhood on the ego development and identity formation of college students. *Journal of Divorce, 3,* 263–271.

Guidubaldi, J. & Cleminshaw, H. (1985). Divorce, family health, and child adjustment. *Family Relations, 34,* 35–41.

Guidubaldi, J. & Perry, J. D. (1985). Divorce and mental health sequelae for children: A two-year follow-up of a nationwide sample. *Journal of American Academy of Child Psychiatry, 24* (5), 531–537.

Gwynn, C. A. & Brantley, H. T. (1987). Effects of a divorce group intervention for elementary school children. *Psychology in the Schools, 24,* 161–164.

Hess, R. D. & Camara, K. A. (1979). Post-divorce family relationships as mediating factors in the consequences of divorce for children. *Journal of Social Issues, 35*(4), 79–95.

Hetherington, E. M. (1972). Effects of father absence on personality development in adolescent daughters. *Developmental Psychology, 7,* 313–326.

Hetherington, E. M. (1979). Divorce: A child's perspective. *American Psychologist, 34,* 851–858.

Hetherington, E. M. (1989). Coping with family transitions: Winners, losers, and survivors. *Child Development, 60,* 1–14.

Hetherington, E. M., Cox, M., & Cox, R. (1982). Effects of divorce on parents and children. In M. Lamb (Ed.), *Nontraditional families: Parenting and child development* (233–288). Hillsdale, N.J.: Erlbaum.

Hetherington, E. M., Cox, M., & Cox, R. (1985). The long-term effects of divorce and remarriage on the adjustment of children. *Journal of the American Academy of Child Psychiatry, 24*(5), 518–530.

Hetherington, E. M. & Parke, R. D. (1979). *Child psychology: A contemporary viewpoint.* New York: McGraw-Hill Inc.

Hurley, E. C., Vincent, L. T., Ingram, T. L., & Riley, M. T. (1984). Therapeutic interventions for children of divorce. *Family Therapy, 9,* 261–268.

Isaacs, M. B. & Leon, G. (1986). Social networks, divorce, and adjustment: A tale of three generations. *Journal of Divorce, 9,* 1–16.

Isaacs, M. B., Leon, G., & Donohue, A. M. (1987). Who are the "normal" children of divorce? On the need to specify population. *Journal of Divorce, 10,* 107–119.

Jacobson, D. S. (1978). The impact of marital separation/divorce on children: II. Interparental hostility and child adjustment. *Journal of Divorce 2*(1), 3–19.

Kalter, N. (1977). Children of divorce in an outpatient psychiatric population. *American Journal of Orthopsychiatry, 47,* 40–51.

Kalter, N. & Rembar, J. (1981). The significance of a child's age at the time of divorce. *American Journal of Orthopsychiatry, 51,* 85–100.

Kalter, N., Riemer, B., Brickman, A., & Chen, J. W. (1985). Implications of parental divorce for female development. *Journal of the American Academy of Child Psychiatry, 24,* 538–544.

Kanoy, K. W. & Cunningham, J. L. (1984). Consensus or confusion in research on children and divorce: Conceptual and methodological issues. *Journal of Divorce, 74,* 45–71.

Kaslow, F. & Hyatt, R. (1982). Divorce: A potential growth experience for the extended family. *Journal of Divorce, 6,* 115–126.

Kelly, J. B. (1988). Longer-term adjustment in children of divorce: Converging findings and implications for practice. *Journal of Family Psychology, 2,* 119–140.

Kelly, J. B. & Wallerstein, J. S. (1976). The effects of parental divorce: Experiences of the child in early latency. *American Journal of Orthopsychiatry, 46,* 20–32.

Kinnaird, K. L. & Gerrard, M. (1986). Premarital sexual behavior and attitudes toward marriage and divorce among young women as a function of their mothers' marital status. *Journal of Marriage and the Family, 48,* 757–765.

Kurdek, L. A. (1981). An integrative perspective on children's divorce adjustment. *American Psychologist, 36,* 856–866.

Kurdek, L. A. & Berg, B. (1983). Correlates of children's adjustment to their parents' divorce. In L. A. Kurdek (Ed.). *Children and Divorce* (pp. 47–60). San Francisco: Jossey-Bass Inc., Publishers.

Kurdek, L. A., Blisk, D., & Siesky, A. E. (1981). Correlates of children's long-term adjustment to their parents' divorce. *Developmental Psychology, 17,* 565–579.

Kurdek, L. A. & Sieksy, A. E. (1979). An interview study of parents' perceptions of their children's reactions and adjustment to divorce. *Journal of Divorce, 3,* 5–17.

Kurdek, L. A. & Siesky, A. E. (1980a). Children's perceptions of their parents' divorce. *Journal of Divorce, 3,* 339–379.

Kurdek, L. A. & Siesky, A. E. (1980b). Effects of divorce on children: The relationship between parent and child perspectives. *Journal of Divorce, 4,* 85–99.

Kurdek, L. A. & Siesky, A. E. (1980c). Sex-role self-concepts of single divorced parents and their children. *Journal of Divorce, 3,* 249–261.

Levitin, T. E. (1979). Children of divorce. *Journal of Social Issues, 35,* 1–25.

Long, N. & Forehand, R. (1987). The effects of parental divorce and parental conflict on children: An overview. *Developmental and Behavioral Pediatrics, 8,* 292–296.

Lopez, F. G. (1987). The impact of parental divorce on college student development. *Journal of Counseling and Development, 65,* 484–486.

Lowery, C. R. & Settle, S. A. (1985). Effects of divorce on children: Differential impact of custody and visitation patterns. *Family Relations, 34,* 455–463.

MacKinnon, C. E., Stoneman, Z., & Brody, G. H. (1984). The impact of maternal employment and family form on children's sex-role stereotypes and mothers' traditional attitudes. *Journal of Divorce, 8,* 51–60.

Maddi, S. R. & Kobasa, S. C. (1984). *The hardy executive: Health under stress.* Chicago: Dorsey Professional Books.

Magid, K. M. (1977). Children facing divorce: A treatment program. *Personnel and Guidance Journal, 55,* 534–536.

McDermott, J. F. (1968). Parental divorce in early childhood. *American Journal of Psychiatry, 124,* 1424–1432.

McKenry, P. C. & Price, S. J. (1984). The present state of family relations research. *Home Economics Journal, 12,* 381–402.

McKenry, P. C. & Price, S. J. (1988). Research bias in family science: Sentiment over reason. *Family Science Review, 1,* 224–233.

Moore, N. E. & Sumner, M. G. (1985). *Support group for children of divorce: A family life enrichment group model.* Paper presented at Annual Meeting of the National Association of Social Workers, New Orleans.

Mueller, D. & Cooper, P. W. (1986). Children of single parent families: How they fare as young adults. *Family Relations, 35,* 169–176.

Omizo, M. M. & Omizo, S. A. (1987). Effects of parents' divorce group participation on child-rearing attitudes and children's self-concepts. *Journal of Humanistic Education and Development, 25,* 171–179.

Pedro-Carroll, J. L. & Cowen, E. L. (1985). The children of divorce intervention program: An investigation of the efficacy of a school based prevention program. *Journal of Consulting and Clinical Psychology, 53,* 603–611.

Peterson, G., Leigh, G. K., & Day, R. D. (1984). Family stress theory and the impact of divorce on children. *Journal of Divorce, 7,* 1–20.

Reinhard, D. (1977). The reaction of adolescent boys and girls to the divorce of their parents. *Journal of Clinical Child Psychology, 6,* 21–23.

Richmond-Abbott, M. (1984). Sex-role attitudes of mothers and children in divorced, single-parent families. *Journal of Divorce, 8,* 61.

Rosen, R. (1977). Children of divorce: What they feel about access and other aspects of the divorce experience. *Journal of Clinical Child Psychology, 6,* 24–27.

Rozendal, F. G. (1983). Halos vs. stigmas: Long-term effects of parent's death or divorce on college students' concepts of the family. *Adolescence, 18,* 948–955.

Rutter, M. (1987). Psychosocial resilience and protective mechanisms. *American Journal of Orthopsychiatry, 57,* 316–331.

Santrock, J. W. (1987). The effects of divorce on adolescence: Needed research perspectives. *Family Therapy, 14,* 147–159.

Santrock, J. W. & Tracy, R. L. (1978). Effects of children's family structure status on the development of stereotypes by teachers. *Journal of Educational Psychology, 70,* 754–757.

Santrock, J. W. & Warshak, R. A. (1979). Father custody and social development in boys and girls. *Journal of Social Issues, 35,* 112–125.

Santrock, J. W., Warshak, R. A., & Elliot, G. L. (1982). Social development and parent child interactions in father-custody and stepmother families. In M. Lamb (Ed.), *Nontraditional families: Parenting and child development.* Hillsdale, N.J.: Erlbaum, 289–314.

Santrock, J. W., Warshak, R. A., Lindbergh, C., & Meadows, L. (1982). Children's and parents' observed social behavior in stepfather families. *Child Development, 53,* 472–480.

Scanzoni, J., Polonko, K., Teachman, J. T., & Thompson, L. (1988). *The sexual bond: Rethinking families and close relationships.* Newbury Park, CA: Sage Publications Inc.

Schwebel, A. I., Fine, M., Moreland, J. R., & Prindle, P. (1988). Clinical work with divorced and widowed fathers: The adjusting family model. In P. Bronstein & C. Cowen (Eds.), *Fatherhood today: Men's changing role in the family.* New York: Wiley, 299–319.

Slater, E. J., Stewart, K., & Linn, M. (1983). The effects of family disruption on adolescent males and females. *Adolescence, 18,* 933.

Springer, C. & Wallerstein, J. S. (1983). Young adolescents' responses to their parents' divorce. In L. A. Kurdek (Ed.), *Children and divorce.* San Francisco: Jossey-Bass, 15–27.

Stevenson, M. R. & Black, K. N. (1988). Paternal absence and sex-role development: A meta-analysis. *Child Development, 59,* 795–814.

Stolberg, A., Camplair, C., Currier, K., & Wells, M. (1987). Individual, familial, and environmental determinants of children's post-divorce adjustment and maladjustment. *Journal of Divorce, 11,* 51–70.

Stolberg, A. L. & Cullen, P. M. (1983). Preventive interventions for families of divorce: The divorce adjustment project. *New Directions for Child Development, 19,* 71–81.

U.S. Bureau of the Census (1990). *Statistical abstract of the U.S.: 1990.* Washington, D.C.

Wallerstein, J. (1983a). Children of divorce: Stress and developmental tasks. In N. Garmezy and M. Rutter (Eds.), *Stress, coping, and development.* New York: McGraw-Hill Inc., 265–302.

Wallerstein, J. (1983b). Children of divorce: The psychological tasks of the child. *American Journal of Orthopsychiatry, 53,* 230–243.

Wallerstein, J. (1984). Children of divorce: Preliminary report of a ten-year follow-up of young children. *American Journal of Orthopsychiatry, 54(3),* 444–458.

Wallerstein, J. (1985a). Children of divorce: Preliminary report of a ten-year follow-up of older children and adolescents. *Journal of American Academy of Child Psychiatry, 24(5),* 545–553.

Wallerstein, J. (1985b). The overburdened child: Some long-term consequences of divorce. *Social Work, 30(2),* 116–123.

Wallerstein, J. (1987). Children of divorce: Report of a ten-year follow-up of early latency-age children. *American Journal of Orthopsychiatry, 57,* 199–211.

Wallerstein, J. & Blackeslee, S. (1989). *Second chances.* New York: Ticknor & Fields.

Wallerstein, J. & Kelly, J. (1974). The effects of divorce: The adolescent experience. In J. Anthony & C. Koupernik (Eds.), *The child in his family: Children at psychiatric risk* (Vol. 3). N.Y.: Wiley.

Wallerstein, J. & Kelly, J. (1976). The effects of divorce: Experiences of the child in later latency. *American Journal of Orthopsychiatry, 46(2),* 256–269.

Wallerstein, J. & Kelly, J. (1980a). *Surviving the Breakup.* New York: Basic Books Inc.

Wallerstein, J. & Kelly, J. (1980b, Jan.) California's children of divorce. *Psychology Today,* 67–76.

Warshak, R. & Santrock, J. W. (1983). The impact of divorce in father-custody and mother-custody homes: The child's perspective. In L. Kurdek (Ed.), *Children and divorce,* San Francisco: Jossey-Bass Inc., Publishers, 29–45.

Weiss, R. (1979). Growing up a little faster: The experience of growing up in a single-parent household. *Journal of Social Issues, 35(4),* 97–111.

Werner, E. E. (1989). High-risk children in young adulthood: A longitudinal study from birth to 32 years. *American Journal of Orthopsychiatry, 59,* 72–81.

Werner, E. E. & Smith, B. S. (1982). *Vulnerable but invincible: A study of resilient children.* New York: McGraw-Hill Inc.

Westman, J. C. (1972). Effect of divorce on child's personality development. *Medical Aspects of Human Sexuality, 6,* 38–55.

Wolchik, S. & A., Braver, S., & Sandler, I. (1985). Maternal versus joint custody: Children's postseparation experiences and adjustment. *Journal of Clinical Child Psychology, 14,* 5–10.

Wolchik, S. A., Sandler, I., Braver, S., & Fogas, B. (1985). Events of parental divorce: Stressfulness ratings by children, parents, and clinicians. *American Journal of Community Psychology, 14,* 59–74.

Zakariya, S. B. (1982, Sept.). Another look at the children of divorce: Summary report of school needs of one-parent children. *Principal, 62,* 34–38.

POSTSCRIPT

Does Divorce Create Long-Term Negative Effects for Children?

Zinsmeister proposes that parents stay together for the sake of the children. According to some studies, children rate divorce second only to the death of a parent as the most stressful event in their lives, and most of them end up not having a close relationship with one of their parents.

Although the number of studies that show negative divorce effects outweighs the number of studies with positive results, Gately and Schwebel use them to illustrate children's resilience. These children developed traits such as a positive personality, self-control, self-reliance, and empathy for others, probably as a result of the divorce.

Is it divorce that creates problems for children, or is it the poverty, family disorganization, and unmet needs accompanying most divorces that cause long-term problems? A common complaint of children of divorce is that there is no adult in whom they can confide.

Suggested Readings

Amato, P. R. (1994, Spring). Life span adjustment of children to their parents' divorce. *The future of children* (143–164). Los Altos, CA: Center for the Future of Children.

Cherlin, A. (1993, Winter). Nostalgia as family policy (emotional and economic effects of divorce on children). *The Public Interest, 110,* 77–85.

Ehrenreich, B. (1996, April 8). In defense of splitting up. *Time, 147,* 80.

Gill, R. (1992, Spring). For the sake of the children (effects of divorce on children). *The Public Interest, 108,* 81–97.

Jones, S. (1993, May). The two-parent heresy (divorce and single parent families can adversely affect children). *Christianity Today, 37,* 20–22.

Lehrman, K. (1993, May). Growing up with divorce. *Vogue, 193,* 182–186.

Robinson, K. (1994, May/June). Which side are you on? *Networker, 18,* 19–23, 26–30.

Roe, C. (1994, Summer). The pros and cons of divorce. *Single Parent, 37,* 26–28.

ISSUE 8

Is Television Violence Viewing Harmful for Children?

YES: Merrilyn O. Johnson, from "Television Violence and Its Effect on Children," *Journal of Pediatric Nursing* (April 1996)

NO: Jib Fowles, from "The Whipping Boy: The Hidden Conflicts Underlying the Campaign Against Violent TV," *Reason* (March 2001)

ISSUE SUMMARY

YES: Merrilyn O. Johnson, MSN, RN, is from the nursing Ph.D. collaborative program at the Medical University of South Carolina and the University of South Carolina, Columbia. She argues that the negative impact of television viewing is so great that it should be included in health professionals' assessments of children and families.

NO: Jib Fowles, a professor of communication at the University of Houston, asserts that although television violence has increased steadily, the violent crime rate has in fact decreased.

The debate over television violence rages on. When asked about violence in contemporary society, many people would respond, "Violence is at epidemic proportions. There is a lot more violence out on the streets now than when I was a kid. It's just not safe to be out anymore. We live in such violent times." There are seemingly endless anecdotes and lots of remorse about more peaceful times. The unison in which society decries the rise in violence begins to disintegrate, however, when one attempts to discern causes for the increases in crimes like murder, rape, robbery, and assault.

One segment of society that is regularly targeted as a contributing cause to the rise in violence is the media, particularly television programming. A common argument is that television is much too violent, especially in children's programming. It has been suggested, for example, that a child will witness in excess of 100,000 acts of simulated violence depicted on television before graduating from elementary school! Children in a lower socioeconomic class may view even more hours of television. Many researchers suggest that this television violence is at least in part responsible for the climbing rates of violent crime, since children tend to imitate what they observe in life.

173

On the other side, critics argue that it is not what is on television that bears responsibility for the surge in violence. They believe that programming is merely reflective of the level of violence in contemporary society. The argument is that while television watching may be associated with violence, that does not mean that it causes violence. As an example, the critics suggest that we have known for some time that aggressive children tend to watch more aggressive television programming. However, does the aggression predispose an interest in aggressive programming, or does the programming cause the aggression? This is a question that sparks hotly contested debates.

Those who believe television viewing is at least partly responsible for aggressive behavior in children want the United States Congress to more closely regulate the ratings, viewing times, and amount of violence that can be shown on American television. Those on the other side of the issue point to the infringement on First Amendment rights of freedom of expression should such intense regulation be imposed on the media.

The following selections are typical of the debate centered around how violence and television affects children. Merrilyn O. Johnson cites studies to support her claim that children watch too much violent TV, to the extent that their health and well-being are negatively affected. Jib Fowles believes that television is used as a "whipping boy," blamed for the ills of society, including the perceived rise in violent acts. Although there are no champions that rise to television's defense, Fowles contends that the attack on television as the source of societal violence is a big lie and is used to cover up society's real problems.

YES

Merrilyn O. Johnson

Television Violence and Its Effect on Children

*For **some** children under **some** conditions **some** television is harmful.*

*For **other** children under **other** conditions it may be beneficial.*

*For **most** children under **most** conditions **most** TV is probably neither particularly harmful nor particularly beneficial.*

—Schramm, Lyle, and Parker (1961)

Although written 33 years ago, the above quote on television (TV) viewing and children is as relevant today as it was then. Does watching violence on TV increase or alter the antisocial or aggressive activity of children? The possibility that widespread watching of violent TV programs by children and youth is increasing the level of violence in American society continues to be the most controversial and emotionally arousing issue related to the TV medium. This is because the concentration of violence portrayed on TV has the potential of generating aggressive behavior, both immediately and in the long term (Joy, Kimball, & Zabrack, 1986, cited in Williams, 1986). *Aggression* in this instance refers to physical aggression with the potential to injure as well as verbal abuse, including threats.

TV may affect its viewers in two possible ways: by displacing other activities and through its content (Williams, 1986). American TV contains the most violence of TV in any Western country (Dietz & Strasburger, 1991). Violent content has not changed appreciably in the past decade despite increasing public awareness and concern. Unfortunately cartoon shows and prime-time programming glorify the use of guns and violence as acceptable, justifiable solutions to complex problems (Dietz & Strasburger, 1991).

Ninety-nine percent of American households contain at least one TV, with two thirds containing two or more sets (A. C. Nielson Company, 1988). Children and adolescents comprise between 10% and 20% of the prime-time viewing audience, and they spend more time watching TV (15,000 h) than they do in school (11,000 h). During this time they witness 180,000 murders, rapes, armed robberies, and assaults.

From Merrilyn O. Johnson, "Television Violence and Its Effect on Children," *Journal of Pediatric Nursing*, vol. 11, no. 2 (April 1996). Copyright © 1996 by Elsevier Health Sciences. Reprinted by permission. References omitted.

175

In 1989, the average child in the United States spent more time watching TV than performing any other activity except sleeping. The Nielson Report on Television (1989) commented that children age 2 to 5 years viewed approximately 27 hours of TV/wk, children age 6 to 11 years viewed more than 23 hours of TV/wk, and adolescents age 12 to 17 years viewed 22 hours of TV/wk. By the time today's children reach 70 years of age, they will have spent 7 years of their lives watching TV (Dietz & Strasburger, 1991). TV therefore represents an influential force in the lives of children and adolescents.

Many variables are involved in the relationship between viewing violence on TV and actual aggressive behavior. Significant developmental and gender variables, family background and attitudes, the viewing context, and the quality and nature of the child's other experiences, as well as his or her perception of TV portrayal, are all important factors that influence TV's impact. Other factors that affect the likelihood of an individual actually performing an aggressive act are characteristics of the viewer, state of arousal, whether the behavior is reinforced, nature of the TV stimuli, and the environment, including the perceived similarity between the observed environment and the viewer's actual environment (Comstock, 1976).

Background Literature

Parents and social critics express concern regarding the possible negative effects that TV viewing has on children. TV influences children, but in what ways and to what extent is the subject of much debate. The research in this area has focused on the relationship between viewing violence on TV and subsequent aggressive behavior. Numerous researchers have examined media violence in many countries using different methods, providing a degree of consistency of results. A small but genuine association appears to exist between media violence and aggression (Heath, Bresolin, & Rinaldi, 1989).

Children are great imitators. Infants as young as 14 months have shown significant and deferred imitation of televised models (Meltzoff, 1988). Bandura postulated that children can learn aggressive behavior from watching characters on TV. His social learning theory suggests that humans learn ways of behaving, as well as appropriateness and effects of behavior, directly from observing real life as well as indirectly through the mass media. Bandura's contention is that the most effective way to teach children desired behavior is to demonstrate the behavior and have the children model it. Thus, in his classic 1963 "Bobo doll" experiments (Bandura, Ross, & Ross, 1963), young children were exposed to televised films in which an adult behaved aggressively toward inflated dolls (Bobo dolls). Children who had viewed this film played more aggressively with a Bobo doll than did children who had not seen the adult model.

The conclusions of the Bobo doll experiment were further validated by Steur, Applefield, and Smith (1971) who found that nursery school children who watched violent TV programs during their breaks displayed more aggression on the playground than children who viewed nonviolent programs. College students also showed more aggressive behavior when exposed to a segment of violent film as opposed to not viewing a film or viewing a neutral film (Berkowitz & Rawlings, 1963). These experiments support the notion that a relationship indeed exists between viewing aggressive behavior and acting aggressively, particularly if the TV aggressor is rewarded for the act.

However, some research reviewers have drawn different conclusions from early research findings, suggesting that no significant effect was found between violence on TV and aggression (Hearold, 1986). Feshbach & Singer (1971) even suggest that exposure to aggressive TV content reduces aggressive behavior in some types of children. Commenting on this latter study, Singer (1989) pointed out that the study was marred by procedural flaws that biased and invalidated the findings. Cook, Kendzienski, and Thomas (1983) argue that there is less consistency of results regarding TV violence and aggression than claimed and that biases may have inflated past estimates. They contend that TV's role is probably small compared with other socialization factors.

Several studies have produced evidence that the introduction of TV increases the level of aggression in the community. Centerwall (1992) compared homicide rates in the United States, Canada, and South Africa and was able to show that homicide rates increased predictably after the introduction of TV to a community. This effect was maximal 10 to 15 years later. Earlier studies in Canadian towns with varying exposure to TV showed that a cohort of first- and second-grade students had an increased rate of aggression in the 2 years after introduction of TV compared with two control groups (Joy, Kimball, & Zabrack, 1986). Singer, Singer, and Rapaczynski (1984) studied elementary school children for 5 years and found on parent report that TV viewing was a major predictor of physical aggression.

A longer-term study shows even more disturbing information. Findings of a study of 875 boys from a semirural US community followed up for 22 years strongly indicated that violence viewing at age 8 years significantly predicted a link between exposure to TV violence at age 8 and antisocial behavior 22 years later (Huesmann, Eron, Lefkowitz, & Walder, 1984).

Reviewing the literature in 1989, Heath, Bresolin, and Rinaldi examined studies for behavioral and attitudinal effects of media violence. They looked at laboratory and field research and concluded that the relationship between exposure to media violence and aggressive behavior appeared to be fairly consistent across studies, but methodological weaknesses introduced bias in favor of this conclusion. The researchers emphasized the importance of the "perceived reality of the message" and discussed the lack of realistic consequences for violence shown on TV. They commented on the difference in viewer response where there was a match between personal experience and the media depiction of violence, as this may reinforce violent behavior patterns. They reviewed intervention programs and found that efforts at training parents and children had not been helpful.

This article provoked a letter from Gadow and Sprafkin (1990) who believed that the correlation between aggression in the media and viewer aggressive behavior had little support. Earlier, Gadow and Sprafkin (1989) had examined 20 field experiments to determine the short-term effects on children's behavior of viewing aggression-laden TV shows. Careful analysis, taking full account of design patterns of these studies, showed that more antisocial behavior occurred after viewing aggressive content on TV. However, there was a significant increase in antisocial behavior after viewing low-aggression or nonaggressive TV as well. They discussed this as a nonspecific arousal response to the medium, concluding that watching wholesome TV may not ameliorate conduct problems. The researchers commented that "television's ability to produce increased levels of social activity (both appropriate and negative) is controversial" (p. 404).

Comstock and Strasburger (1990) recommend further research of the scripting of TV programs and of interventions that may assist children in coping with them. In closing they say that

> competition among media ensures that the amount of violence in television, as well as in films, will not be lower in the future. In fact, it may become even greater in graphicness and ferocity. Intervention and remedy therefore, fall to parents, the school, and the community" (p. 42).

In the 4 years since this article was written, we indeed have seen an increase in the phenomena of violence such as Schwarzenegger's "Terminator" movies, "Power Rangers," and the "Ninja Turtles" movies and TV shows. Testimony to Senate hearings in 1993 indicates that many members of the public have concerns about the increasing violence depicted on TV. (Testimony of Judith Myers-Walls and Ken Auletta, 1993). The community has responded by requiring warnings before violent programs on TV; however, at present no data are available to show any effect of these warnings.

The recent growth of cable TV and video movie rentals has increased the number of potential sources of positive and negative programming that may be viewed by children. Competition for a share of the audience appears to have led to greater exploitation of sex and violence in shows on TV. However, there is continued debate as to whether exposure to such programs is universally damaging to children. After analyzing the public debate, court decisions, and scientific consideration of cause and effect, Lande (1993) warns that the role of the viewer is pivotal and that the focus of research should shift to identifying and describing the vulnerable viewer. This concern about features that make an adaptive response to violence difficult is also evident in an article on real violence by Groves, Zuckerman, Marans, and Cohen (1993), and the ensuing correspondence (Butler, 1993; Kosta, 1993).

One group that can be considered to be at intensified risk are the individuals suffering from major psychiatric illnesses. In a forensic hospital the elimination of Music Television (MTV) cable programs from units led to a significant decrease in the frequency of overt aggressive behavior (Waite, Hilbrand, & Foster, 1992). It was postulated that the removal of MTV withdrew a source of cues and arousal for aggressive behavior. These dynamics, observed in adults, are consistent with the experiments of the Bobo dolls in children, and this study may be reasonably projected to the pediatric viewing group because they lack the internal capacity to modify their responses to the stimulus of programs like MTV. The "Beavis and Butthead" controversy also arose because MTV claimed that the satirical quality of the writing could not be recognized by the children and the blurring of the distinction between real and imaginary was claimed to have produced some negative behaviors in children viewing the program. It must be noted that although many concerns are voiced and anecdotal incidents cited, no research has been done on the effect of "Beavis and Butthead" on young children.

The group of children who have little parental input and are "amoral quick learners out there eager to act out any new TV excitement" represent a group who are at high risk for viewing related violence because "Their teacher is a television set" (Coleman, 1993). Modification of their viewing habits and responses to programs will require specific targeted approaches that need to be further developed. Collaboration of educators, psychiatrists, sociologists, pediatricians, nurses, and other health professionals is desirable in this circumstance, and because health care professionals and teachers are consistent "parental-like" figures and are dispersed in the community, this is an acceptable teaching role for nurses.

As evidenced by the review of literature, there are much conflicting data on the influences of media and TV violence. However, it seems to be in the best interest of the child to restrict access and exposure to media violence. Despite many efforts of public and professional groups this is difficult to achieve, particularly within the political system of the United States (Anonymous, 1994). If exposure cannot be restricted, then careful adult supervision with interpretation of the meaning of violence is imperative.

Strategies for Anticipatory Guidance Related to TV

Because TV is woven into the fabric of today's family life, children's best interests would be served by limiting TV's use and function within the family rather than hoping to rid society of it altogether (Cohen, 1993). If, as mentioned above, TV has its effect by its content and by displacing other activities, then efforts to contain its negative effects must address both these aspects. The nursing profession is uniquely positioned to offer assistance with this effort. Pediatric and community health nurses interact with many families in different roles and settings. Their advice is heeded well, be it offered in the more affluent private pediatric practice or in the clinics of less prosperous neighborhoods, where the nurse is often the most positive, nonthreatening professional the family meets. It is helpful to include the issue of TV violence in anticipatory guidance given to families whatever the environment.

Based on assessment of individual family style, parents' cognition, and social resources available to the family, some useful nursing strategies to assist in creating a balance between TV watching and other activities for children and adults, include the following: (a) educate parents (at an appropriate learning level) about normal child development with emphasis given to the effect that visual media, especially TV, can have on early child development (presentations at Parent-Teacher Association meetings and information sharing in parent newsletters and flyers sent home from schools and daycare centers); (b) encourage parents to spend time with their children; (c) support parents in exercising control over the use of TV in the homes; (d) encourage parents to be role models for their children by participating in activities other than TV viewing and by changing their own TV viewing habits; (e) encourage children to engage in physical activities and exercise; (f) introduce children to games such as Candyland, Monopoly, cards, and other board games; (g) encourage reading as an alternate form of entertainment; (h) counsel parents in the provision of structured bedtime rituals that include reading and talking and less TV; (i) discourage the acquisition of a second TV set or cable TV in households with unsupervised young children; and (j) advise parents against the use of TV as a babysitter or as a reward or punishment.

Family styles are so diverse today that these strategies may not be suitable in every case. However, health care providers need to present options and encourage families to choose the most appropriate ones to best meet the needs of the children.

Strategies to mediate the impact of the content of TV programs on children would include the following: (a) parents watch TV with children to determine the suitability of programs and explain what is being viewed; (b) while watching TV with children, parents provoke discussion and ask questions regarding program accuracy and content; (c) parents block or do not subscribe to cable channels that are considered undesirable for children's viewing; (d) parents foster other creative activities such as active play or production of theatrical, musical, dance, or visual arts activities where children participate in the imaginative experience.

Recommendations for Community Action

The mounting evidence of effects to some children of watching violence on TV is enough to alarm parents, nurses, teachers, and legislators, but the media industry has been slow to respond. It is gratifying to see that cable TV has instituted a violence rating system and that time-control locks for TV receivers are available. Advocacy organizations for positive children's programming include Action for Children's Television and the American Academy of Pediatrics. TV exists to sell audiences to advertisers, so economic pressure on advertisers creates change.

It is essential for health care professionals to play a role in educating the public regarding optimal TV viewing habits. As part of a standard health care package, information for parents on developmentally appropriate TV for children and how it educates and influences them should be readily available. Nurses can be involved in the development and testing of such interventions. Parents can become involved with helping their children to develop critical viewing skills while limiting viewing time and providing TV substitutes (eg. reading, sports, hobbies). Being a fitting role model for children is the responsibility of every adult.

Another critical area requiring the involvement of health care professionals is that of policymaking and legislative initiatives to ensure that high-quality children's TV programming is required for TV station license renewal. Building coalitions with other groups to monitor and improve TV for children would be most beneficial. Professionals in health care roles can also conduct more research to further define the link between TV violence and childhood aggression. In the past this has been undertaken by psychologists, sociologists and media specialists, with less research documented by educators and those in the business of caring for children's general health and well-being. It is essential that future research be interdisciplinary in nature to address the issue of TV violence from a holistic perspective and to raise the understanding of the effect of repeated exposure to TV violence on the behavior of impressionable infants and children. Nursing has much to offer teams that develop and promote scientifically developed interventions to prevent childhood violence.

Summary

The literature points to the negative impact on children of viewing violence on TV. It is essential that nurses concerned with the health and well-being of children include TV violence as a major issue in their work with individual clients and in their community activities. This would include interventions with families to affect family TV viewing habits and involvement in political action by petitioning Congress and the Federal Communications Commission to regulate violence on TV. As professionals, nurses can assist in the investigation and testing of the effectiveness of these interventions.

Finally, we must remember, in the words of Dorothy Singer (1989),

> Professionals and parents must be aware of all sources of input for their children, not only peers, textbooks, teachers, and relatives but also from the subtle "stranger" in the living room who talks to children daily with complex messages of fear, violence, materialism, and, only infrequently, with messages of sharing, friendship, and concern for others (p. 446).

Jib Fowles

NO

The Whipping Boy

Although television violence has never been shown to cause hostile behavior, its sinister reputation lives on. This is because the issue masks a variety of other struggles. Many of these conflicts are suppressed because they may pose a threat to social order or are considered unseemly topics for public discussion. Hence, we hear only the polite versions of the conflicts between races, genders, and generations, although these struggles roil national life. Because they are denied full expression, such conflicts are transferred into other debates, including and perhaps especially the issue of television violence.

Television violence is a whipping boy, a stand-in for other clashes, real or imagined. As one astute observer put it a few years back during a previous cycle of panic, "The debate about children and media violence is really a debate about other things, many of which have very little to do with the media."

There are several reasons why television violence has become such an exemplary whipping boy. First, it is a large target, present in one form or another in virtually every household in America. Second, if one puts on blinders, there might seem to be some correspondence between the mayhem on the television screen and real-life aggression; both televised entertainment and the real world deal in hostilities. Third and most important, television violence attracts no champions; the very idea of defending it seems silly to most people. Even industry representatives rarely get beyond conciliatory statements when they are compelled to address the matter. In one survey, 78 percent of entertainment industry executives expressed concern about the content of the action dramas they helped produce. In 1993 Ted Turner, perhaps the most conspicuous industry leader at the time, said in congressional testimony that television was "the single most important factor causing violence in America." The object of derision simply stands still and takes all the abuse that can be heaped on it.

What are the real conflicts that are being displaced? Most entail the stronger overwhelming the weaker, but in some conflicts the weaker retaliate through moral exertion. Here is a brief examination of the most important conflicts.

From Jib Fowles, "The Whipping Boy: The Hidden Conflicts Underlying the Campaign Against Violent TV," *Reason* (March 2001). Adapted from *The Case for Television Violence* (Sage Publications, 1999). Copyright © 1999 by Jib Fowles. Reprinted by permission of Sage Publications, Inc.

High vs. Low

The attack on television violence is, at least in part, an attack by the upper classes and their partisans on popular culture. In this interpretation, which has been broached repeatedly for a quarter-century, the push to reform television is simply the latest manifestation of the struggle between the high and the low, the dominant and the dominated.

The United States is often regarded as a virtually classless society. Indeed, the overwhelming majority of Americans identify themselves as members of a "middle" class. Everyday experience, however, points in a different direction. Americans constantly make class judgments about one another. They quickly note outward appearances and speech patterns. When necessary, one person learns about the other's occupation and education, where he lives and what car he drives, and locates that person socially. Notions of class rank notoriously crop up in courtship and marriage. Characters in films and television programs radiate class information about themselves to audience members who know precisely how to read such clues.

Perhaps the preeminent living theorist and researcher into matters of class and culture is Pierre Bourdieu. He is best known for his work on the segmentation of society according to preferences in aesthetic taste (for instance, going or not going to art museums). At the center of Bourdieu's work is the concept of *habitus,* an idea similar to that of the English word, *habit.* Habitus is the system of predispositions ingrained in a particular group or social class. It manifests itself in similar thoughts, behaviors, expressions, and leisure pursuits. The shared habitus unites and defines the social entity. Habitus, however, does not shackle individuals; in Bourdieu's scheme, there is ample room for idiosyncratic action.

Another concept special to Bourdieu is *capital,* approximately equivalent to social power. In addition to conventional economic wealth, there are several other kinds of capital in Bourdieu's system. Cultural capital (preferences gained primarily through education), symbolic capital (prestige and honors), and social capital (whom one knows) work together with financial capital to define a person's location in the overall social structure. Social action then becomes a function of class habitus and personal capitals. A final term from Bourdieu's work is *reproduction,* which is the manner by which social classes reproduce themselves and, in doing so, preserve status differences. For Bourdieu, the reproduction of habitus is the key work of a social class.

Although Bourdieu does not discuss television in his magisterial work, *Distinctions* (1984), it does not take much imagination to extend his analysis. He writes in his opening pages that taste (cultural capital) functions as a marker of social class; therefore, different preferences (such as watching television violence or not) can be used to situate a person hierarchically. According to this system, an attack on the most popular medium, on television and especially its violent content, would also be an attack by the dominant class on the habitus of the dominated. To reconfirm social distinctions and maintain exclusivity, members of the dominant class need only profess an opposition to television violence. (Ironically, Bourdieu, mustering all the trappings of a

French intellectual, himself attacked television in a series of lectures published in English in 1998, calling the medium "a threat to political life and to democracy itself.")

In the derisive vocabulary of this dominant class, violent content is delivered via the "mass media." This term is used so much that it seems unremarkable, but repetition has concealed its derogatory nature. Programming is not received by an undifferentiated horde; it is received by individuals. In fact, there is no mass, there are no masses. As the cultural critic Raymond Williams wrote in 1958, "The masses are always the others, whom we don't know, and can't know. . . . Masses are other people. There are in fact no masses; there are only ways of seeing people as masses." When dominant Americans chastise the nonexistent phenomena of the "masses" and their "mass medium" of television, with its evil content, what they are really endeavoring is to disparage and suppress the culture of dominated Americans.

The class nature of this conflict is evident in the string of congressional hearings that have addressed television violence. Consider the five such congressional hearings held between 1988 and 1995. Of the 36 non-industry witnesses who testified against television violence, only seven were women. None was black or Hispanic. The 29 white males were identified as presidents, professors, directors, representatives, senators, senior scientists, and other distinguished titles that suggested they were well advanced in their careers. It is this patrician sector of society that for reasons of its own leads the attack on rowdy television violence.

The means by which one enters into society's dominant segment, and in doing so learns to affect reproachful views on television violence, is the academy. The general veneration that greets the academy is a sign of its near-sacred station and of the importance of its role in, as Bourdieu would view it, the reproduction of the dominant class and its habitus. Although the rewards of academics are middling in terms of financial capital, the cultural capital they accrue cannot be surpassed. To have a college degree—only about one-quarter of American adults do—is to have the credential of the dominant; not to have a college degree is to remain forever among the dominated.

Academics strive to regard television with condescension or an affected indifference. "A studied, conspicuous ignorance about television," communication professor Ellen Seiter wrote in 1996, "is a mark of distinction (like all distinctions, it is valued because it is so difficult to maintain)." Professors' general attitude toward television becomes more pointed when the topic of television violence is discussed; they are quick to assert piously that television is dangerously violent. Among college communication teachers, two-thirds of a 1991 sample of 486 instructors agreed that television "increased aggressive behavior." Of 68 scholars who had published papers or reports specifically on television's effects, 80 percent concurred that television violence produced aggressiveness.

Professors researching television's effects, therefore, seem to occupy a doubly honored position. Not only are they, like their colleagues, performing the crucial service of reproducing the dominant classes, but they also are breathing life into a key issue in the struggle between the dominant and the dominated. They may devote their entire careers to demonstrating the dangers of television violence and are bound to receive approbation from the dominant class as a result. No wonder the position of television effects researcher has proven so attractive.

Yet when a given skirmish over violence has exhausted itself and a lull sets in, members of the dominant class revert to their un-self-conscious viewing of televised mayhem. Even college professors watch TV. During one lull in the violence debate, a 1982 study found that media professors did not restrict their children's viewing any more than the rest of the population did.

Us vs. Them

Perhaps the most striking conflict concealed in the debate over television violence involves the fabrication and control of "the Other." The best-known treatment of the concept of the Other is Edward Said's *Orientalism* (1978). The Orient, argued Said, was one of Europe's "deepest and most recurring images of the Other." It was "almost a European invention" that served as "a Western style for dominating, restructuring, and having authority over the Orient." Superiority over the Other was one motive for this phenomenon; another was self-definition. "The Orient," Said wrote, "has helped to define Europe (or the West) as its contrasting image, idea, personality, experience."

Thus the Other, the "not-us," is a fabrication used both to regulate those classified as the Other and to distinguish the culture of those doing the classifying. It is also a mechanism for emphasizing differences and disregarding similarities in order to maintain group solidarity. The Other differs conceptually from the mass in that the mass can be a part of "us," even if a discredited part, whereas the Other remains outside.

In the United States, the Other is often primarily a Dark Other—blacks and, to a lesser extent, Hispanics. The Dark Other is the recipient of an undeniable assault that plays out in racially charged terms. One form of the assault on the Dark Other is the War on Drugs. This "war" promotes definitions of legal and illegal drugs that have favored whites at the expense of the Dark Other; alcohol and prescription tranquilizers (both of whose records of extensive abuse and human damage are well documented) enjoy legal protection, whereas drugs associated with black culture, such as marijuana and cocaine (the health effects of which, on examination of the data, appear to be negligible), are proscribed. Of course, there is nothing inherent in these drugs that allocates them to the legal or illegal categories. These allocations are socially determined.

The anti–television violence crusades are part of this same assault. People do not worry about their own viewing of violent shows, and in fact they are so at peace with it that they are less likely to acknowledge the violence at all. They worry extensively, however, about what the Dark Other is watching. As British media scholar David Buckingham noted in 1997, "Debates about the negative effects of the media are almost always debates about other people."

"People like us" project a scenario onto the Dark Other in which viewing entertainment violence leads to real-life criminal behavior. This scenario is false in every detail—there exists no uniform Dark Other, and symbolic violence does not produce aggression—but it is upheld due to the emotional conviction behind it and the handy availability of rationalizing "scientific proof." Fears of the Dark Other—fears of difference, of being preyed on, of having one's culture overturned, of invalidating one's identity—are denied expression elsewhere but are allowed to sneak into the attack on television violence. In this way, the Dark Other, his culture, his viewing habits, and his behaviors are disparaged.

There is a curious twist to all this, however—a complexity revealing much about the intricacies of social life. Whereas whites push off the Dark Other with vigor, at the same time they subtly beckon him back. Cultural theorists Peter Stallybrass and Allon White observe that whatever is excluded and displaced to the Other then becomes an object of fascination and is summoned back. The desire for cultural homogeneity produces instead a heterogeneous mix. Thus whites are fascinated by the music, dance, clothing styles, and behavior of blacks. Whites study black athletes, seeking to learn about the prowess of the Other. Whites welcome black entertainers, even when (or especially when) black actors are involved in violent scenarios.

Old vs. Young

Adults who enlist in the anti-television crusade always insist that it is "impressionable youths" whom they wish to protect. In the guise of shielding youths, however, adults are trying to contain and control them.

This generational conflict emerges in contemporary polls: A 1997 survey by Steve Farkas and Jean Johnson of 2,000 randomly selected American adults found them ill disposed toward both younger children and adolescents. The majority of respondents used harsh terms to characterize 5-to-12-year-olds, such as "lacking discipline," "rude," and "spoiled." Two-thirds of the respondents were very critical of teenagers, calling them "irresponsible" and "wild." According to the report, "Most Americans look at today's teenagers with misgiving and trepidation, viewing them as undisciplined, disrespectful, and unfriendly." Six hundred teenagers were also surveyed, however; they viewed things differently. Most felt happy in their lives and in their relationships with adults. These discrepant attitudes indicate much about the essential nature of generational strife—of who deprecates whom.

Antagonism toward the young can be especially strong in an adult population configured like that of the United States—one that is aging rapidly due to the baby boom phenomenon. As subculture researcher Dick Hebdige observes, in the consciousness of adult society, "Youth is present only when its presence is a problem, or is regarded as a problem." Overall, adults feel threatened by the next generation.

Social scientist Charles Acland has argued that "youth's complex relationship with popular culture as a live and expressive domain is menacing because the uses of culture cannot be policed completely." With adults able only partially to supervise the "menace" of popular culture, children and adolescents turn to their television shows, their movies, their computer games, and their music as an escape from adult restraint. Passing through a difficult stage in life, indeed perhaps the most strenuous one of all, youths turn to television violence for the vicarious release it can offer.

The consumption of symbolic violent content correlates negatively with age. According to a 1993 study commissioned by the Times Mirror Center for People and the Press, age is the single most significant factor in the viewing of television violence: Younger viewers watch much more than do older viewers. Cultural critic James Twitchell suggests that "if you study the eager consumers of vulgarities, you will soon see that this audience is characterized not so much by class (as we tend to assume, due in part to Marxist interpretations of the culture industry) as by maturity."

Youths do not think it probable that there could be any transfer from television's violence to aggression in the real world; of all age groups, they are the least likely to believe there is a connection. Elizabeth Kolbert, a *New York Times* reporter, interviewed three teenage felons on the subject in 1994 and noted, "The three teenagers . . . all scoffed at the notion that what young people see on the screen bore any relation to the crimes they committed."

Weaker vs. Stronger

There are at least two cases where the anti-television crusade allows a weaker group to mount an attack against a stronger target. The first relates to the struggle between masculinity and femininity. As the male expresses dominion and the female resists it, everything in culture becomes gendered, or has reference to gender. This pervasive rivalry would be expected to find its way into the anti-television campaign as another camouflaged conflict between the dominant and the dominated, but in this instance the thrust is completely reversed. That is, when the struggle between genders enters into the debate over television violence, it does so as an act of resistance by the female against the male—as a small counterstrike.

The power of males is most pointedly realized in the violence some of them direct toward women. Alert to the chance of male animosity, women are prone to feeling wary of violence even in its flattened, symbolic form on the television screen. The figment may draw too close to the real thing, whether experienced or imagined, to permit the degree of unimpeded pleasure that male viewers might enjoy. In surveys females are more likely than males to report there is "too much violence in television entertainment" and have been so since the general question was first asked in 1972. When queried about the amount of violence on specific action programs, women viewers will perceive more of it than will men, presumably because of their awareness of and uneasiness about the vicious content.

The recurring moral crusade against television violence affords women a choice opportunity for retribution. Seemingly untainted by any overt hostility on its own part, the movement to purify televised entertainment, one that all agree is to be rhetorical only, seems to be shielded from any possibility of retaliatory strikes. How much contention against males is bound up in the 1994 assertion of Barbara Hattemer, president of the National Family Foundation, that "as media violence is absorbed into a person's thoughts, it activates related aggressive ideas and emotions that eventually lead to aggressive behavior"? How much gender strife is exposed in the hyperbolic 1996 statement of Carole Lieberman, chairperson of the National Coalition Against Television, that "more lives are damaged or destroyed by the effects of on-screen violence than by any other medical problem"? She has forgotten heart disease, cancer, and other maladies, and she has done so for a particular reason.

The second case of a counterstrike against a stronger group involves religion. Many of the groups organized in opposition to television violence have religious ties. Here, neither the contestants nor their motives are camouflaged. The partisans on the attacking side are explicit and vociferous; they stand for religiosity, conservative beliefs, and "family values," and they are against licentiousness, media excesses, and symbolic violence. Those under attack—the entertainment industries and, by extension, all sorts of permissive people—respond first with incomprehension and then with annoyance, wishing the conservative and fundamentalist contingent would disappear. It would be easy for the political left to ignore the religious right if the latter did not comprise a well-defined and adamant voting bloc.

This cultural axis could hardly be more different from class antagonism. Social classes are stacked from bottom to top. Here, the axis and its poles can be understood as horizontal, stretching from the most conservative to the most free-thinking. Those gathered at the conservative and evangelical pole come from a wide range of social strata, although they are frequently depicted by their opponents as occupying lower-status positions exclusively. Seeking certainty in the literal word of the Bible, often believing in creationism and patriarchal traditions, and adhering to longstanding customs and attitudes, those clustered at this pole are often moved to take issue with the novelties of social transitions and the uncertainties of modern life.

Fundamentalists rail against the expanding, heaving tableau of television violence, and in organized fashion they strike out against it. The American Family Association (AFA), headed by the Rev. Donald Wildmon, has objected strenuously to video carnage. In 1993 Randall Murphree, editor of the association's *AFA Journal,* wrote: "Violence on the small screen continues to invade America's homes as television offers more graphic murders, bloodier assaults, and general mayhem. And all the while, the dramatic effects on society grow more and more alarming." In 1997 the AFA announced that, by its count, violent incidents in prime time network programs had increased 31 percent from the previous year—an increase far in excess of those measured by other monitors. As an example of the AFA's activities, in August 1997 its "Action Alert" roused its members to contact CBS and "express your concerns about their dangerous agenda of expanding the limits of violence on television through [the cop drama] *Brooklyn South.*"

The issue of television violence affords groups such as the AFA the sanctioned opportunity to carry out a cultural attack—to have at their opponents, to condemn immoral depictions and the entertainment industry that produces and distributes them. Doing so, fundamentalism affirms its presence to others through an issue that is allowed to capture media attention and affirms its role to itself as a guardian of traditional mores. Television violence allows conservative forces the opportunity to carry their standard forward.

As religious conservatives react negatively to social changes of greater and lesser profundity, they may be performing an important service for American civilization. American culture is venturing into areas rarely if ever visited before, and never on such a large scale (for example, in matters of widespread individuality or of social inclusiveness). Some sort of conservative movement may prove useful, much like a sea anchor during turbulence, for steadying the vessel of culture.

The Big Lie

The widely held belief that television fantasy violence stimulates aggression in the real world and should be censured is what propaganda experts might call "a big lie"—a grotesque fabrication to which all unreflectingly subscribe. What makes this particular big lie different from the propagandists' is that it is not bestowed on an acquiescent population by some cabal; rather, this is one that we all repeatedly tell one another, duping ourselves as we dupe others. We do this for reasons of convenience: By repeating this uncontroverted big lie with ever-increasing volume, we can easily vent some of our own hostilities regarding other, truly confounding social conflicts.

While censure is generally directed by the stronger party toward the weaker, in some instances it flows in the opposite direction. Within the gender wars, and in the invectives of the religious right, condemnations are directed by weaker parties toward stronger targets. But whether the chastising energy flows from the stronger toward the weaker or from the weaker toward the stronger has nothing to do with the actualities of television violence.

Whatever its immediate source, the energy that breathes life into the whipping boy of television violence has its ultimate origins in fear—fear of disorder that, in the extreme, could overturn society. As Charles Acland has written, "A society is always concerned with normalization, with the organization of its order, to assure the continuation of its structures and distribution of power." Although social order is a perpetual preoccupation, at this point in history it would seem to be an obsessive one; witness the outsized emphasis on the containment of crime at a time when crime is on the decline and the reckless hysteria of the War on Drugs. Sociologist Graham Murdock refers to the "fear about the precarious balance between anarchy and order in the modern age." Exactly why this fearful fixation on social order should be occurring now is open to question. Its existence, however, should not be doubted. Indeed, the need to strengthen social controls has a correlate in Americans' increasing imposition of self-controls: Per capita alcohol consumption and cigarette smoking have been on the decline and health club memberships on the rise for most of the past 30 years.

Television is new enough that it is not embraced without reservations, and it has not yet accumulated the social equity that would allow it to be shielded by nostalgia. In addition to its relative novelty, it is enormous, filling up the day (television viewing trails only work and sleep in terms of expended time), and can be menacing on this count. Because everyone has access to television, its use cannot be regulated, and thus for those who want to control it, the medium is believed to be out of control and threatening. The rise of television, observes media scholar Richard Sparks, "has been taken to signify the drift of history beyond willed control or direction. The censure of television bears witness to the fear of the future."

General apprehension about the course of history is in several senses the opposite of video violence—the passivity of fear vs. the frenzy of aggression, the amorphous vs. the detailed, and the actual vs. the symbolic. The two find each other as if magnetized, whereupon the flaying of the whipping boy begins.

POSTSCRIPT

Is Television Violence Viewing Harmful for Children?

Almost everyone has access to television if they so choose. There is hardly any other medium so pervasive in American society as television. What is the relationship of television viewing to violent acts? Those who believe that television viewing is the root of all evil support unplugging the "boob tube" and going back to the good old days of reading, listening to the radio, and swapping stories while sitting by the fireplace. At the other end of the continuum, those that argue that television is merely the next evolution of communication technology would promote "going with the flow," grinning and bearing television—for it is surely here to stay—and stop worrying about it. After all, they say, television is ultimately harmless; it cannot make you do anything you do not want to do.

What should be done to effectively address this problem? Is it realistic to revert back to the days prior to the television era? Or should we just relax and stop worrying about the effects of television? After all, many say, children are resilient; they will eventually come to terms with TV's impact on their lives. How much truth lies in Johnson's contention that children's television viewing of violent behavior is associated with antisocial behavior later on in life? Is it more a matter of parental involvement with their children while they are watching television than *what* children watch? Would it be an overreaction to more closely censor television programming? Would programming quality then be forfeited? How should we respond to Fowles's contention that television is being used as the simple explanation for societal violence when the reason is much more complex?

School-aged children are the most targeted when it comes to television advertising. There are more commercial breaks per hour for this type of programming than for others. Additionally, with the widespread access to cable television, children have ever-increasing access to adult programming, many times in unsupervised homes. Some research suggests that although children who spend excessive amounts of time watching television tend to do poorly in school, others who spend a moderate amount of time in front of the set perform better scholastically than those who watch no television at all. Logically, there must be middle-ground solutions to the issue of children, television viewing, and violence.

Perhaps if parents could accept the inevitable, that television is not only here to stay but viewing choices are expanding almost daily, then society could move past this dichotomy of thinking of television as simply good or bad. Television viewing could be thought of as an active endeavor rather than a passive one. Parents could become more involved with their children as they watch television. Through modeling, parents could teach children to be skeptical about television advertisements, point out the differences between fantasy and reality, and explain that the moral values being portrayed on the tube are different from values that are important to the parents.

On the other hand, it is true that television viewing can be overdone. Children who watch TV excessively versus play actively are more likely to be overweight. If children are watching TV to excess, they are not communicating with adults in the family; they are not learning family values but values portrayed on TV. Studies that provide information on violence and its causes can lend additional insight into the role that a variety of societal factors play in perpetuating violence.

Family: Single Parenting

This Single Parenting page of ParentsPage.com focuses on issues concerning single parents and their children. Although the articles cover issues concerning single parents of children from infancy through adolescence, most of the articles deal with middle childhood.

http://parenting.ivillage.com

National Institute on Out-of-School Time

Directed by the Wellesley College Center for Research on Women, this National Institute on Out-of-School Time project aims to improve the quality and quantity of school-age child care nationally.

http://www.niost.org

National Black Child Development Institute

At this site, the National Black Child Development Institute provides resources for improving the quality of life for African American children through public education programs.

http://www.nbcdi.org

National Clearinghouse for English Language Acquisition

This National Clearinghouse for English Language Acquisition was formely called the National Clearinghouse for Bilingual Education. This Web site is funded by the Department of Education and includes information on the latest legislation and conferences, as well as links to bilingual educational materials.

http://www.ncela.gwu.edu/

Action for Healthy Kids

This is a nonprofit organization formed specifically to address the epidemic of overweight, undernourished and sedentary youth by focusing on changes at school. The organization's goal is to improve children's nutrition and increase physical activity, which will in turn improve their readiness to learn.

http://www.actionforhealthykids.org

PART 3

Middle Childhood

*M*iddle childhood, or school age, is the period from ages five through twelve. The rate of a child's growth generally declines until the later part of this stage of development. Perhaps the most important experience during middle childhood is schooling. As a child progresses through this stage, new significant others outside the family emerge in the child's life. Children gain a broader understanding of the similarities and differences among them. The peer group (especially same-sex peers), teachers, and media personalities take on increased importance for the child. This section examines issues related to schooling, language development, and self-care.

- Does Marriage Improve Living Standards for Children?

- Are Stepfamilies Inherently Problematic for Children?

- Is Television Viewing Responsible for the Rise in Childhood Obesity?

- Do Bilingual Education Programs Help Non-English-Speaking Children Succeed?

- Is Gay Adoption and Foster Parenting Healthy for Children?

ISSUE 9

Does Marriage Improve Living Standards for Children?

YES: Wade F. Horn, from "Healthy Marriages Provide Numerous Benefits to Adults, Children, and Society," *Insight on the News* (March 18, 2002)

NO: Stephanie Coontz and Nancy Folbre, from "Marriage, Poverty, and Public Policy," *The American Prospect Online,* http://www.prospect.org/webfeatures/2002/03/coontz-s-03-19.html (March 19, 2002)

ISSUE SUMMARY

YES: Wade F. Horn, who heads the Marriage Initiative for President George W. Bush, asserts that marriage can remedy the ills of society, including family poverty and poor living standards for children.

NO: Stephanie Coontz, author and family advocate, and Nancy Folbre, professor of economics at the University of Massachusetts, contend that improving the living standards of children is a complicated issue, which needs to be approached from many different angles in order to make improvements.

There is no doubt that living with two parents who are married and who want to be together, is good for children, psychologically and economically. Having two married parents means that there is a possibility for two incomes, which would provide a higher standard of living for children and would make it more likely that the children will not grow up in poverty. Presently, the majority of children living in poverty live with a single parent, usually their mom.

And yet, is the issue that simple? Should we merely request or require that parents marry? Will that make everything all right? Will children's living standards improve if their parents get married? One-third of poor children live within a two-parent family. If the premise that marriage improves living standards for children is true, what happened to these families?

The complicated issue involving the living standards of children and marriage promotion has become intertwined with the issues of welfare reform fund reauthorization. The whole issue of how marriage influences children's living standards recently emerged in the American political agenda. Key personnel in the George W. Bush administration, led by Wade F. Horn, decided that parents need to be married to each other in order to move families out of poverty and to improve living standards for children. Horn asserts that marriage would solve the problem of children living in poverty. This idea prompted a slew of opposition from some family professionals and public-policy analysts.

As welfare reform has evolved, funding for Temporary Assistance for Needy Families (TANF) has also changed. While improving living standards for children has always been states' prominent goal, by moving families from welfare to work, states have been allowed to choose their own method of using federal dollars to accomplish this goal. The individuation of states has complicated this issue. Some states choose to provide affordable child care, education, and job training as a way to move families from welfare to work, and in so doing, they have managed to improve living standards for children. With the marriage promotion initiative, states that show higher levels of marriage rates receive more federal dollars for the welfare reform initiative. Although there is no empirical evidence that this type of programming works, states are likely to adopt programs that promote marriage, regardless of whether or not these programs are effective in improving living standards for children. Some states do this merely to increase funding levels.

The issue is not merely about living standards for children. It has evolved into the issue of making poor people get married in order to keep children from enduring a lifetime of poverty. In the following selections, the issue is debated within the present political climate. Horn presents the merits of marriage within the poor population. Horn states that the issue is simple: the government should promote marriage as a way to improve family life in general and more specifically for the children involved. In the opposing selection, Stephanie Coontz and Nancy Folbre describe why marriage within poor families is not always feasible or wise. They contend that this issue is more complicated than Horn suggests.

Wade F. Horn

 YES

Healthy Marriages Provide Numerous Benefits to Adults, Children, and Society

The case for marriage is beyond debate. Marriage is the most stable and healthy environment for raising children. Men and women who are married have been shown to be happier and healthier. And they make more money over time than their single counterparts. Communities with more households headed by married couples are beset by fewer social ills, such as crime and welfare dependency, than communities where marriage is less prevalent.

We really can't argue—or, at least, the data say we shouldn't argue—about the benefits of marriage to children, adults and society. But I do grant that it is reasonable to debate the proper role of government in promoting marriage and that, indeed, reasonable people can disagree on whether government has a place in the marriage debate. I for one, noting that marriage is related directly to child well-being, conclude that government has no choice but to promote healthy marriages.

Let's pose the question this way: Since we know marriage can help adults be happier and healthier, and help children grow up happier and healthier, don't we have a responsibility to figure out ways to help low-income couples who want to be married enjoy a strong, supportive marriage? Of course we do.

Before I lay out my vision for how government can begin to make this happen, allow me a pre-emptive strike against the criticism that descends every time I unequivocally state that government should support and promote healthy marriages. Let me discuss four things that promoting marriage is not about.

First, it is not about government matchmaking or telling anybody to get married. Obviously, government has no business doing that. Choosing to get married is a private decision. Government should, and will not get into the business of telling people who, or even whether, to marry. I can state without hesitation that the Bush administration has no plans to create a federal dating service. We have no plans to add an entirely new meaning to the famous phrase, "Uncle Sam Wants You!"

Second, promoting marriage cannot, intentionally or inadvertently, result in policies that trap anyone in an abusive relationship. Seeing more Americans married is not our goal. Seeing more Americans enjoying healthy marriages is our goal. Healthy marriages are good for children and adults alike. Abusive marriages are not good for anyone.

Abuse of any sort by a spouse cannot be tolerated under any circumstances, and no marriage-promotion effort should provide comfort to spouse or child abusers. The good news is that good marriages are not a matter of luck but, rather, a matter of skill. We can teach couples the skills necessary to have good marriages. We can teach couples how to negotiate conflict and how not to allow unresolved anger to escalate. Marriages that last a lifetime and marriages that dissolve after a short while often face equal amounts of conflict. The difference is that couples who stay married have learned to manage this conflict constructively. We have proven strategies for teaching these skills to couples; standing by and not sharing these skills with low-income couples is irresponsible.

Third, when we talk about promoting marriage we are not talking about withdrawing support and services for single-parent families. As noted, we are for marriage because that's what the data say is best for kids. There is no data suggesting that taking away support from single mothers helps children in any way. Many single parents make heroic efforts to raise their children despite incredible pressures. Promoting marriage and supporting single parents is not, and must not be, mutually exclusive. Together, they are part of an integrated effort to promote child well-being.

Finally, marriage promotion is not the same as cohabitation promotion. For too long, we have treated marriage as if it were a dreaded "M" word. Too afraid to say "marriage," we have instead talked about "committed relationships." But shacking up isn't getting married. Common sense says so. So does research. There is something fundamentally different about the commitment two people make within a marriage relationship versus a cohabiting relationship. In a cohabiting relationship, the commitment of each of the partners primarily is self-serving. By contrast, the marriage commitment is about serving one's spouse. This is a fundamental difference, and one that ought to be reflected in our social policy.

I recommend the following principles for government marriage promotion:

Government must resolve that it will not merely be "neutral" about marriage. For many behaviors government is rightly neutral, for others it is not. For example, the government is not neutral about home ownership because it is good for communities when people own their homes. Furthermore, the government is not neutral about charitable giving because charitable giving is good for society. In the same way, government should not be neutral about healthy marriages because they contribute directly to the general strength of a good and sound society.

First of all, we must remove disincentives for marriage. Under current law if couples (especially low-income couples) marry, our tax code and social welfare system punish them. But striking these disincentives from our laws and policies, while a very important first step, only will bring us to the state of being neutral on marriage. We must go beyond that, into active support of marriage.

More than 90 percent of adults in the United States marry at some point during their lifetimes, and the vast majority enter marriage believing it to be a lifetime commitment. Surveys consistently document that most Americans see marriage as an important life goal. Clearly, providing active support for couples who want to marry and stay married is consistent with the values of the vast majority of Americans.

In doing so, government must not be paralyzed by the unknown. What we don't know about marriage promotion cannot be allowed to stand in the way of what we do know. Some have argued that we don't know enough about marriage promotion and, therefore, we should do nothing. They are partially correct. We have much to learn about promoting and supporting healthy marriages. But there is much we do know.

For example, thanks to a nascent marriage movement in our country, we do know that premarital-education programs work. We know that programs that assign mentoring couples to newlyweds do work. We know that good marriages are a result not of luck or chance but hard work and skill. We know that these skills can be taught. Finally, we know that programs designed to save even the most troubled marriages do work. Yes, there still is much to be learned, but we know enough about what works that standing by and doing nothing would be a tragic mistake.

New research constantly is shedding more light on our path. For example, research is debunking the myth that low-income, inner-city men and women who have children out of wedlock are not linked romantically and have no interest in marriage. A recent study by researchers at Princeton and Columbia universities revealed that 48 percent of unmarried urban couples were living together at the time their child was born. Eighty percent were involved in an exclusive romantic relationship. And half believed their chances of marrying— not at sometime to somebody, but to each other—were "certain" or "near certain." In other words, drive-by pregnancies are an especially insidious urban legend.

Now that we understand the goal for marriage promotion—helping couples who choose marriage develop the skills they need to build healthy marriages—it is time to explore specific actions the government can take. A number of proposals have been put forth. Here are five of my favorites—ideas that have the best chance of improving child well-being by strengthening the institution of marriage:

- Put marriage in the hospital. Hospitals should do more than talk about paternity establishment. They can talk about marriage as well. In most cases, hospital personnel stop at telling a young man that he must establish paternity. Doing so is extremely important. But hospital personnel should also ask the simple question, "Have you considered getting married?" If the answer is "yes," the couple can be referred to helpful services, such as premarital education. If the answer is "no," that's fine. But we can't be afraid to say the "M" word in the labor and delivery ward.

- Develop a referral system for premarital education. Schools, clinics, job-training sites and welfare offices all offer opportunities to provide referrals to premarital education.
- Provide marital-enrichment services through social programs dedicated to strengthening families. Head Start provides a perfect example. Many children in Head Start live with a married mother and father. While Head Start centers routinely provide parenting-education classes, I don't know of a single Head Start program providing marriage-education classes. Head Start represents a perfect opportunity to teach parents the skills they need to maintain a long-term, healthy marriage. We should seize this and similar opportunities.
- Create public-education campaigns highlighting the benefits of healthy marriages. The government funds numerous public-education campaigns promoting various healthy behaviors. Marriage can and should be added to this list.
- Increase support for intervention services, including mentoring programs, so that troubled marriages can be made whole and strong once again.

It no longer is a question of whether government should do this, but of how. It's time to get started right away, before another generation of children misses out on the benefits of a married mom and dad.

**Stephanie Coontz and
Nancy Folbre**

 NO

Marriage, Poverty, and Public Policy

One of the stated objectives of welfare legislation passed in 1996 was "to end dependence by promoting marriage." With this legislation coming up for reauthorization, many policymakers want to devote more public resources to this goal, even if it requires cutting spending on cash benefits, child care, or job training. Some states, such as West Virginia, already use their funds to provide a special bonus to couples on public assistance who get married.[1] In December 2001, more than fifty state legislators asked Congress to divert funds from existing programs into marriage education and incentive policies, earmarking dollars to encourage welfare recipients to marry and giving bonus money to states that increase marriage rates. On February 26, 2002, President Bush called for spending up to $300 million a year to promote marriage among poor people.[2]

Such proposals reflect the widespread assumption that failure to marry, rather than unemployment, poor education, and lack of affordable child care, is the primary cause of child poverty. Voices from both sides of the political spectrum urge us to get more women to the altar. Journalist Jonathan Rauch argues that "marriage is displacing both income and race as the great class divide of the new century."[3] Robert Rector of the Heritage Foundation claims that "the sole reason that welfare exists is the collapse of marriage."[4] In this briefing paper, we question both this explanation of poverty and the policy prescriptions that derive from it.

Marriage offers important social and economic benefits. Children who grow up with married parents generally enjoy a higher standard of living than those living in single-parent households. Two parents are usually better than one not only because they can bring home two paychecks, but also because they can share responsibilities for child care. Marriage often leads to higher levels of paternal involvement than divorce, non-marriage, or cohabitation. Long-term commitments to provide love and support to one another are beneficial for adults, as well as children.

Public policies toward marriage could and should be improved.[5] Taxes or benefit reductions that impose a marriage penalty on low-income couples are inappropriate and should be eliminated. Well designed public policies could play a constructive role in helping couples develop the skills they need to develop healthy and sustainable relationships with each other and their children. It does not follow, however, that marriage promotion should be a significant component of anti-poverty policy, or that public policies should provide a "bonus" to couples who marry.

The current pro-marriage agenda in anti-poverty policy is misguided for at least four reasons:

- Non-marriage is often a result of poverty and economic insecurity rather than the other way around.
- The quality and stability of marriages matters. Prodding couples into matrimony without helping them solve problems that make relationships precarious could leave them worse off.
- Two-parent families are not immune from the economic stresses that put children at risk. More than one third of all impoverished young children in the U.S. today live with two parents.

Single parenthood does not inevitably lead to poverty. In countries with a more adequate social safety net than the United States, single parent families are much less likely to live in poverty. Even within the United States, single mothers with high levels of education fare relatively well.

In this briefing paper, we summarize recent empirical evidence concerning the relationship between marriage and poverty, and develop the four points above in more detail. We also emphasize the need to develop a larger anti-poverty program that provides the jobs, education, and child care that poor families need in order to move toward self-sufficiency.

The Economic Context

Children living with married parents generally fare better than others in terms of family income. In 2000, 6 percent of married couple families with children lived in poverty, compared to 33 percent of female householders with children.[6] Mothers who never marry are more vulnerable to poverty than virtually any other group, including those who have been divorced.[7]

But the low income associated with single parenthood reflects many interrelated factors. Income is distributed far more unequally in the United States than in most other developed countries, making it difficult for low-wage workers (male or female) to support a family without a second income. Women who become single mothers are especially likely to have inadequate wages, both because of pre-existing disadvantages such as low educational attainment and work experience and because the shortage of publicly subsidized child care makes it difficult for them to work full time. In 2000, only 1.2 percent of children of single mothers with a college degree who worked full-time year round lived in poverty.[8] For single mothers with some college working full-time, the poverty rate was less than 8 percent.[9]

Whether single or married, working parents face high child care costs that are seldom factored into calculations of poverty and income. Consider the situation of a single mother with two children working full-time, full year round at the minimum wage of $5.15 an hour, for an income of $10,712. If she files for and receives the maximum Earned Income Tax Credit, she can receive as much as $3,816 in public assistance. But the EITC phases out quickly if she earns much more than the minimum wage, and her child care costs are very high. Unless she is lucky enough to have a family member who can provide free child care, or to find a federally subsidized child care slot, more than 20 percent of her income will go to pay for child care.[10] Federally subsidized child care remains quite limited. Most families who made a transition from welfare to employment in the 1990s did not receive a subsidy.[11]

The high cost of child care helps explain why the economic position of single parents has improved little in recent years despite significant increases in their hours of market work.[12] It may also explain why single parents are likely to live in households with other adults who can share expenses with them. About 40 percent of births to single mothers take place among cohabitors, and much of the increase in nonmarital childbearing in recent years reflects this trend rather than an increase among women living without a partner.[13] The economic stress associated with reductions in welfare benefits over the past six years may have increased the pressure on single mothers to cohabit, often with partners who are unwilling or unlikely to marry.[14]

On both a symbolic and a practical level, marriage facilitates the income pooling and task sharing that allows parents to accommodate family needs.[15] Not surprisingly, many low-income families consider marriage the ideal arrangement for child rearing.[16] The Fragile Families and Child Welfare project currently underway in about twenty cities shows that about 50 percent of unmarried parents of newborns live together and hope to marry at some point.[17] Lower expectations among some couples were associated not with disinterest in marriage but with reports of drug or alcohol problems, physical violence, conflict and mistrust.[18]

The advantages of marriage, however, do not derive simply from having two names on a marriage certificate, and they cannot be acquired merely by going through a formality. Rather, they grow out of a long-term and economically sustainable commitment that many people feel is beyond their reach.

Causality Works Both Ways

Liking the abstract idea of marriage and being able to put together a stable marriage in real life are two very different things. Unemployment, low wages, and poverty discourage family formation and erode family stability, making it less likely that individuals will marry in the first place and more likely that their marriages will deteriorate. These economic factors have long-term as well as short-term effects, contributing to changes in social norms regarding marriage and family formation and exacerbating distrust between men and women. These long-term effects help explain why African-Americans marry at much lower rates than other groups within the U.S. population. Poverty is a cause as well as a consequence of non-marriage and of marital disruption.[19]

Dan Lichter of Ohio State University puts it this way: "Marriage can be a pathway from poverty, but only if women are 'marriageable,' stay married, and marry well."[20] Precisely because marriage offers economic advantages, individuals tend to seek potential spouses who have good earnings potential and to avoid marriage when they do not feel they or their potential mates can comfortably support a family. Ethnographic research shows that low-income women see economic stability on the part of a prospective partner as a necessary precondition for marriage.[21] Not surprisingly, men increasingly use the same calculus. Rather than looking for someone they can "rescue" from poverty, employed men are much more likely to marry women who themselves have good employment prospects.[22]

Poor mothers who lack a high school degree and any regular employment history are not likely to fare very well in the so-called "marriage market." Teenage girls who live in areas of high unemployment and inferior schools are five to seven times more likely to become unwed parents than more fortunately situated teens.[23] A study of the National Longitudinal Survey of Youth confirms that poor women, whatever their age, and regardless of whether or not they are or have ever been on welfare, are less likely to marry than women who are not poor. Among poor women, those who do not have jobs are less likely to marry than those who do.[24]

It is easy to spin a hypothetical scenario in which marrying off single mothers to an average male would raise family incomes and reduce poverty. But unmarried males, and especially unmarried males in impoverished neighborhoods, are not average. That is often the reason they are not married. Researchers from the Center for Research on Child Well-Being at Princeton University report results from the Fragile Families Survey showing that unmarried fathers were twice as likely as married ones to have a physical or psychological problem that interfered with their ability to find or keep a job, and several times more likely to abuse drugs or alcohol. More than 25 percent of unmarried fathers were not employed when their child was born, compared to fewer than 10 percent of married fathers.[25]

Poor mothers tend to live in neighborhoods in which their potential marriage partners are also likely to be poorly educated and irregularly employed. Low-earning men are less likely to get married and more likely to divorce than men with higher earnings.[26] Over the past thirty years, labor market opportunities for men with low levels of education have declined substantially.[27] Several studies suggest that the decrease in real wages for low-income men during the 1980s and early 1990s contributed significantly to lower marriage rates in those years.[28]

This trend has been exacerbated by the high incarceration rates for men convicted of non-violent crimes, such as drug use. While in jail, these men are not available for women to marry and their diminished job prospects after release permanently impair their marriageability. High rates of incarceration among black males, combined with high rates of mortality, have led to a decidedly tilted sex ratio within the African-American population, and a resulting scarcity of marriageable men.[29] One study of the marriage market in the 1980s found that at age 25 there were three unmarried black women for every black man who had adequate earnings.[30] As Ron Mincy of Columbia University emphasizes, simple pro-marriage policies are likely to offer less benefit to African-American families than policies encouraging responsible fatherhood and paternal engagement.[31]

In short, the notion that we could end child poverty by marrying off impoverished women does not take into account the realities of life among the population most likely to be poor. It is based on abstract scenarios that ignore the many ways in which poverty diminishes people's ability to build and sustain stable family relationships.

Quality Matters

Happy, healthy, stable marriages offer important benefits to adults and children. But not all marriages fit this description. Marital distress leads to harsh and inconsistent parenting, whether or not parents stay together. Studies show that a marriage marked by conflict, jealousy and anger is often worse for children's well-being than divorce or residence from birth in a stable single-parent family.[32] For instance, research shows that while children born to teenagers who were already married do better than children born to never-married teens, children born to teen parents who married *after* the birth do worse on some measures, probably because of the high conflict that accompanies marriages entered into with ambivalence or under pressure. Some research suggests that, among low-income African-American families, children from single-parent homes show higher educational achievement than their counterparts from two-parent homes.[33]

The idea that marriage can solve the problems of children in impoverished families ignores the complex realities of these families. The Fragile Families study shows that many low-income parents of new born children already have children from previous relationships. Thus, their marriages would not create idealized biological families, but rather blended families in which child support enforcement and negotiation among stepparents would complicate relationships.[34] A recent study of families in poor neighborhoods in Boston, Chicago and San Antonio also reveals complex patterns of cohabitation and coparenting.[35]

Marriage to a stepfather may improve a mother's economic situation, but it does not necessarily improve outcomes for children and in some cases leads to more problems than continued residence in a stable single-parent family. Even if programs succeed in getting first-time parents married, there is no guarantee that the couples will stay married. Research shows that marriages contracted in the 1960s in order to "legitimate" a child were highly likely to end in divorce.[36] Multiple transitions in and out of marriage are worse for children psychologically than residence in the same kind of family, whatever its form, over long periods of time.[37]

Women and children in economically precarious situations are particularly vulnerable to domestic violence.[38] While it may be true that cohabiting couples are more prone to violence than married couples, this is probably because of what social scientists call a "selection effect": People in non-abusive relationships are more likely to get married. Encouraging women in an unstable cohabiting relationship to marry their partners would not necessarily protect them or their children. Indeed, the first serious violent episode in an unstable relationship sometimes occurs only after the couple has made a formal commitment.[39]

Even when it does not take a violent form, bad fathering can be worse than no fathering. For instance, the National Center on Addiction and Substance Abuse at Columbia University found that while teens in two-parent families are, on average, much less likely to abuse drugs or alcohol than teens in one-parent ones, teens in two-parent families who have a poor to fair relationship with their father are *more* likely to do so than teens in the average one-parent family.[40]

Furthermore, even good marriages are vulnerable to dissolution. The current risks of a marriage ending in divorce are quite high, although they have come down from their peak in 1979–81. It is now estimated that approximately 40 percent of marriages will end in divorce, and the risk of divorce is elevated among people with low income and insecure jobs. Sociologist Scott South calculates that every time the unemployment rate rises by 1 percent, approximately 10,000 extra divorces occur.[41] Comparing the income of single-parent families and married-couple families in any particular year leads to an overly optimistic assessment of the benefits of marriage, because it ignores the possibility of marital dissolution.

Marriage may provide a temporary improvement in a woman's economic prospects without conferring any secure, long-term protection for her children. Indeed, if marriage encourages mothers to withdraw time from paid employment, this can lower their future earnings and increase the wage penalty that they incur from motherhood itself.[42]

Two Parent Families Are Also Under Stress

Poverty among children is not confined to single-parent families. In 2000, about 38 percent of all poor young children lived in two-parent homes.[43] These families have been largely overlooked in the debates over anti-poverty programs and marriage. Indeed, the campaign to increase marriage has overlooked one of the most important public policy issues facing the United States: the growing economic gap between parents, whether married or unmarried, and non-parents.

The costs of raising children have increased in recent years, partly because of the expansion of opportunities for women in the labor market and partly because of the longer time children spend in school. The lack of public support for parenting has also contributed to a worsening of the economic position of parents relative to non-parents.[44] Unlike other advanced industrial countries, the United States fails to provide paid family leaves for parents, and levels of publicly subsidized support for child care remain comparatively low. Most employment practices penalize workers who take time away from paid responsibilities to provide family care.[45] The high cost of parenting in this country helps explain many of the economic disadvantages that women face relative to men.[46] It may also help explain why many men are reluctant to embrace paternal responsibilities.

The Need for a Better Social Safety Net

The association of single parenthood with poverty is not inevitable. In Canada and France, single mothers—and children in general—are far less likely to live in poverty. Sweden and Denmark, with higher rates of out-of-wedlock births, have much lower rates of child poverty and hunger than does the United States. The reason for the difference is simple: These countries devote a greater percentage of their resources to assisting families with children than we do.[47] Similarly, dramatic differences in child poverty rates within our country reflect differences in tax, child care, and income assistance policies across states.[48]

Fans of the 1996 welfare reform law point to a dramatic decline in the welfare rolls since its enactment. Much of this decline is attributable to the economic boom and resulting low unemployment rates of the late 1990s. Despite promises that work requirements and time limits would lead to a more generous package of assistance for those who "followed the rules," cash benefits have declined. Between 1994 and 1999, the real value of maximum benefits fell in most states, with an overall decline in inflation-adjusted value of about 11 percent.[49] Average benefits declined even more, as recipients increased their earnings. Indeed, the declining value of benefits is another reason why caseloads have fallen.[50]

Punitive attitudes, as well as time limits, have discouraged many eligible families from applying for assistance. The Census Bureau estimates that less than 30 percent of children in poverty resided in a family that received cash public assistance in 1998.[51] Take-up rates for Food Stamps and Medicaid have declined in recent years.[52] The implementation of the new Children's Health Insurance program has been quite uneven. As a result, states have saved money, but many children have gone without the food or medical care they needed. Public support for child care increased on both the federal and the state level. Still, most families who made a transition from welfare to work in the late 1990s did not receive a subsidy.[53]

During the economic boom of the late 1990s, increases in earnings among single parents helped make up for declining welfare benefits. As a result, poverty rates among children declined from a high of about 21 percent in 1996 to about 16 percent in 2000.[54] But these figures do not take into account the costs of child care and other work-related expenses, and they offer little hope for the future of children in low-income families as unemployment rates once again begin to climb.[55]

The most important federal policy promoting the welfare of low income families is currently the Earned Income Tax Credit (EITC), a fully refundable tax credit aimed at low-income families with children. Because benefits are closely tied to earnings, and phase out steeply after family income reaches $12,460, the EITC imposes a significant penalty on two-earner married couples, who are less likely to benefit from it than either single parent families or married couples with a spouse at home. This penalty is unfair and should be eliminated.

Other problems with the EITC, however, should be addressed at the same time. Families with two children receive the maximum benefit, which means that low-income families with three or more children do not receive any additional assistance. More than a third of all children in the country live in families with three or more children. Partly as a result of limited EITC coverage, these families are prone to significantly higher poverty rates.[56] Furthermore, the EITC is phased out in ways that penalize middle income families, who currently enjoy less public support for child rearing than the affluent.[57] An expanded unified tax credit for families with children could address this problem.[58]

Given the pressing need for improvements in basic social safety net programs and the threat of rising unemployment, it is unconscionable to reallocate already inadequate Temporary Assistance to Needy Families (TANF) funds to policies designed to promote marriage or provide a "marriage bonus." There is little evidence that such policies would in fact increase marriage rates or reduce poverty among children. Indeed, the main effect of marriage bonuses would probably be to impose a "non-marriage" penalty that would have a particularly negative impact on African-American children, who are significantly less likely to live with married parents than either whites or Hispanics.[59] As Julianne Malveaux points out in her discussion of the Bush proposal, "a mere $100 million can be considered chump change. But the chump who could have been changed is the unemployed worker who misses out on job training because some folks find those programs—but not marriage-promotion programs—a waste."[60]

Well-designed programs to help individuals develop and improve family relationships may be a good idea. However, they should not be targeted to the poor, but integrated into a larger provision of public health services, or built into existing health insurance programs (mandating, for instance, that both public and private health insurance cover family counseling). Such programs also should not be limited to couples who are married or planning to marry. Fathers and step-fathers who are not living with their biological children also need guidance and encouragement to develop healthy, nurturing relationships. Gay and lesbian families—who are currently legally prohibited from marriage—also merit assistance.

Public policies should not penalize marriage. Neither should they provide an economic bonus or financial incentive to individuals to marry, especially at the cost of lowering the resources available to children living with single mothers. Such a diversion of resources from public assistance programs penalizes the children of unmarried parents without guaranteeing good outcomes for the children of people who are married. A variety of public policies could help strengthen families and reduce poverty among all children, including a broadening of the Earned Income Tax Credit, expansion of publicly subsidized child care, efforts to promote responsible fatherhood, improvements in public education and job training, and efforts to reduce income inequality and pay discrimination. Unlike some of the pro-marriage policies now under consideration, these policies would benefit couples who wish to marry but would not pressure women to enter or remain in intimate relationships they would not otherwise choose.

Notes

1. Alexandra Starr, "Shotgun Wedding by Uncle Sam?" *Business Week,* June 4, 2001.

2. Cheryl Wetzstein, "States Want Pro-Family Funds," *The Washington Times,* December 10, 2001; Robin Toner and Robert Pear, "Bush Urges Work and Marriage Programs in Welfare Plan," *New York Times,* February 27, 2002.

3. Jonathan Rauch, "The Widening Marriage Gap: America's New Class Divide," *National Journal,* Friday, May 18, 2001.

4. Cheryl Weitzstein, "Unwed Mothers Set a Record for Births," *The Washington Times,* April 18, 2001.

5. See Jared Bernstein, Irv Garfinkel, and Sara McLanahan, *A Progressive Marriage Agenda,* forthcoming from the Economic Policy Institute.

6. U.S. Bureau of the Census, "Historical Poverty Statistics—Table 4. Poverty Status of Families, by Type of Family, Presence of Related Children, Race, and Hispanic Origin: 1959–2000." Available at http://www.census.gov. In 1999, 36 percent of single-mother households lived in poverty. *Poverty in the U.S. 1999.* Current Population Reports, P60–210 (Washington, D.C.: Government Printing Office, 2000).

7. Alan Guttmacher Institute, "Married Mothers Fare the Best Economically, Even if They Were Unwed at the Time They Gave Birth," *Family Planning Perspectives* 31, no. 5: pp. 258–60, September, 1999; Ariel Halpern, "Poverty Among Children Born Outside of Marriage: Preliminary Findings From the National Survey of America's Families" (Washington, D.C.: The Urban Institute, 1999).

8. Calculations by Arloc Sherman, Children's Defense Fund, based on the March 2001 Current Population Survey.

9. Ibid. See also Neil G. Bennett, Jiali Li, Younghwan Song, and Keming Yang, "Young Children in Poverty: A Statistical Update," released June 17, 1999. New York: National Center for Children in Poverty, http://cpmcnet.columbia.edu/dept/nccp/99uptext.html.

10. Linda Giannarelli and James Barsimantov, *Child Care Expenses of America's Families,* Occasional Paper Number 40 (Washington, D.C.: Urban Institute, 2000).

11. Rachel Schumacher and Mark Greenberg, *Child Care After Leaving Welfare: Early Evidence From State Studies* (Washington, D.C.: Center for Law and Social Policy, 1999).

12. Kathryn H. Porter and Allen Dupree, "Poverty Trends for Families Headed by Working Single Mothers, 1993–1999," Center on Budget and Policy Priorities, August 16, 2001. For full article: http://www.cbpp.org/8-16-01wel.pdf.

13. Pamela Smock, "Cohabitation in the U.S.: An Appraisal of Research Themes, Findings, and Implications," *American Review of Sociology* 26, no. 1 (2000): pp. 1–20.

14. Gregory Acs and Sandi Nelson, "'Honey, I'm Home.' Changes in Living Arrangements in the Late 1990s," *New Federalism: National Survey of America's Families* (The Urban Institute), June 2001, pp. 1–7. A new study by Johns Hopkins researchers, presented on February 20, 2002 at a welfare forum in Washington D.C., however, shows that these partnerships are unstable and may not be better for children than single-parent households. See Robin Toner, "Two Parents Not Always Best for Children, Study Finds," *New York Times,* February 20, 2002.

15. Many dual-earner families with preschool age children include a parent who works evenings and nights in order to provide care during the day while their husband or wife is at work. See Harriet Presser, "Employment Schedules Among Dual-Earner Spouses and the Division of Household Labor by Gender," *American Sociological Review* 59, no. 3 (June 1994): pp. 348–364.

16. Kristen Harknett and Sara McLanahan, "Do Perceptions of Marriage Explain Marital Behavior? How Unmarried Parents' Assessments of the Benefits of Marriage Relate to Their Subsequent Marital Decision"; and Marcia Carlson, Sara McLanahan, and Paula England, "Union Formation and Stability in Fragile Families," papers presented at the meetings of the Population Association of America, Washington D.C., April 2001.

17. More details on the Fragile Families study are available at http://crcw. princeton.edu/fragilefamilies/nationalreport.pdf.

18. Maureen Waller, "High Hopes: Unwed Parents' Expectations About Marriage," *Children and Youth Services Review* 23 (2001): pp. 457–84.

19. Sara McLanahan, "Parent Absence or Poverty: Which Matters More?" pp. 35–48 in Greg Duncan and Jeanne Brooks-Gunn, eds., *Consequences of Growing Up Poor* (New York: Russell Sage Foundation, 1997). On the impact of poverty in creating non-marriage and marital disruption, see Aimee Dechter, "The Effect of Women's Economic Independence on Union Dissolution," Working Paper Np. 92–98 (1992).

    Center for Demography and Ecology, University of Wisconsin, Madison, WI; Mark Testa et al., "Employment and Marriage Among Inner-City Fathers," *Annals of the American Academy of Political and Social Science* 501 (1989), pp. 79–91; Karen Holden and Pamela Smock, "The Economic Costs of Marital Dissolution: Why Do Women Bear a Disproportionate Cost?" *Annual Review of Sociology* 17 (1991), pp. 51–58. On the association of low income with domestic violence see Kristin Anderson, "Gender, Status, and Domestic Violence," *Journal of Marriage and the Family* 59 (1997), pp. 655–670; A. M. Moore, "Intimate Violence: Does Socioeconomic Status Matter?" in A. P. Gardarelli, ed., *Violence Between Intimate Partners* (Boston: Allyn and Bacon, 1997), pp. 90–100; A. J. Sedlack and D. D. Broadhurst, *Third National Incidence Study of Child Abuse and Neglect: Final Report* (Washington D.C.: Department of Health and Human Services, 1996).

20. Daniel T. Lichter, *Marriage as Public Policy* (Washington, D.C.: Progressive Policy Institute, September 2001).

21. Kathryn Edin, "A Few Good Men: Why Poor Mothers Don't Marry or Remarry?" *The American Prospect,* January 3, 2000, p. 28; Kathryn Edin and Laura Lein, Making Ends Meet: How Single Mothers Survive Welfare and Low-Wage Work (New York: Russell Sage, 1998).

22. Valerie Oppenheimer and Vivian Lew, "American Marriage Formation in the 1980s," in Karen Mason and An-Magritt Jensen, eds., *Gender and Family Change in Industrialized Countries* (Oxford: Oxford University Press, 1994), pp. 105–38; Sharon Sassler and Robert Schoen, "The Effects of Attitudes and Economic Activity on Marriage," *Journal of Marriage and the Family* 61 (1999): pp. 148–49.

23. John Billy and David Moore, "A Multilevel Analysis of Marital and Nonmarital Fertility in the U.S.," *Social Forces* 70 (1992), pp. 977–1011; Sara McLanahan and Irwin Garfinkel, "Welfare Is No Incentive," *The New York Times,* July 29, 1994, p. A13; Elaine McCrate, "Expectations of Adult Wages and Teenage Childbearing," *International Review of Applied Economics* 6 (1992), pp. 309–328; Ellen Coughlin, "Policy Researchers Shift the Terms of the Debate on Women's Issues," *The Chronicle of Higher Education,* May 31, 1989; Marian Wright Edelman, *Families in Peril: An Agenda for Social Change* (Cambridge: Harvard University Press, 1987), p. 55; Lawrence Lynn and Michael McGeary, eds., *Inner-City Poverty in the United States* (Washington, D.C.: National Academy Press, 1990), pp. 163–67; Jonathan Crane, "The Epidemic Theory of Ghetto and Neighborhood Effects on Dropping Out and Teenaged Childbearing," *American Journal of Sociology* 96 (1991), pp. 1226–59; Sara McLanahan and Lynne Casper, "Growing Diversity and Inequality in the American Family," in Reynolds Farley, *State of the Union,* vol. 2, pp. 10–11; Mike Males, "Poverty, Rape, Adult/Teen

Sex: Why 'Pregnancy-Prevention' Programs Don't Work," *Phi Delta Kappan,* January 1994, p. 409; Mike Males, "In Defense of Teenaged Mothers," *The Progressive,* August 1994, p. 23.

24. Diane McLaughlin and Daniel Lichter, "Poverty and the Marital Behavior of Young Women," *Journal of Marriage and the Family* 59, no. 3 (1997): pp. 582–94.

25. Wendy Single-Rushton and Sara McLanahan, "For Richer or Poorer?" manuscript, Center for Research on Child Well-Being, Princeton University, July 2001, p. 4; Kathryn Edin, "What Do Low-Income Single Mothers Say About Marriage?" *Social Problems* 47 (2000), pp. 112–33.

26. Robert Nakosteen and Michael Zimmer, "Man, Money, and Marriage: Are High Earners More Prone than Low Earners to Marry?" *Social Science Quarterly* 78 (1997): pp. 66–82.

27. Francine D. Blau, Lawrence W. Kahn and Jane Waldfogel, "Understanding Young Women's Marriage Decisions: The Role of Labor and Marriage Market Conditions," *Industrial and Labor Relations Review* 53, no. 4 (July 2000): pp. 624–48.

28. Robert Nakosteen and Michael Zimmer, "Men, Money, and Marriage," *Social Science Quarterly* 78 (1997); Frank F. Furstenberg, Jr., "The Future of Marriage," *American Demographics* 18 (June 1996), pp. 39–40; Francine Blau, Lawrence Kahn, and Jane Waldfogel, "Understanding Young Women's Marriage Decisions," *Industrial and Labor Relations Review* 53 (2000): pp. 624–48.

29. William A. Darity, Jr. and Samuel L. Myers, Jr., "Family Structure and the Marginalization of Black Men: Policy Implications," in *The Decline in Marriage Among African Americans: Causes, Consequences, and Policy Implications,* ed. M. Belinda Tucker and Claudia Mitchell-Kernan (New York: Russell Sage Foundation, 1995), pp. 263–308.

30. Daniel T. Lichter, D. McLaughlin, F. LeClere, G. Kephart, and D. Landry, "Race and the Retreat From Marriage: A Shortage of Marriageable Men?" *American Sociological Review* 57 (December 1992): pp. 781–99.

31. Ron Mincy, Columbia University, personal communication, February 18, 2002.

32. Mavis Hetherington, *For Better or for Worse: Divorce Reconsidered* (New York: W. W. Norton, 2001); Paul Amato and Alan Booth, "The Legacy of Parents' Marital Discord," *Journal of Personality and Social Psychology* 81 (2001), pp. 627–638; Andrew Cherlin, "Going to Extremes: Family Structure, Children's Well-Being, and Social Science," *Demography* 36 (November 1999): pp. 421–28.

33. Elizabeth Cooksey, "Consequences of Young Mothers' Marital Histories for Children's Cognitive Development," *Journal of Marriage and the Family* 59 (May 1997), pp. 245–62; Juan Battle, "What Beats Having Two Parents? Educational Outcomes for African American Students in Single- Versus Dual-Parent Families," *Journal of Black Studies* 28 (1998), pp. 783–802.

34. Ron Mincy and Chen-Chung Huang, "'Just Get Me to the Church . . .': Assessing Policies to Promote Marriage Among Fragile Families," manuscript prepared for the MacArthur Foundation Network on the Family and the Economy Meeting, Evanston, Illinois, November 30, 2001. Contact Ron Mincy, School of Social Work, Columbia University.

35. Research by Andrew Cherlin and Paula Fomby at Johns Hopkins University, as reported in Robin Toner, "Two Parents Not Always Best for Children," *New York Times,* February 21, 2002.

36. Frank Furstenberg, Jeanne Brooks-Gunn, and S. Philip Morgan, *Adolescent Mothers in Later Life* (New York: Cambridge University Press, 1987).

37. Frank Furstenberg, "Is the Modern Family a Threat to Children's Health?" *Society* 36 (1999): p. 35.

38. Richard Gelles, "Constraints Against Family Violence," *American Behavioral Scientist* 36 (1993), pp. 575–86; A. J. Sedlack and D. D. Broadhurst, *Third National*

Incidence Study of Child Abuse and Neglect: Final Report (Washington, D.C.: Department of Health and Human Services, 1996); Kristin Anderson, "Gender, Status and Domestic Violence," *Journal of Marriage and the Family* 59 (1997), pp. 655–670; Jacqueline Payne and Martha Davis, "Testimony of NOW Legal Defense and Education Fund on Child Support and Fatherhood Initiatives," submitted to the United States House Human Resources Subcommittee of the Ways and Means Committee, June 28, 2001.

39. Catherine Kenney and Sara McLanahan, "Are Cohabiting Relationship More Violent Than Marriages?" manuscript, Princeton University; E. D. Leonard, 1994, "Battered Women and Criminal Justice: A Review," doctoral dissertation cited in Todd Migliaccio, "Abused Husbands: A Narrative Analysis," *Journal of Family Issues* 23 (2002), pp. 26–52; K. D. O'Leary et al., "Prevalence and Stability of Physical Aggression Between Spouses: A Longitudinal Analysis," *Journal of Consulting and Clinical Psychology* 57 (1989), pp. 263–68.

40. National Center on Addiction and Substance Abuse at Columbia University, "Back to School 1999—National Survey of American Attitudes on Substance Abuse V: Teens and Their Parents," August 1999. See also Irvin Molotsky, "Study Links Teenage Substance Abuse and Paternal Ties," *New York Times*, Aug. 31, 1999.

41. "Census Bureau Reports Poor Two-Parent Families Are About Twice as Likely to Break Up as Two-Parent Families Not in Poverty," *New York Times*, January 15, 1993, p. A6; Don Burroughs, "Love and Money," *U.S. News & World Report*, October 19, 1992, p. 58; Scott South, Katherine Trent, and Yang Shen, "Changing Partners: Toward a Macrostructural-Opportunity Theory of Marital Dissolution," *Journal of Marriage and Family* 63, no. 3 (2001): 743–754. Also see note 17.

42. Michelle Budig and Paula England, "The Wage Penalty for Motherhood," *American Sociological Review* 66 (2001): pp. 204–225; Heather Joshi, Pierella Paci, and Jane Waldfogel, 1999. "The Wages of Motherhood: Better or Worse," *Cambridge Journal of Economics* 23, no. 5 (1999): pp. 543–564. Jane Waldfogel, "The Effect of Children on Women's Wages," *American Sociological Review* 62: 2 (1997): pp. 209–217.

43. "Young Children in Poverty: A Statistical Update," June 1999 Edition. Released June 17, 1999, prepared by Neil G. Bennett, Jiali Li, Younghwan Song, and Keming Yang. New York: National Center for Children in Poverty, http://cpmcnet.columbia.edu/dept/nccp/99uptext.html. Data for 2000 from CPS, http://ferret.bls.census.gov/macro/032001/pov/new01_003.htm.

44. Nancy Folbre, *Who Pays for the Kids? Gender and the Structures of Constraint* (New York: Routledge, 1994); Ann Crittenden, *The Price of Motherhood* (New York: Metropolitan Books, 2001); Sylvia Ann Hewlett and Cornell West, *The War Against Parents* (New York: Houghton Mifflin, 1998).

45. Joan Williams, *Unbending Gender: Why Family and Work Conflict and What to Do About It* (New York: Oxford University Press, 2000).

46. Ann Crittenden, *The Price of Motherhood. Why the Most Important Job in the World Is Still the Least Valued* (New York: Henry Holt, 2001).

47. Timothy Smeeding, Barbara Boyle Torrey and Martin Rein, "Patterns of Income and Poverty: The Economic Status of Children and the Elderly in Eight Countries," in John L Palmer, Timothy Smeeding, and Barbara Boyle Torrey, eds., *The Vulnerable* (Washington, D.C.: Urban Institute Press, 1988); Susan Houseknecht and Jaya Sastry, "Family 'Decline' and Child Well-Being: A Comparative Assessment," *Journal of Marriage and the Family* 58 (1996); Sara McLanahan and Irwin Garfinkel, "Single-Mother Families and Social Policy: Lessons for the United States From Canada, France, and Sweden," pp. 367–83 in K. McFate, R. Lawson, W. J. Wilson eds., *Poverty, Inequality, and the Future of Social Policy: Western States in the New World Order* (New York: Russell Sage Foundation, 1995). Michael J. Graetz and Jerry L. Mashaw, *True Security: Rethinking American Social Insurance* (New Haven: Yale University Press, 1999).

48. Marcia K. Meyers, Janet C. Gornick, and Laura R. Peck, 2001, "Packaging Support for Low-Income Families: Policy Variation Across the U.S. States," *Journal of Policy Analysis and Management* 20, no. 3: pp. 457–483.

49. Table 7–6, *Green Book 2000*. Committee on Ways and Means, U.S. House of Representatives, 106th Congress Available at http://www.access.gpo.gov/congress/wm001.html.

50. President's Council of Economic Advisors, *The Effects of Welfare Policy and the Economic Expansion of Welfare Caseloads: An Update* (Washington, D.C.: Council of Economic Advisors, 1999).

51. *2000 Kids Count Data Online*, http://www.aecf.org/kidscount/kc2000/sum_11.htm.

52. Jennifer Steinhauer, "States Proved Unpredictable in Aiding Uninsured Children," *New York Times*, September 28, 2000. See also Leighton Ku and Brian Bruen, "The Continuing Decline in Medicaid Coverage," Series A, no. A–37 (Washington, D.C.: Urban Institute, 1999); Sheila Zedlewski and Sarah Brauner, "Are the Steep Declines in Food Stamp Participation Linked to Falling Welfare Caseloads?" Series B, no. B–3 (Washington, D.C.: Urban Institute, 1999).

53. Rachel Schumacher and Mark Greenberg, *Child Care After Leaving Welfare: Early Evidence From State Studies* (Washington, D.C.: Center for Law and Social Policy, 1999). On the added costs of child care and care-giving activities for low-income families, see Jody Heymann, *The Widening Gap: Why America's Working Families Are in Jeopardy and What Can Be Done About It* (New York: Basic Books, 2000).

54. Bureau of the Census, Current Population Reports, *Money Income and Poverty in the U.S.*, 1999. Figures for 2000 from http://ferret.bls.census.gov/macro/032001/pov/new17_008.htm.

55. Patricia Ruggles, *Drawing the Line: Alternative Poverty Measures and Their Implications for Public Policy* (Washington, D.C.: The Urban Institute Press, 1990); Constance Citro and Robert Michael, eds., *Measuring Poverty: A New Approach* (Washington, D.C.: National Academy of Science, 1995); Jared Bernstein, Chauna Brocht, Maggie Spade-Aguilar, *How Much Is Enough? Basic Family Budgets for Working Families* (Washington, D.C.: Economic Policy Institute, 2000).

56. Robert Greenstein, "Should EITC Benefits Be Enlarged for Families With Three or More Children?" Washington, D.C.: Center on Budget and Policy Priorities, 2000. http://www.cbpp.org/3-14-tax.htm.

57. David Ellwood and Jeffrey B. Liebman, "The Middle Class Parent Penalty: Child Benefits in the U.S. Tax Code," manuscript, John F. Kennedy School of Government, Harvard University, Boston, MA, 2000.

58. Robert Cherry and Max Sawicky, "Giving Tax Credit Where Credit Is Due," Briefing Paper (Washington, D.C.: Economic Policy Institute, April 2000). Available at http://www.epinet.org/briefingpapers/eitc.html.

59. Ronald B. Mincy, "Marriage, Child Poverty, and Public Policy," *American Experiment Quarterly*, 4: 2 (Summer 2001): pp. 68–71. See also Wendy Sigle-Rushton and Sara McLanahan, "For Richer or Poorer?" manuscript, Center for Research on Child Well-Being, Princeton University.

60. Julianne Malveaux, "More Jobs, Not More Marriages, Lift Poor," *U.S.A. Today*, February 22, 2002, p. 15A.

POSTSCRIPT

Does Marriage Improve Living Standards for Children?

In order to improve living standards for children, Horn maintains that parents need to be married. Horn asserts that the U.S. government must take a stand and become pro-marriage. In doing so, the government must remove tax disincentives for marriage and revamp the welfare system so that it does not punish married couples. Horn states that government programs should include pre-marriage education and teach couples the skills they need to help their marriage succeed. Horn provides specific techniques to encourage marriage among welfare recipients.

In the opposing selection, Coontz and Folbre cite evidence that shows that poor families need job training, increased education, and affordable child care in order to work their way out of poverty and to provide a higher standard of living for their children. Coontz and Folbre site the number of single parents who have high levels of education, work at well-paying jobs, and live at a middle-class standard of living. For these parents, the lack of marriage has not caused them to live in poverty.

Coontz and Folbre also show how dangerous marriage can be for single mothers and their children. The fathers to whom the mothers might marry are twice as likely to abuse alcohol or drugs and are likely to physically abuse them and their children. Marriage would not take these mothers and their children out of poverty and improve their standard of living, but might push them deeper into a desperate way of living, assert Coontz and Folbre.

Does marriage improve children's standard of living? Have we looked for complicated answers to this question and overlooked an obvious way to help children in our society by encouraging their parents to marry? Should the government promote marriage as a healthy lifestyle instead of being afraid to say the "M" word? What is wrong with promoting married parents and children? On the other hand, could this marriage promotion initiative backfire? Instead of helping children could it actually hurt them? Will the pressure to marry in order to move from welfare to work put additional stress on the family and cause increased child abuse and neglect? Society has a commitment to help children live at a standard of living that encourages positive growth and development. How society can achieve this goal is highly debatable.

ISSUE 10

Are Stepfamilies Inherently Problematic for Children?

YES: David Popenoe, from "The Evolution of Marriage and the Problem of Stepfamilies: A Biosocial Perspective," in Alan Booth and Judy Dunn, eds., *Stepfamilies: Who Benefits? Who Does Not?* (Lawrence Erlbaum, 1994)

NO: Lawrence A. Kurdek, from "Remarriages and Stepfamilies Are Not Inherently Problematic," in Alan Booth and Judy Dunn, eds., *Stepfamilies: Who Benefits? Who Does Not?* (Lawrence Erlbaum, 1994)

ISSUE SUMMARY

YES: Professor of sociology David Popenoe contends that children from single-parent families and stepfamilies are more likely to have emotional problems and health problems and to do poorly in school than children from intact families with two biological parents.

NO: Psychologist Lawrence A. Kurdek maintains that multiple-divorce families, not stepfamilies, differ from two-parent families and that stepfamilies are not inherently problematic for children.

Asking the question, Are stepfamilies inherently problematic for children? triggers memories of the fairy tale "Cinderella," with her wicked stepmother and stepsisters. Although professional family associations such as the National Council of Family Relations and the Stepfamily Association have worked to dispel the Cinderella stepfamily myth, it is still a powerful image. Most people grow up believing that they will marry, have their own biological children, and live happily ever after. This does not always happen. All kinds of events can happen to change the way lives unfold. Changes in physical and mental health, abuse, loss of income, and changing needs of spouses are just a few of the things that can alter the fairy-tale ending of which many people dream.

For the past 20 years divorce has become more common, and, as a result, there is an increasing number of stepfamilies being formed. Most of these families result from divorce and remarriage, but some are formed due to the death of a spouse, single-parent marriage, or other circumstance. Because the research on divorce and stepfamilies is clouded with conflicting findings and research design flaws, how these family forms affect the development of children is also unclear.

Studies of children from divorced families and stepfamilies often take a negative approach. Researchers study what is wrong with the behavior of children from different family types rather than how children have adapted their behavior to survive life transitions. Conversely, society may have become so accustomed to validating divorce and remarriage that the needs of children have become ignored.

In the following selections, David Popenoe and Lawrence A. Kurdek present opposing views on the stepfamily's effect on children. Popenoe proposes that stepfamilies are not a useful alternative to the intact family and that they are a breeding ground for all kinds of problems for children. Kurdek refutes Popenoe's argument with four specific points of his own. He maintains that family life has changed and that family stability for stability's sake is not an appropriate societal value.

David Popenoe

 YES

The Evolution of Marriage and the Problem of Stepfamilies: A Biosocial Perspective

One of the fastest growing family types in every advanced industrial nation has been the stepfamily. . . .

Since 1960 . . . the chances of spending part or all of one's childhood outside an intact family have grown dramatically. According to various estimates, the chances that a child born around 1980 will not be living at age 17 with both biological parents have increased to over 50% (Hernandez, 1993). . . . In 1960, an estimated 83% of all children are living with their two married, biological parents; by 1990, this figure was 58%. . . . More than 9 out of 10 stepchildren live with their biological mother and a stepfather. . . .

The Problem of Stepfamilies

Many, and perhaps most stepfamilies today lead contented home lives and produce happy and successful children. But a growing body of evidence suggests that the increase of stepfamilies has created serious problems for child welfare. . . . Contrary to the view of some social scientists in recent years, who believed that the effects of family fragmentation on children were both modest and ephemeral, there is now substantial evidence to indicate that the child outcomes of these alternative family forms are significantly inferior to those of families consisting of two biological parents. Compared to those in intact families, children in single-parent and stepfamilies are significantly more likely to have emotional and behavioral problems, to receive the professional help of psychologists, to have health problems, to perform poorly in school and drop out, and to leave home early. Moreover, some of these negative effects have been shown to persist into adult life.

Social scientists used to believe that, for positive child outcomes, stepfamilies were preferable to single-parent families. Today, we are not so sure. Stepfamilies typically have an economic advantage, but some recent studies indicate that the children of stepfamilies have as many behavioral and emotional problems as the children of single-parent families, and possibly more (e.g., Kiernan, 1992). . . .

Certain problems are more prevalent in stepfamilies than in other family forms. A common finding is that stepparents provide less warmth and communicate less well with their children than do biological parents (Thomson, McLenahan, & Curtin, 1992). A number of studies have found that a child is far more likely to be abused by a stepfather than by the biological father. . . . Compared to children in intact and single-parent households, . . . "stepchildren are not merely disadvantaged,' but imperiled" (Wilson & Daly, 1987, p. 230).

As in single-parent families, a major problem of the stepfamily phenomenon is the net loss of fathering in children's lives. . . . Many studies have shown that stepfathering acts to diminish contact between original fathers and their biological children (Furstenberg & Nord, 1985; Furstenberg, Nord, Peterson, & Zill, 1983; Mott, 1990; Seltzer & Bianchi, 1988). In their turn, stepfathers take a considerably less active role in parenting than do custodial biological fathers, according to many studies, and frequently become disengaged from their stepchildren following the establishment of a stepfamily. . . .

Another problematic aspect of stepfamilies is their high breakup rate, higher than that of two-biological-parent families. According to the most recent census data, more than 62% of remarriages among women under age 40 will end in divorce, and the more that children are involved, the higher the redivorce rate. . . . By one estimate, about 15% of all children born in recent decades will go through at least two family disruptions before coming of age (Furstenberg, 1990).

In summary, according to the available evidence, stepfamilies tend to have less cohesive, more problematic, and more stressful family relationships than intact families, and probably also than single-parent families. Put more strongly by a recent article in *Psychology Today,* stepfamilies "are such a minefield of divided loyalties, emotional traps, and management conflicts that they are the most fragile form of family in America" ("Shuttle Diplomacy," 1993).

Biosocial Bases of Family Life

In order to better understand the special problems that stepfamilies pose, it is necessary to delve into the fundamental biosocial nature of human family life. . . .

From the perspective of evolutionary biology, the organization of the human nuclear family is based on two inherited biological predispositions that confer reproductive success, one that operates between parent and child, and the other between parent and parent. The first is a predisposition to advance the interests of genetic relatives before those of unrelated individuals. . . . With respect to children, this means that men and women have likely evolved to invest more in children who are related to them than in those who are not. . . .

The second biological predisposition is for males and females to have some emotional affinity for each other beyond the sexual act, and to establish pair bonds. We tend to fall in love with one person at a time. Although we think of love attachments as being highly social in character, they also have a strong biological component. There exists an "affective attachment" between men and women that causes us to be infatuated with each other, to feel a sense of well-being when we are together with a loved one, and to feel jealous when others attempt to intrude into our relationship. Around the world today, almost all adults pair-bond with someone of the opposite sex for at least a portion of their lives, and monogamous relationships are the rule. . . .

One fundamental reason for family instability is that, at heart, human beings are probably more self-interested than truly altruistic, even toward our own relatives and intimates. We act, first and foremost, in the interest of self-survival. But another reason is that the male–female bond, especially when compared to the mother–infant bond, is notoriously fragile. Although marriage is universal, divorce has also been a central feature of human social life. . . .

Possibly the most disintegrating force acting on the human pair bond is the male sexual drive. . . . Universally, men are the more sexually driven and promiscuous, while women are more relationship-oriented. . . .

Sexual and Reproductive Strategies

. . . Biologically, the primary reproductive function for males is to inseminate, and for females is to harbor the growing fetus. . . . Males, therefore, have more incentive to spread their numerous sperm more widely among many females, and females have a strong incentive to bind males to themselves for the long-term care of their more limited number of potential offspring.

The woman's best reproductive strategy is to ensure that she maximizes the survivability of the one baby she is able to produce every few years through gaining the provision and protection of the father. . . . The man's best strategy, however, may be twofold. He wants his baby to survive, yes, and for that reason he may provide help to his child's mother. But, at the same time, it is relatively costless to him . . . to inseminate other women, and thereby help to further insure that his genes are passed on. . . .

Why aren't all men promiscuous cads? Because, in addition to the pull of the biological pair-bonding and parenting predispositions discussed previously, virtually all human societies have established strong cultural sanctions that seek to limit male promiscuity and protect the sanctity of the family. . . .

If a man is to stay with one woman rather than pursue many different women, according to sociobiologists, the "paternal certainty" of his offspring is extremely important. A woman can be certain about her own offspring, but a man cannot be. . . . [A] male tends to invest in his mate's children only when his paternal confidence is high. . . .

Cultural Contexts

. . . During the most recent stages of the development of the human species, rapidly paced cultural evolution has overtaken slow-moving biological evolution as the main force of social change (Hallpike, 1986; Scott, 1989). One result is that family structures around the world today are widely variable, determined more by cultural differences than by biological predispositions. . . .

Associated with the rise of horticultural and agrarian societies was fundamental shift in people's attitudes toward reproduction (Lancaster & Lancaster, 1987). . . .

[W]ith increased density of population and wealth, people came to perceive that resources were limited, that major differentials existed between who survived and who did not, and that survival was very much dependent on who controlled the most resources. It was no longer sufficient merely to rear as many offspring as possible and hope that they would survive to reproduce. Reproductive strategies became individually tailored to maximize the use and control of resources. It was necessary to try to guarantee children access to resources in the form of education or inheritance, for example, so that they would have an advantage over other parents' children.

Marriage and Divorce in Premodern Societies

The new perception of resource scarcity in complex societies generated a dramatic transformation in family life and kinship relations, including concern for the "legitimacy" of children, the rise of inheritance laws, and the careful control of female sexuality. The nuclear family gave way to the complex, extended family; the conjugal unit became imbedded in an elaborate kinship network. The father role of authority figure and head of household grew in importance, whereas the status of women deteriorated. . . .

Through the institutionalization of cultural norms and sanctions, complex societies have become heavily devoted to socially controlling male and female sexual strategies. The most important social institution serving this purpose is marriage. Marriage can be defined simply as "a relationship within which a group socially approves and encourages sexual intercourse and the birth of children" (Frayser, 1985, p. 248). . . . Throughout most of recorded history, until recently, most marriages were arranged (although the principals typically had a say in the matter); they were less alliances of two individuals than of two kin networks, typically involving an exchange of money or goods.

Various theories have been put forth to explain the fundamental purposes of marriage. But certainly one purpose is, as noted previously, to hold men to the pair bond, thereby helping to ensure high quality offspring and, at the same time, helping to control the open conflict that would result if men were allowed unlimited ability to pursue the "cad" strategy with other men's wives. . . .

Marriage and Divorce in Urban-Industrial Societies

. . . In urban-industrial societies, reproductive concerns about the quantity of children have largely given way to concerns about quality. Children in these societies require massive parental investments if they are to succeed, and childrearing has become extraordinarily expensive in terms of time and money. . . .

The modern nuclear family that accompanied the emergence of urban-industrialism and cultural modernity in the West was distinctly different from its preindustrial predecessor. . . . The new family form was emotionally intense, privatized, and child-oriented; in authority structure, it was relatively egalitarian; and it placed a high value on individualism in the sense of individual rights and autonomy. . . .

The big winners from the emergence of the modern nuclear family . . . were . . . children. In preindustrial Europe, parental care of children does not seem to have been particularly prominent, and such practices as infanticide, wet nursing, child fosterage, and the widespread use of lower status surrogate caretakers were common (Draper & Harpending, 1987). . . . Draper and Harpending (1987) suggested that one of the greatest achievements of the modern nuclear family was the return to the high-investment nurturing of children by their biological parents, the kind of parenting characteristic of our hunter-gatherer ancestors. . . .

Family stability during this era, together with parental investments in children, may have been greater than at any other time in history. Cultural sanctions concerning marriage were powerfully enforced, and thanks to ever lowering death rates and low divorce rates, both parents were typically able to see their children through to adulthood. This remarkably high family stability helps to explain why the family situation in the United States today appears so troubled, particularly in the minds of the older generation.

Recent Family and Cultural Change in America

In the past half century, the U.S. family has been on a social roller coaster. The ups and downs have been quite astonishing. Following World War II, the United States entered a two-decade period of extraordinary economic growth and material progress. Commonly referred to as simply "the 50s," it was the most sustained period of prosperity in U.S. history. Together with most other industrially developed societies of the world, this nation saw improvements in the levels of health, material consumption, and economic security that had scant historical precedent. For most Americans, the improvements included striking increases in longevity, buying power, personal net worth, and government-sponsored economic security.

The 1950s was also an era of remarkable familism and family togetherness, with the family as an institution undergoing unprecedented growth and stability within the middle and working classes. The marriage rate reached an all-time high, the birth rate returned to the high levels of earlier in the century, generating the baby boom, and the divorce rate leveled off. Home, motherhood, and child-centeredness reigned high in the lexicon of cultural values. A higher proportion of children were growing up in stable, two-parent families than ever before in U.S. history.

Beginning in the 1960s, however, a series of unanticipated social and cultural developments took place that shook the foundations of the modern nuclear family. . . . Men abandoned their families at an unprecedented rate, leaving behind broken homes and single-parent, female-headed households. Women relinquished their traditional mother/housewife roles in unexpectedly large numbers and entered the labor force. The percentage of births taking place outside of marriage skyrocketed. Highly permissive sexual behavior became acceptable. . . .

Not only did the modern nuclear family become fragmented, but participation in family life went into a precipitous decline. . . .

Underlying these family-related trends was an extraordinary shift in cultural values and self-definition. . . . Trust in, and a sense of obligation toward, the larger society and its institutions rapidly eroded; the traditional moral authority of social institutions such as schools, churches, and governments withered. What emerged, instead, was a new importance given by large segments of the population to the personal goal and even moral commandment of expressive individualism or "self-fulfillment" (Bellah, Madsen, Sullivan, Swidler, & Tipton, 1985). . . .

The institution of marriage was particularly hard hit. . . .

The marriage rate has steadily declined over the past few decades, from 76.7 marriages per 1,000 unmarried women in 1970, to 54.2 in 1990. The divorce rate, although it has leveled off, remains at an historically high level. Marriage has become a voluntary relationship which individuals can make and break at will. As one indicator of this shift, the legal regulation of marriage and divorce has become increasingly lax. In summary, fewer people ever marry, those who marry do so at a later age, a smaller proportion of life is spent in wedlock, and marriages are of a shorter duration (Espanshade, 1985).

. . . One of the significant attitudinal changes of recent years is the rising acceptance of divorce, especially when children are involved. . . .

The high voluntary dissolution of marriages might not be a serious problem if only adults were involved although, even then, it certainly generates considerable instability and anxiety. The problem is that young children, if they are to grow up successfully, still need strong attachments to parents. The evidence strongly suggests that parental bonds with children have suffered in recent years, and that the tremendous parenting advantages of the modern nuclear family are on the wane. . . .

The Social Response to Stepfamilies

The decline of marriage and the increase of divorce are, of course, the major contributors to the recent growth of stepfamilies. . . .

It is surely the case, especially in view of the diminution of kinship and neighborhood groupings, that stepfamilies need our collective help and understanding more than ever. But we should not confuse short-run actions aimed at helping stepfamilies with long-run solutions. If the argument presented [here] is correct, and the family is fundamentally rooted in biology and at least partly activated by the "genetically selfish" activities of human beings, childrearing by nonrelatives is inherently problematic. It is not that unrelated individuals are unable to do the job of parenting, it is just that they are not as likely to do the job well. Stepfamily problems, in short, may be so intractable that the best strategy for dealing with them is to do everything possible to minimize their occurrence.

Unfortunately, many members of the therapeutic and helping professions, together with a large group of social science allies, now take the view that the trend toward stepfamilies cannot be reversed. . . .

A close companion to this belief in stepfamily inevitability and optimum fit with a changing society is the view that we should now direct most of our attention toward understanding the familial processes of stepfamilies, and seek to develop social policies and interventions that will assist children's adjustment to them. . . . Once stepfamilies become more common and accepted, it is argued, and once our society comes to define the roles of stepparenthood more clearly, the problems of stepfamilies will diminish.

This may be a largely incorrect understanding of the situation. The reason why unrelated stepparents find their parenting roles more stressful and less satisfying than biological parents is probably due much less to social stigma and to the uncertainty of their obligations, as to the fact that they gain fewer intrinsic emotional rewards from carrying out those obligations. . . .

If, as the findings of evolutionary biology strongly suggest, there is a biological basis to parenting, we must question the view, widespread in the social sciences, that parenthood is merely a social role anyone can play if only they learn the part. . . .

The biosocial perspective presented in this essay leads to the conclusion that we as a society should be doing much more to halt the growth of stepfamilies. It is important to give great respect to those stepfamilies that are doing their job well, and to provide both assistance and compassion for those that are experiencing difficulties. But such efforts should not overshadow the paramount importance of public policies designed to promote and preserve two-biological-parent families, and of endeavors to reverse the cultural drift toward radical individualism and the decline of marriage.

References

Bellah, R. N., Madsen, R., Sullivan, W. M., Swidler, A., & Tipton, S. M. (1985). *Habits of the heart: Individualism and commitment in american life.* Berkeley: University of California.

Daly, M., & Wilson, M. (1987). The Darwinian psychology of discriminative parental solicitude. *Nebraska Symposium on Motivation.*

Draper, P., & Harpending, H. (1987). Parent investment and the child's environment. In J. B. Lancaster, J. Altmann, A. S. Rossi, & L. R. Sherrod (Eds.), *Parenting across the life span: Biosocial dimensions* (pp. 207–235). New York: Aldine De Gruyter.

Espenshade, T. J. (1985). The recent decline of american marriage. In K. Davis (Ed.), *Contemporary marriage* (pp. 53–90). New York: Russell Sage Foundation.

Frayser, S. (1985). *Varieties of sexual experience: An anthropological perspective on human sexuality.* New Haven, CT: HRAF Press.

Furstenberg, F. F., Jr. (1990). Divorce and the American family. *Annual Review of Sociology, 16,* 379–403.

Furstenberg, F. F., Jr., & Nord, C. W. (1985). Parenting apart: Patterns of childbearing after marital disruption. *Journal of Marriage and the Family, 47*(4), 893–905.

Furstenberg, F. F., Jr., Nord, C. W., Peterson, J. L., & Zill, N. (1983). The life course of children of divorce: Marital disruption and parental contact. *American Sociological Review, 48*(2), 656–658.

Hallpike, C. R. (1986). *The principles of social evolution*. Oxford: Clarendon.

Hernandez, D. J. (1993). *America's children*. New York: Russell Sage Foundation.

Kiernan, K. E. (1992). The impact of family disruption in childhood on transitions made in young adult life. *Population Studies, 46,* 213–234.

Lancaster, J. B., & Lancaster, C. S. (1987). The watershed: Change in parental-investment and family formation strategies in the course of human evolution. In J. B. Lancaster, J. Altmann, A. S. Rossi, & L. R. Sherrod (Eds.), *Parenting across the life span: Biosocial dimensions* (pp. 187–205). New York: Aldine de Gruyter.

Mott, F. L. (1990). When is father really gone? Paternal-child contact in father absent homes. *Demography, 27*(4), 499–517.

Scott, J. P. (1989). *The evolution of social systems*. New York: Gordon & Breach.

Seltzer, J. A., & Bianchi, S. M. (1988). Children's contact with absent parents. *Journal of Marriage and the Family, 50,* 663–677.

Shuttle diplomacy. (1993, July/August). *Psychology Today,* p. 15.

Thomson, E., McLanahan, S. S., & Curtin, R. B. (1992). Family structure, gender, and parental socialization. *Journal of Marriage and the Family, 54*(2), 368–378.

Wilson, M. I., & Daly, M. (1987). Risk of maltreatment of children living with stepparents. In R. J. Gelles & J. B. Lancaster (Eds.), *Child abuse and neglect: Biosocial dimensions* (pp. 215–232). New York: Aldine de Gruyter.

Lawrence A. Kurdek **NO**

Remarriages and Stepfamilies Are Not Inherently Problematic

My strongest reactions to [professor of sociology David] Popenoe's chapter ["The Evolution of Marriage and the Problem of Stepfamilies: A Biosocial Perspective," in Alan Booth and Judy Dunn, eds., *Stepfamilies: Who Benefits? Who Does Not?*] were disappointment and irritation. . . . I had expected a critical review of the factors that determine both relationship commitment (e.g., Kurdek, 1993a) and relationship stability (e.g., Kurdek, 1993b) in remarriages involving children. No such review was presented.

Instead, Popenoe uses a biosocial perspective to make sweeping claims about the nature of family life that result in the conclusion that society should do more to halt the growth of stepfamilies. . . .

Children of Stepfamilies Have as Many Behavioral and Emotional Problems as the Children of Single-Parent Families, and Possibly More

My response to this claim has four parts: (a) comparisons between family structures should include mention of the size of any obtained differences between these family structures, (b) comparisons among divorce-related family structures need to take into account the number of parental divorces experienced, (c) the key family structure comparison involves stepfamilies and single divorced-parent families, and (d) comparisons involving stepfamilies need to consider the structural heterogeneity of stepfamilies. I expand on each of these parts.

In their influential meta-analysis of parental divorce and children's well-being, Amato and Keith (1991) presented information on the nature of differences between children in intact families and children in stepfamilies. True to the pattern Popenoe describes, relative to children in intact families, those in stepfamilies had more conduct problems, lower psychological adjustment, and lower self-esteem. . . . Although reliable, the differences between the two groups are fairly weak. . . .

Based on evidence from the life events, attachment, and family process literatures, there is reason to expect that the children and adolescents most at risk for behavioral and emotional problems are not those in stepfamilies, but those who have experienced multiple parental divorces and, consequently, multiple parenting transitions. Although evidence on this point is limited, it is consistent.

Studies that have examined the effects of parenting transitions on child and adolescent outcomes have typically compared four groups. These are children living continuously with both biological parents, children who have experienced one parental divorce and live with a single mother, children who have experienced one parental divorce and have made the additional transition to living with a mother and stepfather, and children who have experienced more than one parental divorce. Because of their relatively small numbers, children living with single divorced fathers and children living in stepmother families are usually excluded (see Kurdek & Fine, 1993).

Across a range of outcome variables and sources of information, it is the multiple divorce group—not the stepfamily group—that differs most strongly and negatively from the two-parent group. In fact, few differences emerge between children living continuously with both biological parents and either children living with a singly divorced mother or children living in a stepfather family. These findings lead to the plausible conclusion that what negatively affects children's well-being is not so much the kind of family structure in which they happen to reside, but the history of the quality and consistency of the parenting they receive. . . .

Despite the emphasis Popenoe places on family structure, he fails to recognize that stepfamilies themselves are quite structurally diverse. To his credit, he does note that stepfamilies may result from parental death, parental abandonment, or parental divorce. However, he does not mention that there may be important differences between stepfather families and stepmother families, or that the remarriage history of each spouse may affect the stability of the remarriage. Nor does he state that a joint consideration of the husbands' and wives' parent and custody status relevant to previous marriages leads to at least nine types of stepfamilies, and highlights the distinction between residential and nonresidential stepfamilies, or that a substantial number of children—as many as 300,000 children for women in second marriages alone—are born into stepfamilies (Wineberg, 1992). Given such diversity within stepfamily structures, the general and unqualified claim that stepfamilies are no better than single-parent families is unfounded.

Stepfamilies Are More Unstable Than Intact Families

Popenoe claims that one problematic aspect of stepfamilies is their high breakup rate. However, a close reading of the limited data on this topic reveals that the findings on this issue are actually inconsistent. Most of the evidence concerns the stability of second marriages. Some of these studies report no difference in the marital stability of second marriers with and without children. Others report slightly higher instability rates for second marriers with children compared to those without children. Still others report that for second-marriers, a slightly increased instability rate occurs only for dissolutions occurring within the first 5 years of remarriage and that the birth of children to a mother in a second marriage increases the stability of that remarriage (Wineberg, 1992).

In short, because stepfamilies are a diverse group, it is misleading to characterize their stability as if they represented a homogeneous group. The current evidence gives every reason to expect that stability rates of remarriages vary by divorce history and parent history of each spouse; length of remarriage; age, gender, and pattern of residence for stepchildren; and whether mutual children are born to spouses in the stepfamily.

A Biosocial Perspective Leads to the Conclusion That Stepfamilies Are Intractably Problematic

Popenoe claims that in order to understand the special problems posed by stepfamilies, one must consider the biosocial nature of human family life. Based on an evolutionary biology perspective, Popenoe states that the organization of the human nuclear family is based on two inherited biological predispositions that confer reproductive success. The first predisposition operates between parents and children and entails advancing the interests of genetic relatives over those of unrelated individuals. The second predisposition operates between parents and concerns affective attachments between males and females. These seem like reasonable propositions.

Popenoe further notes that family instability can be linked to the fact that human beings are more interested in themselves than in their own relatives, results from men being more sexually driven and promiscuous than women, and that because human pair bonds are fragile, men and women follow different reproductive strategies: Men inseminate as many women as possible, whereas women withhold reproductive access until they can be certain that the male will commit his resources to his offspring.

I see two major problems with using these points to support the argument that childrearing by nonrelatives is inherently problematic. First, Popenoe ignores evidence that although the roles consistent with each gender's reproductive strategy do a reasonable job of accounting for differences between men and women in sexual attraction and mate selection, these same roles actually contribute to relationship problems and relationship instability. In what he termed the *fundamental paradox*, Ickes (1993) noted a tension between what genes predispose us to do in finding a mate and what current culture prescribes us to do in living happily with that mate. That is, although our evolutionary past may account for partner attraction, our cultural present accounts for how nonexploitative, equal partner relationships are established and maintained.

Second, Popenoe does not use the term *paternal investment* very clearly, but I assume he means that biological fathers in stable marriages are directly—and not just genetically—involved in childrearing. However, most of the normative descriptive data on this topic indicate that although fathers believe they should be directly involved in their children's lives, most are not (Thompson & Walker, 1989). . . .

Thus, the bystander role played by some stepfathers may be functionally similar to the indirect parenting role played by some biological fathers. . . .

Family Life in the 1950s Was Better Than Contemporary Family Life

I agree with Popenoe that it is important to place family life within a larger sociocultural context. Further, no one could disagree that divorce rates began to accelerate in the 1960s. However, I strongly disagree with Popenoe's claim that the 1950s were an era of remarkable familism and family togetherness. Certainly, marital stability rates were high at this time in history. Nonetheless, there is ample evidence that stable marriages are not necessarily happy or healthy marriages. In addition, prospective longitudinal studies that have assessed the same group of children when they lived with both parents as well as when they lived with a divorced single parent indicate that the relatively adverse functioning of children who have experienced parental divorce is predicted by conditions in the intact family that existed well before the divorce. . . .

What irritates me most about the claim of familism in the 1950s is that it seems to value marital stability for stability's sake. Home, motherhood, and children did rank high among U.S. cultural values, yet current data on middle-aged persons who were children during this era strongly suggest that what transpired in many of these families belied these values. That is, the culture of the family was at odds with the conduct of the family. How can Popenoe extol the somewhat superficial endorsement of familism during this era in light of evidence that many children in these highly stable families were exposed to an interconnecting web of family conflict, domestic violence, harsh and inconsistent discipline, alcoholism, and, in some instances, abuse and neglect? Two biological parents were physically present in many of these families, but at what cost?

The Family Is Being Deinstitutionalized

Popenoe rightly notes that marriage as a social institution has evolved in form and function to adapt to new economic, social, cultural, and even psychological settings. But for some reason, Popenoe does not seem to think that the current nature of the institution of marriage reflects this continuous process of economic, social, cultural, and psychological change. One of the most peculiar aspects to Popenoe's chapter is that although he endorses a grand model of change (the biosocial, evolutionary perspective), he urges us as members of society to put an end to a family form that could be viewed as the result of the very economic, social, cultural, and psychological changes that preceded it.

. . . Like it or not, women are no longer economically dependent on their husbands. Like it or not, women no longer need to define themselves in terms of their social roles as wives and mothers. Like it or not, women benefit from participating in roles other than or in addition to that of mother. Like it or not, men and women are going to renege on vows of lifetime commitments to one person because life with that one person sometimes reaches intolerable limits that could not be foreseen at the time of marriage. Finally, like it or not, as a result of these economic, social, cultural, and psychological dimensions of contemporary life, many children will experience the stresses associated with parenting transitions.

References

Amato, P. R., & Keith, B. (1991). Parental divorce and the well-being of children: A meta-analysis. *Psychological Bulletin, 110,* 26–46.

Ickes, W. (1993). Traditional gender roles: Do they make, and then break, our relationships? *Journal of Social Issues, 49,* 71–85.

Kurdek, L. A. (1993a). *Determinants of relationship commitment: evidence from gay, lesbian, dating heterosexual, and married heterosexual couples.* Manuscript submitted for publication.

Kurdek, L. A. (1993b). Predicting marital dissolution from demographic, individual-differences, interdependence, and spouse discrepancy variables: A 5-year prospective longitudinal study of newlywed couples. *Journal of Personality and Social Psychology, 64,* 221–242.

Kurdek, L. A., & Fine, M. A. (1993). The relation between family structure and young adolescents' appraisals of family climate and parenting behavior. *Journal of Family Issues, 14,* 279–290.

Thompson, L., & Walker, A. J. (1989). Women and men in marriage, work, and parenthood. *Journal of Marriage and the Family, 51,* 845–872.

Wineberg, H. (1992). Childbearing and dissolution of the second marriage. *Journal of Marriage and the Family, 54,* 879–887.

POSTSCRIPT

Are Stepfamilies Inherently Problematic for Children?

Popenoe maintains that the intact, two-biological-parent family is the only type of family that is appropriate for children. He goes a step further by saying that stepfamilies are so harmful to children that they should be stopped.

Are stepfamilies inherently problematic for children? How do children in stepfamilies fare compared to families in which the mother lives with a number of boyfriends? This type of family form is not considered a stepfamily but could be very unstable for children. How do children from stepfamilies compare to children with two biological parents who are abusive to them? Is it better to be with stepparents who may not treat you warmly, as Popenoe argues, than to be with biological parents who beat you?

On the other hand, history is full of examples in which blood relatives were treated differently than relatives who came into the family through marriage or some other means. Inheriting land or a title as the first-born son or as the lineage associated with royalty has always depended upon being related by blood versus being adopted or being an in-law. Popenoe recognizes that having a son or daughter that is part of one's genetic material is a powerful concept. Whether or not this genetic tie interferes with parenting styles is debatable.

Suggested Readings

Amato, P. R. (1993). Children's adjustment to divorce: Theories, hypotheses, and empirical support. *Journal of Marriage and the Family, 55,* 23–38.

Cherlin, A. J., & Furstenberg, F. F. (1994). Stepfamilies in the United States: A reconsideration. *Annual Review of Sociology, 20,* 359–381.

Ganong, L. H., & Coleman, M. (1994). *Remarried family relationships.* Thousand Oaks: Sage Publications.

McLanahan, S., & Sandefur, G. (1994). *Growing up with a single parent: What hurts? What helps?* Cambridge, MA: Harvard University Press.

ISSUE 11

Is Television Viewing Responsible for the Rise in Childhood Obesity?

YES: The Henry J. Kaiser Family Foundation, from "The Role of Media in Childhood Obesity," *Issue Brief—The Henry J. Kaiser Foundation* (February 2004)

NO: Center for Science in the Public Interest, from "Dispensing Junk: How School Vending Undermines Efforts to Feed Children Well," *Center for Science in the Public Interest* (May 2004)

ISSUE SUMMARY

YES: The Henry J. Kaiser Family Foundation, a private non-profit foundation focusing on major health care issues facing the nation, cites research studies that show that the more children watch television, the more likely they will be overweight. They also contend that the rise in childhood obesity can be traced to the increased use of media.

NO: The Center for Science in the Public Interest, a consumer advocacy organization on nutrition and health, views the high-calorie, non-nutritious foods found in school vending machines as the culprit in the rise in childhood obesity rates.

T he rise in childhood obesity is considered an epidemic because the rates of childhood overweight have grown so rapidly in such a short amount of time. According to the Centers for Disease Control and Prevention, National Center for Health Statistics, since 1980 the proportion of overweight children has more than doubled. The rate for teens has tripled since 1980. Currently, 10 percent of 2 to 5-year-olds are overweight, and 15 percent of 6 to 19-year-olds are overweight. The numbers go up to 20 percent for 2 to 5-year-old children, and 30 percent for 6 to 19-year-old children when you add in those at risk for being overweight. Children of color are at greater risk with four out of 10 Mexican-American and African-American children being overweight.

Childhood obesity is the term used to describe the problem in the population while individual children are generally referred to as being overweight.

Children would not be referred to as obese, but would be classified as overweight. Overweight and at risk for being overweight are terms used to define children whose height and weight fall within a certain range on a chart referred to as the BMI (body mass index). The BMI measures the ratio of weight to height. BMI measures for children are age- and gender-specific because children's body fat varies with age and gender. A child's BMI is plotted on a growth curve that reflects that child's age and gender. This plotting yields a value, BMI for age, that provides a consistent measure across age groups. Percentile scores indicate how a particular child compares with other children of the same age and gender. The Centers for Disease Control classifies children above the 95th percentile for their age and gender as overweight. Children are considered at risk for being overweight if they fall between the 85th and 95th percentile for age and gender. Healthy children have a BMI of 6 to 85 percent, and underweight children have a BMI of less than 5 percent.

Why is the rise in childhood obesity considered such a problem? Along with being overweight comes a host of physical and mental health problems such as diabetes, high blood pressure, depression, and poor body image. The health care costs for these medical conditions are exorbitant, not to mention the reduced quality of life for the children. The probability that overweight children will become overweight adults is 50 percent; thus, these health care issues may follow the child into adulthood. The subsequent reduced productivity levels of adults, whose overweight condition follows them into adulthood, have economic and social implications. Instead of contributing to society and the economy, individuals may be relying on these institutions to take care of them.

What are the reasons that we are seeing such a rise in childhood overweight? In the following selections, personnel from The Henry J. Kaiser Family Foundation propose that the rise in childhood obesity is due to the influence of the media, specifically the huge numbers of hours of television that children watch. Personnel from The Center for Science in the Public Interest assert that the high-calorie, low-nutrient food found in school vending machines encourages children to develop poor eating habits and leads to their being overweight.

The Henry J. Kaiser
Family Foundation

 YES

The Role of Media in Childhood Obesity

Introduction

In recent years, health officials have become increasingly alarmed by the rapid increase in obesity among American children. According to the Centers for Disease Control and Prevention (CDC), since 1980 the proportion of overweight children ages 6–11 has more than doubled, and the rate for adolescents has tripled. Today about 10 % of 2- to 5-year-olds and 15 % of 6- to 19-year-olds are overweight. Taking into consideration the proportion who are "at risk" of being overweight, the current percentages double to 20 % for children ages 2–5 and 30 % for kids ages 6–19. Among children of color, the rates are even higher: 4 in 10 Mexican American and African American youth ages 6–19 are considered overweight or at risk of being overweight.

According to the American Academy of Pediatrics, the increase in childhood obesity represents an "unprecedented burden" on children's health. Medical complications common in overweight children include hypertension, type 2 diabetes, respiratory ailments, orthopedic problems, trouble sleeping, and depression. The Surgeon General has predicted that preventable morbidity and mortality associated with obesity may exceed those associated with cigarette smoking. Given that an estimated 80 % of overweight adolescents continue to be obese in adulthood, the implications of childhood obesity on the nation's health—and on health care costs—are huge. Indeed, the American Academy of Pediatrics has called the potential costs associated with childhood obesity "staggering."

In an effort to seek the causes of this disturbing trend, experts have pointed to a range of important potential contributors to the rise in childhood obesity that are unrelated to media: a reduction in physical education classes and after-school athletic programs, an increase in the availability of sodas and snacks in public schools, the growth in the number of fast-food outlets across the country, the trend toward "super-sizing" food portions in restaurants, and the increasing number of highly processed high-calorie and high-fat grocery products.

The purpose of this issue brief is to explore one other potential contributor to the rising rates of childhood obesity: children's use of media.

During the same period in which childhood obesity has increased so dramatically, there has also been an explosion in media targeted to children: TV shows and videos, specialized cable networks, video games, computer activities and Internet Web sites. Children today spend an average of five-and-a-half hours a day using media, the equivalent of a full time job, and more time than they spend doing anything else besides sleeping. Even the very youngest children, preschoolers ages six and under, spend as much time with screen media (TV, videos, video games and computers) as they do playing outside. Much of the media targeted to children is laden with elaborate advertising campaigns, many of which promote foods such as candy, soda, and snacks. Indeed, it is estimated that the typical child sees about 40,000 ads a year on TV alone.

For the first time, this report pulls together the best available research, going behind the headlines to explore the realities of what researchers do and do not know about the role media plays in childhood obesity. In addition, the report lays out media-related policy options that have been proposed to help address childhood obesity, and outlines ways media could play a positive role in helping to address this important public health problem.

Pediatricians, child development experts, and media researchers have theorized that media may contribute to childhood obesity in one or more of the following ways:

- The time children spend using media displaces time they could spend in physical activities;
- The food advertisements children are exposed to on TV influence them to make unhealthy food choices;
- The cross-promotions between food products and popular TV and movie characters are encouraging children to buy and eat more high-calorie foods;
- Children snack excessively while using media, and they eat less healthy meals when eating in front of the TV;
- Watching TV and videos lowers children's metabolic rates below what they would be even if they were sleeping;
- Depictions of nutrition and body weight in entertainment media encourage children to develop less healthy diets.

The research to date has examined these issues from a variety of perspectives ranging from health sciences and public health, to child development and family relations, to advertising and mass communications. These investigations have been methodologically diverse, and the results have often been mixed. As with any research, caution must be used when comparing the outcomes of studies because of variations in the methods and measures used. For example, some studies are regional, while others use large, nationally representative samples. Some focus on specific demographic subsets, such as 6th-grade girls, while others are broader. Some studies rely on detailed data sets, others on fairly simplistic measures. For example, television use may be measured through self-reports, parental reports, or detailed diaries. Likewise, body fat may be assessed through multiple clinical measures or by self-reports of height and weight.

The following section of this report reviews the major research that has been conducted on the key issues concerning media and childhood obesity, and summarizes the major findings.

DEFINING CHILDHOOD OBESITY

The phrases "obese," "overweight," and "at risk for being overweight" are commonly used in the public health community. With regard to children, the terms "obese" and "overweight" are generally used interchangeably in the medical literature. The Body Mass Index (BMI), which measures the ratio of weight to height, is a standard tool used to define these terms. BMI definitions for children and adolescents are age- and gender-specific in order to accommodate growth patterns. The Centers for Disease Control and Prevention (CDC) classify children as "overweight" if they are above the 95th percentile for their age and sex, and "at risk of being overweight" if they are between the 85th and 95th percentile.

Research on Media and Childhood Obesity

Do major studies find a relationship between childhood obesity and the time children spend using media? The first major evidence that children's media consumption may be related to their body weight came in a 1985 article by William Dietz and Stephen Gortmaker in the journal *Pediatrics,* and it was dramatic. An analysis of data from a large national study of more than 13,000 children, the National Health Examination Survey (NHES), found significant associations between the amount of time children spent watching television and the prevalence of obesity. The authors concluded that, among 12- to 17-year-olds, the prevalence of obesity increased by 2 % for each additional hour of television viewed, even after controlling for other variables such as prior obesity, race, and socio-economic status. Indeed, according to the authors, "only prior obesity had a larger independent effect than television on the prevalence of obesity." In a commentary published in 1993, the authors went on to note that another interpretation of their findings is that "29 % of the cases of obesity could be prevented by reducing television viewing to 0 to 1 hours per week."

Since then, several more studies have found a statistically significant relationship between media use and rates of obesity, while others have found either a weak relationship or no relationship at all. In addition to the Dietz and Gortmaker study, other large-scale national studies have found a correlation between media use and body weight:

- Analysis of data from a nationally representative survey of more than 700 kids ages 10–15, conducted in the late 1980s, concluded that "the odds of being overweight were 4.6 times greater for youth watching more than 5 hours of television per day compared with those watching for 0–1 hours," even when controlling for prior overweight, maternal overweight, race, and socio-economic status. The authors concluded, "Estimates of attributable risk indicate that more [than] 60 % of overweight incidence in this population can be linked to excess television viewing time."

- Data from the 1988–1994 waves of the National Health and Nutrition Examination Surveys (NHANES) were analyzed to explore the relationship between TV watching and obesity among 8- to 16-year-olds. The study concluded that "television watching was positively associated with obesity among girls, even after controlling for age, race/ethnicity, family income, weekly physical activity, and energy intake." The study did not find a correlation for boys.
- Another analysis of the 1988–1994 NHANES data found that among 8- to 16-year-olds, both boys and girls "who watched the most television had more body fat and greater BMIs than those who watched less than 2 hours a day."
- A study based on the CDC's 1999 Youth Risk Behavior Survey which sampled more than 12,000 high school students nationwide, found that watching television more than 2 hours a day was related to being overweight; these findings were consistent for the entire student population, controlling for race, ethnicity, and gender.
- A later study found a link between television viewing and obesity using a different methodology. The Framingham Children's Study was a longitudinal study in which slightly more than 100 children were enrolled as preschoolers and followed into early adolescence. In this study, published in 2003, the authors found that "television watching was an independent predictor of the change in the child's BMI" and other measures of body fatness. They noted that the effect of TV viewing was "only slightly attenuated" by controlling for factors such as the child's body-fat measures at the time they were enrolled in the study, and their parents' BMI or education. The authors concluded that "television watching is a risk factor for change in body fat, not simply reflective of more obese children tending to watch more television as a consequence of their obesity making it difficult to exercise."

Other studies—one from a nationally representative cross-sectional sample and the others from specific regions or communities—have not found a relationship between television viewing and childhood obesity:

- A recent analysis of data from a national study of more than 2,800 children ages 12 and under, which relied on detailed time-use diaries, found a "striking" lack of relationship between time spent watching television and children's weight status. On the other hand, this study did find a relationship between obesity and time spent playing video games, although that relationship was not linear: Children with higher weight played moderate amounts of games, while those with low weight played electronic games either very little or a lot.
- A 1993 study of 6th- and 7th-grade girls in Northern California found that over a two-year period "baseline hours of after-school television

viewing was not significantly associated with either baseline or longitudinal change in BMI." The authors argued that their study "refutes previous suggestions that . . . television viewing is causally related to obesity."

- A study of nearly 200 preschoolers in Texas observed the children for several hours on each of four different days a year, over the course of three years, recording the amount of TV the children watched and their physical activities. This study found that although television watching was weakly negatively correlated with physical activity levels, it was not associated with body composition.

In evaluating this research, it is important to note that some of these studies are cross-sectional rather than longitudinal—that is, they take a specific point in time and look at whether TV viewing is associated with obesity. One problem with this approach is that while a study may indicate a relationship between TV viewing and being overweight, it does not prove that the TV viewing *caused* the increased weight. Controlling for other risk factors such as socio-economic status and parental body weight (as many studies do) can help clarify the results. Another problem with the cross-sectional approach is that the causal relationship could run in the opposite direction: that is, being obese may cause children to engage in more sedentary (and isolated) activities, including watching more television.

Longitudinal studies can help address the causality issue; however, the results of these studies have varied. As noted above, the two-year longitudinal study of adolescent girls in Northern California did not find a causal relationship between children's weight and the time they spent with media. On the other hand, the Framingham Children's Study, which tracked preschoolers through early adolescence, did find such a relationship. The authors of the latter study have theorized that the effects of media use on body weight may emerge slowly over time, and hence were not revealed in the two-year study in Northern California. It has also been argued that the lack of effect in that study may be due to factors specific to the sample of 6th- and 7th-grade girls in Northern California. Additionally, the study of 700 10- to 15-year-olds referenced above used height and weight data from 1986 and compared it to TV viewing and BMI measures in 1990. These authors concluded that "no evidence was found for a selective effect of overweight; i.e., children who were overweight in 1986 were unlikely to watch more television in 1990 than were children who were not overweight."

Others argue that the only way to truly demonstrate a causal relationship is through an experimental trial; for example, reduce TV viewing and see whether that affects children's weight when compared to a control group. Several interventions of this nature have been found to have a positive impact in reducing children's body weight.

Do experimental interventions that reduce children s media time result in weight loss?   Experimental trials are considered the best way of determining whether there is a causal relationship between television viewing and childhood obesity. Some experiments have incorporated reductions in media time as part of a more comprehensive program involving diet and increased physical activity as well. Another experiment used reduced media time as the only intervention, yet still found an impact on children's weight and body fatness.

- During the 1996–97 school year, Stanford University researchers conducted a randomized controlled trial in which they reduced the amount of time a group of about 100 3rd- and 4th-graders in Northern California spent with TV, videos, and video games. Two matched elementary schools were selected to participate, one of which served as the control group. The intervention involved a "turnoff" period of no screen time for 10 days followed by limiting TV time to 7 hours per week, as well as learning media literacy skills to teach selective viewing. At the end of a 6-month, 18-lesson classroom curriculum, students who received the intervention achieved statistically significant reductions in their television viewing and meals eaten in front of the TV set, as well as decreases in BMI, triceps skinfold thickness, waist circumference, and waist-to-hip ratio. While these changes were not accompanied by reduced high-fat food intake or increased physical activity, the findings do appear to demonstrate the feasibility of decreasing body weight by reducing time spent with screen media.
- Another school based intervention found improved diet, increased physical activity, and decreased television time to be effective. The study, which measured prevalence, incidence, and remission of obesity among ethnically diverse middle-school boys and girls, involved a randomized controlled field trial with five intervention and five control schools. Classroom teachers in math, science, language arts, social studies, and physical education incorporated lessons within the existing curricula over two years. The lessons focused on decreasing television viewing to 2 hours per day, increasing physical activity, reducing consumption of high-fat food, and increasing servings of fruits and vegetables. For each hour television viewing was reduced, the prevalence of obesity was reduced among girls in the intervention schools compared with the control schools; no similar effect was found for boys. The program also resulted in an increase in girls' consumption of fruits and vegetables.
- A family-based weight-control program found that decreasing sedentary behaviors (such as screen media use) is a viable alternative to increasing physical activity in treating childhood obesity. Families with obese children ages 8–12 were randomly assigned to one of four groups that included dietary and behavior-change information, but differed in whether they tried to decrease sedentary activities or increase physical activity. Results indicated that significant decreases in percent of overweight and body fat were associated with decreasing sedentary behaviors such as watching TV or videos, or playing video or computer games.

These interventions indicate that reducing the time children spend with media may indeed be an effective way to address childhood obesity. Researchers, health professionals, and advocates have theorized several ways media may contribute to childhood obesity. The following sections summarize some of the major scientific studies in order to provide an understanding of media's potential influence on the incidence of overweight among children and adolescents in the United States.

Does the time children spend using media displace time spent in more physical activities? From toddlers to teens, American youth are spending a substantial part of every day of their lives using media. But the time children spend using media does not necessarily mean a decrease in time spent in physical activities. Surprisingly, few studies have examined this relationship, and results have been mixed. Some studies have found a weak but statistically significant relationship between hours of television viewing and levels of physical activity, while others have found no relationship between the two.

- A study of 6th- and 7th-grade adolescent girls in four Northern California middle schools found that the number of hours they spent watching TV after school was negatively associated with their level of physical activity; however, the relationship accounted for less than 1 % of the variance and there was no connection with body weight.
- A study of a small sample of preschool children in Texas, conducted in a naturalistic setting, found a weak but statistically significant relationship between TV viewing and physical activity, although it did not find a relationship between viewing and body weight.
- A recent national telephone survey of parents of children ages 4–6 found that children who spent more than two hours watching TV the previous day spent an average of a half-hour less playing outside that day than did other children their age.
- A review of data from the 1999 National Youth Risk Behavior Study, which includes a nationally representative sample of more than 15,000 high school students, found that among white female students only, time spent watching TV was associated with being sedentary.
- A survey of close to 2,000 9th-graders in Northern California found a weak but statistically significant relationship between TV viewing and physical activity for white males only.
- A study of national data from the 1988–1994 NHANES found no relationship between TV viewing and the number of bouts of vigorous physical activity, although it did find a statistically significant relationship between TV viewing and body weight.

While logic suggests that extensive television viewing is part of a more sedentary lifestyle, the evidence for this relationship has been surprisingly weak to date. In order for this relationship to be true, as one study noted, children who watch less TV would have to be choosing physically vigorous activities instead of TV, rather than some other relatively sedentary pastime such as reading books, talking on the phone, or playing board games.

Another possibility is that the act of watching TV itself actually reduces children's metabolic rate, contributing to weight gain. One study of 8- to 12-year-olds found that TV viewing decreased metabolic rates even more than resting or sleeping, but several other studies found no such effect.

The fact that most studies have failed to find a substantial relationship between the time children spend watching TV and the time they spend in physical activity may suggest that the *nature* of television viewing—that is, how children watch and what they watch—may be as or more important than the number of hours they watch.

Do the food ads children are exposed to on TV influence them to make unhealthy food choices? Many researchers suspect that the food advertising children are exposed to through the media may contribute to unhealthy food choices and weight gain. Over the same period in which childhood obesity has increased so dramatically, research indicates that the number of ads children view has increased as well. In the late 1970s, researchers estimated that children viewed an average of about 20,000 TV commercials a year; in the late 80s, that estimate grew to more than 30,000 a year. As the number of cable channels exploded in the 1990s, opportunities to advertise directly to children expanded as well. The most recent estimates are that children now see an average of more than 40,000 TV ads a year.

The majority of ads targeted to children are for food: primarily candy (32 % of all children's ads), cereal (31 %), and fast food (9 %). One study documented approximately 11 food commercials per hour during children's Saturday morning television programming, estimating that the average child viewer may be exposed to one food commercial every 5 minutes. According to another study, even the two minutes of daily advertising targeted to students in their classrooms through Channel One expose them to fast foods, candy, soft drinks, and snack chips in 7 out of 10 commercial breaks.

A review of the foods targeted to children in commercials on Saturday morning television indicates that the nutritional value has remained consistently low over the past quarter-century. Over the years, the most prevalent foods advertised have been breakfast cereals. Up until the 1990s, the next most-advertised products were foods high in sugar, such as cookies, candy, and other snacks. By the mid-1990s, canned desserts, frozen dinners, and fast foods overtook ads for snack foods. The data indicate that ads for these high-fat and high-sodium convenience foods have more than doubled since the 1980s. While studies vary as to the exact percentages, the same pattern emerges: a predominance of ads for high-sugar cereals, fast food restaurants, and candy, and an absence of ads for fruit or vegetables.

The effect of food advertising on children The vast majority of the studies about children's consumer behavior have been conducted by marketing research firms and have not been made publicly available. Clearly, the conclusion advertisers have drawn is that TV ads can influence children's purchases—and those of their families. Fast food outlets alone spend $3 billion in television ads targeted to children. Recent years have seen the development of marketing firms, newsletters, and ad agencies specializing in the children's market. The New York Times has noted that "the courtship of children is no surprise, since increasingly that is where the money is," and added that marketing executives anticipate that children under 12 will spend $35 billion of their own money and influence $200 billion in household spending in 2004. The enthusiasm of marketers can be felt in the

Februray 2004 edition of Harris Interactive's "Trends and Tudes" newsletter, which notes that "This generation has become a huge consumer group that is worthy of attention from many businesses seeking to maximize their potential. Kids, teens and young adults spend significant amounts of their own money, and they influence the shopping behavior of their parents, their siblings, their relatives, and other adults in their lives."

Scientific studies that are available in the public realm back up these marketing industry assessments of the effectiveness of advertising directed at children. Studies have demonstrated that from a very young age, children influence their parents' consumer behavior. As many parents can attest after a trip down the grocery aisle with their children, television viewing has also been found to impact children's attempts to influence their parents' purchases at the supermarket. For example, several studies have found that the amount of time children had spent watching TV was a significant predictor of how often they requested products at the grocery store, and that as many as three out of four requests were for products seen in TV ads. These studies have also found that children's supermarket requests do indeed have a fairly high rate of success.

One study found that among children as young as 3, the amount of weekly television viewing was significantly related to their caloric intake as well as their requests and parent purchases of specific foods they saw advertised on television. Another study manipulated advertising shown to 5- to 8-year-olds at summer camp, with some viewing ads for fruit and juice, and others ads for candy and Kool-Aid. This study found that children's food choices were significantly impacted by which ads they saw.

Experimental studies have demonstrated that even a brief exposure to food commercials can influence children's preferences. In one study, researchers designed a randomized controlled trial in which one group of 2- to 6-year-olds from a Head Start program saw a popular children's cartoon with embedded commercials, and the other group saw the same cartoon without commercials. Asked to identify their preferences from pairs of similar products, children who saw the commercials were significantly more likely to choose the advertised products. Preference differences between the treatment and control group were greatest for products that were advertised twice during the cartoon rather than only once.

Researchers are beginning to document a link between viewing television and children's consumption of fast foods and soda, a possible result of exposure to food advertising. A recent study found that students in grades 7–12 who frequently ate fast food tended to watch more television than other students. Another study found that middle-school children who watched more television tended to consume more soft drinks.

Other evidence of television's potential impact on children's dietary habits indicates a negative relationship between viewing television and consuming fruits and vegetables. The USDA's Dietary Guidelines recommend that youth eat three to five daily servings of fruits and vegetables, yet only 1 in 5 children meet the guideline, and one-quarter of the vegetables consumed reportedly are french fries. In a recent study, more than 500 middle school students from ethnically diverse backgrounds were studied over a 19-month period to determine whether daily television and video viewing predicted fruit and vegetable consumption. Using a linear regression analysis, researchers found that for each additional hour of television viewed per day, daily servings of fruits and vegetables decreased among adolescents. The researchers who conducted the study conclude that this relationship may be a result of television advertising.

Some researchers believe that TV ads may also contribute to children's misconceptions about the relative health benefits of certain foods. One of the earlier studies found that 70 % of 6- to 8-year-olds believed that fast foods were more nutritious than home-cooked foods. Another study showed a group of 4th- and 5th- graders a series of paired food items and asked them to choose the healthier item from each pair (for example, corn flakes or frosted flakes). Children who watched more television were more likely to indicate that the less healthy food choice was the healthier one. These results replicated the results of an earlier study conducted with children of the same age.

Do cross-promotions between food products and popular TV and movie characters encourage children to buy and eat more high-calorie foods?   Recent years have seen what appears to be a tremendous increase in the number of food products being marketed to children through cross-promotions with popular TV and movie characters. From SpongeBob Cheez-Its to Hulk pizzas and Scooby-Doo marshmallow cereals, today's grocery aisles are filled with scores of products using kids' favorite characters to sell them food. Fast food outlets also make frequent use of cross-promotions with children's media characters.

A recent article in the New York Times business section noted that "aiming at children through licensing is hardly new. What has changed is the scope and intensity of the blitz as today's youth become unwitting marketing targets at ever younger ages through more exposure to television, movies, videos and the Internet." One food industry executive was quoted as saying that licensing "is a way to . . . infuse the emotion and popularity of a current kids' hit into a product."

Some promotions involve toys based on media characters that are included in the food packages or offered in conjunction with fast food meals. McDonald's and Disney have an exclusive agreement under which Happy Meals include toys from top Disney movies. In the past, Happy Meals have reportedly also included toys based on the Teletubbies TV series, which is aimed at pre-verbal babies. Burger King has also featured Teletubbies tie-ins, along with Rugrats, Shrek, Pokemon and SpongeBob. More than a decade ago, researchers were finding that the typical "kid's meal" advertised to children consisted of a cheeseburger, french fries, soda, and a toy. One study found that about 1 in 6 (16.9 %) food commercials aimed at children promise a free toy. In addition to the use of toys as an incentive in marketing food to children, many commercials use cartoon characters to sell products, which research has shown to be particularly effective in aiding children's slogan recall and ability to identify the product.

A recent example of the effectiveness of this technique is the growth in the dried fruit snack market. Almost half (45 %) of fruit snacks had licensing agreements in 2003 compared to 10 % in 1996. Sales have increased substantially every year since 1999: 5.6 % in 2000, 8.7 % in 2001, 3.2 % in 2002, and 5.5 % in 2003. Marketing experts attribute the sales growth to children's influence on their parents' purchasing decisions and parental beliefs that dried fruit snacks are healthier than other sweets.

Do depictions of nutrition and body type in entertainment media encourage children to develop less healthy diets and eating habits?   Over the years, some critics have argued that TV, movies, and magazines have promoted unrealistically thin body types as the ideal, possibly encouraging teen girls to engage in unhealthy dieting or eating disorders. But after years of an imbalance toward depictions of thin characters, the true weight-related health emergency among young people is, paradoxically, obesity. This paradox has yet to be explained.

Some advocates note that television gives children and teens contradictory messages about dietary habits and ideal body type: be thin but eat fatty foods, sugary sweets, and salty snacks. They point out that on the one hand, the stories media tell are about thin people who are popular and successful, while on the other hand, thin and average-size people on TV can eat whatever they want and almost never gain weight.

Some advocates and researchers also have criticized TV producers for not including more depictions of obese characters, and for negatively portraying the obese characters that do make it onto the screen. On the other hand, it could be argued that portraying obesity as an unhealthy and undesirable characteristic—and associating it with overeating—sends an *appropriate* message to youth. And while some critics fault the media for leaving obese characters off the screen, adding to stigmatization and isolation, other critics complain that too many minority characters are overweight.

NO

Dispensing Junk: How School Vending Undermines Efforts to Feed Children Well

Executive Summary

In September and October 2003, 120 volunteers in 24 states (including the District of Columbia) surveyed the contents of 1,420 vending machines in 251 schools, including 105 middle and junior high schools, 121 high schools, and 25 schools with other combinations of these grade levels (e.g., 7th–12th grades).

The results suggest that the overwhelming majority of options available to children in school vending machines are high in calories and/or low in nutrition. **In both middle and high schools, 75% of beverage options and 85% of snacks were of poor nutritional quality.** The most prevalent options are soda, imitation fruit juices, candy, chips, cookies, and snack cakes. The high prevalence of junk food in school vending machines does not support students' ability to make healthy food choices or parents' ability to feed their children well.

This is of concern because 1) 74% of middle/junior high schools and 98% of senior high schools have vending machines, school stores, or snack bars, 2) children are in school for a substantial portion of the week, and 3) obesity rates are rising rapidly in children and teens.

Given the rising obesity rates and children's poor eating habits, the time has come to ensure that school environments support healthy eating and parents' efforts to feed their children well. A number of policies and programs should be put in place or strengthened to address childhood obesity. **One important strategy is for federal, state, and/or local governments, schools, and school districts to enact policies to ensure that foods sold out of vending machines, school stores, fundraisers, a la carte, and other venues outside of the school meal programs are healthful and make a positive contribution to children's diets.**

At the federal level, Congress should give the U.S Department of Agriculture (USDA) authority to establish and enforce regulations for all food sales anywhere on school campuses throughout the school day as a condition for participating in the National School Lunch Program or School Breakfast

Program. USDA has strong nutrition policies for school meals. It also should set nutrition standards for foods and beverages sold outside those meals.

States, cities, school districts, and schools also could implement strong nutrition standards for foods and beverages sold out of vending machines, school stores, a la carte (snack lines), fundraisers, and other venues outside of the school meal programs. We recognize that school budgets are tight and that the sale of foods in schools provides much-needed revenue. However, a number of schools around the country have replaced soda in school vending machines with healthier beverages and have not lost money.

Introduction

Vending machines are prevalent in schools, yet quantitative data regarding their contents are lacking. Such data would be important to have because most children eat diets of poor nutritional quality, with too much saturated fat, sodium, and refined sugars and too few nutrient-rich fruits, vegetables, and whole grains. Those nutrient imbalances can lead to heart disease, high blood pressure, cancer, dental cavities, and other health problems. In addition, children's calorie intake has increased (and they are insufficiently active) and, as a result, rates of overweight in children have increased. While obesity is a complex, multi-factorial problem, over-consumption of soft drinks and snack foods plays a key role.

Junk food in school vending machines undermines parents' efforts to feed their children well. (This is especially problematic when children have diet-related health problems, such as high cholesterol or diabetes.) When parents send their child to school with lunch money, they do not know whether the child will buy a balanced school lunch or a candy bar and a soda. Long cafeteria lines, short lunch periods, and activities during the lunch period mean that some students rely on foods from vending machines rather than buy lunch from the cafeteria line.

The food industry is taking advantage of schools' financial problems by offering them incentives to sell low-nutrition foods in schools. But bridging school budget gaps by selling junk food to students is a shortsighted approach. In the long run, society is sure to spend more money treating the resulting obesity and diet-related diseases, such as diabetes, heart disease, cancer, and osteoporosis, than schools can raise by selling soda and snack foods to students.

There are ways schools can raise money without jeopardizing children's health. A number of schools in Maine, California, Minnesota, Pennsylvania, and elsewhere have replaced soda with healthy beverages and not lost revenue. In addition to selling healthy foods, schools can sell gift wrap or candles, sponsor fun runs, host car washes, or conduct other profitable fundraisers that do not undermine children's health.

Methods

In late September and early October 2003, 120 individuals in 24 states (including Arkansas, California, Connecticut, the District of Columbia, Illinois, Iowa, Maine, Maryland, Michigan, Mississippi, Missouri, Montana, New Mexico,

New York, North Carolina, North Dakota, Ohio, Oregon, Pennsylvania, South Carolina, South Dakota, Vermont, Washington, and Wisconsin) surveyed the contents of vending machines in their local middle and high schools. The individuals collecting the data were primarily health professionals, employees of health organizations, and school employees. Volunteers surveyed a total of 1,420 vending machines in 251 schools, including 105 middle and junior high schools, 121 high schools, and 25 schools with other combinations of these grade levels.

School sites included both urban and rural schools, schools in a range of socioeconomic areas, and schools ranging in size from 110 to 2,600 students. Vending machines in areas accessible only to teachers and staff were not included.

The average number of vending machines per high school was eight. Some high schools had only one vending machine, while others had as many as 22 vending machines. The average number of vending machines per middle or junior high school was four. Some middle and junior high schools had only one vending machine, while others had up to 10 vending machines.

Vending machines were assessed by counting the number of slots per machine for each beverage or snack category and totaling the number of slots in all machines. Study participants were given a standardized survey form . . . and protocol. Participants had the opportunity to participate in a pre-survey conference call to discuss the protocol and methods for the survey. Participants sent their completed surveys to the Center for Science in the Public Interest (CSPI) for data aggregation and analysis.

The categorization of foods and beverages as "healthier" and "less healthful" was based on and generally in accordance with the nutrition standards for school foods developed by a national panel of experts convened by the California Center for Public Health Advocacy. The following types of beverages were categorized as "healthier" options: water, fruit juice containing at least 50% real juice, low-fat (1%) or fat-free milk (regular or flavored), and diet drinks. The following types of beverages were categorized as "less healthful" options: soda pop (regular), fruit drinks containing less than 50% real juice, whole or 2% milk, sports drinks, iced tea, and lemonade. Only 1% of the options in beverage vending machines ended up being categorized into the "other" category.

The following types of snacks were categorized as "healthier" options (which includes healthy foods and nutritionally-improved versions of unhealthy vending snacks): low-fat chips, pretzels, crackers, Chex Mix, fruits, vegetables, granola bars, cereal bars, nuts, trail mix, low-fat cookies, and other low-fat baked goods. While some of the options are not the healthiest products—high in sodium or made with refined flour—they are considered healthier alternatives to common vending options. The following types of snacks were categorized as being of "poor nutritional quality": regular chips, crackers with cheese, candy, cookies, snack cakes, and pastries. Foods that did not fit into these categories were categorized as "other." Just 2% of the options in snack vending machines ended up being categorized into the "other" category.

Table 1

Beverages Available in Middle and High School Vending Machines

Beverage Type	Middle Schools Percent of Total (Number of Slots)	High Schools Percent of Total (Number of Slots)	Middle Schools, High Schools, & Other Secondary Schools Combined Percent of Total (Number of Slots)
Soda (regular)	28 (1110)	39 (3489)	36 (4860)
Fruit drinks (less than 50% real juice)	17 (664)	12 (1079)	13 (1801)
Sports drinks	17 (671)	11 (994)	13 (1826)
Iced tea, lemonade, or other sweetened drink	9 (362)	8 (752)	9 (1167)
Whole or 2% milk (including flavored)	1 (46)	3 (268)	3 (367)
Water	13 (515)	11 (1001)	12 (1611)
Fruit juices (at least 50% real juice)	8 (295)	6 (563)	7 (896)
Diet soda	4 (149)	6 (555)	6 (769)
Low-fat/1% or fat-free milk (including flavored)	1 (47)	2 (177)	2 (276)
Other drinks	2 (64)	<0.5 (13)	1 (77)
TOTAL	100 (3,923)	98 (8,891)	102 (13,650)

Results

The vending machine options in middle and high schools were markedly similar. In middle-school vending machines, 73% of beverage options and 83% of snack options were of poor nutritional quality. In high-school vending machines, 74% of beverage options and 85% of snack options were nutritionally-poor options.

The types of beverages available in middle and high school vending machines are listed in Table 1. **Seventy percent of those beverages were sugary drinks such as soda pop, juice drinks, iced tea, and sports drinks.** Of the sodas available in vending machines for both high schools and middle schools, 86% of soda slots were regular sugary sodas and 14% were diet. 12% of the beverages available were water. Of the "juices" offered, two-thirds (67%) were juice drinks that contained less than 50% juice. Only 5% of beverage options were milk. The majority (57%) of milks offered in school vending machines were the fattier types (either whole or 2%), with 43% of the milk either low-fat (1%) or fat-free.

The types of snacks available in middle and high school vending machines are listed in Table 2. The snack items most commonly available were: candy (42%), chips (25%), and sweet baked goods (13%), which together accounted for 80% of snacks available in school vending machines.

Children need fruits and vegetables to provide key nutrients and reduce future risk of heart disease and cancer. Yet of 9,723 total snack slots, only

Table 2

Snacks Available in Middle and High School Vending Machines

Snack Type	Middle Schools Percent of Total (Number of Slots)	High Schools Percent of Total (Number of Slots)	Middle Schools, High Schools, & Other Secondary Schools Combined Percent of Total (Number of Slots)
Candy	38 (882)	43 (3028)	42 (4062)
Chips (regular)	24 (555)	25 (1787)	25 (2391)
Cookies, snack cakes, and pastries	14 (310)	13 (928)	13 (1270)
Crackers with cheese or peanut butter	7 (154)	4 (306)	5 (484)
Chips (low-fat) or pretzels	7 (152)	5 (332)	5 (489)
Crackers or Chex Mix	2 (52)	3 (235)	3 (303)
Granola/cereal bars	2 (56)	1 (103)	2 (171)
Low-fat cookies and baked goods	2 (44)	1 (106)	2 (155)
Nuts/trail mix	2 (41)	1 (89)	1 (141)
Fruit or vegetable	<0.5 (8)	<0.5 (18)	<0.5 (26)
Other snacks	2 (39)	3 (178)	2 (231)
TOTAL	100 (2,293)	100 (7,110)	100 (9,723)

26 slots contained a fruit or vegetable. Only 7% of the beverage options were fruit juice (i.e., contained greater than 50% real juice). This finding highlights the potential value of increasing the number of refrigerated snack vending machines in schools to provide more fruits and vegetables to children.

Rationale for Improving School Foods

I. Schools Should Practice What They Teach

This study found that most choices available in school vending machines are of poor nutritional quality. Current school vending practices are not supportive of healthy eating.

Schools should practice what they teach. Selling low-nutrition foods in schools contradicts nutrition education and sends children the message that good nutrition is not important. The school environment should reinforce nutrition education in the classroom to support and model healthy behaviors.

II. The Sale of Low-Nutrition Foods in Schools Undermines Parents' Ability to Feed Their Children Well

Parents entrust schools with the care of their children during the school day. The sale of low-nutrition foods in schools makes it difficult for parents to ensure that their children are eating well. This is especially problematic when children have diet-related conditions, such as diabetes, high cholesterol, or overweight.

Without their parents' knowledge, some children spend their lunch money on the low-nutrition foods from vending machines rather than on balanced school meals. Long cafeteria lines, short lunch periods, or activities during the lunch period lead some students to purchase foods from a vending machine rather than a lunch from the cafeteria line.

III. Children's Eating Habits and Health

Obesity rates have doubled in children and tripled in adolescents over the last two decades. As a result, diabetes rates among children also have increased and type 2 diabetes can no longer be called "adult onset" diabetes. Also, 60% of obese children have high cholesterol, high blood pressure, or other risk factor for cardiovascular disease. While obesity is a complex, multi-factorial problem, over-consumption of soft drinks and snack foods plays a key role.

While low levels of physical activity are an important part of the problem, children are clearly eating more calories now than in the past. Between 1989 and 1996, children's calorie intake increased by approximately 80 to 230 extra calories per day (depending on the child's age and activity level). Soft drinks and low-nutrition snack foods are key contributors to those extra calories. Children who consume more soft drinks consume more calories and are more likely to be overweight than kids who drink fewer soft drinks. A recent study found that a school-based nutrition education program that encouraged children to limit their soda consumption reduced obesity among the children.

Consumption of soft drinks also can displace from children's diets healthier foods like low-fat milk, which can help prevent osteoporosis, and juice, which can help prevent cancer. In the late 1970s, teens drank almost twice as much milk as soda pop. Twenty years later, they are drinking twice as much soda pop as milk. The number of calories children consume from snacks increased by 30% (from 460 to 610 calories) between 1977 and 1996.

The health benefits of eating fruits and vegetables are well-documented; eating enough fruits and vegetables is important for preventing cancer, heart disease, high blood pressure, and other diseases. People who eat five or more servings of fruits and vegetables each day have half the cancer risk of those who eat fewer than two servings per day. However, children are not consuming enough fruits and vegetables to receive maximum health benefits. The average 6 to 11 year old eats only 3.5 servings of fruits and vegetables a day, achieving only half the recommended seven servings per day for this age group. Fewer than 15% of elementary-school-aged children eat the recommended five or more servings of fruits and vegetables daily. While fruit juices can have as many calories as soda, they provide important nutrients and health benefits that soda does not.

Milk is an important source in children's diets of essential vitamins and minerals, such as calcium and vitamins A and D. Since 98% of maximum bone density is reached by age 20, it is especially important that children get enough calcium. However, milk is also the largest source of saturated fat in children's diets. While low-fat and fat-free milk make important contributions to children's diets, whole and 2% milk contribute to children's risk of heart disease.

IV. Short-Term Profits from Selling Junk Food in Schools Pale in Comparison with the Long-Term Costs for Diet-Related Diseases

While schools are facing serious budget gaps, it is shortsighted to fund schools at the expense of our children's health. Diet- and obesity-related diseases, such as diabetes, heart disease, and cancer, cause disabilities and affect quality of life. The financial costs also are staggering. Annual medical spending attributed to obesity is estimated to be $75 billion per year, and half of that amount is financed by federal taxpayers through Medicare and Medicaid. From 1979 to 1999, annual hospital costs for treating obesity-related diseases in children rose threefold (from $35 million to $127 million).

The federal government also spends large amounts of money treating other diet-related diseases such as heart disease, cancer, diabetes, stroke, and osteoporosis through the Medicaid and Medicare programs and federal employee health insurance. Those diseases have their roots in childhood. According to the USDA, healthier diets could save at least $71 billion per year in medical and related costs.

V. Schools That Stop Selling Soda and Junk Food Are Not Losing Money

Even in the short-term, schools are finding that they can raise funds without undermining children's diets and health. A number of schools and school districts including Aptos Middle School (CA), Folsom Cardova Unified School District (CA), Monroe High School (CA), Venice High School (CA), Vista High School (CA), Fayette County Public Schools (KY), Old Orchard Beach Schools (ME), School Union 106 (ME), Shrewsbury School District (MA), North Community High School (MN), McComb School District (MS), Whitefish Middle School (MT), Sayre Middle School (PA), and South Philadelphia High School (PA) have improved the nutritional quality of school foods and beverages and not lost money.

Venice High School in Los Angeles eliminated unhealthy snack and beverage sales on campus. The school vending machines now offer a variety of waters, 100% juices and soy milk as well as a variety of healthy snacks including granola and cereal bars. After one year, snack sales in the student store were up by over $1,000 per month compared to the same time the previous year. Two years after the changes, snack sales per month had roughly doubled ($6,100 in May 2002 compared with $12,000 in March 2004). The students also raise significant funds with fundraisers that do not undermine children's health, such as a celebrity basketball game, car washes, and holiday gift wrapping.

Old Orchard Beach Schools in Maine wrote school vending policies that led to the removal of sodas and junk foods, and replaced them with water,

100% fruit juices, and healthier snack options. The vending machine signage was changed to advertise water instead of soda pop. Vending revenues have remained the same as they were prior to the changes.

North Community High School in Minneapolis replaced most of its soda vending machines with machines stocked with 100% fruit and vegetable juices and water and slightly reduced the prices of those healthier options. As a result, the sale of healthier items increased and the school has not lost money.

Though school vending is lucrative, it often represents only a small percentage of total school budgets. Soft drink contracts generate between $3 and $30 per student **per year;** even the most profitable contracts provide less than 0.5% of a school district's annual budget. In addition, the money raised from vending machines in schools is not a donation from the soft drink and snack food industries—it comes from the pockets of children and their parents.

VI. School Foods Can Be Improved at the Federal, State, or Local Level

States and localities have historically left the development of nutritional guidance to the federal government. The federal government has developed the Food Guide Pyramid, *Dietary Guidelines for Americans*, and nutrition facts labeling standards for packaged foods.

In addition, unlike other aspects of education that are primarily regulated at the state and local level, school foods have historically been regulated at the federal level—by Congress and the U.S. Department of Agriculture (USDA). The National School Lunch Program was created in 1946 under the Truman administration, "as a measure of national security, to safeguard the heath and well-being of the Nation's children and to encourage the domestic consumption of nutritious agricultural commodities and other food."

The federal government invests enormous resources in the school meal programs ($8.8 billion in FY 2003, including cash payments and commodities) and has strong nutrition standards for those meals, as well as provides technical assistance and support for states and local food service authorities to meet those standards. Selling junk foods in school vending machines undermines that investment.

USDA sets detailed standards and requirements for the foods provided through the school meal programs, including which foods are served, the portion sizes of those foods, and the amounts of specific nutrients that school meals must provide over the course of a week. In contrast, foods sold in vending machines, a la carte lines, fund-raisers, and other venues outside the school meal programs are not required by the USDA to meet comparable nutrition standards. The USDA currently has limited authority to regulate those foods.

For foods sold outside of school meals, USDA restricts only the sale of "Foods of Minimal Nutritional Value" (FMNV). A FMNV provides less than 5% of the Reference Daily Intake (RDI) for eight specified nutrients per serving. During meal periods, the sale of FMNV is prohibited by federal regulations in areas of the school where USDA school meals are sold or eaten. However,

FMNV can be sold anywhere else on-campus—including just outside the cafeteria—at any time. In addition, many nutritionally poor foods are not considered FMNV despite their high contents of saturated or trans fat, salt, or refined sugars, including chocolate candy bars, chips, and fruitades (containing little fruit juice), and thus can be sold anywhere on school campus anytime during the school day.

In order for USDA to set nutrition standards for all foods sold on school campuses throughout the school day, Congress needs to grant USDA additional authority. Implementation of those nutrition standards could be required as a condition for participating in the school meal programs.

States and cities have express authority to set nutrition standards in addition to the federal standards for foods sold out of school vending machines, a la carte lines, and other venues outside of the meal programs. A number of states have set or are working to set stronger nutrition standards for such foods (for examples, see http://cspinet.org/schoolfood/school_foods_kit_part3.pdf). Such state and local actions are needed given the limitations of current federal regulations.

Modest improvements in vending machine offerings can significantly reduce the calorie content of items purchased by students. . . .

Conclusions

This study found that the overwhelming majority of beverage and snack options in school vending machines are of poor nutritional quality. While foods and beverages sold in school vending machines are not the sole cause of childhood obesity, improving school nutrition environments is a key step toward ensuring that children have access to foods that promote their health and well-being. (For more information and model policies regarding other approaches to addressing nutrition, physical activity, and obesity, visit www.cspinet.org/nutritionpolicy.)

With skyrocketing childhood obesity rates, it is urgent that schools, school districts, and local, state, and federal governments enact policies to ensure that all foods and beverages available in schools make a positive contribution to children's diets and health. . . .

POSTSCRIPT

Is Television Viewing Responsible for the Rise in Childhood Obesity?

Authors of numerous research reports and surveys, which have appeared in the popular press as well as professional journal articles, agree that there is an increase in the rate of childhood obesity in the United States. Where the debate begins is over the reasons for this obesity epidemic. The Kaiser Foundation believes media is the culprit, while the Center for Science in the Public Interest feels vending machines in the schools are the cause of the problem. A balanced perspective would include both of these variables in explaining childhood overweight in addition to other factors such as parental influence, community access to exercise and nutritious food, economic cost of nutritious food, neighborhood safety, and education.

A review of the extensive literature that has been emerging on childhood obesity shows there are a multitude of reasons cited for the epidemic. Almost every American institution has been blamed as being responsible for the increase in children's weight. Grocery stores, schools, communities, families, restaurants, fast food, media, and the economy have had a role in making children overweight. Specifically, grocery stores are accused of stocking high-fat, high-calorie foods; the cost of healthy foods such as fruits and milk are more than processed snack foods and sodas. Schools house vending machines full of foods with little nutritive value and loads of calories; often school officials hesitate to get rid of the offending machines because they depend on them for revenue to purchase needed school supplies. There has been a reduction in the amount of hours and level of intensity of physical education classes in the schools, thus children do not get a chance to burn off calories in school the way they have in the past.

Other institutions have encouraged overeating while discouraging physical activity. Communities and neighborhoods do not lend themselves to exercise with few sidewalks for walking and few parks in which to play. Children do not feel safe enough in their neighborhoods to go out and play after school. Full-service restaurants and fast food venues have super sized their portions and encourage people to overeat. Buffets lure people to overeat by offering "all you can eat" for a lower price than a nutritious meal with vegetables and reasonable portions.

There is an overwhelming amount of media available to encourage sedentary behavior. Watching television, surfing the Web, and playing video games create an environment that discourages physical activity. Interestingly enough, research studies show that when children reduce time watching TV, physical exercise time does not necessarily increase; the children may replace this TV time with other sedentary activities like reading, talking on the phone, or playing board games.

The work/family dilemma of too little time shows up in family schedules that are hectic and leave little time for family meals together. Eating together as a family has been associated with reducing child weight. Parents may be contributing to childhood obesity by providing too much and the wrong type of food as well as not encouraging more physical activity of their children or themselves.

Although there are many factors that contribute to childhood obesity, will the concern for reducing childhood weight turn into an obsession with weight and lead to other types of problems? Already there is a concern among educators that more eating disorders such as anorexia or bulimia will emerge. In addition, there may be more of a tendency for overweight children to be discriminated against and develop a poor body image which can ultimately lead to mental illness and depression.

Related Readings

Bruss, M.B., Morris, J., & Dannison, L. (August 2003). Prevention of childhood obesity: Sociocultural and familial factors. *Journal of the American Dietetic Association, 103,* 1042–1046.

Golan, M., & Crow, S. (February 2004). Targeting parents exclusively in the treatment of childhood obesity: Long term results. *Obesity Research, 12,* 357–361.

Greaser, J., & Whyte, J.J. (September 2004). Childhood obesity: Is there effective treatment? *Consultant, 44,* 1349–1354.

McTaggart, J. (October 2004). The trouble with kids today: Childhood obesity is a complex problem, but supermarkets can be part of the solution. *Progressive Grocer, 83,* 26.

Van Staveren, T. & Dale, D. (September 2004). Childhood obesity problems and solutions: Food choices and physical activity at school and at home, underlie the childhood obesity problem. *The Journal of Physical Education, Recreation, and Dance, 75,* 44–51.

ISSUE 12

Do Bilingual Education Programs Help Non-English-Speaking Children Succeed?

YES: Stephen Krashen, from "Bilingual Education: Arguments for and (Bogus) Arguments Against," in James E. Alatis and Ai-Hui Tan, eds., *Georgetown University Round Table on Languages and Linguistics 1999: Language in Our Time: Bilingual Education and Official English, Ebonics and Standard English, Immigration and the Unz Initiative* (Georgetown University Press, 2001)

NO: Rosalie Pedalino Porter, from "The Case Against Bilingual Education," *The Atlantic Monthly* (May 1998)

ISSUE SUMMARY

YES: Stephen Krashen, professor of education at the University of Southern California, contends that good bilingual education programs provide background knowledge of subject matter and literacy in the child's native language. Then, the program provides English input using English as a second language technique along with sheltered subject matter teaching in English. Krashen argues against assertions that immersion is more successful than bilingual education.

NO: Rosalie Pedalino Porter, director for the Institute for Research in English Acquisition and Development (READ), states that bilingual education is a failed endeavor. Porter cites drop-out rates and parental sentiment as evidence as to why bilingual education should be discontinued.

There is little consistency among bilingual programs throughout schools in the United States. Numerous types of bilingual programs are being implemented. Each program is different, and each comes with its own set of advocates and opponents. For example, one school may have a program in which every subject is taught in the child's native tongue, with a small amount of class time reserved for English instruction. In another school, the child may start out being taught in Spanish, for example, and within 3–5 years be transitioned into an English-only classroom. In yet another school, a child may be immersed into English-only classes with a small amount of time reserved for tutoring in his or her native language.

Since bilingual education first became a political issue in the 1960s, it has been hotly debated. A child who does not speak English has as much of a right to an education as a child who does speak English. However, parents, politicians, researchers, and educators cannot seem to agree as to the best way to educate non-English-speaking children. When children are taught in their native language only, opponents argue that they may lack sufficient immersion into the culture and appropriate fluency in the dominant language (i.e. English), which is necessary to succeed in our society. When a child is taught in an English-only classroom, opponents argue that this leads to the student (especially one who is middle-school age and older) disliking school. These students do not understand what is being said. This, in turn, leads to disenchantment with the educational system and an alarmingly high number of non-English-speaking students becoming dropouts.

Even in more successful bilingual education programs, in which students are oriented to the language and happenings of an English-speaking classroom before being "immersed," there are other problems. These types of programs may take much longer to integrate the students into English-only classrooms. This, in turn, leaves the non-English-speaking students in danger of falling behind the other students academically, which could cause them to be in school more years than their English-speaking counterparts.

In the following selections, you will read two sides of the argument over whether or not bilingual education programs help non-English-speaking children succeed. Stephen Krashen details what successful bilingual education really is and then responds to the common criticisms of bilingual education. Rosalie Pedalino Porter discusses the origins of bilingual education. She calls it a "failed endeavor" and gives examples to support her case.

As you read the following selections, put yourself in the positions of politician, parent, educator, and student. Which approach to educating non-English-speaking students do you believe is most effective? Which teaching methods are economically and politically feasible? Which methods lead to integration into English-speaking society most effectively? And finally, is it the responsibility of the schools to preserve the child's native culture, or should that be left to the family?

Bilingual Education: Arguments for and (Bogus) Arguments Against

Introduction

It is helpful to distinguish two goals of bilingual education. The first is the development of academic English and school success, and the second is the development of the heritage language. Good bilingual education programs achieve both goals, but my focus in this report is on the first.

Confusion about the first goal is understandable: How can children acquire English, their second language, while being taught in their first language? This occurs for two reasons: First, when we give a child good education in the primary language, we give the child knowledge, knowledge that makes English input more comprehensible. A child who understands history, thanks to good history instruction in the first language, will have a better chance understanding history taught in English than a child without this background knowledge. And more comprehensible English input means more acquisition of English.

Second, there is strong evidence that literacy transfers across languages, that building literacy in the primary language is a short-cut to English literacy. The argument is straightforward: If we learn to read by understanding the messages on the page (Smith, 1994; Goodman, 1982), it is easier to learn to read if we understand the language. And once we can read, we can read: The ability transfers to other languages.

The empirical support for this claim comes from studies showing that the reading process is similar in different languages, studies showing that the reading development process is similar in different languages, and that correlations between literacy development in the first language and the second language are high, when length of residence is controlled. All the above is true even when the orthographies of the two languages are very different (Krashen, 1996).

Good bilingual programs thus have these characteristics:

1. They provide background knowledge through the first language via subject matter teaching in the first language. This should be done to

the point so that subsequent subject matter instruction in English is comprehensible.

2. They provide literacy in the first language.
3. Of course they provide comprehensible input in English, through ESL and sheltered subject matter teaching. In sheltered classes, subject matter is taught to intermediate second language acquirers in a comprehensible way. (Sheltered classes are for intermediates; they are not for beginners and not for advanced acquirers or native speakers. It is extremely difficult to teach subject matter to those who have acquired none or little of the language. Beginners should be in regular ESL, where they are assured of comprehensible input. Including more advanced students in sheltered classes is problematic because their participation may encourage input that is incomprehensible to the other students. There is substantial evidence supporting the efficacy of sheltered subject matter teaching for intermediate level, literate students; Krashen, 1991).

A Sample Program

The "gradual exit" model is one way of doing a bilingual program that utilizes these characteristics. In the early stage, non-English speaking students receive all core subject matter in the primary language. At the next stage, limited English proficient children receive sheltered subject matter instruction in those subjects that are the easiest to make comprehensible in English, math and science, which, at this level, do not demand a great deal of abstract use of language.

Putting sheltered subject matter classes at this stage insures that they will be comprehensible. Students in sheltered math, for example, have had some ESL, giving them some competence in English, and have had math in the primary language, giving them subject matter knowledge. These two combine to help make sheltered math comprehensible. Those forced to do subject matter in the second language immediately, without any competence in second language, have neither of these advantages. The gradual exit program appears to be the fastest way of introducing comprehensible subject matter teaching in English.

Note also that while the child is doing sheltered math, she is developing additional background knowledge and literacy through the first language in subjects that are more abstract, social studies and language arts. This will serve to make instruction in English at later stages more comprehensible.

In later stages, math and science are done in the mainstream and other subjects, such as social studies, are taught in sheltered classes in English. Eventually, all subjects are done in the mainstream. In this way, sheltered classes function as a bridge between instruction in the first language and the mainstream.

Once full mainstreaming is complete, advanced first language development is available as an option. This kind of plan avoids problems associated with exiting children too early from first language instruction (before the English they encounter is comprehensible) and provide instruction in the first language where it is most needed. This plan also allows children to have the advantages of advanced first language development.

In the gradual exit program, the second language is not delayed. It is introduced as soon as it can be made comprehensible. Quite early on, students in these programs do a considerable amount of serious academic work in English, well before they reach the very high levels required for official reclassification. The gradual exit model is thus not subject to the criticism that bilingual education programs delay exposure to English for years.

The Evidence for Bilingual Education

Evidence supporting bilingual education is of several kinds: (1) the results of program evaluations; (2) the effect of previous education on immigrant children's academic performance; (3) the effect of measured first language ability on immigrant children's second language acquisition. This framework also helps explain the strong impact of SES on school success for immigrant children and why some are successful without bilingual education.

Program evaluations. I would like to suggest a somewhat different approach in evaluating and reviewing research on bilingual education, relaxing one requirement that others adhere to strictly, but insisting on others. The one I insist on is the definition of bilingual education: A program can be considered a properly organized bilingual education program when it provides (a) subject matter teaching in the primary language without translation to the point that subject matter instruction in the second language is made comprehensible; (b) literacy development in the primary language; (c) comprehensible input in the second language. My prediction is that full bilingual programs, with all three conditions met, will be superior to those with fewer conditions met. I also insist that studies have adequate sample sizes and that the programs run for at least one year (which may be far too short to show an effect).

Other reviewers have required that there be some kind of control for experimental-comparison group differences that may have existed before the study began. Everyone agrees that randomization is the best way to do this. Lacking randomization, another technique is to statistically control for differences, in pretest scores and/or background differences. In this review, I relax this requirement and allow studies to enter the analysis where there is no compelling reason to suspect that the groups come from different populations. The logic behind this approach was presented in Krashen (1996): With a large number of post-test studies of this kind, randomization is present.

My conclusions are these: In all published studies in which these conditions are met, bilingual education is a winner. Children in bilingual programs acquire more of the second language than those in all-English programs (Mortensen, 1984), even eventually doing as well as native speakers of English (de la Garza and Medina, 1985; Burnham-Massey and Pina, 1990). Results of studies in other countries are similar (Fitzpatrick, 1987; Modiano, 1968 [literacy instruction in L1 only]; Appel, 1984; Verhoeven, 1991 [literacy only]).

In addition, apparent counterexamples, cases in which bilingual education was thought to be inferior, do not meet the conditions outlined above.

In these comparisons, bilingual ed. is not described or inaccurately described, sample sizes are small, and/or real comparisons are not made.

For example, Rossell and Baker (1996) present ten studies which "immersion" is considered to be better than bilingual education. Six are actually comparisons of different versions of Canadian immersion, a program that satisfies all three of the characteristics given above: They are all bilingual education. In all versions of Canadian immersion, children obtain enough background knowledge and develop enough literacy through the first language, both in school and at home, to make subject matter taught in the second language comprehensible (Krashen, 1996). Thus, those with more comprehensible input in the second language acquire more of it, since factors (a) and (b) are fully satisfied. In several other cases, categorization is inaccurate: What Rossell and Baker consider to be "immersion" and "submersion" are actually bilingual education; comparisons that Rossell and Baker consider to be between bilingual education and submersion or immersion are really comparisons of different versions of bilingual education (e.g., El Paso and McAllen; see Krashen, 1996). . . .

Natural experiments. Two natural experiments meet the criteria outlined above: Spanish-speaking children who had all their schooling in the U.S. were compared to those who had some of their education in Mexico. In one case, all children were in a bilingual program (Gonzales, 1989); the study thus compared the impact of some first language instruction with more. In the other study, education in the U.S. was all-English (Ferris and Politzer, 1981). In the former case, sixth graders with some education in Mexico did better than all-U.S. educated comparisons in English reading, while in the latter there was no difference between the groups in English writing in junior high school, but the Mexican-educated children had higher grades in English, and, according to teacher reports, were more dedicated students. Ferris and Politzer also report that the socioeconomic status of those with schooling in Mexico was lower than that of the all-U.S. educated group.

Impact of education in L1. Also consistent with this theoretical stance are studies showing that those with more education in the primary language are more successful in English language acquisition, a result that confirms the powerful influence of subject matter knowledge and literacy gained through the first language.

Here is just one example: Gardner, Polyzoi and Rampaul (1966) studied the impact of education in the first language on progress in intensive ESL classes for Kurdish and Bosnian adult immigrants to Canada who had "virtually no English" when they arrived (p. 3). The subjects were classified into three groups, those with a great deal of formal education (mean = 15 years), those with some (mean = 7 years) and those with no formal education.

[Another measure] presents the gains made by each group on tests of oral and written English after participation in intensive ESL (20 hours per week, for 1 to 1.5 years). For both measures, it is clear that the higher the level of literacy in the primary language, the greater the gains. This was true of both measures, and extremely powerful in the written test, in which preliterates' posttest scores were lower than the high literates' pretest scores.

The strong impact of first language education on English development has been confirmed in several other studies (Chiswick, 1991; Chiswick and Miller, 1995; Espanshade and Lu, 1997).

SES as defacto bilingual education. Our framework helps explain the consistent positive relationship between SES and English language development (Krashen, 1996). Children from wealthier families have, most likely, more and better education in their primary language, caregivers who are better able to help them with schoolwork (in their primary language), and have more access to print in general.

Immigrant success. The research presented here helps explain why some immigrants did well in school without bilingual education: They came with a good education in their own country, making instruction in English much more comprehensible (Krashen, 1996; Tse, 1997). Such cases are arguments for bilingual education, not against it.

Bogus Arguments Against Bilingual Education

Many of the arguments used to attack the effectiveness of bilingual education violate one or more of the principles presented here.

Is immersion successful? In several cases, the media has claimed success for "immersion" when no comparison was made at all with similar children under bilingual education.

Orange According to the Los Angeles Times (Orange County edition) "A controversial new English immersion program in the Orange Unified School District appears to help many students learn to speak the language faster than traditional bilingual programs" (April 18, 1998). The article, which appeared in the middle of the Proposition 227 campaign, announced that "almost a quarter of the district's 4,132 elementary students in the immersion program had advanced their fluency by at least one level in the first five months of study." Orange, the Times reported, dropped bilingual education the year before and "went with English immersion."

A closer look shows that this did not occur at all: First, while Orange claimed that they dropped bilingual education, their current English immersion program used at least some first language support, supplied by paraprofessionals. Even more serious, no comparison was made of the progress made by children in the current program and children in the older program. Finally, the progress was not remarkable. I concluded (Krashen, 1999) that at the rate these children were progressing, for those starting with no English, after one year fewer than half would be ready for sheltered subject matter instruction in English, and fewer than 20% would be ready for the mainstream in one and a half years.

McQuillan (1998) analyzed a more recent report from the same district, and also concluded that children were not doing very well under the "immersion" plan. The district, for example, claimed that 81% of the immersion students could understand English in specially taught classes. McQuillan points out, however, that three-quarters of the children were already advanced enough in English to do a modified program before the new program began! In addition, only six of the 3,549 students were ready for regular classes after one year (the time limit imposed by Proposition 227), a dismal 1% reclassification rate, and, in agreement with my findings, only about half who began with no English were ready for "sheltered" classes after one year. Finally, once again Orange did not compare their students' progress with progress under older programs. . . .

Taft   In another case, the comparison group was completely inappropriate. Children at the Taft School in Santa Ana scored at the 48th percentile in English reading on the CTBS in Spring, 1997, well above the district average of 22.5 and the highest in the district. Taft's principal credited the school's English immersion philosophy for some of this performance (*Education Week*, January 14, 1998). But Taft's students are clearly more advantaged than others in the district. . . .

Taft lies two standard deviations above the mean for free/reduced lunch as well as for percent of limited English proficient students. The correlation between reading scores and SES status (as measured by % free/reduced lunch) was nearly perfect (r = .926)(Krashen, 1999).

Taft's "success" has, most likely, nothing to do with the absence of bilingual education. In fact, some of it could be due to "de facto" bilingual education, the superior education in the primary language that more advantaged children tend to have. . . .

Is bilingual education responsible for dropouts?   The circumstantial argument is this: Hispanic students have a large dropout rate. Hispanic students are the biggest customer of bilingual education programs. Therefore bilingual education causes dropouts.

False. Only a small percentage of Hispanic students are enrolled in bilingual education: In California, for example, only 15% were in full bilingual programs. In addition, the only empirical study of the impact of bilingual education on dropouts, Curiel, Rosenthal, and Richek (1986), reported fewer dropouts among bilingual education students than among comparison students.

What accounts for dropout rates? Not surprisingly, competence in English (McMillan, Kaufman and Klein, 1997). But if bilingual education results in better English development, as claimed above, this finding is an argument *for* bilingual education.

A large number of studies confirm that other factors count, such as socioeconomic class, time spent in the U.S., the presence of print, and family factors. Hispanic students are well behind majority children in these areas.

What is especially interesting is that *these background factors appear to be responsible for much if not all of the difference in dropout rates among different ethnic groups.* In other words, when researchers control for these factors, there is little or no difference in dropout rates between Hispanics and other groups. (Rumberger, 1995; Rumberger, 1983; Fernandez, Paulsen, and Hiranko-Nakanishi, 1996; Warren, 1996; White and Kaufman, 1997; Pirog and Magee, 1997). Rumberger (1995), for example, concluded that " . . . Black, Hispanic, and Native American students have twice the odds of dropping out compared to White students . . . however, after controlling for the structural characteristics of family background—particularly, socioeconomic status—the predicted odds of dropping out are no different than those for White students" (p. 605). Rumberger (1983) confirms that Hispanic students often drop out because they have to go to work. When dropouts were asked why they dropped out, only 4% of the Hispanic students mentioned poor performance in school, compared to 8% of comparisons. But 38% of the Hispanic students mentioned economic factors, compared to 22% of the other students.

Bilingualism, Bilingual Education, and Earnings

. . . Chiswick and Miller (1998) suggest that bilingualism itself leads to lower earnings. On the basis of an analysis of data from the 1990 census, based on males ages 25–64 born in the U.S., they claim:

1. Those who speak only English earned more in 1989 than those who reported that another language was spoken in their home, even when factors such as schooling, years in the labor market, amount worked, marital status, and urban/rural were controlled. Overall, English-onlys (those who only heard English at home) earned about 8% more.
2. Even those who grew up in homes with another language who reported that they spoke English "very well" earned less than English-onlys.

Chiswick and Miller conclude that there is "no statistical support for the proposition that bilingualism, as measured in this study, enhances earning in the U.S. It does provide support for the proposition that whatever detracts from full proficiency in English has an adverse effect on earnings" (p. 15).

However:

• Those who really suffered were Native American, Hispanic, and "Mexican" men (for some reason, "Mexican" was not considered "Hispanic"). Even those who reported they spoke English "very well" earned less than English-onlys, 16%, 9%, and 7% respectively. Other groups had either a much smaller gap (3% for "white-non Hispanic) and none at all for Black and Asian-origin men. Chiswick and Miller also found that Hispanics who speak English "very well" but who live in "high concentration Spanish states" earned 11% less than English-onlys, but those other states were only 4% lower. These results suggest that language may not have been the central issue in determining earnings, a possibility that Chiswick and Miller present.

- All other studies of heritage language show rather positive effects of bilingualism: Those who develop their heritage language, in addition to acquiring English, do slightly better in school and on the job market (research reviewed in Krashen, 1998). The overwhelming majority of children of immigrants report higher competence in English than in the heritage language by the time they are in high school (Krashen, 1996). Thus, most of those who speak another language at home probably do not develop it to high levels, for a variety of factors. Language shift is powerful. Most of Chiswick and Miller's subjects were, most likely, weak heritage language speakers. Their data is thus consistent with the hypothesis that high development of the heritage language is positive, and that weak development of the heritage language is a disadvantage.

Public Opinion

Our discussion of theory helps us interpret some opinion polls on bilingual education.

The polls clearly show that the public is not against bilingual education. Respondents last year in both Los Angeles and Texas agreed either that "Students should be taught in their native language for a brief time—a year or two" (Texas poll = 38% agreement. Los Angeles Times poll = 39%), or that first language instruction "should last as long as teachers and parents think it is necessary." (Texas poll = 36% agreement. Los Angeles Times poll = 25% agreement.) Thus, 74% of Texans surveyed supported some use of the first language in school and 64% of those surveyed in Los Angeles. Only a small percentage supported English only (Texas = 24%; Los Angeles = 32%). (Details in Krashen 1999.) . . .

When polls seem to indicate that the public is against bilingual education, a closer look reveals that this is not so.

- In some cases, the public is simply expressing support for children learning English, a goal we all agree with. In fact, this explains much of the success of Proposition 227: Many people thought they were simply "voting for English" (Krashen, 1999). Of course, when parents say they want children to learn English, this should not be interpreted as a rejection of bilingual education.
- When parents reject bilingual education explicitly, they reject versions of it that few bilingual education advocates would support, i.e., versions in which all instruction is in the first language "until children are ready to learn English." As noted earlier, I think children are ready for English the first day of school (Krashen, 1999).
- Some polls ask if parents are willing to delay subject matter for English, that is, take time for English study before children learn subject matter. This is an unreasonable question: In good bilingual education programs, children get both maximum subject matter instruction

and make maximum progress in acquiring English at the same time. The former helps the latter, as explained earlier in this paper.

- Some polls ask if parents are willing to delay English while the children are instructed in their native language. This is also an unreasonable question: In good bilingual programs, there is no delay of English.

Postscript: What Happened in California?

I suspect that many voters did not know what they were voting for when they supported Proposition 227: They thought that a "yes" vote was simply a vote for English. My evidence comes not only from the countless number of people I talked to, people who told me that they were voting for Prop. 227 because "I'm for English," but also from the [Los Angeles] Times poll of April 13, discussed in the text, showing clear support for the use of the first language in school and little support for "English-only."

If voters had known what was really in 227, they would have voted differently. This was confirmed in our study. Jim Crawford noted that the following kind of question, closely following the description of 227 on the ballot, was typically asked of voters in polls: "There is an initiative on the June primary ballot that would require all public school instruction to be conducted in English and for students not fluent in English to be placed in a short-term English immersion program. If the June primary were being held today, would you vote for or against this measure?"

This kind of question can be easily interpreted as "Are you in favor of children getting intensive English instruction?" and did not reflect what was in Proposition 227. A more accurate question, Crawford suggested, would be one like this one: "There is an initiative on the June primary ballot that would severely restrict the use of the child's native language in school. This initiative would limit special help in English to one year (180 school days). After this time, limited English proficient children would be expected to know enough English to do school work at the same level as native speakers of English their age. The initiative would dismantle many current programs that have been demonstrated to be successful in helping children acquire English, and would hold teachers financially responsible if they violate this policy. If passed, schools would have 60 days to conform to the new policy. If the June primary were being held today, would you vote for or against this measure?"

Students in my language education class asked 251 voters either question 1 or question 2 and the data was analyzed by Haeyoung Kim. The difference between the responses to the two questions was huge (and statistically significant): While 57% supported the original version, only 15% supported the modified version, a result that confirmed our suspicions that few people knew what was in Proposition 227, and if they had known, most would have not supported it.

Unfortunately, despite numerous attempts, we were unable to get crucial information about 227 to many voters.

References

Appel, Rene. 1984. *Immigrant children learning Dutch.* Dordrecht, The Netherlands: Foris.

Burnham-Massey, Laurie, and Pina, Marilyn. 1990. Effects of reading instruction on English academic achievement of LEP children. *Reading Improvement* 27: 129–132.

Chiswick, Barry. 1991. Speaking, reading, and earnings among low-skilled immigrants. *Journal of Labor Economics* 9: 149–170.

Chiswick, Barry, and Miller, Paul. 1995. The endogeneity between language and earnings: International analyses. *Journal of Labor Economics* 13: 246–288.

Chiswick, Barry, and Miller, Paul. 1998. The economic cost to native-born Americans of limited English language proficiency. Report prepared for the Center for Equal Opportunity. August, 1998.

Crawford, James. 1999. *Bilingual education: History, politics, theory and practice.* Fourth Edition. Los Angeles: Bilingual Educational Services.

Cummins, Jim. 1989. *Empowering minority students.* Los Angeles, CA: California Association for Bilingual Education.

Curiel, Herman; Stenning, Walter; and Cooper-Stenning, Peggy. 1980. Achieved reading level, self-esteem, and grades as related to length of exposure to bilingual education. *Hispanic Journal of Behavioral Sciences* 2(4): 389–400.

Curiel, Herman; Rosenthal, James; and Richek, Herbert. 1986. Impacts of bilingual education on secondary school grades, attendance, retentions and dropout. *Hispanic Journal of Behavioral Sciences* 8(4): 357–367.

Espenshade, Thomas, and Haishan Fu. 1997. An analysis of English-language proficiency among U.S. immigrants. *American Sociological Review* 62: 288–305.

Fernandez, Roberto; Paulsen, Ronnelle; and Hiranko-Nakanishi, Marsha. 1989. Dropping out among Hispanic youth. *Social Science Research* 18: 21–52.

Ferris, M. Roger, and Politzer, Robert. 1981. Effects of early and delayed second language acquisition: English composition skills of Spanish-speaking junior high school students. *TESOL Quarterly* 15(3): 263–274.

Fitzpatrick, Finbarre. 1987. *The open door.* Multilingual Matters.

Gardner, Sheena; Polyzoi, Eleoussa; and Rampaul, Yvette. 1996. Individual variables, literacy history, and ESL progress among Kurdish and Bosnian immigrants. *TESL Canada* 14: 1–20.

Gersten, Russell. 1985. Structured immersion for language minority students: Results of a longitudinal evaluation. *Educational Evaluation and Policy Analysis* 7: 187–196.

Glenn, Charles. 1998. Rethinking bilingual education: Changes for Massachusetts. *READ Abstracts, Research and Policy Review,* August, 1998.

Gonzales, L. Antonio. 1989. Native language education: The key to English literacy skills. In D. Bixler-Marquez, J. Ornstein-Galacia, and G. Green (Eds.), *Mexican-American Spanish in its societal and cultural contexts* (pp. 209–224). Rio Grande Series in Languages and Linguistics 3. Brownsville, Texas: University of Texas, Pan American.

Goodman, Kenneth. 1982. *Language, literacy, and learning.* London: Routledge & Kegan Paul.

Krashen, Stephen. 1991. Sheltered subject matter teaching. *Cross Currents* 18: 183–188.

Krashen, Stephen. 1996. *Under attack: The case against bilingual education.* Culver City, CA: Language Education Associates.

Krashen, Stephen. 1998. Heritage language development: Some practical arguments. In Stephen Krashen, Lucy Tse, and Jeff McQuillan (Eds.), *Heritage language development.* Culver City, CA: Language Education Associates.

Krashen, Stephen. 1999. *Condemned without a Trial: Bogus arguments against bilingual education.* Portsmouth, NH: Heinemann.

Krashen, Stephen, and Crawford, Jim. 1999. The research, the scientific method, and the Delaware-Massachusetts argument. *NABE News* 22(5): 14–15.

Krashen, Stephen, and McQuillan, Jeffrey. 1998. Do graduates of bilingual programs really earn less? A response to Lopez and Mora. *NABE News* 22(3): 506.

Lopez, Mark, and Mora, Marie. (1998). The labor market effects of bilingual education among Hispanic workers. *READ Perspectives* 5(2): 33–54.

McMillen, Marilyn; Kaufman, Phillip; and Klein, Steve. 1997. *Dropout rates in the United States: 1995*. Washington: US Dept of Education. NCES 97–473.

McQuillan, Jeff. 1998. Is 99% failure a "success"? Orange Unified's English immersion program. *Multilingual Educator* 21(7): 11.

Modiano, Nancy. 1968. National or mother tongue language in beginning reading: A comparative study. *Research in the Teaching of English* 2: 32–43.

Moore, Fernie Baca, and Parr, Gerald. 1978. Models of bilingual education: Comparisons of effectiveness. *The Elementary School Journal* 79(2): 93–97.

Mortensen, Eileen. 1984. Reading achievement of native Spanish-speaking elementary students in bilingual vs. monolingual programs. *Bilingual Review* 11(3): 31–36.

Pirog, Maureen, and Magee, Chris. 1997. High school completion: The influence of schools, families, and adolescent parenting. *Social Science Quarterly* 78: 710–724.

Ramos, Francisco, and Krashen, Stephen. 1997. Success without bilingual education? Some European cases of de facto bilingual education. *CABE Newsletter* 20(6): 7, 19.

Rumberger, Russell. 1983. Dropping out of high school: The influence of race, sex, and family background. *American Educational Research Journal* 20(2): 199–220.

Rumberger, Russell. 1995. Dropping out of middle school: A multilevel analysis of students and schools. *American Educational Research Journal* 32(3): 583–625.

Rossell, Christine. 1990. The effectiveness of educational alternatives for limited-English proficient children. In Gary Imhoff (Ed.) *Learning in Two Languages* (pp. 71–121). New Brunswick, NJ: Transaction Publishers.

Rossell, Christine, and Baker, Keith. 1996. The educational effectiveness of bilingual education. *Research in the Teaching of English* 30(1): 7–74.

Shin, Fay, and Simon Kim, S. 1998. Korean parent perceptions and attitudes of bilingual education. In R. Endo, C. Park, J. Tsuchida and A. Abbayani (Eds.) *Current issues in Asian and Pacific American education*. Covina, CA: Pacific Asian Press.

Shin, Fay, and Gribbons, Barry. 1996. Hispanic parent perceptions and attitudes of bilingual education. *Journal of Mexican American Educators*, pp. 16–22.

Shin, Fay, and Lee, Bo V. 1996. Hmong parents: What do they think about bilingual education? *Pacific Educational Research Journal* 8(1): 65–71.

Smith, Frank. 1994. *Understanding reading*. Fifth edition. Hillsdale, NJ: Erlbaum.

Tse, Lucy. 1997. A bilingual helping hand. *Los Angeles Times,* Dec. 17, 1997.

Verhoeven, L. 1991. Acquisition of biliteracy. *AILA Review* 8: 61–74.

Warren, John. 1996. Educational inequality among White and Mexican-origin adolescents in the American Southwest: 1990. *Sociology of Education* 69: 142–158.

White, Michael, and Kaufman, Gayle. 1997. Language usage, social capital, and school completion among immigrants and native-born ethnic groups. *Social Science Quarterly* 78(2): 385–398.

NO

Rosalie Pedalino Porter

The Case Against Bilingual Education

Bilingual education is a classic example of an experiment that was begun with the best of humanitarian intentions but has turned out to be terribly wrongheaded. To understand this experiment, we need to look back to the mid-1960s, when the civil-rights movement for African-Americans was at its height and Latino activists began to protest the damaging circumstances that led to unacceptably high proportions of school dropouts among Spanish-speaking children—more than 50 percent nationwide. Latino leaders borrowed the strategies of the civil-rights movement, calling for legislation to address the needs of Spanish-speaking children—Cubans in Florida, Mexicans along the southern border, Puerto Ricans in the Northeast. In 1968 Congress approved a bill filed by Senator Ralph Yarborough, of Texas, aimed at removing the language barrier to an equal education. The Bilingual Education Act was a modestly funded ($7.5 million for the first year) amendment to the Elementary and Secondary Education Act of 1965, intended to help poor Mexican-American children learn English. At the time, the goal was "not to keep any specific language alive," Yarborough said. "It is not the purpose of the bill to create pockets of different languages through the country . . . but just to try to make those children fully literate in English."

English was not always the language of instruction in American schools. During the eighteenth century classes were conducted in German, Dutch, French, and Swedish in some schools in Pennsylvania, Maryland, and Virginia. From the mid nineteenth to the early twentieth century, classes were taught in German in several cities across the Midwest. For many years French was taught and spoken in Louisiana schools, Greek in Pittsburgh. Only after the First World War, when German was proscribed, did public sentiment swing against teaching in any language but English.

These earlier decisions on education policy were made in school, church, city, or state. Local conditions determined local school policy. But in 1968, for the first time, the federal government essentially dictated how non-English-speaking children should be educated. That action spawned state laws and legal decisions in venues all the way up to the Supreme Court. No end of money and effort was poured into a program that has since become the most controversial arena in public education.

❧❦❧

In simplest terms, bilingual education is a special effort to help immigrant children learn English so that they can do regular schoolwork with their English-speaking classmates and receive an equal educational opportunity. But what it is in the letter and the spirit of the law is not what it has become in practice. Some experts decided early on that children should be taught for a time in their native languages, so that they would continue to learn other subjects while learning English. It was expected that the transition would take a child three years.

From this untried experimental idea grew an education industry that expanded far beyond its original mission to teach English and resulted in the extended segregation of non-English-speaking students. In practice, many bilingual programs became more concerned with teaching in the native language and maintaining the ethnic culture of the family than with teaching children English in three years.

Beginning in the 1970s several notions were put forward to provide a rationale, after the fact, for the bilingual-teaching experiment. José Cárdenas, the director emeritus of the Intercultural Development Research Association, in San Antonio, and Blandina Cárdenas (no relation), an associate professor of educational administration at the University of Texas at San Antonio, published their "theory of incompatibilities." According to this theory, Mexican-American children in the United States are so different from "majority" children that they must be given bilingual and bicultural instruction in order to achieve academic success. Educators were convinced of the soundness of the idea—an urgent need for special teaching for non-English-speaking children—and judges handed down court decisions on the basis of it.

Jim Cummins, a bilingual-education theorist and a professor of education at the University of Toronto, contributed two hypotheses. His "developmental interdependence" hypothesis suggests that learning to read in one's native language facilitates reading in a second language. His "threshold" hypothesis suggests that children's achievement in the second language depends on the level of their mastery of their native language and that the most-positive cognitive effects occur when both languages are highly developed. Cummins's hypotheses were interpreted to mean that a solid foundation in native-language literacy and subject-matter learning would best prepare students for learning in English. In practice these notions work against the goals of bilingual education—English-language mastery and academic achievement in English in mainstream classrooms.

Bilingual education has heightened awareness of the needs of immigrant, migrant, and refugee children. The public accepts that these children are entitled to special help; we know that the economic well-being of our society depends on maintaining a literate population with the academic competence for higher education and skilled jobs. The typical complaint heard years ago,

"My grandfather came from Greece [or Sicily or Poland] and they didn't do anything special for him, and he did okay," no longer figures in the public discussion.

Bilingual education has brought in extra funding to hire and train para-professionals, often the parents of bilingual children, as classroom aides. Career programs in several school districts, among them an excellent one in Seattle that was in operation through early 1996, pay college tuition for para-professionals so that they may qualify as teachers, thus attracting more teachers from immigrant communities to the schools. Large school districts such as those in New York and Los Angeles have long had bilingual professionals on their staffs of psychologists, speech therapists, social workers, and other specialists.

Promoting parental understanding of American schools and encouraging parental involvement in school activities are also by-products of bilingual education. Workshops and training sessions for all educators on the historical and cultural backgrounds of the rapidly growing and varied ethnic communities in their districts result in greater understanding of and respect for non-English-speaking children and their families. These days teachers and school administrators make an effort to communicate with parents who have a limited command of English, by sending letters and school information to them at home in their native languages and by employing interpreters when necessary for parent-teacher conferences. In all these ways bilingual education has done some good.

⋅◉⋅

But has it produced the desired results in the classroom? The accumulated research of the past thirty years reveals almost no justification for teaching children in their native languages to help them learn either English or other subjects—and these are the chief objectives of all legislation and judicial decisions in this field. Self-esteem is not higher among limited-English students who are taught in their native languages, and stress is not higher among children who are introduced to English from the first day of school—though self-esteem and stress are the factors most often cited by advocates of bilingual teaching.

The final report of the *Hispanic Dropout Project* (issued in February) states,

> While the dropout rate for other school-aged populations has declined, more or less steadily, over the last 25 years, the overall Hispanic dropout rate started higher and has remained between 30 and 35 percent during that same time period . . . 2.5 times the rate for blacks and 3.5 times the rate for white non-Hispanics.

About one out of every five Latino children never enters a U.S. school, which inflates the Latino dropout rate. According to a 1995 report on the dropout situation from the National Center on Education Statistics, speaking Spanish at home does not correlate strongly with dropping out of high school; what does correlate is having failed to acquire English-language ability. The NCES report states,

> For those youths that spoke Spanish at home, English speaking ability was related to their success in school. . . . The status dropout rate for young Hispanics reported to speak English 'well' or 'very well' was . . . 19.2 percent, a rate similar to the 17.5 percent status dropout rate observed for enrolled Hispanic youths that spoke only English at home.

In the past ten years several national surveys of the parents of limited-English schoolchildren have shown that a large majority consider learning English and having other subjects taught in English to be of much greater importance than receiving instruction in the native language or about the native culture. In 1988 the Educational Testing Service conducted a national Parent Preference Study among 2,900 Cuban, Mexican, Puerto Rican, and Asian parents with children in U.S. public schools. Although most of the parents said they wanted special help for their children in learning English and other subjects, they differed on whether their children should be taught in their native languages. Asian parents were the most heavily opposed to the use of native languages in the schools. Among Latino groups, the Puerto Rican parents were most in favor, the Mexicans somewhat less, and the Cubans least of all. A large majority of the parents felt that it is the family's duty, not the school's, to teach children about the history and traditions of their ancestors. When Mexican parents were asked if they wanted the school to teach reading and writing in Spanish and English, 70 percent answered yes. But when they were asked if they wanted Spanish taught in school if it meant less time for teaching English, only 12 percent were in favor.

In the most recent national survey of Latino parents, published by the Center for Equal Opportunity, in Washington, D.C., 600 Latino parents of school-age children were interviewed (in Spanish or English) in five U.S. cities— Houston, Los Angeles, Miami, New York, and San Antonio. A strong majority favored learning English as the first order of business for their children, considering it more important than learning other subjects, and much more important than reading and writing in Spanish.

Having begun quietly in the 1980s and gained momentum in the 1990s, Latino opposition to native-language teaching programs is now publicly apparent. Two actions by communities of Latino parents demonstrate this turn of events.

A hundred and fifty parents with children in Brooklyn public schools filed a lawsuit in September of 1995, charging that because their children routinely remained segregated in bilingual programs in excess of three years, and in some cases in excess of six years, contrary to section 3204 (2) of the State Education Law, these children were not receiving adequate instruction in English, "the crucial skill that leads to equal opportunity in schooling, jobs, and public life in the United States."

New York State law limits participation in a bilingual program to three years, but an extension can be granted for up to three years more if an individual review of the student's progress seems to warrant it. And here is the nub of the lawsuit: thousands of students are routinely kept in native-language classrooms for six years or longer without even the pretense of individual progress reviews.

Unfortunately, even with the help of a strong champion of their cause, Sister Kathy Maire, and the pro bono services of a prestigious New York law firm, Paul, Weiss, Rifkind, Wharton & Garrison, the parents lost their case. Under New York law these parents in fact have the right not to enroll their children in bilingual classes, or to remove them from bilingual classes, but in practice pressure from school personnel is almost impossible to overcome. Teachers and principals tell parents that their children will fail in English-language classrooms. They play on ethnic pride, asserting that children of a Latino background need to be taught in Spanish to improve their self-esteem.

In May of last year the Court of Appeals of the State of New York ruled that there could be no further appeals. But the publicity attracted by the case may encourage other Latino parents to take action on behalf of their children. And one concrete improvement has already occurred: the New York City Board of Education announced an end in 1996 to the automatic testing for English-language skills that children with Spanish surnames had undergone when they started school.

On the other coast an equally irate group of Latino parents moved against the Ninth Street School in Los Angeles. Seventy families of mostly Mexican garment workers planned the protest through Las Familias del Pueblo, a community organization that provides after-school child care. Typical of the protesters are Selena and Carlos (I have changed their names, because they are undocumented immigrants), who left the poverty of a rural Mexican village in 1985 to come to work in Los Angeles. Their children were born in Los Angeles, but the school insisted that they not be taught in English until they had learned to read and write in Spanish, by the fourth or fifth grade. The parents complained to the school for years that children who lived in Spanish-speaking homes and neighborhoods needed to study in English in the primary grades, when children find it easier to learn a language than they will later on.

Persistent stonewalling by administrators finally moved the parents to keep their children out of school for nearly two weeks in February of 1996, a boycott that made national news. The parents demanded that their children be placed in English-language classes, a demand that has since been met. The school administrators waited too long to make this change: the previous spring only six students (about one percent of enrollment) had been deemed sufficiently fluent in English to "graduate" to regular classrooms in the next school year.

In the early 1970s almost all the students in bilingual classes spoke Spanish. Today, of the three million limited-English students in U.S. public schools, more than 70 percent speak Spanish at home; the rest speak any of 327 other languages. California alone enrolls 1.4 million limited-English children in its schools—one of every four students in the state. According to the 1990 U.S. census, 70 percent of limited-English students are concentrated in California, Florida, Illinois, New Jersey, New York, and Texas.

⚬✦⚬

Controversy over native-language education is at the boil in California. In our most multicultural state, where minorities now constitute 46 percent of the population, a revolution is brewing. In 1987 the California legislature failed to reauthorize the Bilingual-Bicultural Education Act, allowing it to expire. However, the California Department of Education immediately notified all school districts that even without the state law the same requirements would be enforced and bilingual programs continued. In July of 1995 the state Board of Education announced two major policy changes: the "preference" for native-language programs would henceforth be revoked and school districts would be given as much flexibility as possible in choosing their own programs; and school districts were ordered to be more diligent in recording evidence of student achievement than in describing the teaching methods used.

Yet in two years only four school districts have succeeded in obtaining waivers from the department, permitting them to initiate English-language programs for limited-English students. Why should schools have to seek waivers when no state or federal law, no court decision, no state policy, bars them from teaching in English? The most important case to date is that of the Orange Unified School District, with 7,000 limited-English students.

Orange Unified applied in early May of last year for permission to focus on English-language teaching in kindergarten through sixth grade while using a small amount of Spanish. The Department of Education strongly opposed the district, as did the California Association for Bilingual Education, California Rural Legal Assistance, and the organization Multicultural Education, Training, and Advocacy (META). Local Latino activists publicly criticized the district's change of plan, and some bilingual teachers resigned.

Nevertheless, the Board of Education last July granted Orange permission to try an English-language program for one year. A lawsuit was filed, and a temporary restraining order granted. But last September, U.S. District Court Judge William B. Shubb lifted the restraining order. In his seventeen-page decision the judge wrote, "The court will not second-guess the educational policy choices made by educational authorities." And he added a ruling with much broader application:

> It is clear that "appropriate action" does not require "bilingual education." . . . The alleged difference between two sound LEP [Limited-English Proficient] educational theories—ESL [English as a Second Language] and bilingual instruction—is inadequate to demonstrate irreparable harm.

The federal court ruling allowed Orange to proceed with its English-language program. But the case was returned to Sacramento County Superior Court, where Judge Ronald B. Robie ruled that nothing in California state law requires primary-language instruction, and therefore no waiver is needed for a district to provide an English-language program; and that federal law permits educational programs not to include native-language instruction. Soon after Robie's ruling the Board of Education rescinded the policy that schools must obtain waivers in order to eliminate bilingual programs. Although the court decision may be appealed, these two actions signal a victory for Orange Unified and have implications for other California districts as well. The legal battle has already cost the Orange district $300,000, which no doubt would have been better spent on students. It is estimated that the new program will cost an additional $60,000 the first year, but the superintendent of Orange Unified schools, Robert French, says, "We're not doing this to save money. We're doing this to save kids."

Ron Unz, a Silicon Valley entrepreneur, has long been concerned about the California education system's failures, especially as they affect its 1.4 million limited-English students. He has decided to put his time, energy, and money into an initiative—"English for the Children"—meant to give all California voters a say on the language of public education. If the initiative passes, in elections to be held on June 2, it will give "preference" to English-language programs for immigrant children, reduce the length of time children may remain in special programs, and make the state spend $50 million a year to teach English to adults. Bilingual programs will be allowed only in localities where parents actually request native-language teaching for their children.*

Last November, Unz and the co-chairman of the drive, Gloria Matta Tuchman, submitted more than 700,000 signatures to put the petition on the California ballot. The drive has the support of several Latino leaders in California, most notably Jaime Escalante, who is its honorary chairman. Escalante is the Los Angeles high school teacher whose success in teaching his Latino students advanced calculus gained him national fame in the film *Stand and Deliver.*

Though some opponents characterize the petition as "anti-immigrant," Unz and Matta Tuchman have strong pro-immigrant credentials. In 1994 Unz ran against the incumbent Pete Wilson in the Republican primary for governor and forcefully opposed the referendum to deny schooling and health benefits to illegal immigrants—a referendum that passed with Wilson's support. Matta Tuchman is a recognized Latina advocate for improved schooling for all immigrant children, but especially Spanish-speakers. The measure is likely to pass, some believe with strong ethnic support. A *Los Angeles Times* poll last October found Latino voters backing the initiative by 84 percent, and Anglos by 80 percent. A more recent survey showed a reduced amount of support— 66 percent of respondents, and 46 percent of Latinos, in favor. But whether or not the initiative passes, bilingual education has had a sufficient trial period to be pronounced a failure. It is time finally to welcome immigrant children into our society by adding to the language they already know a full degree of competency in the common language of their new country—to give these children the very best educational opportunity for *inclusion.*

---

*[It did pass.—Eds.]

POSTSCRIPT

Do Bilingual Education Programs Help Non-English-Speaking Children Succeed?

Is bilingual education effective? Depending on the way research is interpreted, and also what is considered "bilingual education," the answer to that question may vary. Even if research were consistent enough to determine the best way to handle bilingual education, we would still be left with the dilemma of dealing with bilingual education when more languages need to be taught. While the majority of children in bilingual classrooms speak Spanish as their native tongue, there are students who speak Portuguese, Korean, Chinese, and any number of other languages. Would it be necessary to implement bilingual programs in every school for every language needed?

Krashen gives three criteria for a successful bilingual program: providing background in the first language, providing literacy in the first language, and providing teaching in English through ESL or sheltered classes. Is this feasible? If it is feasible, is it enough to successfully integrate non-English-speaking students into American society? Will they be just as prepared for college as a native English speaker?

Porter states that parents of children in bilingual classrooms typically do not want their children there, and they are afraid that their child is missing out on valuable instruction in English. She suggests that we give up on bilingual education, but what does she suggest be implemented in its place? Is what she suggests just another form of bilingual education?

The controversy over the efficacy of bilingual education continues in states, provinces, counties, school districts, and even in individual schools and homes. Arguments ensue over the statistics and what the research means. But one must not lose sight of the most important thing in this battle—the children. What approaches provide the best possible education for the non-English-speaking students involved? As debates spiral round and round, we need to remember why we are debating in the first place. The reason for the debate is the children, who are more precious than the politics of securing funding for programs.

Suggested Readings

Crawford, J. (1999). *Bilingual education: History, politics, theory, and practice* (4th ed.). Los Angeles: Bilingual Educational Services.

Krashen, S. (1996). *Under attack: The case against bilingual education.* Culver City, CA: Language Education Associates.

Shin, F., & Grobbons, B. (1996). Hispanic parent perceptions and attitudes of bilingual education. *Journal of Mexican American Educators,* 16–22.

ISSUE 13

Is Gay Adoption and Foster Parenting Healthy for Children?

YES: National Adoption Information Clearinghouse, from *Gay and Lesbian Adoptive Parents: Resources for Professionals and Parents* (National Clearinghouse on Child Abuse and Neglect Information/ National Adoption Information Clearinghouse, April 2000)

NO: Paul Cameron, from "Gay Foster Parents More Apt to Molest," *Journal of the Family Research Institute* (November 2002)

ISSUE SUMMARY

YES: The National Adoption Information Clearinghouse (NAIC) presents facts regarding gay and lesbian adoptive parents. The NAIC gives current information on the background and laws regarding homosexual parenting, and confronts the issues and concerns many people have regarding homosexual adoption, including the idea that children are molested by homosexual parents.

NO: Dr. Paul Cameron, of the Family Research Institute, presents his case against allowing homosexuals to become parents—foster parents in particular. He mainly discusses case study information regarding the proclivity for homosexual parents to molest foster children.

$\mathbf{A}$ current topic being hotly debated in our society is gay and lesbian marriage. On the heels of this topic comes a closely related one regarding the fitness of homosexuals to raise children. Does sexual orientation affect parenting skills? Are gay and lesbian parents likely to promote homosexual behavior in their children? Will children learn to become homosexual from their gay parents? Are children at greater risk of molestation if they are raised in a homosexual household? These are just a sampling of the multitude of questions that some segments of our society have raised as we embrace this highly controversial and volatile issue. While there are segments of the heterosexual population that do not disfavor homosexual parenting, there are many concerns and fears that others have about homosexual parents. The question is whether or not any of those concerns have merit.

Those opposed to homosexual parenting, foster parenting and adoption fear for the effects it may have on the children. Will children in these homes experience ridicule by their peers when a child tells a friend that they have two moms and no dad? Are young boys who are being raised by gay men being exposed to a lifestyle that is morally wrong? Will this exposure cause these boys to "turn gay"? Those opposed also worry about the safety of the children. In particular, they fear that children living in these environments could be molested by a parent or family friend. Furthermore, some groups have claimed that the children themselves will become gay because they are learning the lifestyle from their parents. The teasing children may endure from their friends because of having homosexual parents are a haunting concern. Those opposed to homosexual parenting also point to the need for children to have both a father and mother figure in order to grow up "normally." Some also contend that the vast majority of religions are vehemently against children being raised in a homosexual family because this is an "unnatural lifestyle."

There are not only homosexual, but heterosexual, segments of society that support the right of gays and lesbians to bear or adopt children and parent them. These groups contend that most of the concerns mentioned above are founded in the deep seated homophobia that exists throughout the world. They point to research on homosexuality which suggests that while homosexual parenting is challenging, especially with respect to children's relations with peers, most of the concerns of the opposition group are not based upon any scientific evidence and therefore are unfounded and without merit. They contend that homosexual parents face the same challenges as any other parent in raising their children. Gays and lesbians can be just as appropriately loving and nurturing as anyone else, and have the right to raise children and experience family life to the same degree that heterosexuals enjoy this right.

In the article that supports gay and lesbian parenting, the National Adoption Information Clearinghouse presents information about adoption in general and how gays and lesbians can initiate the adoption process as well. The article addresses many of the concerns that segments of society have regarding homosexual parenting. Current laws regarding adoption, by homosexual parents, are also presented. Dr. Paul Cameron, from the Family Research Institute, in his article that opposes homosexual parenting, argues that one of the most worrisome concerns that people have regarding homosexual parenting—children being molested—is occurring, yet social workers and placement agencies are choosing to overlook it.

As you read the following articles, realize that your personal beliefs and value system will heavily influence how you respond to each article. The issue of homosexuality and homosexual rights is one of the more divisive controversies in our society. As a personal challenge, read each article with the intent of not supporting one side or the other. Instead, try your best to understand the points made in the article that is more opposite of your views on homosexual parenting. Remember, to understand a point of view different than yours does not necessarily mean that you condone such a view. It merely aids you in seeing things from a different perspective.

Gay and Lesbian Adoptive Parents: Resources for Professionals and Parents

Introduction

Gay men and lesbians have always adopted, though in the past they usually hid their sexual orientation. Today, just as they are becoming visible in all other aspects of U.S. society, they are being considered more seriously as potential adoptive parents. This change has been aided by the increase in the number of gay and lesbian biological parents in the United States.

In 1976, there were an estimated 300,000 to 500,000 gay and lesbian biological parents; as of 1990, an estimated 6 to 14 million children *have* a gay or lesbian parent.[1] And, between 8 and 10 million children are being *raised* in gay and lesbian households.[2] The US Department of Health and Human Services, Adoption and Foster Care Analysis Reporting System (AFCARS), estimated in 1999 there were approximately 547,000 children in foster care in the United States, of which 117,000 are legally free and therefore eligible for adoption. But, in 1997, there were qualified adoptive families (including single parents) available for only twenty percent of these children. It is also estimated that approximately ten percent of the U.S. population—or 25 million individuals—are homosexual.[3]

Based on these increasing numbers, can gay and lesbian individuals be realistically and automatically excluded from consideration as potential adoptive parents?

Despite this increase in gay and lesbian parenting, social workers may have reservations when considering gay adoptive parents for a child. They might wonder how the children will be raised and how they will feel about themselves and their parents. Will they be embarrassed because they have two mothers or two fathers, or because their single mother dates women or their unmarried father has a boyfriend? Will their friends tease them? Will they be more likely to be homosexual than will children raised by heterosexual parents? And most important, how will having been raised by gay or lesbian parents affect them as they grow into adulthood?

This fact sheet addresses the issues faced both by social workers evaluating prospective gay or lesbian adoptive parents and by gays and lesbians considering

From *Adoption Information Clearinghouse*, April 2000.

adoption. An extensive list of sources of support and information that may be helpful to gay and lesbian adoptive parents and adoption professionals is available online at `http://naic.acf.hhs.gov/pubs/f_gay/f_gayh.cfm`, or by contacting the Clearinghouse at `naic@caliber.com` or (888) 251-0075.

The Status of Gay and Lesbian Parenting

Defining the family structure of gay and lesbian parents can be a challenging task. The most common type of homosexual household is step or blended families. These are gay and lesbian parents who had their biological children in a former heterosexual relationship, then "came out, and created a new family with another partner. Other types of family structures include single gay or lesbian parents and couples having children together. Both of these family types may be created through adoption, but more frequently reproductive technology is being utilized.[4]

There has been some research on biological families with gay and lesbian parents. This research focuses mainly on children born to donor-inseminated lesbians or those raised by a parent, once married, who is now living a gay lifestyle. While research on these situations has not addressed all the issues relevant to adoptive parenting; this information is invaluable for social workers struggling with difficult decisions, for gay men and lesbians who want to be parents, for their families and friends, and for anyone seeking information on this nontraditional type of family.

Unfortunately, the effects on children of being raised by lesbian and gay adoptive parents cannot be predicted. The number of homosexuals who have adopted is unknown, and because of the controversial nature of the issue, their children are often reluctant to speak out. Testimony of children who have grown up in gay households may turn out to provide the best information about the results of gay parenting.

Research studies, often conducted by individuals or organizations with a vested interest in the outcome, are contradictory. Studies linked to conservative political and religious groups show negative effects on children of gay and lesbian parents; while, studies which support homosexual parenting are said to reflect the bias of those who are themselves gay or who support gay rights. Clearly, what are needed are definitive studies that would follow larger numbers of children over a long period of time. That research, when completed, will provide more definitive information for the debate.

In the meantime, it is critical to address the issues and concerns so that social workers can examine their own personal biases to make informed decisions and gay and lesbian adoptive families can receive the support they need to thrive.

Issues and Concerns

"What Is Sexual Orientation?"

The American Psychological Association defines sexual orientation as "one of four components of sexuality and is distinguished by an enduring emotional, romantic, sexual or affectionate attraction to individuals of a particular gender. The three other components of sexuality are biological sex, gender identity (the psychological sense of being male or female) and social sex role (the adherence to cultural norms for feminine or masculine behaviors)."[5]

For most people sexual orientation emerges in early adolescence without any prior sexual experience. Sexual orientation is different from sexual behavior because it refers to innate feelings and self-concept and may not be expressed in behavior. Understanding the source of sexual orientation depends on which side of the nature versus nurture debate you fall. Some theories point to genetic or inborn hormonal factors; others to early childhood life experiences. Many believe sexual orientation is shaped at an early age through a combination of biological, psychological and social factors.[6]

"Children Will Be Molested by Homosexual Parents"

There is no legitimate scientific research connecting homosexuality and pedophilia. Sexual orientation (homosexual or heterosexual) is defined as an adult attraction to other adults. Pedophilia is defined as an adult sexual attraction or perversion to children.[7] In a study of 269 cases of child sex abuse, only two offenders where found to be gay or lesbian. More relevant was the finding that of the cases involving molestation of a boy by a man, seventy-four percent of the men were or had been in a heterosexual relationship with the boy's mother or another female relative. The conclusion was found that "a child's risk of being molested by his or her relative's heterosexual partner is over one hundred times greater than by someone who might be identifiable as being homosexual."[8]

"Children Will Be Teased and Harassed"

Children of gay men and lesbians are vulnerable to teasing and harassment, particularly as they approach adolescence, when any sign of difference is grounds for exclusion. How much of a problem is it? Is it likely to cause lasting psychological damage?

Gay and lesbian parents are well aware of the difficulties that a child may face—many have dealt with prejudice all of their lives. Most see it as an opportunity for ongoing discussion that will help their children grow as people.

Abby Ruder, a therapist, lesbian, and adoptive mother, acknowledges that children will be teased, and takes great pains to prepare her gay and lesbian clients for some of the problems that their children will face. She feels that families should have a plan for dealing with society's attitude toward them. "Children with gay or lesbian parents need to be taught when it's okay to tell people and when not to. A family doesn't have to be 'out' all of the time. My 9-year-old . . . has become very adept at knowing when to tell people that she has two mommies."

Wendell Ricketts and Roberta Achtenberg, in the article "Adoption and Foster Parenting for Lesbians and Gay Men: Creating New Traditions in Family" from *Homosexuality and Family Relations*, address social workers grappling with the issue by asking, ". . . should children be sheltered from every experience in which their difference might challenge prejudice, ignorance, or the status quo (or in which they would be 'exposed' to the difference of others)? Agencies conforming to such a standard must ask themselves whether it is their function to honor the system that generates stigma by upholding its constraints." They continue, "Teasing is what children do. Does this mean that child welfare policy must be set at a level no higher than the social interactions of children?"

In custody cases involving a gay or lesbian parent, courts have considered the fact that a child might be teased as contrary to the best interests of the child. They argue that the stigma attached to having a gay or lesbian parent will damage a child's self-esteem. This has been refuted in many studies. Research has found that although children of gays and lesbians do report experiencing teasing because of their parent(s), their self-esteem levels are no lower than those of children of heterosexual parents.[9]

In 1984 the Supreme Court heard a case, *Palmore v Sidoti*, in which a Florida man sought custody of his daughter on the grounds that his white ex-wife was now married to a black man and that this would expose his daughter to the stigma of living in an interracial family. The Court ruled that the girl should stay with her mother, saying that under the Equal Protection Clause of the Fourteenth Amendment, "private biases may be outside the reach of the law, but the law cannot, directly or indirectly, give them effect." Although the Court's ruling dealt specifically with racial prejudices, several researchers have mentioned the case as a rebuttal to the argument that placing a child in a family subject to social stigma is automatically contrary to the child's best interests.[10]

Nonetheless, social workers and even some gay men and lesbians considering adoption wonder if it is in the best interest of a child to be raised by homosexual parents. "It can be too hard a transition for some children, especially those who are older and have already formed preconceived notions about homosexuality," explains therapist Ruder. "Younger children usually have an easier time adjusting to a gay and lesbian parented home. They haven't learned the societal biases against gays and lesbians yet." When a gay person is being considered as a potential adoptive parent for an older child, the child should be told about the person's sexual orientation and asked his feelings about it. If the child is comfortable with the information, the caseworker can proceed to the next step.

Gay and lesbian adoptive parents must also think about how they will explain to younger children, in age-appropriate language, not only how and why the child was adopted but also about the parents' sexual orientation. Both are complex subjects that should be addressed a number of times as the child grows and matures, each time adding new information as the child asks and is able to absorb and understand more. Then both topics become accepted facts of family life.

"Children Raised in Homosexual Households Will Become Gay"

The bulk of evidence to date indicates that children raised by gay and lesbian parents are no more likely to become homosexual than children raised by heterosexuals. As one researcher put it, "If heterosexual parenting is insufficient to ensure that children will also be heterosexual, then there is no reason to conclude that children of homosexuals also will be gay."[11]

Studies asking the children of gay fathers to express their sexual orientation showed the majority of children to be heterosexual, with the proportion of gay offspring similar to that of a random sample of the population. An assessment of more than 300 children born to gay or lesbian parents in 12 different samples shows no evidence of "significant disturbances of any kind in the development of sexual identity among these individuals."[12]

"Children Will Develop Problems Growing Up in an 'Unnatural' Lifestyle"

Courts have expressed concern that children raised by gay and lesbian parents may have difficulties with their personal and psychological development, self-esteem, and social and peer relationships. Because of this concern, researchers have focused on children's development in gay and lesbian families.

The studies conclude that children of gay or lesbian parents are no different than their counterparts raised by heterosexual parents. In "Children of Lesbian and Gay Parents," a 1992 article in *Child Development,* Charlotte Patterson states, "Despite dire predictions about children based on well-known theories of psychosocial development, and despite the accumulation of a substantial body of research investigating these issues, not a single study has found children of gay or lesbian parents to be disadvantaged in any significant respect relative to children of heterosexual parents."

Psychiatrist Laurintine Fromm, of the Institute of Pennsylvania Hospital, agrees with that finding. "[The] literature . . . does not indicate that these children fare any worse [than those of heterosexual parents] in any area of psychological development or sexual identity formation. A parent's capacity to be respectful and supportive of the child's autonomy and to maintain her own intimate attachments, far outweighs the influence of the parent's sexual orientation alone."

What the Law Says

Only one state, Florida, specifically bars the adoption of children by gay and lesbian adults. Similar legislation was introduced in Utah prohibiting unmarried couples, including same-sex couples, from adopting children. The bill claims it is not in a child's best interest to be adopted by persons "cohabiting in a relationship that is not a legally valid (binding) marriage." The bill passed the State of Utah's House and Senate in February 2000 and is waiting the Governor's signature. The Governor has pledged to sign it.

Yet, in April 2000, Vermont lawmakers approved legislation that makes the State the first in the nation to recognize same-sex couples' right to form "civil unions." Partners in a civil union would be given the same benefits of married couples—the ability to transfer property, to make medical decisions for each other, to be eligible for inheritance, and the necessity to dissolve the union in Family Court (equivalent to a divorce). More than 30 other states have tried to avoid such unions through the passage of the Defense of Marriage Act. The act defines marriage as a union between a man and a woman and denies recognition of same-sex marriages performed elsewhere.

Legislation has also been introduced in Mississippi that would ban gay and lesbian couples from adoption and forbid the State of Mississippi from recognizing gay and lesbian adoptions that have previously been granted by other state courts—an unprecedented provision. Anti-sodomy statutes in 19 states and the lack of legal recognition of homosexual couples complicate adoption in the states that don't specifically prohibit gay and lesbian adoption.

Professor William Adams Jr., co-counsel in a case challenging Florida's ban on adoptions by gays and lesbians, has noted courts are increasingly turning to expert testimony to resolve questions in gay rights cases. He theorizes that there are several factors contributing to this trend, among them the courts' desire to justify their decisions in light of the controversy surrounding the issue and the efforts of gay litigants and civil rights organizations to provide the court with information. Although Adams sees this as a positive step, he comments, "citation to social science data should not be mistaken for a court's full understanding of it, however, because courts sometimes struggle to make sense of the research, or strain to ignore it."[13]

Nine states—California, Massachusetts, New Jersey, New Mexico, New York, Ohio, Vermont, Washington and Wisconsin—and the District of Columbia have allowed openly gay or lesbian individuals or couples to adopt. Although some joint adoptions have been successful, the most common practice is for a single person to apply as the legal adoptive parent of the child. Couples who both want custody then apply for a second parent, or coparent, adoption.

Second parent adoption or the adoption by non-marital partners, leaves the parental rights of one legally recognized parent intact and creates a second legally recognized parent for the adoptive children. Second parent adoption, which has become routine for children of heterosexual stepparents, is the only way for gay couples to both become legal parents of their children.[14] Although state statutes generally provide a "stepparent exception," these exceptions emphasize the existence of a legal marriage between the biological parent and the stepparent.[15]

This growing practice was tested in a landmark case in Vermont in 1993. Jane Van Buren had given birth to two boys through anonymous donor insemination. According to the law, only Ms. Van Buren was considered their parent—her partner, Deborah Lashman, had no legal standing. The couple filed a petition for a second parent adoption, asking the probate court to allow Ms. Lashman to adopt the children while leaving Ms. Van Buren's parental rights intact. The court denied the adoptions because Ms. Lashman was not married to the biological parent. On June 18, 1993, the Vermont Supreme Court unanimously reversed the decision of the lower court and awarded joint custody to the couple.[16] With this decision, the Vermont Supreme Court became the first State Supreme Court to recognize lesbian co-parent adoptions. As a result of this finding, other couples are likely to find second parent adoptions easier to accomplish in Vermont and other areas of the country.

Second parent adoptions (by unmarried couples) have been granted by the courts (the approvals were generally from the lower level courts) in 21 states and the District of Columbia: Alabama, Alaska, California, Illinois, Indiana, Iowa, Maryland, Massachusetts, Michigan, Minnesota, Nevada, New Jersey, New Mexico, New York, Ohio, Oregon, Pennsylvania, Rhode Island, Texas, Vermont and Washington.[17]

Types of Adoption

Depending on the type of adoption gay and lesbian parents are interested in—public, private, independent, open or international—there may be different considerations involved in disclosing sexual orientation. How open prospective adoptive parents are about their homosexuality depends upon the couples' personal feelings on disclosure, whether direct questions are asked and what the laws in the State of residency are.

One important point for all prospective adoptive parents to be aware of is—the difference between not sharing private information and deliberately lying at any time in the adoption process. Although it is completely legal to omit information regarding homosexuality, it is illegal to lie about it when confronted directly.[18] Let it be clear that failing to tell the truth is considered fraud and raises the opportunity for either an adoption not being finalized or a possible disruption.

Public Agency Adoption

Success in adopting from the public child welfare system depends on the State adoption law and the attitude of the agency. For example, in New York and California, gay and lesbian prospective adoptive parents are protected against discrimination. It is illegal for public agencies in those states to reject adoptive parents on the basis of sexual orientation. However, that is not a guarantee that prejudices don't exist. Social workers who are uncomfortable with homosexuality may find the prospective adoptive parents unsuitable for other reasons.[19]

Each state decides independently who can adopt. Since, the final decision is made by judges at the county level, the availability of adoption as an option to openly gay and lesbian couples is influenced by the political and social community in which the family lives. The court's decision hinges on the "best interest" of the child, a concept interpreted differently by different judges.

Private Agency Placements

Private agencies establish their own criteria for the prospective adoptive parents. Age, religion, fertility status, marital status and sexual orientation all may be agency considerations. Some private agencies may disregard sexual orientation, and present the prospective parent as a single adopter who lives with another adult who will share the responsibilities of raising the child. This omission of sexual orientation is based on the agency's judgement and relevancy to the applicant's parenting qualifications.

Independent and Open Adoption

An independent adoption is an adoption facilitated by those other than case-workers associated with an agency. They may be a physician, an attorney, or an intermediary and are illegal in some states. In an independent adoption the placement decision (within the provisions of the state statute) is completely up to the families involved. However, independent adoption does not necessarily mean an open adoption. An open adoption involves some amount of initial and/or ongoing contact of birth and adoptive families. The adoptive and birth parents agree upon the birth parents' role, future communication and the degree of openness prior to adoption. Being honest with the birth parents from the first contact allows gay and lesbian adoptive parents the opportunity to have a relationship without the possibility of a disrupting secret.

International Adoption

Adopting a child from a foreign country may involve finding an agency willing to accept the adoptive parents' sexual orientation, disclosing the information to the contacts in the sending country, and presenting the information to the foreign government. However, conservative, or religious and often developing countries may not be as receptive to gay and lesbian couples. Adoptive parents need to be aware that foreign governments and courts are making placement decisions based on their cultural standards and what they feel is in the best interest of the child.

The Social Worker's Dilemma

Placement Decisions

The debate goes on and will continue as long as there are conflicting views about homosexuality. Considering these different views, should social workers place children with gay men or lesbians? To make the best placement decision for children, social workers need to answer the following questions:

- Is this person or couple caring, nurturing, and sensitive to others?
- Do they have the qualities needed to parent a child?
- What are their individual strengths and weaknesses?
- How do their strengths/weaknesses complement the needs of the child?
- Do they have the capacity to nurture a child not born to them?

In addition, for prospective homosexual adoptive parents, Denise Goodman, Ph.D., a consultant and trainer in Ohio, firmly believes that workers need to have a holistic understanding that includes finding out answers to questions about their homosexuality:

> "I counsel workers to ask homosexual applicants where they are in their individual development. Have they recently come out? Are they comfortable with their self-image and with being gay? Having a positive self-image will provide a model for an adopted child. I want to know about

family support and how those who are important in their lives view them and their idea of adopting. I ask questions about the stability of their relationship and try to see how committed they are to each other. Do they have wills? Have they bought a home? Do they share finances? Once you know more about their situation, you can help them access appropriate resources and connect them with other gay or lesbian adoptive parents."

Goodman, who has trained thousands of social workers in Ohio, sees the opportunity for change, but has a few concerns:

"While it is gratifying to see social workers become more open, if agency administrators are not fully behind the workers, little will change. Families will be approved and never hear about an available child; those who aren't open about their sexuality will receive a child, while "honest" applicants will wait, or other issues will surface so that a family is not accepted."

If a sense of trust and openness is established between a social worker and applicant, the worker can help to decide when privacy is the best route or when an applicant can be more outspoken. It ultimately depends on state laws and the views of presiding judges.

Professional Prejudices and Policy Decisions

Adoption professionals need to be aware of their own personal prejudices and prejudgments when working with gay and lesbian prospective adoptive parents. Experiences and beliefs come from family background and values, religious beliefs, and community views on homosexuality and will affect social workers' and agency staff's ability to assess the couple.[20] Ann Sullivan, of the Child Welfare League of America, suggests in her article "Policy Issues in Gay and Lesbian Adoption," that professionals consider several key issues:

- The client is the child in need of an adoptive family. All families should be given equal consideration and the potential resources available weighed for the placement of the child.
- No single factor should be the determining factor in assessing suitability for adoption.
- In considering gay and lesbian prospective adoptive parents, sexual orientation and the capacity to nurture a child are separate issues and should not be confused in the decision making process.
- Each placement decision should be based on the strengths and needs of the individual child and the perceived ability of the prospective adoptive family to meet those needs and develop additional strengths.

Coping with the Agency Preference Hierarchy

Many gay and lesbian prospective adoptive parents are troubled by the feeling that adoption agencies offer them the children who are the most difficult to place: those with physical, mental, or emotional disabilities; those who are older; children of color; and members of sibling groups.

"Often gay parents will get harder children because it's the last resort," Bob Diamond, the former Executive Director of AASK Northern California in Oakland, admits. "A lot of social workers will say, 'Well, no one is going to take this kid except gay people.' Being homosexual is not usually seen as a positive factor," he adds, noting that single people in general are usually treated as "second-class citizens" by most adoption agencies.[21]

Roberta Achtenberg, Executive Director of the National Center for Lesbian Rights in San Francisco, bluntly confirms that there is an unspoken ranking within the adoption network. "The hierarchy prefers white, married, middle or upper middle class couples, and these couples don't want the special needs kids. The less preferred children then go to unmarried couples of all kinds, single individuals, and gay people. The children are less preferred, and the recipients are less preferred."

What strikes psychologist April Martin, author of *The Lesbian and Gay Parenting Handbook*, as ironic is that the same bureaucracies that believe that lesbians and gay men are not suitable parents will place children who require the most highly skilled parenting with them. She and others have pointed out that nontraditional families have unique strengths that make them excellent, and in some cases, the best homes for certain children. Among them is an ability to accept differences, to understand what it is like to be in the minority, to demonstrate flexible gender roles, to be open about sexuality with children who have been sexually abused, and to understand the special needs of homosexual children.

April Martin suggests that gays and lesbians who want to adopt younger, healthier children can find them by working with private agencies or by working directly with birthparents. Some birthparents have specifically chosen openly gay households for their children.

Life After Adoption

Explaining Sexuality to Children

All families at one time or another will have "the" discussion on sexuality. For gay and lesbian families this can be an even more sensitive subject. However, a healthy family, regardless of sexual orientation, shares the same core values—love and respect, commitment and understanding. It is especially important when talking with children to stress what these values mean to the family and to recognize that there are many different cultures, communities and families around the world.

The Family Pride Coalition, a national advocacy and support organization, offers several suggestions for parents discussing sexuality with their children:[22]

- Be honest about your own identity and comfort level.
- If you are uncomfortable, let your children know you find this hard to talk about, but that you feel it is important for families to talk about difficult things.

- Listen closely to your child and when possible, let your children take the lead. Let them ask questions. Take cues about their level of understanding from the questions they ask and interact at that level.
- Be as clear as you can be about your own feelings connected to sexuality, coming out, privacy, and family values.
- Consider your childís age and how much information they need.

Getting Support

Once an adoption is completed, the business of family life begins. Like all adoptive parents, gay men and lesbians are seeking ways to incorporate their children into their lives and to help them make a smooth transition. They also want to meet other homosexuals who have taken on the challenge of parenting. There are a growing number of support groups to meet these needs.

Len and Fernando, a multiethnic gay couple who adopted 3-year-old Isabel as a toddler, are members of an active group in the Philadelphia area. "Speaking to the parents of older children gives us ideas of how to cope with issues as they come up. Most of the members are women. We could use a few more men!"

Isabel, who is African-American, has the chance to meet other African-American adopted children and enjoys the many activities planned for families. Their group is part of a larger support network, Philadelphia Family Pride, that serves more than 250 gay and lesbian families in the Delaware Valley. In addition to giving its members a chance to socialize, the group's advocacy and educational projects encourage parents to work with teachers on adoption, race, and alternative family issues that affect their children. Members participate in conferences, receive local and national newsletters, and learn about books and articles for themselves and their children. Older children of gay parents have formed their own network, Colage—Children of Lesbians and Gays Everywhere.

A vital support network of family and friends is important for any family— adoptive, biological, one with heterosexual parents, or one with homosexual parents. Some gay and lesbian adoptive parents have found that even if their parents had a difficult time accepting their homosexuality, the parents readily accept their new role as grandparents. It is almost as if having children makes them more like mainstream families. "Our parents reacted to our desire to parent pretty much the same way they reacted to our coming out," says Tim Fisher, father of two and former Executive Director of the Family Pride Coalition (formerly Gay and Lesbian Parents Coalition International). "They said, 'We love you . . . but let's not talk about it.' With the kids, they have softened their tone a little. They are grandparents who adore their grandchildren."

Conclusion

The increasing number of gay men and lesbians choosing to adopt has brought the issue of gay and lesbian parenting to the forefront. Social workers are being asked to look carefully at their own feelings and to make reasonable judgments about what is in the best interest of children who need families. And, the increasing number of children needing adoptive families puts pressure on workers to find appropriate families.

The questions linger—should stable, nurturing, mature applicants be turned away on the basis of sexual orientation? What if a substantial number of children face the possibility of never achieving permanency, when they could have been adopted by a gay or lesbian family?

Endnotes

1. Sullivan, A., (1995). Issues In *Gay and Lesbian Adoption: Proceedings of the Fourth Annual Peirce-Warwick Adoption Symposium*, Washington, DC: Child Welfare League of America.

2. Editors of the *Harvard Law Review*. (1990). *Sexual Orientation and the Law*. Cambridge, MA: Harvard University Press.

3. Sullivan, A.

4. Rohrbaugh, J.B. Lesbian Families: Clinical Issues and Theoretical Implications. (1992). *Professional Psychology: Research and Practice*, 23: 467–473.

5. Blommer, S.J. (undated). Answers to Your Questions About Sexual Orientation and Homosexuality: A Fact Sheet. Washington, DC. American Psychological Association.

6. Blommer, S.J.

7. Lesbian and Gay Rights Project—ACLU. (1999). ACLU Fact Sheet—Overview of Lesbian and Gay Parenting, Adoption and Foster Care. New York, NY: American Civil Liberties Union.

8. Carole, J. Are Children at Risk for Sexual Abuse by Homosexuals? (1994). *Pediatrics*, 94 (1):

9. Huggins, S.L. A Comparative Study of Self-Esteem of Adolescent Children of Divorced Lesbian Mothers and Divorced Heterosexual Mothers. (1989). *Journal of Homosexuality*, 18 (1/2): 123–135.

10. Adams, W. E. Whose Family Is It Anyway? The Continuing Struggle for Lesbians and Gay Men Seeking to Adopt Children. (1996). *New England Law Review*, 30 (3): 579–621.

11. Bigner, J. J., Bozett, F. W. 1990. Parenting by Gay Fathers. In: *Homosexuality and Family Relations*. Bozett, F. W., Sussman, M. B. New York, NY: Haworth Press, Inc.

12. Patterson, C. J. Children of Lesbian and Gay Parents. (1992). *Child* Development: 1025–1039.

13. Adams, W. E.

14. Lambda Legal Defense and Education Fund. (1997). Lesbian and Gay Parenting: A Fact Sheet. New York: NY: Lambda Legal Defense and Education Fund.

15. Mishra, D. The Road to Concord: Resolving the Conflict of Law Over Adoption by Gays and Lesbians. (1996). Columbia Journal of Law and Social Problems, 30 (1): 91–136.

16. Patterson, C. J.

17. Lambda Legal Defense and Education Fund.

18. Martin, A. (1993). The Lesbian and Gay Parenting Handbook. New York, NY: HarperCollins Publishers, Inc.

19. Martin, A.

20. Sullivan, A. Policy Issues in Gay and Lesbian Adoption. (1995). Adoption and Fostering, 19 (4): 21–25.

21. Perry, D. Homes of Last Resort. (1993). The Advocate: 46.

22. Cronin, M. E. (1999). Guide to Talking with Your Child About California's Knight Initiative. San Diego, CA: Family Pride Coalition.

NO

Paul Cameron

Gay Foster Parents More Apt to Molest

No matter how professionals in our society extol the virtues of 'science,' if empirical evidence goes against their beliefs, they often ignore it or avoid it. The employment of homosexuals as foster parents is a perfect case in point.

When a 16-year-old foster son was molested and raped by two gay foster parents in Vermont, Tom Moore, Deputy of the State's Social and Rehabilitation Services, told me on June 25, 2002 that neither he nor the Commissioner knew of any evidence about the molestation rates of children by homosexual foster parents. He was apparently echoing his boss, Commissioner William Young, who the papers quoted as saying "I don't know of any screening instrument for [sexual molestation]. Certainly, sexual preference doesn't have anything to do with it, or religious beliefs or socioeconomic status. It's so frustrating because there isn't a predictor." (*Rutland Herald* 6/21/02)

Really? Traditional common sense holds that married parents are likely to be the best foster placement, and homosexuals among the worst, in part because of the risks of sexual molestation. But tradition holds almost no weight for these bureaucrats. How can this be? Can the traditions that worked to build arguably the world's most successful culture be ignored without injuring society? What kind of belief-system is so much better that it should be followed instead?

When I interviewed the reporter who wrote the story for the *Rutland Herald*, he refused to specify whether what he had called the "male couple" in the newspaper story was in fact a homosexual couple. He said that the *Rutland Herald* never released the sexual orientations of those accused of crimes. When I spoke with his editor, she repeated the policy. The "male couple" certainly acted as though they were gay, but the newspaper staff wasn't about to say or print it.

Fortunately, those at the District Court of Vermont were not so protective of 'sexual orientation privacy.' They provided the entire record. The rest of the story about the 16-year-old fit traditional common sense perfectly.

It turns out that the natural parents of the boy who was victimized strenuously objected to the placement of their hard-to-control son with these two gays. Yet, following a policy laid down 15 years ago, their objections were

From *Journal of the Family Research Institute*, vol. 17, no. 7, November 2002. Copyright © 2002 by Dr. Paul Cameron. Reprinted by permission.

ignored. Additionally, when the boy complained to the Department that his new foster parents had asked him whether he had engaged in anal intercourse with his brother, the Department, through David Stanley, its Case Worker, concluded that the boy had been 'coached' to say this by his natural parents. Stanley said the gay foster parents denied saying such a thing and he believed them. So as far as the case worker was concerned, the boy had lied, so he was forced to stay with the 'male couple.'

Soon thereafter, the men gave the boy a magazine containing depictions of scantily clad men. They told the boy to 'masturbate to these pictures.' The boy complied, and hid the magazine under his bed.

Here, another factor of the case supported traditional common sense. Traditional thought holds that homosexuals have difficulty containing their sexual desires for youth. And sure enough, even in the face of all this investigation and conflict about possible molestation, the boy was with these homosexuals only two more weeks before they began to rape him!

Think of it. The investigation had already put these two gays 'on notice,' and yet this warning kept them from acting upon their temptation for only two weeks. Then, both men, who were in a 'committed relationship' with one another, had their way sexually with the boy. Sometimes, just one of them raped the boy alone, sometimes it happened when they were together. The boy managed to escape only by pretending that the sex was OK, and then fleeing to a hospital when the 'family' went to town to shop.

As it turned out, the men's magazine was the 'clincher' when the boy fingered his foster 'parents.' Because the magazine was where the boy said it was, the police were able to get the men to confess.

Notice what happened here. Vermont's child protective agency, without evidence of any sort, adopted a new policy 15 years ago that discarded tradition. Why? Because traditional common sense relegated homosexuals as 'not suitable for foster-placement' status. The child protective agency thought it had a 'better way.'

What was this 'better way?' What is this belief system that is so much better than traditional thought?

I filed a Freedom of Information request regarding this case and the policy changes that had been instituted by the agency, asking 17 specific questions. Some of these included: how many foster parents or foster parent pairs who have been involved in foster parenting a child or children were homosexual? Did your department conclude that the 16-year-old boy's claim was false that his foster parents had asked him whether he performed anal intercourse with his brother?

Less than a month later, Jody Racht, the Assistant Attorney General for Vermont, informed me that asking specific questions rather than "access to identified public records" fell outside of "any provision of state law."

So while certain policies had apparently been established to protect homosexuals—both in the child protective agency and at the *Rutland Herald*—neither institution would explain their basis. They just followed 'the policy.'

So what was this 'better way?'

Deputy Commissioner Moore said that, because of privacy and confidentiality concerns, no follow-up of placements with homosexuals had been conducted, nor were any contemplated. This strategy of 'deliberate ignorance' is not unique to Vermont. Over the past 10 years, I have talked with representatives of the District of Columbia, El Paso County (Colorado Springs, CO), and Seattle, WA—jurisdictions which place foster children with homosexuals—and gotten the same replies. In Colorado Springs, the wishes of the family regarding the placement of a 6-year-old boy—whose lesbian mother was judged unsuitable to parent—were overridden by child protective services in favor of the 'right of homosexuals to keep their children.' The little boy was given to a lesbian couple instead of his married aunt—an aunt who had been chosen by the extended family as the 'best fit' for the boy.

The social work representatives in the other three jurisdictions with whom I had contact said that since the National Association of Social Workers (NASW) declared homosexuals to be foster parents 'as fit' as heterosexuals, they believed that they were as unlikely to sexually abuse their charges as non-homosexuals. Indeed, the 1987 NASW resolution decrying "resistance to using single parents, . . . including lesbian and gay parents, as potential foster care and adoption resources" was passed, in substantial part, to counter the traditional belief that children placed with homosexual foster parents would be at higher risk of sexual exploitation.

NASW Influence

This NASW resolution and the new 'theory' behind it has informed social workers for the past 15 years. In one high profile case in 1992, the faculty of the Saint Cloud State University Social Work Department told potential students that this new 'theory' trumped not only traditional common sense, but also any religious beliefs. These faculty decreed that 'social homophobia' is a form of "human oppression." And citing the NASW code of ethics (Sec. 2.3), they noted that "accepting gay and lesbian people does not mean accepting them as individuals while simultaneously abhorring their behavior. . . . The only legitimate position of the social work profession is to abhor the oppression that is perpetrated in gay and lesbian people and to act personally and professionally to end the degradation in its many forms." That is, this 'new faith statement' must trump any other belief—including traditional religious beliefs like Christianity.

Is the NASW claim that homosexual and unmarried foster parents are 'as fit' as married heterosexuals warranted? No empirical literature concerning the issue appears to exist—although the evidence regarding the general parenting of homosexuals suggests that it is inferior to that of the married. Under the current system for placing foster children, putting the NASW claim to an empirical test cannot be done. The bureaucrats who could track the success of homosexual foster parents refuse to do so, and—citing privacy and confidentiality concerns—also prevent outsiders from doing it.

The 'faith' of the social worker profession, consisting of resolutions passed by a tiny committee within the NASW, is sufficient. No evidence is required! What a maddening mess! Fortunately, I found a way to bypass the current bureaucratic strategy of 'deliberate ignorance' regarding foster placements with homosexuals. My strategy exploited recent changes in the technology of newspaper publishing.

Here Is What I Did

While a successful foster-parenting outcome does not make the news, a highly unsuccessful outcome does. If homosexual foster parents do not differ from non-homosexuals, gross failure at foster parenting—such as the sexual molestation of foster kids—ought to occur at rates approximately proportionate to the frequencies of homosexual and heterosexual foster parents. Lexis-Nexis Academic Universe, an internet search service, scans the whole text of over 50 regional and national newspapers, largely in the U.S., but also including major papers in Australia, England, Canada, and New Zealand (e.g., *Baltimore Sun, Boston Globe, Independent* [England], *Ottawa Citizen* [Canada]).

This past summer, I examined every news story from 1989 through 2001 that included "child molestation"—a total of 5,492 stories. The findings were double-checked by also running "foster" against this database in early September, 2002. Only news stories or first-person accounts were tallied, not editorials nor opinion pieces, so the stories basically covered recent events, not reflections on older items.

This technique is obviously different from a comparison study where matched parents—homosexual and heterosexual—are randomly drawn from the total set of foster parents to see how they stack up. News stories are limited in the content they cover, nor are they necessarily consistent from reporter to reporter or paper to paper. Nonetheless, this method has its advantages. News stories are reports about 'the real world,' and not just responses to questionnaires from people who know they are being questioned or scrutinized.

Only a few of the news stories listed the sexual preferences of the perpetrators. Nevertheless, following the classification of method of infection for AIDS by the U.S. Centers for Disease Control, I was able to classify the perpetrators by the kinds of sex they engaged in (e.g., 'male with male' was considered homosexual, 'male with female' heterosexual). Since marital status is generally provided in stories about child molestation, where it was not reported, the perpetrator was assumed to be unmarried.

What I Found

Thirty stories about molestation of foster kids were located. They were numbered by date of the first newspaper story about the molestation, from 1 to 30. The location and date are given below. In 22 stories foster children were sexually abused. Five stories bore upon the character of the foster parent or guardian, though no foster child was reported as having been sexually molested. In three stories, foster caregivers molested their charges as they were held in group quarters.

Result #1. In 22 stories, the perpetrator(s) molested foster children:

1. Arlington, VA (3/2/89): An unmarried man, who had had boys placed in his home for 10 years, was charged with having sex with one of the foster boys (this was counted as one homosexual male perpetrator, one victim).

2. San Diego (3/1/89): A mother (who was married to an oft-absent husband in the military) and son lost their foster day care license when charges of possible molestation of two children were filed against her (counted as a female perpetrator and two victims of unknown sex).

4. Los Angeles (6/6/90): A man and wife lost their license when the man was accused of molesting two foster daughters (counted as a heterosexual male perpetrator and two girl victims).

7. St. Louis (10/21/90): An unmarried man, both a foster parent to one boy and the supervisor of a unit at a children's home, was convicted of molesting his foster son as well as 4 other boys at the home (counted as a homosexual male perpetrator and one boy victim).

8. British Columbia, Canada (3/26/92): A man (marital status not provided) was released from prison for molesting a 14 year old foster daughter (counted as a male heterosexual perpetrator and one girl victim).

10. Los Angeles (7/8/93): A man and wife lost their foster care license when the man was charged with molesting 2 of his foster daughters (counted as a male heterosexual perpetrator and 2 girl victims).

11. St. Petersburg, FL (1/11/94): An unmarried man was convicted of molesting his 12-year-old foster son (counted as a homosexual male perpetrator and one boy victim).

12. Maryland (4/16/94): An unmarried judge was charged with molesting his 17-year-old foster son (counted as a homosexual male perpetrator and one boy victim).

13. San Francisco (12/13/94): A married man was convicted of molesting boys and girls, including 3 foster children (counted as one homosexual male perpetrator and 3 victims of unknown sex).

15. Atlanta (1/30/97): A married man molested his 12-year-old foster son (counted as a homosexual male perpetrator and one boy victim).

17. Connecticut (3/22/97): A man and wife lost their foster care license when he was accused of molesting his foster son (counted as a homosexual male perpetrator and a boy victim).

18. New York (6/29/97): An apparently unmarried foster mother sexually molested her foster daughter from the time she was age 5 until she was 17 (counted as a homosexual female perpetrator and a female victim).

19. Seattle (12/3/97): An unmarried couple molested an 8-year-old foster daughter (counted as a homosexual female perpetrator and a male heterosexual perpetrator and a female victim).

21. England (12/5/98): An unmarried foster parent was convicted of molesting his 12-year-old foster son (counted as a homosexual male perpetrator and a boy victim).

22. Atlanta (2/27/99): An unmarried foster parent was convicted of molesting his 3 foster children, a girl and two boys (counted as a homosexual male perpetrator and a girl and two boy victims).

23. Boston (11/3/99): A married foster parent was convicted of molesting "foster children" (counted as a male perpetrator with 2 victims of unknown sex).
24. Toronto (4/3/00): A married foster parent was convicted of molesting a foster daughter (counted as a heterosexual male perpetrator and a girl victim).
25. San Diego (4/25/00): A married foster parent was convicted of molesting two twin 9-year-old foster daughters (counted as a heterosexual male perpetrator and two girl victims).
26. San Diego (6/23/00): A unmarried foster father was charged with sexual improprieties with his foster son, 11, and hiring him out for sex with other men (counted as a homosexual male perpetrator and a boy victim).
28. San Diego (9/24/00): An unmarried openly homosexual male, living with a partner who was a convicted homosexual child molester (the partner had sexually abused his own son and daughter), was given custody of an 11-year-old foster son. He then raped him. Over the years the foster father also offered his foster son to others who were sexually interested in the boy. At least three individuals accepted the foster-father's offer (counted as a homosexual male perpetrator and a boy victim).
29. Los Angeles (7/10/01): An unmarried woman pled no contest to the accusation of sexually abusing her 12-year-old foster daughter, and then lost her foster-care license (counted as a homosexual female perpetrator and a female victim).
30. St. Louis (12/31/01): An unmarried foster father was charged with molesting 2 foster sons, both 13 years old (counted as a homosexual male perpetrator and two boy victims).

Comment: It is noteworthy that in two of the 12 stories involving gays, the homosexual not only molested his foster son, but prostituted him as well. Something seems to be morally 'wrong' with homosexuals.

Result #2. Five stories concerned the character of the foster parent:

3. Boston (5/18/89): An unmarried man had illicit pictures of boys. Although he had been convicted of child molestation on a boy in 1967 (and given a suspended sentence), starting in 1977 the Massachusetts Probation Department used him as a placement for "24 adolescent males during the past 12 years."
5. Seattle (8/28/90): An unmarried man, with whom 5 foster children were currently living, admitted to molesting two boys, 14 and 15, in his Scout troop. He had been dishonorably discharged from the Navy for "similar incidents involving young boys."
6. St. Louis (8/31/90): An unmarried child molester had a 14-year-old boy placed in his home by the Missouri Division of Family Services. The boy's older brother also lived with the man. The child molester had been convicted of attempted rape of and then stabbing a 12-year-old boy. It is not clear whether he had had sex with the foster boys.
9. Los Angeles (12/29/92): A man and wife lost their foster care license when the man was charged with molesting 2 of his daughters from a previous marriage.

20. Seattle (11/3/98): A unmarried foster parent of a boy was accused of molesting 5 boys. The boys were apparently from a church youth group he assisted.

Comment: Is it a statistical fluke that 3 of the 4 gay foster parents above already had 'a record of child molestation' and yet were given boys to foster parent? Perhaps. But the bias that child protective services seem to exhibit in favor of homosexuals offers a more chilling possibility. While the 'fox' is not running the henhouse, there appear to be a considerable number of 'foxes' in these agencies—and in the current climate of ceding victimhood status to gays, even the non-foxes are inclined to 'give homosexuals a second chance.'

Result #3. In three stories, children in a group home were molested:

14. Los Angeles (5/2/96): For the second time in the year, the state initiated action to revoke the foster home license of Gay and Lesbian Adolescent Social Services because an additional number of boys reported having been molested by male staff members (counted as 3 homosexual male perpetrators and 6 boy victims).
16. Wales, Great Britain (2/4/97): Dozens of staff members at 30 children's homes sexually abused 180 victims, "most . . . were boys, some as young as 8."
27. Los Angeles (8/30/00): At least 3 male counselors raped at least 3 boys and a girl at group homes. One of the perpetrators was single, and at least one boy he raped obtained a judgment against him. There were no follow-on stories about the other perpetrators.

Comment: These stories suggest character flaws inherent to the homosexual lifestyle—flaws that put children under the care of homosexuals at considerable hazard. Note that although there are a lot of girls in children's homes, the boys appear to be at special risk. And why was a homosexual social service allowed to run group homes?

What Do These Stories Suggest?

A pattern of disproportionate molestation of foster children by those who engage in homosexuality is evident in each of the three sets of stories above. The 22 stories involving molestation of foster children, in particular, bear directly upon whether homosexual or unmarried foster parents commit more sexual offenses against their charges. Of the 22 stories, 15 (68%) involved homosexual molestation. Of the 23 perpetrators, 19 (83%) were men, and 4 (17%) were women. Of the 19 men, 12 (63%) engaged in homosexuality. Three (25%) of these 12 were married, while 9 were single. Seven (37%) of the 19 male perpetrators practiced heterosexuality. Of these 7, at least 5 (71%) were married and at least one was single.

Of the 4 women, 3 engaged in homosexuality and were unmarried. The other was married but her sexual proclivities were not revealed. Overall, of the 22 perpetrators whose marital status was known, 13 (59%) were single.

In the 22 stories, among the 32 foster children who were victimized, at least 12 (38%) were girls and at least 13 (41%) were boys. Since 2.5 of the girls were victimized by females (counting the girl who was victimized by the unmarried man and woman as being 0.5 homosexually and 0.5 heterosexually victimized), altogether, out of the 28 victims of perpetrators where a sexual preference could be determined, 8.5 (30%) were victimized by heterosexuals and 19.5 (70%) by homosexuals. Also, of the 32 children, at least 15 (43%) were victimized by the unmarried.

So What Does This Evidence Indicate About Gay Foster Parents?

Undoubtedly, only a fraction of child molestation by foster parents over the 13 years I examined was included in any news stories. If they did 'make the paper,' many—like the molestation of the boy in Vermont in 2002 that led me to conduct this study—only made the local newspaper, not the newspapers covered by Academic Universe. But there is no reason to believe that this sample was biased against those who engage in homosexuality. Indeed, a number of the newspapers included in Academic Universe have editorialized in favor of special social protections for those who engage in homosexuality (e.g., *Los Angeles Times*, *New York Times*, *Boston Globe*). And these same newspapers have also expressed support for 'marital status nondiscrimination.' So they would seemingly little reason to 'pick on' gay foster parents.

That at least 15 of the 22 instances of molestation of a foster-child by a foster parent involved those who engaged in homosexuality is sharply at odds with the National Association of Social Workers' (NASW) 1987 resolution decrying "resistance to using single parents, . . . including lesbian and gay parents, as potential foster care and adoption resources." It also flies in the face of the NASW's appeal to its members to 'correct' this 'injustice.'

The empirical evidence is lined up against the NASW—of the 21 stories where the sexual proclivities of the perpetrator could be determined, 71% implicated homosexuals! Likewise, at least 57% of the 22 perpetrators were unmarried, and they accounted for at least 47% of the 32 child victims.

Homosexuality was also a disproportionate problem in the other 8 stories. When they are around or 'in charge' of kids, homosexuals are far more apt to seek to have sex with them. Nevertheless, we hear a lot from talk show hosts that homosexuals are no more apt to molest kids—tell that to the children who were victimized in these stories!

These news stories suggest that homosexuals and unmarried individuals are more apt to molest their foster charges. Because of this, they would not seem to be 'as fit' foster parents as married heterosexuals. The boy in story number 28, despite being raped, desired to return to live with the perpetrator. So he was apparently willing to 'live with molestations,' perhaps because there were other compensatory benefits in the arrangement. However, no matter how 'great' a parent they might be otherwise, there is no way someone can be a 'fit' foster parent if they sexually abuse their placements.

In a study FRI published earlier this year, interviews with 57 children with gay parents revealed that living in a homosexual home was a trying experience for children. In addition, the largest comparison study done to date—58 kids with married parents, 58 kids with cohabiting heterosexual parents, and 58 kids with homosexual parents—reported that the children with homosexual parents did less well at school, less well socially, and often gave evidence of personal distress. Thus, there is no particular reason to believe that either homosexuals or the unmarried generally compensate for their sexual weaknesses by offering exceptional foster-service in 'other areas.'

If the welfare of children is regarded as the most important consideration in foster-placement, these findings that the unmarried and those who engage in homosexuality are more likely to sexually molest their foster children suggest that the traditional aversion to their use as foster parents is rational and reasonable. Our society makes a lot of noise about 'protecting the children' and 'for the sake of the children.' But our foster system—which may process almost half a million kids every year—is being run throughout the country according to an alien, anti-child social philosophy.

Organizations like the NASW and many child protective service agencies across the land should lose their federal and state funding, until and unless they quit using kids' lives as bricks to reinforce unproven assertions that 'homosexuals are just as good' or that 'the unmarried are just as good.' Kids who need foster care are usually already under considerable stress—they don't need social revolutionaries putting them in highly sexually-charged environments.

POSTSCRIPT

Is Gay Adoption and Foster Parenting Healthy for Children?

There are increasing types of unique family forms that are coming to light as we move more deeply into the twenty-first century. Gay and lesbian-headed families are perhaps the most prominent of these forms. As a consequence, these new family forms challenge the traditional notions of who should be a parent and how families should look. Gay and lesbian families force us as a society to examine the relation between gender and parenting, the role of society in family life and biological relations as prerequisite to the formation of a family. Is, for example, a lesbian mother, who is the biological parent of her seven-year-old daughter, and the mother's partner, who is committed to loving and caring for the seven year old, a family in the legal sense? Is it necessary for a family to be a "legal" family for the children within the family to develop into well-adjusted adults? Are these non-traditional homosexual families significantly different than common law–type heterosexual families?

With the need for qualified foster parents and adoptive parents for older children rising, should society automatically disqualify foster and adoptive parents because of their sexual orientation? It is true that there are many heterosexual married couples ready and waiting to adopt newborns in this country, but the need for reliable foster parents and adoptive parents for older children is great. Would it be better for a child to be raised in a loving home, rather than moved from placement to placement, regardless of the sexual orientation of the parents? Some advocates for homosexual parenting rights suggest that children raised in gay and lesbian families will develop a greater capacity for empathy, tolerance for others, and a healthy respect for differences among people than those children raised in traditional, heterosexual families because these children are forced to embrace these issues more overtly. Is teaching tolerance and respect for differences not a significant goal for *all* parents in the twenty-first century? If this is so, perhaps there is an advantage to being raised by homosexual parents!

The intensity of the beliefs and feelings behind the arguments for each side of the issue of homosexual parenting is immense. This is, however, but one issue in the ongoing dialogue of what is moral and what is immoral in our society. Some factions believe that it is immoral to raise a child without exposing that child to a religion. Atheists, however, are allowed to adopt and raise children and be foster parents. Others feel that adulterers, chronic gamblers and those that abuse drugs and alcohol are immoral. Clearly, there are countless families where children are raised as parents grapple with these issues. Who decides where we draw the line as to who is moral and who

302

is not when it comes to raising children? With such powerful feelings and emotions coming from the adults involved in this argument, it is most important to remember that we, as a community, should be working toward what is best for the children, rather than satisfying the urge to be right in our beliefs.

Related Readings

American Academy of Pediatrics. (February 2002). Technical report: Co-parent or second-parent adoption by same sex parents. *Pediatrics, 109,* 341–349.

American College of Pediatrics. (2004). Homosexual parenting: Is it time for a change? <http://www.acpeds.org/?CONTEXT=art &%20cat=22&art=50&BISKIT=2920801063>

Beaucar, K. (July 18, 2001). Homosexual parenting studies are flawed, report says. http://www.foxnews.com/story/0,2933,29901, 00.html <http://www.foxnews.com/story/0,2933,29901, 00.html>

Cameron, P., & Perrin, E. (April 22, 2002). *Insight on the News, Symposium on Adoption by Gay or Lesbian Couples, 18,* 40–47.

Phillips, D., & Phillips, R. (July 2001). Homosexual parenting. *The Australian Family.* http://www.family.org.au/journal/2001/ j20010728.html <http://www.family.org.au/journal/2001/ j20010728.html>

Ray, V., & Gregory, R. (Winter 2001). School experiences of the children of lesbian and gay parents. *Family Matters,* 28–39.

Tasker, F. (1999). Children in lesbian-led families: A review. *Clinical Child Psychology and Psychiatry, 4,* 153–166.

On the Internet . . .

Positive Parenting

This Positive Parenting site contains informaiton and articles related to how parents and educators can communicate more effectively with children and adolescents. Most of the linked information is specific to adolescence.

> http://www.positiveparenting.com

CYFERNet

The Children, Youth, and Families Education and Research Network (CYFERNet), sponsored by the U.S. Department of Agriculture's Cooperative Extension Service, provides practical research-based information in health, child care, family strengths, science, and technology.

> http://www.cyfernet.org

The American Academy of Child and Adolescent Psychiatry Home Page

Here the American Academy of Child and Adolescent Psychiatry provides information as a public service to assist families and educators in socializing children and adolescents.

> http://www.aacap.org

Adolescent Health On-Line

This Adolescent Health On-Line site of the American Medical Association (AMA) provides extensive information on adolescent health issues and the AMA's Guidelines for Adolescent Preventive Services (GAPS) program. It also links to numerous other sites related to adolescent health issues.

> http://www.ama-assn.org/ama/pub/category/
> 1974.html

PART 4

Adolescence

*M*any people use the term teenage years to describe adolescence. This is the period of time from ages 13 through 19. During this period of development the child experiences puberty, and there are dramatic physical changes that occur as the child becomes a young adult. Much less obvious than the physical changes are the cognitive and emotional changes in children at this stage of development. In early adolescence the child is increasingly able to think on an abstract level. Adolescents also undertake the process of identity development, defining who they are. This final section considers some of the key issues related to decisions about values and sexuality that teens make as they move through adolescence.

- Should Children Who Are at Risk for Abuse Remain With Their Families?

- Is the Welfare of Disadvantaged Children Improving?

- Is Abstenence-Only Sex Education Effective?

- Can Memories of Childhood Sexual Abuse Be Recovered?

ISSUE 14

Should Children Who Are at Risk for Abuse Remain With Their Families?

YES: Lisa Kolb, from "Family Preservation in Missouri," *Public Welfare* (Spring 1993)

NO: Mary-Lou Weisman, from "When Parents Are Not in the Best Interests of the Child," *The Atlantic Monthly* (July 1994)

ISSUE SUMMARY

YES: Lisa Kolb, a public information specialist, asserts that the family preservation model is the best way to help families in crisis. Family preservation keeps all the family members together in the home while helping the family solve its problems.

NO: Freelance writer Mary-Lou Weisman argues that orphanages and out-of-home placements are necessary for children whose parents abuse or neglect them. She maintains that society has an obligation to take children away from parents who are doing serious harm to them and that some children have their only real family experience when living in an institutional setting.

Newspaper headlines and television accounts of parents who neglect, abuse, or even kill their children show that the unthinkable does happen. Parents, the very people who are obligated to nurture and protect their children, do not always meet their children's needs. Parents may forfeit their responsibility to nurture and provide for their children because of drug addiction, mental illness, an abusive childhood, or poor parenting skills.

In the past, children who did not have parents or family members to care for them were sent to orphanages, but presently these children are placed in foster homes, residential treatment centers, or small group care homes. In addition to these types of placements, another alternative, family preservation, has emerged. In the 1980s the large numbers of children who needed foster care exceeded the number of foster homes available. Thus, the idea of family preservation became a popular alternative to out-of-home placement for needy children.

Family preservation is a model of intervention that is family centered and available 24 hours a day, seven days a week. Social workers spend a lot of time with families in their caseload and try to build on the strengths of the family to help create a more functional family unit. At first family preservation was seen to be a cost-effective answer to helping battered children. Now it has come under fire from some critics, who contend that it does more harm than good because the characteristics and standards of the programs have become so varied.

Can all families be served by the family preservation model, and are children protected from abuse during the treatment period? Are children in out-of-home placements or foster care protected from abuse? Studies provide conflicting answers to these questions. Proponents from each side point to cases of abuse and poor care in foster care as well as in family preservation situations.

How can society best care for children who are at risk for abuse or worse? Should the whole family (including children) be kept together and worked with in that context? Should children be placed in foster care until the family's problems are solved? Should children be taken away from parents entirely and sent to an institution for the rest of their childhood?

What do the children think about these choices? When faced with being removed from their home, no matter what the reason, most children probably want to stay at home. Often children will defend their parents before authorities even if their home situation is not safe. In these cases, who intervenes for children when parents cannot meet their responsibilities and when the children themselves want what may be harmful to them? How can society keep its children safe?

In the following selections, Lisa Kolb states that children are further damaged when they are removed from their homes as their families deal with crises. She sees family preservation as a successful way to solve families' problems while keeping children at home and argues that it works because parents value the family unit. On the other hand, Mary-Lou Weisman presents evidence that some children are not safe with parents who physically and emotionally scar their children. She maintains that society must bite the bullet, take children out of their abusive homes, and put them where they will survive and thrive.

Lisa Kolb

 YES

Family Preservation in Missouri

It's 3:00 A.M. in a small, rural town in southwest Missouri. Vanessa Johnston, a family preservation services (FPS) worker, is combing the streets looking for Heidi, one of her clients. Earlier that night, Vanessa learned that Heidi, a 19-year-old single mother, had been accosted by "Stacey," a "friend." Stacey had heard a rumor that Heidi was involved with Stacey's boyfriend, so she had set out to even the score: she surprised Heidi in the dark stairwell leading to her apartment and beat her up.

Heidi has a habit of running when things get rough. Finding no trace of her client, and knowing Heidi's penchant for hitching rides with truckers, Vanessa heads for the local truck stop. She has to talk with only a few drivers to find out that Heidi, with her infant son in tow, has hitched a ride to Oklahoma City.

Vanessa goes back to her office and waits. She knows the rumor about Heidi and Stacey's boyfriend is unfounded, and she wonders how Heidi has been affected by Stacey's assault. She knows that Heidi has felt that Stacey was her only friend, the one person she could trust.

After several hours, the telephone rings: it's Heidi, asking for help to get back home. Vanessa arranges for the bus ride back to Missouri, goes home, and gets ready for work.

Welcome to the world of an FPS worker. The work is harried, and time is a precious commodity. The job is frustrating: one step forward can be followed by two steps backward. And it is emotionally draining—six weeks of being on 24-hour call can take its toll. But it is encouraging: to see a family learn from its mistakes is what this job is all about. Frustrated and eager for a change, many social workers, caseworkers, and others are willing to accept the challenge and take on the daunting job description that comes with FPS.

. . . [F]amily preservation services are designed to protect children who are at immediate risk of out-of-home placement, by providing immediate, intensive, comprehensive, 24-hour, in-home services to these children and their families. FPS is guided by these premises:

- Children have a right to their families.
- The family is the fundamental resource for nurturing children.
- Parents should be supported in their efforts to care for their children.

- Families are diverse and have a right to be respected for the special cultural, racial, ethnic, and religious traditions that make them distinct.
- Children can be reared well in different kinds of families, and one family form should not be discriminated against in favor of another.

Operating statewide since October 1992, FPS is working for a large number of Missouri families. The state measures success by the number of children who remain safely in their homes rather than being removed and placed in foster care. From October 1991 to September 1992—roughly the year before FPS was operating statewide—the program reported serving 656 families. According to the Department of Social Services, Division of Family Services (DFS), which administers the program, 128 of those families ended up having children placed outside the home.

Since it began operating statewide, the program has succeeded in diverting about one-third of the children who otherwise would have entered foster care. Statewide preliminary data show that in the six months to a year following completion of FPS, 81.93 percent of FPS families are intact. A year or more following FPS, 77.89 percent of FPS families are intact.

Vanessa started with the program in November 1991 and had worked with only eight other families before Heidi and her baby. Vanessa identifies the benefits of a program like FPS, which is designed to deal with long-term issues by meeting immediate needs: "We know families will still cycle [in and out of various services] after they've gone through the program, but we hope that what they learned through FPS will help them to pull themselves up and not sink so low the next time."

For Vanessa, one of the most attractive qualities of FPS is the program's flexibility. FPS allows her the latitude to tailor her services to meet the specific needs of her client families. Typically, FPS workers

- teach problem-solving skills to family members;
- teach families how to cope with future crises without relying on harmful behavior;
- provide information to families regarding other sources of assistance;
- teach family members life skills, such as finding an apartment, bargain hunting, nutrition, and money and management;
- focus all services on empowering families to solve their own problems and avert crises.

Statewide, FPS has 114 full-time workers: 36 are employees of DFS, and 78 are working under contract. FPS also has four part-time workers, three in-house and one contractual.

FPS workers must meet a number of requirements:

- They must have a master's degree in social work, counseling, psychology, or a related field. Or, with the approval of DFS, they can have a bachelor's degree and extensive experience in treatment of families in crisis. Vanessa has a bachelor of arts degree in psychology and five and a half years' experience with DFS in investigations, foster care, and casework.

- They must have experience working with children and their families.
- They must demonstrate knowledge of crisis intervention, communications skills, and family education methods.
- They must demonstrate a willingness to work a nonstructured, flexible schedule, routinely including evenings and weekends.
- Contracted workers must meet applicable state licensing criteria.

FPS workers are assigned two families at a time and work with those families for six weeks. The two assignments rarely begin and end at the same time, so there is frequent overlap of cases. Though she could use as much as two weeks between cases to complete the required paperwork—since she has little time to work on anything but the family's needs while the case is in progress—the demand for FPS is so great that Vanessa usually gets no more than two to five days between family assignments.

Vanessa's personality is ideally suited for FPS's nondirective approach. Her ability to act as mother, confidant, and counselor, coupled with her innate sense of when to advise, when to pull back, and when to listen, are key to her rapport with families in crisis. Vanessa admits she works best when encouraging family members to identify their problems and arrive at their own solutions. Although each FPS worker has his or her own style, Vanessa emphasizes that the priority in each FPS case is the same—to make all families safe. If she accomplishes nothing else in her six weeks with a family, Vanessa strives to instill one vitally important attitude: "respect for the kids and their view of the world."

The six-week time frame forces FPS workers to prioritize the elements that are critical to keeping a family together. Vanessa's work with Heidi on parenting and other life skills had to wait until mother and son had a roof over their heads. Kima and Jerry, Vanessa's other FPS family, were not searching for food and shelter, but rather salvation for their marriage.

Heidi and Zach

Like many clients, Heidi chose FPS as the less of two evils. Faced with the removal of her son, Heidi reluctantly allowed FPS into her life for one simple reason: "Zach is all I have." Many of Vanessa's clients have a history of physical or sexual abuse, and Heidi's background is no different. Her childhood in Alabama was little more than a series of new addresses and new guardians, and she did not develop relationships with any of them. Her parents divorced when she was very young. The few times she lived with them were brief, unpleasant interruptions in her travels from one foster home to another. When she turned 18, Heidi aged out of the Alabama foster care system and finally escaped the instability of foster care; but she found that life in an Alabama group home was not much better. She soon ran away to Arkansas, then to Mt. Vernon, Missouri, where she met Micky.

Within a year, Heidi found herself homeless and pregnant with Micky's child. She delivered Zach while living in an area home for unwed mothers. But, restless and longing for her old lifestyle, Heidi soon left to run with her baby's 15-year-old father and his friends. The drugs, alcohol, and delinquency of the group led to the intervention of DFS and Vanessa.

Immediately, Vanessa learned that, with Heidi, she would have to shelve her counselor's hat. Heidi's past had left her stubborn and independent, with a deep mistrust of adults and no tolerance for advice. Heidi likes the fact that FPS allows her to retain control over her own life: "Vanessa doesn't tell me what to do—the decisions are mine to make. I'm learning to trust in myself. I'm a good person."

With Vanessa's help, Heidi was able to begin pursuing her lifelong dream of becoming a nurse. Daycare, provided by FPS, allowed Heidi to work on her general equivalency diploma (GED); and she scored well in preliminary testing. For the first time in her life, she not only is setting goals but also is working to meet them. "I'll do it," she says, "if it takes me till I'm 80."

Vanessa's teaching methods allowed Heidi to learn by example. "My families learn much more from what I do," she says, "than from what I say." For Heidi, many of life's most mundane tasks—including looking for an apartment—were a mystery; and, as Vanessa explained, "You can't ask about something you know nothing about." Armed with a newspaper, a telephone book, and a map, Vanessa talked Heidi through the procedure—looking in the classified section, calling apartment managers for details, and filling out applications.

The scarcity of rental housing in the area limited Heidi's options, and her monthly income—$234 from Aid to Families with Dependent Children and $200 in food stamps—prevented her from qualifying for federal housing. Finding nothing more suitable, Vanessa and Heidi were forced to make do with a small, windowless basement apartment for $100 a month. With money from the Crisis Intervention Fund, an FPS emergency fund earmarked for high-priority needs, Vanessa took Heidi to garage sales, teaching her to bargain-shop for kitchen items, other household goods, and baby clothes for Zach. One of Vanessa's FPS coworkers obtained a used sleeper sofa, chairs, and a lamp to complete the apartment's furnishings.

Although the apartment soon looked livable, Vanessa worried about the steep, dark stairwell leading to the apartment and the lack of heating or air conditioning. Heidi objected to turning on the gas stove for fear of an explosion, but Vanessa explained that utilities are a good way to establish credit. Meanwhile, Vanessa would look for a used microwave oven.

Vanessa also subtly tried to change Heidi's nutritional habits and attitudes about medical care. Heidi, a frail 80 pounds, frequently skipped meals; and this sometimes would carry over to 4½-month-old Zach, who needed regular feedings of formula. Vanessa was concerned that Heidi would not prepare balanced meals for Zach as his nutritional needs changed. She learned that Heidi occasionally would fix instant soup or other one-step preparation foods if she had access to a microwave. Vanessa knew that Heidi was concerned about Zach staying on target with his weight gain, and she hoped this would entice Heidi to do more cooking.

Whereas Heidi did not seem very concerned about her own health, Vanessa did begin to see improvements in her concern for Zach's health.

Heidi would become defensive at the suggestion of seeking medical care for herself, and she ignored her doctor's diagnosis of strep throat and recommendation for a tonsillectomy. With Vanessa's encouragement, however, Heidi began to understand the importance of regular checkups for Zach, who had developed a chronic cough soon after he was born. Heidi was afraid of the "hurt" that doctors cause and the bad-tasting medicine they prescribe, but Vanessa helped her to see that these were the only ways to make Zach better. Watching Heidi follow Zach's medication schedule gave Vanessa a renewed sense that mother and son would make it—together.

As determined as she was to become a better mother, Heidi experienced an equally strong pull to return to her old lifestyle on the streets, running with Micky and his friends. Vanessa had to suppress her own maternal instincts. As a mother of three, she knew that if Heidi were her own child, she likely would have reacted to Heidi's involvement with Micky and his friends by criticizing their behavior and prohibiting Heidi from seeing them. But Vanessa knew that reaction not only would be a waste of time, but also would damage her relationship with Heidi.

As an FPS worker, Vanessa strongly believes that it is neither her position nor beneficial to her clients for her to judge them. She realizes that Micky's role as Zach's father is important to Heidi and that it is unlikely that his influence and that of his friends will diminish.

During a scheduled visit, Vanessa found Micky and his friends at Heidi's apartment. Vanessa's theory is that every moment spent with a family is "teachable," so she turned what could have been a wasted afternoon into a group counseling session by including the entire group in her discussion with Heidi. By opening a discourse about their influence on Zach's well-being, Vanessa believes Micky, and perhaps some of his friends, came away with a sense of the consequences of their actions. Heidi says Micky likes her involvement with FPS and that he admits he has gained a new perspective through Vanessa.

Vanessa's presence gradually began to have a calming effect on Heidi's life. Heidi describes her past experiences with the Department of Social Services (DSS) as having had a "bad thing" with the agency. But she says her relationship with Vanessa is "okay"—a glowing endorsement from the reserved teenager. "DDS has always been rude," Heidi says. "They make me feel like they don't have the time. FPS is making me think some of them do care. Maybe they do."

Kima and Jerry

Vanessa met Kima and Jerry as their two-year marriage was showing signs of breaking up. Jerry, a 25-year-old unemployed welder, was starting to drink; and drinking made him mean. Kima had plenty of experience with abusive men, and she wasn't going to risk Jerry's angry words turning to violence. Fed up, she had filed for divorce; and, as a would-be single mother of three with no job, she saw FPS as the only way to keep her family together.

Kima's nightmare had begun in her early teens. After months of sexually abusing her, Kima's stepfather one day had escalated his assault to a violent rape, after which he had left her tied in an abandoned barn. She escaped by breaking a window and sawing herself free with a shard of glass. The stepfather, serving an eight-year sentence for the crime, was threatening Kima from prison. Family members who were in contact with him warned her about his plans to find her when he was released. In fact, shortly after his release early in 1993, he was rearrested for attempting to poison the water supply of Sarcoxie, Missouri, a town close to where Kima lived.

Although her stepfather's incarceration gave Kima a sense of release from the pain he had caused, she had had other equally devastating relationships in the years since—sadly, a common occurrence for sexual abuse victims. Kima's oldest son, Travis, 7, was born out of a later rape. Then a boyfriend killed his and Kima's 6½-month-old son. Kima has two other children, Megan, 5, and Miles, 11 months; only Miles is Jerry's child.

Kima and Jerry's first contact with DFS came after Jerry jerked a crying Miles out of his crib, breaking his arm. Although the doctor who treated Miles's injury originally suspected abuse, his final report called the incident "accidental." Jerry now feels DFS is suspicious of him, and his disdain for what he believes was an unfair investigation has left both Kima and Jerry with a blatant distrust of DFS.

Despite this mistrust, Kima saw FPS as the only way to save her marriage, something she very much wanted to preserve. Middle-class values are important to Kima. Her father, killed when she was 11, was a positive influence on her life; and she wants the same for her children. Referred to the program by a DFS worker, the couple was willing to work with FPS because they saw it as an answer to their marital troubles, not acknowledging that the children were at issue.

"I just wanted Jerry to realize he is an equal partner," Kima said. "You can't take 90 percent and give 10. I realize he had a lot of problems growing up. I guess I just wanted us both to start fresh. It's easier for Jerry to talk with someone else present—he's not as apt to walk out."

Jerry says he and Kima immediately accepted Vanessa by "detaching" her from DFS. "I kind of had feelings . . . I didn't know Vanessa or anything about her. I wasn't sure if I was ready to talk to an outsider. But she's strong on offering suggestions. She's even told us several times she'd leave if we wanted her to. I thought we'd have to sit in a circle and play a game. Everything was to our advantage, because it helped."

Kima and Jerry's problems escalated after Kima lost her job with a local trucking company. Until then, it had not been important to Kima that Jerry work—she was willing to do almost anything to keep the peace: "When Jerry is unhappy, the whole house suffers." But when the loss of Kima's paycheck forced Jerry to look for employment, the tension began to mount. Although Jerry eventually landed a job at an area factory, one with good wages and benefits as well as safe working conditions, he found many excuses to skip work. After three weeks, Jerry had clocked in for only seven shifts.

Now that Kima was unemployed, she had time to begin work on her GED, and FPS enabled her to do that. Since Travis was in the first grade and Megan was enrolled in Head Start, Miles was the only child needing daycare. Unfortunately, Mt. Vernon happens to have the highest teen pregnancy rate in Missouri, which makes state-funded daycare scarce. After Kima completes her GED, she plans to attend college full-time. Through Vanessa, Kima learned that many area colleges have daycare facilities on campus. "FPS points out opportunities," Kima says. "I always knew I had college potential, but until I met Vanessa, I wasn't aware what was available in this area."

Kima and Jerry seemed to be getting past the communication barriers that had caused so many of their problems. "Overall, I feel Jerry has more consideration and respect for me," Kima said. "He has learned to voice his anger rather than just letting it build up. He has been harsh with the kids in the past; but he has learned that if we are to respect his feelings, he has to respect ours. You can't solve your problems when you're angry."

Vanessa points out that FPS's nondirective approach doesn't always work for her. Sometimes, she explains, the atmosphere is just right for physical violence to erupt: "After all, FPS strives to build a rapport while family members are learning to vent their frustrations. Some families become so comfortable with my presence that they forget I'm there and start swinging. That's the time to become very directive."

During counseling, Jerry admitted that he often became frustrated with the children when they would not help Kima around the house. Vanessa helped turn a major point of conflict between Kima and Jerry into a workable solution by developing a chore chart with a reward system for the children. "They learned that there are certain things that have to be done," Kima said. "Now they know that Mom isn't going to do everything for them."

Jerry admitted he had been self-centered and that his moods had made life hard for Kima and the children, but he seemed unwilling to share the decision-making with his wife. Money management had been a problem, and Jerry's new role as the breadwinner gave him a sense of ownership over his paycheck. For instance, the rent was due and the family needed a second car; but Jerry went out and bought a motorcycle. Vanessa worried that Kima and Jerry would be evicted since they were already behind on their rent. Their finances for the coming month looked no better. Because Jerry had missed so much work, his paycheck was going to be short; and, though they had applied, the family was not yet receiving food stamps.

Vanessa's first inclination was to dip into the program's Crisis Intervention Fund. FPS workers have discretion over how and when to use the money, and they do not usually make clients aware that the money is available, so that families do not become dependent on it. FPS workers spend an average of $350 from this fund per family, and Vanessa already had nearly depleted Kima and Jerry's share. Vanessa thought better of bailing Kima and Jerry out of their financial troubles. "Jerry lost his safety net when Kima lost her job," Vanessa said. "These are hard lessons for Jerry, and it's too bad the whole family has to suffer. He needs to learn." The family did manage to scrape by, but later had to move when the landlord raised the rent.

Most FPS workers are women, but Jerry's respect for male authority made Vanessa wonder if he would be more inclined to open up with a male counselor. Jerry dispelled those fears, however: "To me it doesn't matter whether it's a male or female counselor as long as they are helping. Vanessa taught me to stop and think before I say anything—but there are still times I wish I would do more thinking."

"I can't speak for all families, but it's been very beneficial for us," Kima said. "Jerry and I talk more than we ever would have before. Jerry's focus used to be on the bad side of things. He would always focus on the bad things the kids did. I guess something from his childhood made him feel like he didn't measure up. Vanessa has helped him see the good things."

FPS workers and their families often develop a closeness that makes it difficult to let go at the end of six weeks. This was the case between Vanessa and Kima and Jerry. When asked if he felt that the progress he and Kima had made with Vanessa would continue, Jerry said, "She's not going to leave our lives—we know where she lives." Vanessa's first FPS family still calls her on occasion, she says, just for reassurance that what they are doing is okay.

After leaving the FPS program, families are assigned aftercare (AC) workers from their home counties. AC workers continue the case plan that the FPS worker has started with the family. To make the transition easier for families, Vanessa is in constant communication with the AC workers to prepare them for the next phase of a family's treatment. "From the very first day I'm with a family, I begin pulling in other services that they can rely on when I'm gone," Vanessa says. "Actually, I guess you could say aftercare begins with that very first session."

Vanessa winds up a whirlwind week with Heidi, Kima, and Jerry with a trip to McDonald County, Missouri, where she will attend a "staffing"—a periodic screening of clients to determine progress and alternative services. The two-hour drive will account for part of the 2,000 miles she puts on her family van each month. Accompanying Vanessa are Angela, a private provider of outpatient therapy from a nearby county, and Keith, an FPS coworker.

The room is filled with social workers, FPS workers, and private providers such as Angela, all of whom offer additional insight to the cases they hear. Amid the often horrifying stories of the plight of area families are the occasional lighthearted jokes and repeated trips to the coffeepot—both necessary for the long meetings. Vanessa relates Heidi's progress, and all are impressed. Vanessa appreciates the recognition from her colleagues, but she warns that Heidi has much work ahead of her. Then Vanessa says she is not taking any more FPS families until she returns from a much-needed vacation. Everyone in the room nods in enthusiastic agreement.

Having already had its final staffing, Kima and Jerry's case is closed for Vanessa. She speaks hopefully of their chances for success, knowing they are better prepared for the inevitable rough turns their lives will continue to take. The AC worker has taken over and will continue to guide them toward services should they need assistance.

Families receive a follow-up survey up to one year after they have completed FPS, and this is an FPS worker's final barometer of the program's impact on each family. Vanessa is not ready to say that FPS has succeeded in

Kima and Jerry's case. If the survey shows that the children still are living with their family, and if Kima and Jerry are talking and not yelling, then she can say that FPS was successful for this family.

Meanwhile, Vanessa steals a few minutes each day for her own family's needs. Her private life is sandwiched between FPS families, but she has no complaints; and the sparkle in her eye reveals her firm belief that she is doing the right thing. She smiles as she relates how her clients' gratitude is rewarding, but misguided. "It's great that some families say they are doing it for me," says Vanessa. "But if I'm the motivation, then I'm out of there, and where do they go? Believe me, they are doing all the work, and they are doing it for their family."

When Parents Are Not in the Best Interests of the Child

Orphanages are not what they used to be. They aren't even called orphanages anymore. The residents no longer sleep in metal beds, twenty to a dormitory room. At the Boys Town campus, just outside Omaha, Nebraska, children live eight to a suburban-style home, two to a bedroom. Bureaus have replaced lockers. Uniforms and standardized haircuts are gone. So are the long wooden tables where, in the orphanages of legend, children sat awaiting their portions of cornmeal mush for breakfast, or bread and gravy for dinner. For instance, at the former St. James Orphanage, in Duluth, Minnesota, known since 1971 as Woodland Hills, young people wearing clothes from places like The Gap and Kmart push plastic trays through a cafeteria line, choosing baked chicken or shrimp and rice. The weight-conscious detour to the salad bar.

In 1910 some 110,000 orphans lived in 1,200 orphan asylums throughout the United States. At the end of 1990, according to data from the American Public Welfare Association, there were approximately 406,000 children in out-of-home placements. About three-quarters of these children were in adoptive and foster homes. About 16 percent, or 65,000, were emotionally disturbed children in need of therapy, most of whom lived in the group homes and residential treatment centers that are the institutional descendants of the orphanage. (The remainder, less than 10 percent, were cared for by a variety of temporary and emergency services.) What little research is available indicates that most of this smaller subset of "homeless" children have been physically or sexually abused, often by the adults charged with their care. At Boys Town, now a residential treatment center—and no longer just for boys—virtually all the girls and nearly half the boys have been sexually abused. The director, Father Val J. Peter, tells of a teenager who asked him on the day she arrived, "Who do I have to sleep with to get along here?"

Child-care workers agree that children in residential treatment today are likely to be far more disturbed than the children who were in need of protective services twenty years ago and who, in turn, were probably more disturbed than the good-hearted orphans with chips on their shoulders who preceded them. These kids have had it with parents—biological, adoptive, or foster—and the feeling is usually mutual. These kids do not trust adults, especially parents. They cannot tolerate the intensity of family life, nor do they behave well enough to attend public school. During a first screening at a residential treatment center a psychiatrist often asks a child, "If you had three wishes, what would they be?" Twenty years ago a typical answer was "I want a basketball," or "I wish my father didn't drink." Today, according to Nan Dale, the executive director of The Children's Village, a residential treatment center for boys in Dobbs Ferry, New York, one is likely to hear "I wish I had a gun so I could blow my father's head off." Child-care professionals call these young people "children of rage." Some of them take antidepressants and drugs to control hyperactivity. In addition to the behavior and attachment disorders common to children who have been abused and moved around a lot, some suffer from having been exposed *in utero* to crack and some from other neurological problems.

Most of the children who live in institutions are between the ages of five and eighteen. According to a 1988 study 64 percent of children in residential treatment centers were adolescents thirteen to seventeen years old. Approximately 31 percent were younger than thirteen, a percentage that has been increasing. According to the same study, the majority, about 70 percent, were male, a factor attributed to the more aggressive nature of the sex. Approximately 25 percent of the children were black, and eight percent were Hispanic.

A group home may house as few as four children, whereas a residential treatment center may be home to a hundred or more, although in either facility usually no more than eight to twelve are housed together, supervised by house parents or by child-care personnel working eight-hour shifts. At Woodland Hills an old three-story red-brick orphanage building has been renovated so that the first floor can be used for administration, classrooms, and the cafeteria. The second- and third-floor dormitory rooms have been divided into meeting rooms, staff offices, and apartments with bedrooms that sleep two.

Unlike the orphanages from which they are descended, most group homes and residential treatment centers are not meant to be long-term abodes. A typical stay at such a center lasts from several months to two years, after which most children return to their birth, foster, or adoptive families. A significant minority, those who either have no homes to return to or do not wish to go home, move on to less restrictive group homes or to independent living arrangements, also under the aegis of the child-welfare system.

History

The first orphan asylum in the United States was established in 1729 by Ursuline nuns, to care for children orphaned by an Indian massacre at Natchez, Mississippi. Thereafter the number of orphanages increased in response to wars, especially the Civil War, and to epidemics of tuberculosis, cholera, yellow fever, and influenza. (Contemporary epidemics such as AIDS, the resurgence of tuberculosis, and the rampant use of crack cocaine have the potential to create another orphan crisis in the twenty-first century.

By the year 2000, it is estimated, 100,000 children, most of them from female-headed households, will lose their mother to AIDS. Senator Daniel Patrick Moynihan, among others, foresees the return of the orphanage as inevitable.)

In spite of the Dickensian reputation that outlives them, orphanages, which began to proliferate in this country in the mid-1800s, represented a significant social reform for their time, just as the group homes and residential treatment centers that took their place are now seen as reforms. Before orphan asylums were common, orphaned, homeless, and neglected children, if they were not living, stealing, and begging on the streets, were housed, along with adults, primarily in almshouses, but also in workhouses and jails. The Victorian conviction that childhood was a time of innocence influenced attitudes toward destitute children. People came to believe that even street urchins could be rescued—removed to a better environment and turned into productive citizens.

Most orphanages were private institutions, the result of the combined efforts of passionately committed "child savers," children's-aid societies, and a variety of mostly religious but also ethnic organizations that raised the money to build and maintain them. But even as the orphanage was becoming the nation's dominant mode of substitute child care, an anti-institutional effort called "placing out" was under way, setting the stage for a debate that continues to this day. By the mid-1800s children were being transported on "orphan trains" from crowded eastern slums and institutions to the West, where they were adopted by farm families in need of extra hands. By the late nineteenth century, in a further move away from institutionalization, cottage-style "homes," which more closely mimicked family life and each of which housed about twenty-five children, began to take the place of large orphanages.

In the twentieth century, psychology—first psychoanalytic theories and then behaviorism—has dominated the field of child welfare. Unlike psychoanalytic theories, which focus on the child's inner personality, behaviorism emphasizes the way the child interacts with his world. In this view a child is not "bad"; his unacceptable behavior is. By changing the behavior, so the thinking goes, one changes the child. Behavioral theories replaced psychoanalytic theories, which were used only to limited effect by Bruno Bettelheim and others in the "homes" and "schools" for emotionally disturbed children which appeared mid-century. The therapeutic hour remains important, but what goes on in the child's life during the other twenty-three hours of the day is seen as potentially even more valuable. (A book by that name, *The Other 23 Hours*, by Albert E. Trieschman, James K. Whittaker, and Larry K. Brendtro, is the classic text of residential treatment.) The goal of residential treatment is to create a "therapeutic milieu," an environment in which everyday events are turned to therapeutic use. Any activity in a child's day—from refusing to get dressed in the morning to answering a question correctly at school to picking a fight—offers the child-care worker an opportunity to teach, change, or reinforce behavior through therapeutic intervention. Residential treatment aims to seize the moment while it is happening and the child's feelings are still fresh.

Policy Versus Reality

Orphanages as such had virtually disappeared by the late 1970s as a result of a decrease in the number of orphans and a growing conviction that children belong in families. That every child needs parents and a home has become an article of faith and a guiding principle for social-policy makers and a matter of federal law as well. The philosophy of "permanency planning," as set forth in the Adoption Assistance and Child Welfare Act of 1980, considers the goal of the foster-care system to be keeping children in families. The law allows for but discourages "out-of-home placement"—institutionalization in group homes or residential treatment centers—and calls for the return of the children to a family, biological or otherwise, whenever possible and as quickly as possible. But for many practitioners in residential treatment the law has become increasingly irrelevant.

Richard Small is the director of The Walker Home and School, in Needham, Massachusetts, a residential and day treatment center for severely disturbed pre-adolescent boys. Writing recently in a professional journal with Kevin Kennedy and Barbara Bender, Small expressed a concern shared by many of his colleagues.

> For at least the past decade, we in the field have been reporting, usually to each other, a worsening struggle to work with a much more damaged group of children and families, and a scramble to adjust our practice methods to meet both client needs and policy directives that may or may not have anything to do with client needs. . . . Those of us immersed in everyday residential treatment practice see these same guidelines as less and less applicable to the real children and families with whom we work. Many of our child clients and their families suffer from profound disruptions of development that we believe are likely to require long-term, multiple helping services, including (but not limited to) one or more time-limited stays in residential treatment. Despite a policy that seems to see clear boundaries between being "in care" (and therefore sick and vulnerable) and "reunified" (and therefore fixed and safe) our experience tells us that many of our clients are likely to live out their lives somewhere between these poles.

In keeping with the goal of permanency planning, institutions are supposed to maintain close communication with the parents of the children they treat. Many centers offer counseling for parents and for the entire family. The Children's Village runs evening and weekend programs especially for parents who have abused their children. At institutions that adhere most closely to the goal of reuniting parent and child, parents are encouraged to visit, and good behavior on the part of children is rewarded with weekend visits home. Green Chimneys, a residential treatment center that serves primarily inner-city kids, regularly transports parents and children in vans between New York City and its campus in Brewster, New York. Nationally, nobody really knows how many families are reunited, for how long or how successfully. Those who work with children in institutions complain that the pressure from departments of social service to reunite parent and child is so intense that the workers sometimes yield to it despite their better judgment.

The objective of residential care is to discharge healthier children into the care of healthier parents—an outcome that authorities agree is desirable in theory but not always likely in fact. In their recent casebook for child-care workers, *When Home Is No Haven,* Albert J. Solit, Barbara Nordhaus, and Ruth Lord write that "one of the hardest tasks for a new worker is becoming reconciled to the inherent contradictions in the Protective Services worker's role. The worker is expected to aim for two goals, which in some instances may be mutually exclusive: reunification of the family, and protection of the child and the child's best interests." . . .

Institutional Family Values

In the paradoxical world of "child protective services," an institution may be the first home some children have ever known, providing their first chance to sit down to meals with other people at regular times, blow out birthday candles, and be taken care of by adults who do not hit or even yell. All but one of the staple ingredients of a happy home life are replicated in the best group homes and treatment centers. Intimacy is purposely missing. Love and family bonding may be what these children will need and be capable of having eventually, but for the moment the emotional thermostat must be set at neutral. These children are believed to be too disturbed to handle the intensity of real family life; that is precisely why they have been institutionalized.

The best institutions offer emotionally disturbed children a chance at a second childhood. They are given the opportunity to shed cynicism, develop self-esteem, and grow back into innocence and vulnerability. Candy will become a treat. This time they will be protected from harm. This time they will come to think of adults as kind and dependable. They will learn to play. They will learn to care about others.

Treatment communities teach Judeo-Christian values—the work ethic and the golden rule. Institutions offer vocational training and courses in computer literacy. At The Children's Village the best computer students teach their newfound skills to other children and adults in the surrounding communities, and The Children's Village has its own Boy Scout troop. The kids at Woodland Hills collect and pack supplies for national and international relief efforts. In addition, they split wood and deliver logs to the elderly in the Duluth community. Boys Town children host Special Olympics games.

A highly controlled environment is required to create a second childhood for severely disturbed children. Safety is the key issue. Keeping these children from harm involves more than keeping them safe from sexual abuse, physical abuse, drugs, and crossfire; they must be kept safe from themselves and their peers. Newly institutionalized children often try to run away. When a young person at Woodland Hills forgets to bring the appropriate book to class, two peers accompany the student back to the dormitory to retrieve it, thereby minimizing the possibility of an escape attempt. At The Children's Village burly guards equipped with walkie-talkies and trained in firm but gentle techniques of physical restraint stand ready to intervene should fights or tantrums develop beyond the regular staff's ability to control them. Children are never left unattended, not even when they sleep. In every one of the twenty-one cottages at The Children's Village one staff member remains awake throughout the night. The children in these cottages are sometimes suicidal. The bedroom doors in all the cottages open into the corridor, so that youngsters cannot barricade themselves in their rooms. Sexually abused children sometimes become sexual predators. At The Villages in Kansas some young girls will not allow anyone to comb their hair; for girls who have been sexually abused, even grooming can be too threatening.

This antidotal second childhood must be highly structured and predictable as well as safe. Treatment communities impose rules, chores, and schedules, and emphasize neatness, cleanliness, and order. "Everybody wakes up at 7:30 in the morning," writes eleven-year-old Robert, describing his day at The Children's Village, where hairbrushes, combs, toothbrushes, and toothpaste tubes are lined up with military precision on bureau tops. "The first thing we do is make our bed, wash our face, brush our teeth, last but not least put on some clothes. We eat our breakfast by 8:15 and do our chores. At 8:45 we go to school. In school the first thing we do is math, then reading and spelling. We go to lunch at 12:00 noon. . . ." Homer, the orphan hero of John Irving's *The Cider House Rules,* thrives on the routine of orphanage life. He enjoys "the *tramp, tramp* of it, the utter predictability of it." "An orphan," Irving writes, "is simply more of a child than other children in that essential appreciation of the things that happen daily, on schedule." A well-structured day serves the child as a kind of armature within which to build a new, less chaotic, inner self. "How to succeed and how to fail is very clear here," says Daniel Daly, the director of research at Boys Town. "These children are looking for consistency and for an environment they can understand." . . .

Paradigms and Politics

[Five] years ago legislation called the Family Preservation Act was vetoed by President George Bush. The bill asked for about $2 billion to strengthen families. About half of that amount was earmarked for "family preservation"—programs to preserve troubled families *before* they broke up, so that fewer children would enter the foster-care system in the first place. Families in crisis would be assigned a licensed social worker, who would be available to them around the clock for a period of about three months, for help with problems ranging from substance abuse to landlord-tenant relations. Parents in imminent danger of abusing their children could find relief in a "respite program." Last year's [1993] budget legislation provided $1 billion for similar purposes, with a substantial portion also to be spent on family preservation. It had the backing of leading child-advocacy groups, including the Child Welfare League of America, the Children's Defense Fund, and The National Association of Homes and Services for Children. The Edna McConnell Clark Foundation has produced media kits claiming that family-preservation programs cost less per family ($3,000 for one family for a year) than family foster care, which it says costs $10,000 per *child,* or institutional care, which costs $40,000 per child.

Directors of some children's institutions are convinced that "family preservation" will take money directly out of institutional pockets. Sam Ross, [founder and executive director of Green Chimneys,] likes to point out that the family, theoretically the best way to rear children, also happens to be the least expensive. He calls this coincidence good news for advocates of family preservation, whom he calls "the liberal-conservative conspiracy." The way Ross sees it, liberal family preservationists believe that residential treatment centers are warehouses for children who could best be served in homes in their own communities. Conservative preservationists are horrified by the cost of residential treatment and are looking for a cheaper alternative. "For once in their lives," Ross says, "they agree on something: let's get rid of residential treatment."

"It makes about as much sense as closing down emergency rooms and intensive-care units in order to lower hospital costs," says Brenda Nordlinger, the executive director of the National Association of Homes and Services for Children.

"Family preservation? Who can be opposed to that?" says David Coughlin, of Boys Town. "But," he warns, "some kids are going to be in trouble all their lives. These kids are always going to need help. You can't just blow across the top of a family for three months and expect their woes to go away."

As of this year [1994] The Villages in Kansas will be responding to pressure from the state, which provides 78 percent of its operating expenses, to institute a family-preservation program in addition to its group-foster-care program. One of the eight Kansas residences will be rededicated as a ninety-day "home away from home" for abused children. Meanwhile, therapists trained by The Villages will work with the abusing parents and the abused children in an effort to reunite the family. "We want to provide the services that the state wants to purchase. We'd be foolish not to," says Mark Brewer, who has been the executive director since last June [1993].

Nan Dale, of The Children's Village, thinks that the fervor to reduce the numbers of children in residential treatment is reminiscent of what is now generally considered the disastrous policy of de-institutionalizing adult mental patients in the 1970s. Program directors are very skeptical about whether preventive-intervention programs are really as successful as their advocates claim. Those who believe that family preservation is being oversold see an ally in John Schuerman, a professor of social work at the University of Chicago. Schuerman has studied preventive-intervention programs and believes that many of the families that were treated and did not split up were not likely to split up in the first place.

Nan Dale is feeling the anti-institutional heat and resenting it. "We're as pro-family a place as you can find. The fact that we serve a child who has been removed from a family does not make us anti-family. We involve parents." Nevertheless, she says, "the lines have been drawn. When the words 'preventive service' got applied to everything up to the doorstep of residential care, some of us had apoplectic fits. We all would have told you that what we did here *was* preventive. We prevent lifetimes in mental hospitals, lifetimes in prisons. All of a sudden some bureaucrat in Washington defines preventive service as preventing placement outside the home, and we become the thing to be prevented." For the first time in anyone's memory The Children's Village, one of the largest and considered one of the best residential treatment centers in the country, has no waiting list. Dale says that children who might once have been sent there are being diverted to less restrictive, less expensive, and less appropriate options, such as foster-home care, on the presumption that a family setting is always better.

"What's in vogue right now is family preservation," says Father Val, of Boys Town. "Just follow the trend. Watch the little lemmings dashing toward the sea. They will tire of family preservation the way they tired of de-institutionalization. It's as if they just discovered that it's a good idea to try to keep kids in families. It's an exegesis of the obvious." Father Val thinks that the need to frame the debate as either anti-family or anti-institution is inevitable, given the longing that human beings feel for simple answers to complex questions. Certainly the people who make child-welfare policy, as well as those who carry it out, believe that the either-or approach is self-defeating. Nevertheless, it persists. Earl Stuck, who was one of the supporters of the Family Preservation Act, acknowledges the problem. "When you try to sell something politically, you have to oversell your case."

David Fanshel was until retirement a professor at the Columbia University School of Social Work. A leader in the field of social work, and foster care in particular, Fanshel was the principal investigator in two major longitudinal studies on foster children in homes and institutions. At a time when many experts are questioning the value of residential treatment and promoting family preservation, Fanshel is going against the tide. He foresees a greater need for residential care in the near future. In fact, Fanshel, for decades one of the leading proponents of permanency planning, has modified his views. He now believes that permanent placement with a family is not an appropriate goal for about a quarter of the older, more seriously damaged and criminally inclined children in the system. He would like to see foster care reorganized into a two-tiered system in which permanent placement would remain the goal for the larger group, and the forestalling of criminal behavior through treatment would be the goal for the other group, which he calls "Subsystem B." He sees institutions playing a significant role in treating such dangerous children. The creation of two subsystems, Fanshel argues, "might help to avoid the inappropriate underfunding of Subsystem B now taking place in the interest of permanency planning."

The debate between family preservationists and those who advocate the wider use of institutions has been going on for decades. Until as late as the 1920s pro-family reformers used the "orphan trains" to place children with farm families. Today their anti-institutional counterparts, in their determination to provide a home for every child, sometimes resort to "adoption fairs," where difficult-to-adopt children are viewed by prospective parents. The social worker who organized one such event told a reporter from *Vogue* that although these fairs can result in the adoption of as many as half the children, "it felt like a slave auction."

Richard Small tells prospective adoptive parents, "If you're going to adopt a child from The Walker School, you're going out of your way to ask for trouble." Small is uncertain about whether it will be possible to find parents for six of the eight children at the school who were recently freed for adoption. One is a very disturbed twelve-year-old boy who has already suffered two failed adoptions. Small is faced with the opposite of King Solomon's conundrum: this time no mothers want the child. How hard should he try to find another adoptive family?

"Another adoption with this boy would be likely to fail," says Small, who also knows that another rejection might harm the boy more than a life-time without parents. On the other hand, can he consign the child to such permanent and profound loneliness? "He has no one," Small says, "abso-lutely no one."

Small talked at length with the boy about the pros and cons of risking another adoption. Together, they had just about made up their minds in favor of life without parents when the boy wondered out loud, "Then who will take me for my driver's license?"

"I wish," Small says, "that there were a place, a group home, where kids could live at those times when they couldn't live at home. We've got a num-ber of youngsters in this society—who knows how many?—who are capable of being connected to people, who wish to be connected, who should be con-nected, but who can't live full-time with the people they're connected to. When they do, terrible things happen to both sides, the kids and the caretak-ers. These kids get placed in families repeatedly and they repeatedly fail. What are we going to do with these children? Right now we either put them in an institution or we put them in a family."

Going Home

A good children's institution is a hard place to leave. In the institutional world the child has the advantage; in the real world the child does not. The experts consult. Parents and children consult. Is the family ready? Is the child ready?

Twenty-five years ago 80 percent of the children who "graduated" from The Children's Village went home to some family member, most likely the mother. But starting about five years ago the percentage began to drop. Today only 55 percent go home to family. Nan Dale, citing her own subjec-tive standard of measurement, the "GFF" (gut-feeling factor), estimates that half of that narrow majority are returning to a home situation that is fragile. At Woodland Hills, where most of the kids are released to the care of their families, David Kern says he feels uneasy about the prospects for success almost half the time. He calls sending vulnerable children home the worst part of the job. While he was at The Villages, Don Harris felt uneasy about returning kids to their parents about 80 percent of the time. "The reality is we can help these kids build some bridges to their families, but they probably will never be able to live with them."

Not sending vulnerable children home can also be the worst part of the job. People who work with institutionalized children continually face a quandary to which they have no satisfactory solution: What should they do when, in spite of everyone's best efforts, family seems not to be in the best interests of the child? What the system has to offer is life in a group home followed by independent apartment living, and then nothing.

Life without parents is a difficult sentence to pronounce upon a child, but it's happening more and more often. "Sometimes children have gone beyond the opportunity to go back and capture what needed to be done between the ages of three and eight," says Gene Baker, the chief psychologist at The Children's Village. "Sometimes the thrust of intimacy that comes with family living is more than they can handle. Sometimes the requirement of bonding is more than they have the emotional equipment to give. As long as we keep pushing them back into what is our idealized fantasy of family, they'll keep blowing it out of the water for us."

POSTSCRIPT

Should Children Who Are at Risk for Abuse Remain With Their Families?

$\mathbf{K}$olb summarizes the family preservation model and documents its success in Missouri. In that program family preservation workers teach family members problem-solving skills and ways to cope with family crises while keeping family members, including children, together as a unit. Family preservation workers in Missouri meet certain educational and experiential requirements and work with two families at a time for six weeks.

Parents choose the family preservation treatment to avoid removal of their children from the home and, according to Kolb, want to preserve the family unit because they value it and want to make it work. Whereas traditional social service focuses on the individual for an indefinite amount of time, Kolb reports that family preservation is more successful because it focuses on the family system for a specific amount of time—four to six weeks.

Policymakers have been instrumental in child welfare in that they have diverted funds from one treatment program to another. When family preservation became a lower-cost alternative to foster care in the 1980s, money was diverted into the family preservation model in lieu of other child protection programs. Was this action in the best interests of the children? Who should decide? Parents? Policymakers? Protective service workers?

Suggested Readings

Berliner, L. (1993, December). Is family preservation in the best interest of children? *Journal of Interpersonal Violence, 8,* 556–557.

Carp, E. W. (1996, June). Two cheers for orphanages. *Reviews in American History, 24,* 277–284.

Craig, C. (1995, Summer). What I need is a mom. *Policy Review, 73,* 41–49.

Ingrassia, M. (1994, April). Why leave children with bad parents? *Newsweek, 123,* 52–58.

McKenzie, R. (1996, May). Revive the orphanage (but don't expect help from child care professionals). *American Enterprise, 7,* 59–62.

Shealy, C. (1995, August). From Boys Town to Oliver Twist: Separating fact from fiction in welfare reform and out-of-home placement of children and youth. *American Psychologist, 50,* 565–580.

Van Biema, D. (1994, December). The storm over orphanages. *Time, 144,* 58–62.

ISSUE 15

Is the Welfare of Disadvantaged Children Improving?

YES: Lisbeth B. Schorr, from "Making the Most of What We Already Know," *Public Welfare* (Spring 1994)

NO: William J. Bennett, from "What to Do About the Children," *Commentary* (March 1995)

ISSUE SUMMARY

YES: Lisbeth B. Schorr, director of the Harvard University Project on Effective Services, contends that organized intervention programs are working to circumvent social problems such as teen pregnancy, juvenile crime, and school dropout rates.

NO: William J. Bennett, former secretary of education and former director of the Office of National Drug Control Policy, sees the decline of the two-parent family and moral confusion as the primary reasons for children's poor living conditions.

Since the 1960s social programs have been established by schools, civic organizations, local agencies, and the federal government to reduce the risk factors that disadvantaged youth face. These programs provide intervention treatments such as after-school activities, counseling programs, and tutoring to reduce the incidence of juvenile delinquency, teen pregnancy, and dropping out of school. Some of these programs, such as Head Start and, more recently, the midnight basketball program, have become well known, but others are less familiar to the public. All the programs have good intentions, and some have evaluation results to confirm their success, but questions are being raised about their efficacy. Are intervention programs really improving the lives of disadvantaged children, or are they masking a larger societal problem?

The Federal Interagency Forum on Child and Family Statistics issued a report in July 1997 on key national indicators of child well-being. Not only are the results of the report useful, but this also marked the first time that national agencies collaborated on trends in the health and education of America's children. The forum was founded in 1994 and includes the Departments of

Agriculture, Commerce, Health and Human Services, Housing and Urban Development, Justice, and Labor; the National Science Foundation; and the Office of Management and Budget. Specifically, the National Institute of Child Health and Human Development, National Maternal and Child Health Bureau, and National Center for Education Statistics were listed as contributors to the report.

The report states that more children know where their next meal is coming from, more children are being read to by parents, more children are being enrolled in preschool programs and also graduating from college, immunization rates are up, and the rate of infant and childhood deaths has decreased. Not all the trends for children were positive, however. The use of illicit drugs and cigarette smoking is up, and crimes against youths have increased. Children in families with annual incomes below $15,000 were 22 times more likely to experience abuse and neglect than families with annual incomes above $30,000.

In the following selections, Lisbeth B. Schorr reports that programs for disadvantaged children are working and have the support of those in power in Washington, D.C. She lists a number of intervention programs that have met their goals and are considered worth the money being spent on them. William J. Bennett takes an opposing view of the status of children in America, pointing to many societal ills that continue to keep children in the lower class and underclass at a disadvantage.

Making the Most of What We Already Know

Human-service administrators probably have the toughest jobs in America. When I reviewed the agenda for your meeting [of the American Public Welfare Association], I was delighted that both welfare reform and health care reform would be so expertly covered, so that I would be free to talk about what we know about the needs of children and families that go beyond income, employment, and access to health care, as well as my favorite subject: what we know about what works in meeting those needs.

I began collecting information that sheds light on this subject almost by accident. In the early 1980s, I was struck with a prevailing sense of helplessness in the face of urgent social problems; and I set out to find examples of programs that worked. I wanted to show that organized interventions—in early education, schooling, health services, social services, and family supports—did indeed change life outcomes among disadvantaged children.

I decided at the outset that I would look for programs that were successful in dealing with problems of consequence—problems that were seen as important because of the enormous toll they take on individual youngsters, their families, and society as a whole: school-age child-bearing, school dropout, delinquency, and long-term welfare dependence. I called these "rotten outcomes."

I then looked at the risk factor research and discovered a strong convergence around the finding that because risk factors interact and multiply the effects of one another, the reduction of any risk factor improves the odds of a favorable outcome. The more risk factors in a particular situation, the greater the damaging impact of each. But the impact is not just additive—risk factors multiply one another's destructive effects.

Youngsters who become pregnant or delinquent or who drop out of school already have been in trouble for many years; many of the troubles that surface in adolescence can be predicted from poor school performance and truancy as early as third or fourth grade. We also know that trouble in elementary school correlates with a number of antecedent risk factors. In addition to poverty, these include

- being born unwanted or to a teenage mother;
- low weight at birth;

- untreated childhood health problems;
- lack of language, reasoning, and coping skills at school entry; and
- failure to develop trusting relationships with reliable and protective adults early in life.

The important news about these risk factors is that every one of them has been successfully attacked through interventions we know how to provide. We now have evidence of

- school-based health clinics that have reduced the rate of teenage childbearing, raised the average age at which youngsters became sexually active, and reduced the number of unwanted births;
- comprehensive prenatal care and nutrition programs that have reduced the proportion of low birth weight babies;
- intensive family support, nurse home-visiting, and childcare programs that have resulted in lower rates of child abuse, fewer children removed from their homes, and fewer mothers dependent on welfare;
- quality preschool programs whose participants, when they become young adults, include fewer dropouts, fewer delinquents, fewer teenage mothers, and fewer youngsters without jobs; and
- reformed elementary schools that were able to so change the climate of the school that whole populations of children who had been failing began to succeed.

As one synthesizes the evidence, it becomes clear that the contention that in the world of social programs "nothing works" is in fact a canard—a myth that cannot be maintained in the face of the research and experience now at hand.

Common Elements

The good news, then, is not only that there are programs that work, but that we now know a lot about how and why they work. As I analyzed the information I had collected to identify common patterns among successful programs, several characteristics emerged:

Successful programs are comprehensive, intensive, flexible, and responsive Staffs in these programs have extensive repertoires and extensive community networks. They have the capacity to respond flexibly to concrete needs for help with food or housing or a violent family member. Sister Mary Paul, who runs a family services program in Brooklyn, says that no one in her program ever says, "This may be what you need, but helping you get it is not part of my job."

Many of these programs provide their staffs with a pool of flexible funds, which they can use at their discretion to help a family buy a wheelchair or a washing machine or to get the car repaired. They respond to the needs of families at times and places that make sense to the family, often at home, at school, or in neighborhood centers and at odd hours, rather than in distant offices once a week on Wednesday afternoons. Job descriptions are broad, boundaries are permeable, and professionalism is redefined.

In my book, *Within Our Reach: Breaking the Cycle of Disadvantage,* I tell the story of a Homebuilders family preservation worker who appeared at the front door of a family in crisis, only to be greeted by a mother's declaration that the one thing she did not need in her life was one more social worker telling her what to do. What she needed, she said, was to get her house cleaned up. The Homebuilders therapist, a master's-level clinical psychologist with supplemental training by Homebuilders, responded by asking the mother if she wanted to start with the kitchen. After they worked together for an hour, the two women were able to talk about the issues that were at the heart of the family's difficulty. It may have been an unorthodox way of forging a therapeutic alliance, but it worked.

I told this story at a meeting some months ago, and a distinguished professor of psychology interrupted to say that that was going too far. What the psychologist had done, she claimed, was unprofessional.

In a sense, of course, she was quite right. In most professions, highest status is conferred on those who deal with issues from which all human complexity and messiness have been removed. Narrowly drawn boundaries that limit what is expected of a professional may be the traditional essence of professionalism, yet they often interfere with professional effectiveness.

Successful programs deal with children as parts of families They recognize that a mother's needs cannot be dealt with in isolation from her children's, and vice versa. They work not alone with one generation, but with two, and often three. Successful Head Start programs and family support centers nurture parents so they can better nurture their children.

Successful programs take into account the real world of those they serve. The clinician treating an infant for recurrent diarrhea sees beyond the patient on the examining table to whether the family needs help from a public health nurse or social worker to obtain nonmedical services. I visited a health center in Mississippi that actually delivers clean water to families who cannot get it any other way.

The effective job-training program knows that unstable childcare can stop a transition to self-sufficiency cold, and that poor-quality child care is likely to interfere powerfully with a young child's chances to climb out of poverty.

Successful programs deal with families as parts of neighborhoods and communities Most successful programs have deep roots in the community. They are not imposed from without—they are not "parachuted" into communities—but are carefully integrated with specific local community needs and strengths so that local communities have a genuine sense of ownership, and programs are in fact designed to respond to the real needs of that particular community.

Staff in successful programs have the time, skills, and support to build relationships of trust and respect with children and families They work in settings that allow them to develop meaningful personal relationships over time and to provide services respectfully, ungrudgingly, and collaboratively.

Psychiatrist James Comer points out that relationship issues are particularly important among low-income people who have given up on helping systems.

None of the programs that succeed are "lean and mean." They have been able to establish a climate that is warm, welcoming, and supportive. The quality and continuity of relationships and support are what make many other activities effective. Home visitors say that respectful, trusting relationships make parent education work.

A careful evaluation of an enhanced prenatal care program in Washington, D.C., found that the most important element that kept women in the program and utilizing health services properly was not the program's cash incentives or even easy access to care; rather it was the "friendly support" of "someone to talk to about pregnancy and other life stresses" that was valued most highly.

Smallness of scale at the point of service delivery also seems to be crucial. Large schools, massive outpatient clinics, and large caseloads vastly complicate the job of personalizing services to respond to individual and family needs. For many children, life trajectories have been changed through a relationship with a caring, attentive adult. And, as those who work as volunteers or as professionals can attest, a caring, attentive adult can come in many forms.

Successful programs have long-term, preventive orientations and continue to evolve over time The people responsible for these programs have no illusion that they can implement the perfect model program. They allow their programs to evolve continually to maintain their responsiveness to individual, family, and community needs over time and to respond to feedback from both front-line staff and participants.

Successful programs combine a highly flexible mode of operation with a clearly articulated sense of mission. They operate in an organizational culture that is outcome oriented rather than rule bound. Their approach is long-term, inclusive, preventive, and empowering.

Countering the System

The successes of these interventions are of enormous importance despite the fact that many of the most successful programs operate in special—and sometimes idiosyncratic—circumstances. But these successes show that something can be done to address social problems previously considered intractable. They provide a vision of what can be achieved. They refute the contention that families in the so-called underclass are beyond the reach of organized services. They show that when high-risk populations get the best of services rather than the worst, life trajectories change. And, by revealing the attributes of success, they contain the information we need to take successful programs to scale.

These attributes of success, of course, are neither counterintuitive nor surprising. When I go around the country making speeches about how effective programs are characterized by flexibility, comprehensiveness, responsiveness, front-line discretion, a family focus, community rootedness, and respectful relationships, practitioners never seem surprised. This is the stuff that most people on the front lines know works—the stuff they know is important.

It is also the stuff that the good ones have to lie, cheat, and connive in order to be able to do.

Recently I received a letter from the director of a community health center who had heard me discuss the attributes of effective programs. She wrote that these attributes describe precisely what she does each day—and that they are precisely the opposite of what she's told to do each day by the large hospital under whose auspices her center operates.

Marc Tucker of the National Center on Education and the Economy says, "When you find an individual school that works, it's almost always because it's running against the grain. You find a teacher or a principal who really doesn't give a damn about the system. They are willing to ignore or subvert every rule in the book in order to get the job done for the kids." You hear the same thing from child protection workers and the staff of job training programs.

Unless we come to grips with the mismatch between the attributes of effective programs and the pressures placed on programs by prevailing systems, successful models will continue to flourish briefly and then disappear or become diluted when special funding and special political protection end, or when they can no longer find a leader who combines the talents of a Mother Theresa, a Machiavelli, and a certified public accountant.

The attributes of effective programs that are now supported by theory, a convergent body of research, and front-line experience in many different disciplines turn out to be totally at odds with the systems within which most programs must function—and which chief executive officers must administer. Successful programs remain the exception and not the rule because existing systems undermine precisely the elements that are the hallmarks of effective programs.

With the tools you are issued, which include categorical financing, rigid rules, hierarchical management techniques, and input-based accountability, of course the front-line practitioners complain that they cannot provide comprehensive, flexible, family-centered, responsive services.

Bright Prospects

So what are the prospects for change, the prospects that you will get some help in operating systems in which ordinary people can achieve superior outcomes, in which effective programs can be sustained—systems that do not depend on a single charismatic leader?

I think the prospects are bright—even though money may be short. Let me tell you why I believe this:

First, I think we have the best shot we have had in a generation to break the cycle of disadvantage, because we have the information we need to do better; and we have a growing consensus that we must do better.

There is increasing recognition that teenage pregnancy, violence, and school failure are not isolated problems that have either isolated or standardized solutions. We know we have the elements of past success to build on, and we know that we cannot do it at bargain basement prices and that we cannot do it overnight. But we can be certain that if it is done well, it will make a difference in the life of this nation.

Marian Wright Edelman of the Children's Defense Fund likes to say that we are at a point in this country today when doing what is right coincides with what we have to do to save our national skins! The people who are committed to social justice can join with those whose highest priority is a workforce that can increase American productivity and win the international economic competition.

Second, I am optimistic about what can be done because human service administrators now have a lot of friends in Washington. From the president on down, the new leadership in Washington is not only competent, but it is respectful of state competence. They see the differences among states and communities not as inconvenient impediments to standardized rule making but rather as critical strengths.

So we have the president declaring

> We're going to give the states, the counties, and the cities the right to design what we call "bottoms-up" initiatives. In other words, you decide what it is you need, tell us what you need, and if it's in a grant proposal that's anywhere under $10 million—or over $10 million if you get approval for it—we will design something to give you the money you need instead of you having to figure out how to walk through the hoops of all the rules and regulations of the hundreds and hundreds of grants in the federal government.

To carry out this charge, the president has created a "community enterprise board" to identify neighborhoods across America, both urban and rural, that are in trouble. These neighborhoods, in the president's words, "will say what they want done. Then my cabinet will sit down and work together and figure out how to do it—not how to tell them how to comply with our rules, but how to do what people need done at the local level."

As columnist Neal Pierce points out, when a city is struggling to assist homeless people, for example, it will now be able to capture not only federal funds earmarked for the homeless, but also monies appropriated for housing, transportation, job training, childcare, health, mental health, and alcohol and drug abuse—keeping just one set of books and adhering to one set of rules.

In exchange for greater flexibility, we will surely see a greater emphasis on outcome accountability, which I think we should welcome. I believe that accountability based on outcomes that reflect common sense and common understanding—such as increasing rates of healthy births, school readiness, and school success—may be the most powerful force to

- focus attention on the mission rather than on the rules,
- permit flexibility and autonomy at the front end,
- encourage cross-systems collaboration,

- promote a community-wide "culture of responsibility" for children and families, and
- provide evidence to funders and the public that programs are indeed achieving their intended purposes.

I believe that efforts to obtain new funds, especially public funds, and to use old funds under new and more flexible rules will succeed only if they are coupled with clear commitments that effectiveness will ultimately be demonstrated in improved outcomes. Especially if one considers discretion at the frontlines as critical, and if one believes that local programs must be able to evolve over time to meet unique local needs, the old ways of ensuring accountability become counterproductive. Legislation or regulations that attempt to ensure quality by imposing detailed procedural protocols interfere profoundly with a program's ability to operate flexibly. But the demands for accountability cannot be dismissed; and the most reasonable way of ensuring that funds are in fact accomplishing their intended purposes, while allowing for front-line creativity, is by documenting results in terms of important, real-world outcomes.

In an outcome-oriented climate, it would be easier to combine publicly funded efforts with the initiatives that several national foundations, including The Ford Foundation, The Pew Charitable Trusts, the Rockefeller Foundation, and the Annie E. Casey Foundation, are now targeting on cross-systems, neighborhood-based efforts to turn around both neighborhood and family disintegration in areas of persistent poverty and social dislocation.

The provision of effective services to populations that heretofore have been neglected or poorly served requires collaboration among individuals and agencies that have previously worked in isolation. But collaboration alone will not improve outcomes. Because fragmentation is such a big problem in existing services, many have come to see the coordination and integration of services as the solution.

Collaboration is hard, and it's a crucial step in solving many current problems; but it is futile to put together services that are of mediocre quality, that are rendered grudgingly, or that are rendered by professionals who do not persevere or do not know how to work collaboratively with families.

Whether we are talking about school-based services, one-stop shopping, or new links between education and other human services, putting together formerly isolated services is essential. But we should not be so dazzled by the feat of putting together formerly isolated pieces of service that we forget to pay attention to the contents of those elements.

That is why I attach so much importance to the many . . . geographically based initiatives that would match the concentration of social problems in urban communities and depleted rural areas with a similar magnitude of fiscal resources and problem-solving capabilities. The factors implicated in persistent poverty and concentrated social dislocation are too intertwined and pervasive for narrow, one-shot interventions. What is needed is a broad attack on many fronts at once. This approach combines comprehensive and responsive services and restructured schools with community development and economic development, sometimes even with reforms to improve housing and public safety, so that they will interact synergistically to achieve a visible level of effectiveness in an entire threatened community.

It is virtually impossible for any child to grow up whole in neighborhoods that society has abandoned, that are left without decent health care, schools, parks, libraries, theaters, youth centers, or even washing machines—neighborhoods where no one can count on being able to land a legal job that will support a family and where no one feels safe.

Everyone agrees that it takes a village to raise a child. But in the inner city, the village has disintegrated. That is why we need bold and comprehensive strategies. Incrementalism will not do it. There are chasms you cannot cross one step at a time. So my third reason for feeling confident is that bold thinking is in.

It became hard, in the last decade, to think boldly. We learned to think small and to content ourselves with fiddling at the margins. But it is rapidly becoming clear that some of our most urgent problems will not be solved unless we dare to adopt a bolder vision—a vision that is built on a shared understanding that we cannot allow the richest country in the world to declare bankruptcy in our civic life. That vision could transform into action—public-private, national, state, and local—the widespread yearning that I see in so many American communities to make life better for all of America's children and families.

William J. Bennett **NO**

What to Do About the Children

At the dawn of the 20th century there was every reason to believe that ours would be (in the title of a best-selling book at the time) "the century of the child." From the early part of the 1900's through the 1950's, despite ups and downs, despite Depression and war, things got better in almost every area touching the welfare of American children: economic security improved, material earnings increased, medicine progressed, family structure was stable, children occupied a valued place in society, and our civic institutions were strong and resilient. In retrospect, it seems as if the midpoint of the century was a high point for the well-being of children.

By the 1960's, however, America began a steep and uninterrupted slide toward what might be called decivilization. Although every stratum of society has been affected, the worst problems have been concentrated within America's inner cities. No age group has remained untouched, but the most punishing blows have been absorbed by children.

In assessing conditions today, it is important to keep perspective: America is *not* in danger of becoming a third-world country; the vast majority of children do not live in sewers of disease and depravity; and most are not violent, sexually promiscuous, or drug-takers. At the same time, however, there is no question that as we approach the end of the last decade of this "American century," the condition of too many of our children is not good. The indicators are well-known: low educational achievement, the decline of the two-parent family, moral confusion, and, for a sizable and increasingly large minority, abuse, neglect, and very bleak prospects for the future.

Consider some real-world facts:

- From 1960 to 1991, the rate of homicide deaths among children under the age of 19 more than quadrupled. Among black teenagers, homicide is now by far the leading cause of death.
- Since 1965, the juvenile arrest rate for violent crimes has tripled, and the fastest-growing segment of the criminal population is made up of children.
- Since 1960, the rate at which teenagers take their own lives has more than tripled.
- The rate of births to unmarried teenagers has increased by almost 200 percent in three decades; the number of unmarried teenagers getting pregnant has nearly doubled in the past two decades.

- Today, 30 percent of all births and almost 70 percent of all black births are illegitimate. By the end of the decade, according to the most reliable projections, 40 percent of all American births and 80 percent of all minority births will be out-of-wedlock.
- During the last 30 years there has been a tripling of the percentage of children living in single-parent families. According to some projections, only 30 percent of white children and only 6 percent of black children born in 1980 will live with both parents through the age of 18.

A useful historical reference point may be 1965, when Daniel P. Moynihan, then an Assistant Secretary of Labor, wrote *The Negro Family: The Case for National Action.* Then, one-quarter of all black children were born out of wedlock; one-half of all black children lived in broken homes at some time before they reached age 18; and 14 percent of black children were on welfare. Moynihan considered this "tangle of pathologies" to be a social catastrophe, and so it was. Today, however, were we to achieve such figures in even one of our major urban centers, we would consider it a stunning accomplishment.

As the figures above demonstrate, these problems are by no means limited to lower-class or minority populations. In addition to everything else, divorce, rampant in all social classes, causes over one million children annually to end up, at least temporarily, in single-parent families. And wherever they live, American children today—especially the teenagers among them—spend relatively minuscule amounts of time with either their fathers or their mothers—or their homework—and vastly greater amounts of time on other things from crime to television.

A few years ago a special commission of political, medical, educational, and business leaders issued a report on the health of America's teenagers titled *Code Blue.* In the words of this report. "Never before has one generation of American teenagers been less healthy, less cared for, or less prepared for life than their parents were at the same age." According to the sociologist David Popenoe, today's generation of children is the first in our nation's history to be less well-off psychologically and socially than its parents.

Nor is the concern limited to the experts. When asked in a recent Family Research Council poll, "Do you think children are generally better off today or worse off than when you were a child?," 60 percent of all Americans—and 77 percent of all black Americans—said children today are "worse off." They are right.

II

The greatest long-term threat to the well-being of our children is the enfeebled condition—in some sectors of our society, the near-complete collapse—of our character-forming institutions. In a free society, families, schools, and churches have primary responsibility for shaping the moral sensibilities of the young. The influence of these institutions is determinative; when they no longer provide moral instruction or lose their moral authority, there is very little that other auxiliaries—particularly the federal government—can do.

Among those three institutions, the family is preeminent; it is, as Michael Novak of the American Enterprise Institute once famously said, the original and best department of health, education, and welfare. But the family today is an agency in disrepair. Writes David Popenoe:

> This period [the 1960's through the 1990's] has witnessed an unprecedented decline of the family as a social institution. Families have lost functions, social power, and authority over their members. They have grown smaller in size, less stable, and shorter in life span. . . . Moreover, there has been a weakening of child-centeredness in American society and culture. Familism as a cultural value has diminished.

And so, too, has fatherhood. Each night in America, four out of ten children go to sleep without fathers who live in their homes, and upward of 60 percent will spend some major part of their childhood without fathers.

In the past, the typical cause of fatherlessness was divorce; its new face is homes headed by never-married mothers. This is "the most socially consequential family trend of our generation" (in the words of David Blankenhorn of the Institute for American Values), and it has seismic social implications. Moynihan warned [more than] 30 years ago that a society which allows a large number of young men to grow up without fathers in their lives asks for and almost always gets chaos. We have come to the point in America where we are asking prisons to do for many young boys what fathers used to do.

❧

There are other signs of decay, particularly of the cultural variety. Television shows make a virtue of promiscuity, adultery, homosexuality, and gratuitous acts of violence. Rap music celebrates the abuse and torture of women. Advertisements are increasingly erotic, even perverse. And many of our most successful and critically-acclaimed movies celebrate brutality, casual cruelty, and twisted sex.

None of these trends takes place in a moral or cultural vacuum. During the last 30 years we have witnessed a profound shift in public attitudes. The pollster Daniel Yankelovich finds that we Americans now place less value on what we owe others as a matter of moral obligation; less value on sacrifice as a moral good, on social conformity, respectability, and observing the rules; less value on correctness and restraint in matters of physical pleasure and sexuality—and correlatively greater value on things like self-expression, individualism, self-realization, and personal choice.

How does all this affect young children? A single, simple statistic tells much: if, in 1951, 51 percent of Americans agreed with the statement, "Parents who don't get along should not stay together for the children," in 1985 that figure had risen to 86 percent.

The social historian Barbara Dafoe Whitehead has observed that the Hallmark company now offers two lines of divorce cards: one set for the newly single adults, the other for children of divorced parents. For the latter, a typical message is piercing in its casualness: "I'm sorry I'm not always there when you need me but I hope you know I'm always just a phone call away." By contrast, one adult card reads, "Think of your former marriage as a record album. It was full of music—both happy and sad. But what's important now is . . . YOU! the recently released HOT NEW SINGLE! You're going to be at the TOP OF THE CHARTS!" As Whitehead comments, What had once been regarded as hostile to children's best interests is now considered essential to adults' happiness."

If the self, in the late Allan Bloom's withering assessment, has become "the modern substitute for the soul," we are also living in an era in which it has become unfashionable to make judgments on a whole range of behaviors and attitudes. This unwillingness to judge has resulted in unilateral moral disarmament, as harmful in the cultural realm as its counterpart is in the military. With the removal of social sanctions in the name of "tolerance" and "open-mindedness," and the devaluing of the idea of personal responsibility, is it any wonder, for instance, that in a recent survey 70 percent of young people between the ages of 18 and 34 said that people who generate a baby out-of-wedlock should not be subject to moral reproach *of any sort?*

It would be supererogatory at this late date to catalogue the role of government in giving form and force to these ideas and beliefs through law and policy. Suffice it to say that from the area of criminal justice, to education, to welfare policy, to the arts, to a whole tangle of sexual and family issues, government has increasingly put itself on the side of the forces of decomposition, not on the side of the forces of restoration. The consequence is that the moral universe we are sending our children into today is more harsh, more vulgar, more coarse, and more violent than the moral universe most of us grew up in—and they are less equipped to deal with it.

We should not flinch from admitting this unsettling truth: we live in a culture which seems dedicated to the corruption of the young, to assuring the loss of their innocence before their time. "It dawned on me recently," the anthropologist David Murray has written, "that we have now become the kind of society that in the 19th century almost every Christian denomination felt compelled to missionize."

III

If the problem is one of moral breakdown, it would be fatuous to suggest that it can be fixed by government intervention. There is, after all, one proposition which has been tested repeatedly over the last three decades and just as repeatedly been found wanting—namely, that we can spend our way out of our social problems. Instead of encouraging government, we need to relimit it—not only, or even primarily, for fiscal reasons, but because the "nanny state" has eroded self-reliance and encouraged dependency, crowding out the character-forming institutions and enfeebling us as citizens.

Still, there are a number of actions government *can* take that would amount to constructive and far-reaching, even radical, reforms. A number of these ideas have been on the table for quite some time, but as the results of the November 1994 elections suggest, Americans may be more ready for fundamental reform today than at any other point in recent history. So we suddenly find ourselves presented with an extraordinary opportunity.

Before getting down to particulars, I would stipulate two general points that should guide any discussion of public-policy solutions to the problems faced by children in America. One of them I borrow from an old principle of medicine: *primum non nocere*—first, do no harm. In many, many cases, the best thing government can do is (to quote Myron Magnet of the *City Journal*) "to *stop* doing what makes the problem worse."

As for the second point, it was well expressed by Alexander Hamilton, who in *The Federalist No. 17* questioned whether "all those things . . . which are proper to be provided for by local legislation [should] ever be desirable cares of a general jurisdiction." To state this in terms of our present situation, there are many responsibilities which would be better handled by states and localities but which have fallen under the jurisdiction of the federal government; they should be devolved back to the smaller "laboratories of democracy."

Within those constraints, government, at one level or another, does have a role to play in improving conditions for the young. Let us look at a few key areas, beginning with the link between welfare and illegitimacy.

Between 1962 and 1992, welfare spending in the United States increased by over 900 percent in 1992 dollars. At the same time, the poverty rate dropped by less than 5 percent—and illegitimacy rates increased over 400 percent. Children are the real victims in this national tragedy. They are being conditioned into the same habits of dependence they are surrounded by, resulting in an almost unbreakable cycle of welfare and "the tangle of pathologies" associated with it.

John J. DiIulio, Jr. of Princeton has put this last point well:

> The problem *is* that inner-city children are trapped in criminogenic homes, schools, and neighborhoods where high numbers of teenagers and adults are no more likely to nurture, teach, and care for children than they are to expose them to neglect, abuse, and violence. . . . Children cannot be socialized by adults who are themselves unsocialized (or worse), families that exist in name only, schools that do not educate, and neighborhoods in which violent and repeat criminals circulate in and out of jail. . . .

Quite a number of serious and thoughtful proposals have been advanced for restructuring the entire system of welfare benefits, of which Charles Murray's is among the most thoroughgoing.[1] In a similar spirit, I would endorse full-scale and far-reaching plans to send welfare back to the states, which have proved the best settings for innovative reform and experimentation.

As for the problem of illegitimacy in particular, one year after legislation is enacted I would recommend ending direct welfare payments to women who have children out of wedlock; enforcing existing child-support laws; and terminating the increase in benefits for women who have children while participating in welfare programs. The success of such reforms, it seems to me, depends critically on their sweep and magnitude; incremental steps will not do the necessary job of altering fundamental assumptions and expectations.

To turn to a point that has been heavily controverted since the elections of November 8 [1994]: in my view, situations will arise which may warrant the removal of a child from the care of his parent(s). To be sure, this should only happen in desperate circumstances and as a last resort. But we cannot ignore the plain fact that there are more and more horrifying cases of abuse, neglect, and parental malfeasence.

While adoption is the best alternative in such circumstances, the concept of orphanages, or group-care homes, should not be dismissed. Such institutions pretty much disappeared from the national scene when government began distributing money in the expectation that poor parents, with federal assistance, would do a better job of raising their children. But in far too many cases that expectation has been resoundingly refuted by experience.

When parents cannot care for their children's basic material, psychological, medical, and moral needs, it is time to look to other institutions. The orphanage—call it a boarding school without tuition—may then be in their best interest. Can anyone seriously argue that some boys would be worse off living in Boys Town than in, say, the Cabrini Green housing project in Chicago, considered by its residents a virtual war zone?

But adoption is certainly preferable. Only 50,000 children are adopted each year in the United States; half are healthy infants and half are older children or children with disabilities. At any given time, however, one to two million homes are waiting to adopt. Provided only the child is young enough, there is, in effect, no such thing as an unwanted child, and this goes even for babies who are not fully healthy. Unfortunately, most potential adopters (and adoptees) are hamstrung by needless barriers.

In addition to the high cost of a private adoption, often as much as $10,000, many couples are automatically excluded from consideration due to race, financial background, age, disability, or home size. Other potential adopters are scared away by lax confidentiality laws, nonbinding adoptions, and the expanded rights of the biological father to reclaim legal custody.

The barriers to adoption are only one side of the problem. Availability is also severely limited. Unwed mothers are often denied information about adoption in prenatal counseling; others decide to abort their pregnancy for economic reasons. (Indeed, it may be partly for this reason that abortion has increasingly become a problem of juveniles: of the one million teenage pregnancies each year, about 400,000 now end in abortion.)[2] Finally, and perhaps most importantly, with the stigma of illegitimacy all but gone in this country, for many young, unwed, pregnant women single motherhood has become a more attractive option than giving a child up for adoption.

Again, there is a limit to what government can do. But again, too, the greatest hope lies in reforms at the state level, such as:

- prohibiting the use of race and/or ethnicity as a disqualification for would-be foster or adoptive parents (in practice this has affected whites seeking to adopt nonwhite babies);

- expediting adoption procedures for infants and children who have been abandoned by their parents and are living in limbo in hospitals, group homes, and/or foster care;
- terminating parental rights and thus making a child available for adoption if by the age of six months—in the case of infants born with positive toxicology—maternal drug use has not ceased, or if a child has been severely abused by its parents;
- enacting model legislation that will require courts to consider the best interests of the child first in all cases concerning custody;
- establishing uniform rules making voluntary surrender/adoption irrevocable at any point past 72 hours after birth;
- restricting payments to biological parents by adoptive parents to necessary expenses related directly to the pregnancy and adoption;
- ensuring that adoptive families are treated with the same respect as other families, free of the fear of intrusion by the state or other parties after an adoption has been finalized.

꒰◌꒱

Then there is divorce—which, in terms of damage to children, can be the most devastating circumstance of all, yet which is conspicuous by its absence from the agenda of policy-makers.

As Karl Zinsmeister of the *American Enterprise* has written: "We talk about the drug crisis, the education crisis, and the problems of teen pregnancy and juvenile crime. But all these ills trace back predominantly to one source: broken families."

The statistics, indeed, are chilling. Children of single-parent families are twice as likely to drop out of high school, or, if they remain in school, have lower grade-point averages, lower college aspirations, and poorer attendance records than the general population. Girls living with only one parent are two-and-a-half times more likely to become teenage mothers. When it comes to crime, according to some studies, 70 percent of juveniles now incarcerated in state-reform institutions have lived either in single-parent homes or with someone other than their natural parents, and 75 percent of adolescent murderers come from single-parent homes.

The divorce rate has nearly doubled since 1960—not coincidentally, the same period in which no-fault divorce laws became popular. Previously, before a divorce was granted, the law had required a showing of fault, such as cruelty, abuse, adultery, or desertion. The recision of these conditions not only significantly increased the number of divorces but transformed marriage into a simple business contract.

Though the incidence of divorce cannot significantly be addressed through public policy, its effects can perhaps be curbed to some degree. My suggestions include braking mechanisms when children are involved, such as mandatory and substantial "cooling-off" periods as well as mandatory counseling; reinstituting fault as an absolute requirement for divorce and in determining the terms of a settlement; and classifying all property as family property, which would affect the distribution of assets in cases where children are involved.

ᴖᴏᴖ

This brings us to institutions outside the home, starting with the schools. Parents all over the country are increasingly aware that the public-education system in America is an embarrassment. As the federal government has taken over more responsibilities for the nation's schools, the quality of education has plummeted. The response of the education establishment and of the teachers' unions to this situation, and to the growing movement for greater parental involvement and local control that has arisen in response to it, has been to advocate pumping more money into the system. This has only served to perpetuate and even escalate the problem.

The signs of failure are everywhere, and need not be reiterated here.[3] Fortunately, there are many potentially good solutions—though more money is not among them. Instead, and yet again, a devolution is in order: the first step toward genuine education reform should be to rein in the federal government. In my judgment, legislation is called for which would restore decision-making responsibilities to state and local authorities, enabling the federal government to give states a block grant with virtually no strings attached. The state, local school districts, and parents would then be in a better position to make their own decisions regarding curriculum, books, standards, discipline, etc. Not only would this lead to a system more accountable to parents, but it would encourage innovation and experimentation.

The next step is to implement reforms at the state level which would foster excellence in the education system. These include open enrollment; charter schools; privatization; performance-testing for students and teachers; a merit-pay system for teachers and administrators; and, above all, school choice, complete with vouchers redeemable at public, private, and religious schools. And to prevent a future trend toward regulatory authority, the federal Department of Education should be dismantled. The limited functions of the department should be carried out by the executive branch in an office of education policy.

ᴖᴏᴖ

What about crime? Between 1985 and 1991, the annual rate at which young men aged 15 to 19 were being killed increased by 154 percent, far surpassing the rate of change in any other group. Twenty percent of high-school students now carry a knife, razor, firearm, or other weapon on a regular basis. As James Q. Wilson recently pointed out, "Youngsters are shooting at people at a far higher rate than at any time in recent history."[4] Or, in the words of Senator Bill Bradley, "The murderers are younger, the guns more high-powered, and the acts themselves occur more and more randomly." This problem will almost certainly get worse before it gets better, as by the end of the decade there will be a half-million more American males between the ages of 14 and 17 than there are today, 30,000 of whom will probably become high-rate offenders.

The justice system spends $20 billion a year to arrest, rehabilitate, and jail juvenile offenders, only to watch 70 percent of them commit crimes again. Here, too, money is evidently not the panacea. Genuine reform of our juvenile-justice laws, which for the most part should take place on the state level, would involve keeping records of juvenile arrests, fingerprinting offenders, and making these records available to adult courts to prevent juvenile criminals from being treated as first-time offenders when they reach the age of 18. I would also strongly recommend legislation at the state level to allow juveniles, 14 or older, to be charged as adults for certain crimes—such as murder, rape, armed robbery, and assault with a firearm.

Genuine reform would also establish consistent, graduated punishments for every offense. It would insist on building and maintaining the facilities needed to keep violent offenders off the streets. It would speed up the criminal-justice system by enacting and enforcing realistic trial provisions. It would prohibit irresponsible judges from unilaterally imposing measures (such as "prison caps") which release violent and repeat offenders back onto the streets. It would require offenders to pay restitution to their victims. And it would create extended sentences in institutional boot camps for repeat offenders and those who failed to participate in the community-service and public-works programs to which they had been sentenced.

⋙⊙⋘

A special subcategory of the overall crime problem is drugs. From the mid-1980's until 1991, significant progress was made on the drug front, with researchers tracking a sharp decline in overall use. But in 1991 use began to rise, and drugs are still a major problem among the young.

According to the latest study from the University of Michigan's Institute for Social Research, one in four students has used illegal drugs before reaching high school; among 8th graders, 13 percent say they have smoked marijuana in the last year, *double* the rate of 1991; and over 40 percent of all 10th graders and nearly 50 percent of all 12th graders have used some illicit drug, including LSD, inhalants, stimulants, barbiturates, and cocaine and crack. This, in the words of the study's principal investigator, Lloyd D. Johnston, is "a problem that is getting worse at a fairly rapid pace," and it is being abetted by a decline in peer disapproval and a general softening of teenagers' attitudes toward drug use.

While the Clinton administration has not formally abandoned the war against drugs, it has abandoned it for all practical purposes. This could have a dire effect on what has already been achieved, incomplete as that is. If we mean to continue our efforts, we will need to do a number of things. They include allowing communities to choose their own antidrug priorities by combining federal antidrug support with that from states and localities; putting the U.S. military in charge of stopping the flow of illegal drugs from abroad, and giving the military control over the entire interdiction process; establishing trade and diplomatic sanctions and eliminating aid to cocaine-source countries that fail to reduce their production of cocaine by 10 percent per year, and by at least 50 percent in five years; and requiring the Attorney

General first to identify all major drug-trafficking organizations known to be operating in the U.S. and then to create a plan to dismantle them.

IV

Drawing up laundry lists of public policy may seem a tedious and academic exercise. It is nevertheless an instructive one, if for no other reason than that it glaringly exposes how *little* has been done, on the most commonsensical level, to address the terrible problems that confront us, and that have accumulated in both number and intensity over the past 30 years. In this sense, thinking concretely about specific, practical reforms offers the hope that, by a concerted national effort, we might yet begin to alleviate some of the worst manifestations of these ills, and even, in time, to reverse course.

And yet, to repeat, even if we were to enact each and every one of the desired reforms in each and every area, we would still be a long way from having healed the broken families of America. Smart, intelligent public policies can and do make a difference. But political solutions are not, ultimately, the answer to problems which are at root moral and spiritual.

"Manners," wrote Edmund Burke two centuries ago,

> are of more importance than laws. Upon them, in a great measure, the laws depend. The law touches us but here and there, and now and then. Manners are what vex or soothe, corrupt or purify, exalt or debase, barbarize or refine us, by a constant, steady, uniform, insensible operation, like that of the air we breathe in. They give their whole form and color to our lives. According to their quality, they aid morals, they supply them, or they totally destroy them.

Can government supply manners and morals if they are wanting? Of course it cannot. What it can supply, through policy and law, is a vivid sense of what we as a society expect of ourselves, what we hold ourselves responsible for, and what we consider ourselves answerable to. There can be little doubt that in this last period of time the message our laws have been sending our young people and their parents has been the profoundly demoralizing one that we expect little, and hold ourselves answerable for still less.

By changing and improving our laws, we might not thereby bring about, but we would certainly *help* to bring about, a climate that would make it easier rather than harder for all of us to grow more civilized; easier rather than harder for us to keep our commitments to one another; easier rather than harder for us to recapture the idea of personal and civic responsibility. This, in turn, would make it easier rather than harder for us to raise our children in safety to adulthood—something which at the moment we are not doing very well at all.

Notes

1. "What To Do About Welfare," *Commentary,* December 1994.
2. Although abortion *per se* is not one of my subjects in this article, let me register here my belief that 1.5 million abortions a year—of which the overwhelming majority are performed on perfectly healthy women in order to prevent the

birth of perfectly healthy children—is a national catastrophe. There is no doubt that such a number must also have a coarsening effect on adults' attitudes toward children and what they need from us.

3. Chester E. Finn, Jr., in "What To Do About Education: The Schools" *Commentary*, October 1994 provides a long list of the appalling details.

4. "What To Do About Crime," *Commentary*, September 1994.

POSTSCRIPT

Is the Welfare of Disadvantaged Children Improving?

Schorr collected information on social programs aimed at reducing risk factors for children in the areas of school-age childbearing (teen parenting), school dropouts, delinquency, and long-term welfare dependence. Programs that are working had some common elements, such as flexibility in responding to family needs, dealing with the whole family system, and community ownership.

Both Schorr and Bennett use statistics to support their views on social intervention results for disadvantaged children. Their views reflect the current discussions being conducted on a larger scale about America's welfare system. Welfare reform proponents want social programs to be held accountable for their expenditure of funds and their success rates.

The goals of welfare reform are to reduce the amount of time that some families can receive public assistance and to build incentives to motivate families to improve their own lives. Proponents assume that in the absence of welfare payments, parents will find jobs, support their families, and develop a sense of pride, initiative, and self-esteem, but are these goals realistic for the people involved? Similarly, proponents of social intervention programs for disadvantaged children believe that their programs will work to reduce risk factors and motivate children to seek a better life, but are their goals realistic? Can they be successful within the context of the larger society? Can the long-term effects of these programs be documented, and can the cycle of poverty and family dysfunction be ended by these interventions?

Suggested Readings

Barry, V. (1995, Winter). What will happen to the children? *Policy Review, 71*, 7–14.

Besharov, D. J. (1996, May). Child abuse reporting. *Society, 33*, 40–46.

Edelman, M. W. (1996, June). Taking a stand. *Emerae, 7*, 58–63.

Murphy, P. T. (1995, May). Preserving chaos. *Commonweal, 122*, 12–15.

Peter, V. J. (1995, November). Welfare reform, the American family, and orphanages: What's best for the children? *USA Today: The Magazine of the American Scene, 124*, 56–60.

Stoesz, D. (1996, June). Suffer the children. *Washington Monthly, 28*, 20–25.

ISSUE 16

Is Abstinence-Only Sex Education Effective?

YES: Kerby Anderson, from "School-Based Health Clinics and Sex Education," *Probe Ministries International,* `http://www.probe.org/docs/clinics.html` (1998)

NO: Advocates for Youth and the Sexuality Information and Education Council of the United States (SIECUS), from "Toward a Sexually Healthy America: Roadblocks Imposed by the Federal Government's Abstinence-Only-Until-Marriage Education Program," a Report of Advocates for Youth and the Sexuality Information and Education Council of the United States (SIECUS) (2001)

ISSUE SUMMARY

YES: Kerby Anderson, president of Probe Ministries International, finds fault with traditional comprehensive sex education. Anderson demonstrates how, in his view, there is a need for abstinence-only sex education by presenting statistics and examples from case studies that support his assertion.

NO: Advocates for Youth helps young people make informed and responsible decisions about their reproductive and sexual health. The Sexuality Information and Education Council of the United States (SIECUS) is a national nonprofit organization that promotes comprehensive education about sexuality and advocates the right of individuals to make responsible sexual choices. In this selection, the organizations compare abstinence-only sex education to comprehensive sex education, outline the shortcomings of abstinence-only sex education, and show support for comprehensive sex education.

An overwhelming majority of people agree that abstinence is the safest choice an adolescent can make regarding sexual activity. Abstinence is the only 100 percent effective way to avoid pregnancy, the hundreds of sexually transmitted diseases that are epidemic, and the severe broken heart that often comes after a breakup with a sexually intimate partner. The problem is that parents and educators cannot agree on the best way to teach children and teenagers about abstinence. One group takes the stance that comprehensive sex education is the best approach. This includes some encouragement toward abstinence, but it also provides information on birth control and protection against sexually transmitted diseases (STDs). There are other parents and professionals who promote abstinence-only sex education. These programs include information on the hazards of sex (pregnancy, STDs, broken hearts, etc.) and also often include sections on self-esteem and standing up to peer pressure.

Advocates for comprehensive sex education argue that many teenagers will have sex. Therefore, they need to be taught about birth control methods and STD prevention techniques. Advocates for abstinence-only sex education argue that teaching about birth control methods and STD prevention sends mixed messages to adolescents. This information may even give them the impression that teachers and parents know and accept that they cannot help themselves from having sex, which is the opposite of what the pro-abstinence movement would like to accomplish.

To intensify the debate, the government established a federal entitlement program for abstinence-only-until-marriage education. When schools and other agencies accept these grants, they must adhere to the rules that come along with them. These rules include requiring schools to teach little about sexuality but instead to send a strong message that sexual activity outside of the context of marriage is psychologically and/or physiologically harmful and therefore should be avoided. For comprehensive sexual education advocates, this is worrisome because they believe that education about sexuality is the best way to empower adolescents to make sound decisions regarding premarital sex.

Kerby Anderson's selection begins by discussing school-based health clinics. The selection quickly moves to a list of arguments against comprehensive sexual education and Anderson's case for abstinence-only sex education. Advocates for Youth and the Sexuality Information and Education Council of the United States (SIECUS) present a history of abstinence education in the United States. They offer definitions of both abstinence and comprehensive sex education, discuss problems with abstinence-only programs, and conclude with research supporting comprehensive sex education programs.

As you read the following articles, think back to high school or put yourself in the position of a parent of an adolescent. Consider what approach you can support and why.

Kerby Anderson **YES**

School-Based Health Clinics and Sex Education

School-Based Health Clinics

As comprehensive sex education curricula have been promoted in the schools, clinics have been established to provide teens greater access to birth control information and devices. Proponents cite studies that supposedly demonstrate the effectiveness of these clinics on teen sexual behavior. Yet a more careful evaluation of the statistics involved suggests that school-based health clinics do not lower the teen pregnancy rate.

The first major study to receive nationwide attention was [at] DuSable High School. School administrators were rightly alarmed that before the establishment of a school-based health clinic, three hundred of their one thousand female students became pregnant. After the clinic was opened, the media widely reported that the number of pregnant students dropped to 35.

As more facts came to light, the claims seemed to be embellished. School officials admitted that they kept no records of the number of pregnancies before the operation of the clinic and that three hundred was merely an estimate. Moreover, school officials could not produce statistics for the number of abortions the girls received as a result of the clinic.

The most often-cited study involved the experience of the clinic at Mechanics Arts High School in St. Paul, Minnesota. Researchers found that a drop in the number of teen births during the late 1970s coincided with an increase in female participation at the school-based clinics. But at least three important issues undermine the validity of this study.

First, some of the statistics are anecdotal rather than statistical. School officials admitted that the schools could not document the decrease in pregnancies. The Support Center for School-Based Clinics acknowledged that "most of the evidence for the success of that program is based upon the clinic's own records and the staff's knowledge of births among students. Thus, the data undoubtedly do not include all births."

Second, an analysis of the data done by Michael Schwartz of the Free Congress Foundation found that the total female enrollment of the two schools included in the study dropped from 1268 in 1977 to 948 in 1979.

Therefore the reduction in reported births could have been merely attributable to an overall decline in the female population at the school.

Finally, the study actually shows a drop in the teen birth rate rather than the teen pregnancy rate. The reduction in the fertility rate listed in the study was likely due to more teenagers obtaining an abortion.

Today, more and more advocates of school-based health clinics are citing a three-year study headed by Laurie Zabin at Johns Hopkins University, which evaluated the effect of sex education on teenagers. The study of two school-based clinics in Baltimore, Maryland, showed there was a 30 percent reduction in teen pregnancies.

But even this study leaves many unanswered questions. The size of the sample was small, and over 30 percent of the female sample dropped out between the first and last measurement periods. Since the study did not control for student mobility, critics point out that some of girls who dropped out of the study may have dropped out of school because they were pregnant. And others were not accounted for with follow-up questionnaires. Other researchers point out that the word abortion is never mentioned in the brief report, leading them to conclude that only live births were counted.

The conclusion is simple. Even the best studies used to promote school-based health clinics prove they do not reduce the teen pregnancy rate. School-based clinics do not work.

Sex Education

For more than thirty years proponents of comprehensive sex education have argued that giving sexual information to young children and adolescents will reduce the number of unplanned pregnancies and sexually transmitted diseases. In that effort nearly $3 billion have been spent on federal Title X family planning services; yet teenage pregnancies and abortions rise.

Perhaps one of the most devastating popular critiques of comprehensive sex education came from Barbara Dafoe Whitehead. The journalist who said that Dan Quayle was right also was willing to say that sex education was wrong. Her article, "The Failure of Sex Education" in the October 1994 issue of *Atlantic Monthly,* demonstrated that sex education neither reduced pregnancy nor slowed the spread of STDs.

Comprehensive sex education is mandated in at least seventeen states, so Whitehead chose one of those states and focused her analysis on the sex education experiment in New Jersey. Like other curricula, the New Jersey sex education program rests on certain questionable assumptions.

The first tenet is that *children are sexual from birth.* Sex educators reject the classic notion of a latency period until approximately age twelve. They argue that you are "being sexual when you throw your arms around your grandpa and give him a hug."

Second, *children are sexually miseducated.* Parents, to put it simply, have not done their job, so we need "professionals" to do it right. Parents try to protect their children, fail to affirm their sexuality, and even discuss sexuality in a context of moralizing. The media, they say, is also guilty of providing sexual misinformation.

Third, *if mis-education is the problem, then sex education in the schools is the solution.* Parents are failing miserably at the task, so "it is time to turn the job over to the schools. Schools occupy a safe middle ground between Mom and MTV."

Learning about Family Life is the curriculum used in New Jersey. While it discusses such things as sexual desire, AIDS, divorce, condoms, and masturbation, it nearly ignores such issues as abstinence, marriage, self-control, and virginity. One technique promoted to prevent pregnancy and STDs is noncoital sex, or what some sex educators call "outercourse." Yet there is good evidence to suggest that teaching teenagers to explore their sexuality through noncoital techniques will lead to coitus. Ultimately, outercourse will lead to intercourse.

Whitehead concludes that comprehensive sex education has been a failure. For example, the percent of teenage births to unwed mothers was 67 percent in 1980 and rose to 84 percent in 1991. In the place of this failed curriculum, Whitehead describes a better program. She found that "sex education works best when it combines clear messages about behavior with strong moral and logistical support for the behavior sought." One example she cites is the "Postponing Sexual Involvement" program at Grady Memorial Hospital in Atlanta, Georgia, which offers more than a "Just say no" message. It reinforces the message by having adolescents practice the desired behavior and enlists the aid of older teenagers to teach younger teenagers how to resist sexual advances. Whitehead also found that "religiously observant teens" are less likely to experiment sexually, thus providing an opportunity for church-related programs to help stem the tide of teenage pregnancy.

Contrast this, however, with what has been derisively called "the condom gospel." Sex educators today promote the dissemination of sex education information and the distribution of condoms to deal with the problems of teen pregnancy and STDs.

The Case Against Condoms

At the 1987 World Congress of Sexologists, Theresa Crenshaw asked the audience, "If you had the available partner of your dreams and knew that person carried HIV, how many of you would have sex, depending on a condom for your protection?" None of the 800 members of the audience raised their hand. If condoms do not eliminate the fear of HIV infection for sexologists and sex educators, why encourage the children of America to play STD Russian roulette?

Are condoms a safe and effective way to reduce pregnancy and STDs? Sex educators seem to think so. Every day sex education classes throughout this country promote condoms as a means of safe sex or at least safer sex. But the research on condoms provides no such guarantee.

For example, Texas researcher Susan Weller, writing in the 1993 issue of *Social Science Medicine*, evaluated all research published prior to July 1990 on condom effectiveness. She reported that condoms are only 87 percent effective in preventing pregnancy and 69 percent effective in reducing the risk of HIV infection. This 69 percent effectiveness rate is also the same as a 31 percent failure rate in preventing AIDS transmission. And according to a study in the *1992 Family Planning Perspectives,* 15 percent of married couples who use condoms for birth control end up with an unplanned pregnancy within the first year.

So why has condom distribution become the centerpiece of the U.S. AIDS policy and the most frequently promoted aspect of comprehensive sex education? For many years the answer to that question was an a priori commitment to condoms and a safe sex message over an abstinence message. But in recent years, sex educators and public health officials have been pointing to one study that seemed to vindicate the condom policy.

The study was presented at the Ninth International Conference on AIDS held in Berlin on June 9, 1993. The study involved 304 couples with one partner who was HIV positive. Of the 123 couples who used condoms with each act of sexual intercourse, not a single negative HIV partner became positive. So proponents of condom distribution thought they had scientific vindication for their views.

Unfortunately, that is not the whole story. Condoms do appear to be effective in stopping the spread of AIDS when used "correctly and consistently." Most individuals, however, do not use them "correctly and consistently." What happens to them? Well, it turns out that part of the study received much less attention. Of 122 couples who could not be taught to use condoms properly, 12 became HIV positive in both partners. Undoubtedly over time, even more partners would contract AIDS.

How well does this study apply to the general population? Not very well. This study group was quite dissimilar from the general population. For example, they knew the HIV status of their spouse and therefore had a vested interest in protecting themselves. They were responsible partners in a committed monogamous relationship. In essence, their actions and attitudes differed dramatically from teenagers and single adults who do not know the HIV status of their partners, are often reckless, and have multiple sexual partners.

And even if condoms are used correctly, do not break, and do not leak, they are still far from 100 percent effective. The Medical Institute for Sexual Health reported that "medical studies confirm that condoms do not offer much, if any, protection in the transmission of chlamydia and human papilloma virus, two serious STDs with prevalence as high as 40 percent among sexually active teenagers."

Abstinence Is the Answer

Less than a decade ago an abstinence-only program was rare in the public schools. Today, directive abstinence programs can be found in many school districts while battles are fought in other school districts for their inclusion or removal. While proponents of abstinence programs run for school board or influence existing school board members, groups like Planned Parenthood bring lawsuits against districts that use abstinence-based curricula, arguing that they are inaccurate or incomplete.

The emergence of abstinence-only programs as an alternative to comprehensive sex education programs was due to both popularity and politics. Parents concerned about the ineffectiveness of the safe-sex message eagerly embraced the message of abstinence. And political funding helped spread the message and legitimize its educational value. The Adolescent Family Life Act, enacted in 1981 by the Reagan Administration, created Title XX and set aside $2 million a year for the development and implementation of abstinence-based programs. Although the Clinton Administration later cut funding for abstinence programs, the earlier funding in the 1980s helped groups like Sex Respect and Teen-Aid launch abstinence programs in the schools.

Parents and children have embraced the abstinence message in significant numbers. One national poll by the University of Chicago found that 68 percent of adults surveyed said premarital sex among teenagers is "always wrong." A 1994 poll for USA Weekend asked more than 1200 teens and adults what they thought of "several high profile athletes [who] are saying in public that they have abstained from sex before marriage and are telling teens to do the same." Seventy-two percent of the teens and 78 percent of the adults said they agree with the pro-abstinence message.

Their enthusiasm for abstinence-only education is well founded. Even though the abstinence message has been criticized by some as naive or inadequate, there are good reasons to promote abstinence in schools and society.

First, teenagers want to learn about abstinence. Contrary to the often repeated teenage claim, not "everyone's doing it." A 1992 study by the Centers for Disease Control found that 43 percent of teenagers from ages fourteen to seventeen had engaged in sexual intercourse at least once. Put another way, the latest surveys suggest that a majority of teenagers are not doing it.

A majority of teenagers are abstaining from sex; also more want help in staying sexually pure in a sex-saturated society. Emory University surveyed one thousand sexually experienced teen girls by asking them what they would like to learn to reduce teen pregnancy. Nearly 85 percent said, "How to say no without hurting the other person's feelings."

Second, abstinence prevents pregnancy. After the San Marcos (California) Junior High adopted the Teen-Aid abstinence-only program, the school's pregnancy rate dropped from 147 to 20 in a two-year period.

An abstinence-only program for girls in Washington, D.C. has seen only one of four hundred girls become pregnant. Elayne Bennett, director of "Best Friends," says that between twenty and seventy pregnancies are common for this age-group in the District of Columbia.

Nathan Hale Middle School near Chicago adopted the abstinence-only program "Project Taking Charge" to combat its pregnancy rate among eighth-graders. Although adults were skeptical, the school graduated three pregnancy-free classes in a row.

Abstinence works. That is the message that needs to be spread to parents, teachers, and school boards. Teenagers will respond to this message, and we need to teach this message in the classroom.

Third, abstinence prevents sexually transmitted diseases (STDs). After more than three decades, the sexual revolution has taken lots of prisoners.

Before 1960, doctors were concerned about only two STDs: syphilis and gonorrhea. Today there are more than twenty significant STDs, ranging from the relatively harmless to the fatal. Twelve million Americans are newly infected each year, and 63 percent of these new infections are in people under twenty-five years of age. Eighty percent of those infected with an STD have absolutely no symptoms.

Doctors warn that if a person has sexual intercourse with another individual, he or she is not only having sexual intercourse with that individual but with every person with whom that individual might have had intercourse for the last ten years and all the people with whom they had intercourse. If that is true, then consider the case of one sixteen-year-old girl who was responsible for 218 cases of gonorrhea and more than 300 cases of syphilis. According to the reporter, this illustrates the rampant transmission of STDs through multiple sex partners. "The girl has sex with sixteen men. Those men had sex with other people who had sex with other people. The number of contacts finally added up to 1,660." As one person interviewed in the story asked, "What if the girl had had AIDS instead of gonorrhea or syphilis? You probably would have had 1,000 dead people by now."

Abstinence prevents the spread of STDs while safe sex programs do not. Condoms are not always effective even when they are used correctly and consistently, and most sexually active people do not even use them correctly and consistently. Sex education programs have begun to promote "outercourse" instead of intercourse, but many STDs can be spread even through this method, and, as stated, outercourse almost always leads to intercourse. Abstinence is the only way to prevent the spread of a sexually transmitted disease.

Fourth, abstinence prevents emotional scars. Abstinence speakers relate dozens and dozens of stories of young people who wish they had postponed sex until marriage. Sex is the most intimate form of bonding known to the human race, and it is a special gift to be given to one's spouse. Unfortunately, too many throw it away and are later filled with feelings of regret.

Surveys of young adults show that those who engaged in sexual activity regret their earlier promiscuity and wish they had been virgins on their wedding night. Even secular agencies that promote a safe-sex approach acknowledge that sex brings regrets. A Roper poll conducted in association with SIECUS (Sexuality Information and Education Council of the United States) of high schoolers found that 62 percent of the sexually experienced girls said they "should have waited."

Society is ready for the abstinence message, and it needs to be promoted widely. Anyone walking on the Washington Mall in July 1993 could not miss the acres of "True Love Waits" pledge cards signed by over 200,000 teenagers. The campaign, begun by the Southern Baptist Convention, provided a brief but vivid display of the desire by teenagers to stand for purity and promote abstinence. For every teenager who signed a card pledging abstinence, there are no doubt dozens of others who plan to do the same.

Teenagers want and need to hear the message of abstinence. They want to promote the message of abstinence. Their health, and even their lives, are at stake.

Toward a Sexually Healthy America: Roadblocks Imposed by the Federal Government's Abstinence-Only-Until-Marriage Education Program

A Brief History of Abstinence-Only-Until-Marriage Education

Government funding of abstinence-only-until-marriage programs is not new. In fact, the federal government has poured large sums of money into such programs for the past 20 years.

AFLA: the birthplace of abstinence-only programs   The U.S. Office of Population Affairs began administering the Adolescent Family Life Act (AFLA) in 1981. This program was designed to prevent teen pregnancy by promoting chastity and self-discipline.[1] During its first year, AFLA received $11 million in federal funds. In fiscal year 2000, AFLA received $19 million.

AFLA's early programs taught abstinence as the only option for teens and often promoted specific religious values. As a result, the American Civil Liberties Union filed suit in 1983 charging that AFLA violated the separation of church and state as defined in the U.S. Constitution. In 1985, a U.S. district judge found AFLA unconstitutional. On appeal in 1988, the U.S. Supreme Court reversed that decision and remanded the case to a lower court.[2]

Finally, an out-of-court settlement in 1993 stipulated that AFLA-funded sexuality education programs must: (1) not include religious references, (2) be medically accurate, (3) respect the "principle of self-determination" regarding contraceptive referral for teenagers, and (4) not allow grantees to use church sanctuaries for their programs or to give presentations in parochial schools during school hours.[3] Within these limitations, AFLA continues to fund abstinence-only programs today.

Abstinence-only-until-marriage education as defined in AFLA has been taught for over two decades and yet there is still no peer-reviewed research that proves it is effective in changing adolescents' behavior. To the contrary, a meta-evaluation of AFLA program evaluations found them "barely adequate" to "completely inadequate."[4]

Congress institutes similar programs through Doolittle amendment
The first Congressional attempt to censor sexuality education using an abstinence-only provision came in 1994 during the reauthorization of the Elementary and Secondary Education Act. Representative John Doolittle (R-CA) introduced an amendment to limit the content of HIV-prevention and sexuality education in school-based programs.

Fortunately, four federal statutes required alterations to the Doolittle amendment. The Department of Education Organization Act (Section 103a), the Elementary and Secondary Education Act (Section 14512), Goals 2000 (Section 319 (b)), and the General Education Provisions Act (Section 438) all prohibited the federal government from prescribing state and local school curriculum standards.

Proponents of abstinence-only programs learned from this that even though they could not legally restrict state and local education programs that they could restrict and define the scope of state and local health policy and funding. They applied their new-found lesson in 1996.

Federal entitlement program promotes abstinence-only-until-marriage
That year, the federal government attached a provision to the popular welfare-reform law establishing a federal entitlement program for abstinence-only-until-marriage education.

This entitlement program, Section 510(b) of Title V of the Social Security Act, funneled $50 million per year for five years into the states. Those states that choose to accept Section 510(b) funds are required to match every four federal dollars with three state-raised dollars and then disperse the funds for educational activities.[5]

Programs that use the funds are required to adhere to a strict eight-point definition, which, among other things, requires them to teach that "sexual activity outside of marriage is likely to have harmful psychological and physical effects."[6] The section 510(b) abstinence-only-until-marriage funds are up for reauthorization in 2001.

Other federal abstinence legislation Funding for unproven abstinence-only-until-marriage education has increased nearly 3,000 percent since the federal entitlement program was created in 1996.[7] In November 1999, opponents of comprehensive sexuality education, family planning, and reproductive rights began a process that successfully secured an additional 50 million federal dollars for abstinence-only-until-marriage programs over the next two years. Although these funds are not part of Section 510(b), they are only available for programs that conform to the strict eight-point definition in 510(b).[8]

These new funds will be awarded directly to state and local organizations by the Maternal and Child Health Bureau through a competitive grant process instead of through state block grants as is the case for 510(b) funds. Many viewed this decision as an attempt by conservative lawmakers to control the funding and prevent money from supporting media campaigns, youth development, and after-school programs that they saw as diluting the abstinence message.[9]

Sexuality Education: Definitions and Comparisons

This section compares two contrasting approaches to teaching young people about their sexuality: *comprehensive sexuality education* and *abstinence-only-until-marriage education*. The differences point to the real public health threat imposed by current federal policy.

Comprehensive sexuality education   These programs emphasize the benefits of abstinence while also teaching about contraception and disease-prevention methods. Ideally, they start in kindergarten and continue through twelfth grade. They provide developmentally appropriate information on a broad variety of topics related to sexuality such as sexual development, reproductive health, interpersonal relationships, affection, intimacy, body image, and gender roles. Comprehensive programs provide opportunities for students to develop communication, decision-making, and other personal skills.

Abstinence-only-until-marriage   These programs, many of which are federally-funded, teach abstinence from all sexual activity as the only morally correct option for unmarried young people. They teach that "a mutually faithful monogamous relationship in the context of marriage is the expected standard of human sexual activity" and that "sexual activity outside of the context of marriage is likely to have harmful psychological and physical effects."[10] These programs, also referred to as abstinence-only programs, censor information on contraception for the prevention of sexually transmitted diseases and unintended pregnancies.

Abstinence-only-until-marriage programs and curricula are, by their very nature, very limited in scope. They typically limit discussion to sexually transmitted diseases, unplanned pregnancies, contraceptive failure rates, and the need to refrain from sexual activity outside of marriage. They often fail to mention basic sexual health information relating to puberty and reproduction and contain no information about pregnancy and disease-prevention methods other than abstinence. Consequently, these abstinence-only-until-marriage programs deny young people the information necessary to make informed, responsible sexual decisions. Some, however, go beyond withholding information by using fear as an educational tool. These programs, often referred to as fear-based, are designed to control young people's sexual behavior by instilling fear, shame, and guilt. They often contain biased information about gender, family structure, sexual orientation, and abortion. . . .

What Is Wrong With Abstinence-Only-Until-Marriage Education Requirements?

SIECUS, Advocates for Youth, and other organizations who support comprehensive sexuality education also support teaching young people about abstinence. They do not, however, support teaching young people *only* about abstinence or using fear and negative messages to motivate behavior.

One of the four primary goals of sexuality education—as set forth by the National Guidelines Task Force, a group of leading health, education, and sexuality professionals—is to "help young people exercise responsibility regarding sexual relationships, including abstinence [and] how to resist pressures to become prematurely involved in sexual intercourse." SIECUS' *Guidelines for Comprehensive Sexuality Education; K–12,* which was created by the Task Force, includes 36 sexual health topics. Abstinence is one of these topics.[11]

SIECUS and Advocates for Youth believe that abstinence is a healthy choice for adolescents and that premature involvement in sexual behavior poses risks. However, data has consistently shown that 50 percent of high school students have engaged in sexual intercourse.[12]

Whether adults agree with young people's actions or not, they cannot ignore the fact that millions of teenagers in the United States are engaging in a range of sexual behavior.[13] That is why all young people need the information, skills, and access to services necessary to make and carry out informed, responsible decisions about their sexuality.

Federally-funded abstinence-only-until-marriage education programs deny young people this very information. In fact, they must adhere to a strict eight-point definition, many aspects of which are in direct opposition to the goals and tenets of comprehensive sexuality education. While the law does not require programs to focus equally on each aspect of the definition, it does state that a federally-funded project "may not be inconsistent with any aspect of the abstinence definition."[14] While some aspects of the law's definition are not objectionable, others run counter to common sense, research, and genuine public health realities and responsibilities. The following section highlights some of the more problematic points of the eight-point definition.

> *Federal Requirement B ". . . teaches that abstinence from sexual activity outside marriage is the expected standard for all school age children."*

Although adults may want this as a standard, it is far from accurate in describing the world of today's teenagers. The reality is that sexual behavior is almost universal among American adolescents. A majority of them date, over 85 percent have had a boyfriend or a girlfriend and have kissed someone romantically, and nearly 80 percent have engaged in deep kissing.[15]

The majority of young people move from kissing to more intimate sexual behaviors during their teen years. Seventy-two percent of teens report "touching above the waist," 54 percent report "touching below the waist," 26 percent report engaging in oral sex, and 4 percent report engaging in anal sex.[16]

According to data from the most recent *Youth Risk Behavior Surveillance System* of the Centers for Disease Control and Prevention (CDC), 50 percent of high school students have had sexual intercourse, a rate virtually unchanged since the study began in 1990.[17] A similar survey of college students found that 80 percent of students 18 to 24 years of age had engaged in sexual intercourse.[18]

In addition, a recent study found that even those young people who remain virgins during their teen years engage in some forms of sexual behavior. Nearly one third of teens who identified themselves as virgins in that study had engaged in heterosexual masturbation of or by a partner, 10 percent had participated in oral sex, and one percent had engaged in anal intercourse.[19]

Teens are engaging in a variety of sexual behaviors every day that place them at risk for unintended pregnancy and STDs, including HIV. There is no research to support the notion that they will stop sexual behavior simply because adults ask them. Yet, the federal definition of abstinence-only-until-marriage education clearly prohibits programs from discussing pregnancy and disease-prevention methods other than abstinence. Such education denies teens the information they need to make informed responsible sexual decisions.

Federal Requirement C ". . . teaches that abstinence from sexual activity is the only certain way to avoid out-of-wedlock pregnancy, sexually transmitted diseases, and other associated health problems."

On the surface, it is hard to argue with this statement. The *Guidelines* state that "abstinence from sexual intercourse is the most effective method of preventing pregnancies and STDs/HIV."[20] However, this point clearly prevents funded programs from discussing the effectiveness of condoms and contraception in preventing unintended pregnancy and disease transmission. In fact, many abstinence-only-until-marriage programs discuss methods of contraception only in terms of their failure rate. After learning that abstinence is the "only certain way" to avoid pregnancy and disease and that condoms and contraceptive methods are not reliable, young people who do become sexually active are less likely to practice prevention techniques.

Some strict abstinence-only-until-marriage programs actually discourage the use of contraception, especially condoms. These programs give teens exaggerated and outdated information about effectiveness and tell them that correct condom use is difficult. In reality, research has shown that using a condom for protection from HIV is 10,000 times safer than not using a condom. But people need to learn how to use condoms correctly if they are going to protect themselves.[21] The CDC states that "studies of hundreds of couples show that consistent condom use is possible when people have the skills and motivations to do so." The CDC pointed out, however, that "people who are skeptical about condoms aren't as likely to use them—but that doesn't mean they won't have sex."[22]

Programs that teach students that condoms or contraception do not work will not necessarily prevent students from having sexual intercourse but will likely prevent them from using protection. These students will, therefore, put themselves at risk for STDs and unintended pregnancy.

In 1979, fewer than 50 percent of adolescents used contraception at first intercourse. In 1988, more than 65 percent used them. In 1990, more than 70 percent used them.[23] Unfortunately, abstinence-only-until-marriage education is likely to reverse these significant strides that youth in the United States have made toward safer sexual behavior in the past two decades.

Federal Requirement D ". . . teaches that a mutually faithful monogamous relationship in the context of marriage is the expected standard of human sexual activity."

Again, while members of Congress or society might wish this as a standard, it is clearly not true in American culture. The concept of chastity until marriage is unrealistic in an age when young people are reaching puberty earlier than ever before, when half of high school students have engaged in sexual intercourse,[24] when 80 percent of college students 18 to 24 years of age have engaged in sexual intercourse,[25] and when the median age of first marriage is 25.9 for men and 24 for women.[26]

A brief look at Americans' behavior indicates that this "expected standard" is highly unlikely in American society. The vast majority of Americans begin having sexual relationships in their teens, fewer than seven percent of men and 20 percent of women 18 to 50 years old were virgins when they were married, and only 10 percent of adult men and 22 percent of adult women report their first sexual intercourse was with their spouse.[27] It is likely this "standard" was never true in America. A third of all Pilgrim brides were pregnant when they were married.[28]

Federally-funded abstinence-only-until-marriage programs are required to teach young people that all unmarried individuals (both adults and youth) *must* remain celibate. While this is a value held by many people in America, it is clearly not universally accepted as truth. Today, there are almost 80 million American adults who are classified as single because they have either delayed marriage, have decided to remain single, have divorced, are widowed, or have entered into gay or lesbian partnerships.[29] It is unreasonable to expect these adults to adhere to this "standard" and it is inaccurate and misleading to tell students that adults are adhering to it.

This part of the definition also seems to assume that all people have an equal chance or desire to enter into a "mutually faithful monogamous relationship in the context of marriage." Many people choose not to marry. Others—like gays and lesbians—are legally barred from marrying. Students enrolled in abstinence-only-until-marriage programs are now essentially learning that the sexual relationships of these people—whether same-sex or opposite-sex—are in conflict with society's standards.

Finally, this part of the definition may prove particularly harmful to young people who are or have been sexually abused. It requires telling these students that the behaviors in which they have involuntarily participated go against society's "expected standard." Such statements are likely to produce additional feelings of guilt and shame in these abused individuals.

Federal Requirement E ". . . teaches that sexual activity outside of marriage is likely to have harmful psychological and physical effects."

There is no sound public health data to support this statement. It is true that unprotected sexual activity can lead to unplanned pregnancies, STDs, and HIV. It is also true that intimate relationships can be harmful for some people. However, the reality is that the majority of people have had sexual relationships prior to marriage with no negative repercussions.

> *Federal Requirement F ". . . teaches that bearing children out-of-wedlock is likely to have harmful consequences for the child, the child's parents, and society."*

In order to comply with this part of the definition, abstinence-only-until-marriage programs must present one family structure as morally correct and beneficial to society. In reality, any American classroom is likely to have children of never-married or divorced parents as well as children of gay, lesbian, and bisexual parents who can never legally marry. Telling these students that their families are the cause of societal problems will likely alienate them and could cause negative feelings about themselves and their families.

In sum, much of this eight-point definition written by Congressional staff under the influence of special interest groups has no basis in public health research.

Research Supports Comprehensive Sexuality Education

Abstinence-only-until-marriage education relies on the notion that young people will "just say no" if they are told to do so. Proponents of this type of education conclude that this is the only way to encourage young people to delay sexual activity until marriage, and consequently, to avoid becoming involved in a pregnancy, infected with an STD, or even emotionally hurt by a failed romance.

There is no proof that these claims are true. There are no published studies in the professional literature that show that abstinence-only programs will result in young people delaying the initiation of sexual intercourse.

To date, there are six published studies of abstinence-only programs. None have found consistent and significant program effects on delaying the onset of intercourse. In fact, at least one has provided strong evidence that the program did not delay the onset of intercourse.[30]

Proponents of abstinence-only-until-marriage programs often conduct their own in-house evaluations and cite them as proof that their programs are effective. However, outside experts have found them inadequate, methodologically unsound, or inconclusive based on methodological limitations.[31]

The CDC's *Research to Classroom Project* identifies curricula that have *shown evidence* of reducing sexual risk behaviors.[32] A recent paper written by the White House Office of National AIDS Policy points out that "none of the curricula on the current list of programs uses an 'abstinence-only' approach." The paper goes on to say that ". . . it is a matter of grave concern that there is such a large incentive to adopt unproven abstinence-only approaches."[33]

Comprehensive sexuality education is effective   On the other hand, numerous studies and evaluations published in peer-reviewed literature suggest that comprehensive sexuality education is an effective strategy to help young people delay their involvement in sexual intercourse.

A review commissioned by the Joint United Nations Programme on HIV/AIDS (UNAIDS) looked at 22 HIV-prevention and comprehensive sexuality education programs and found that they delayed the onset of sexual activity, reduced the number of sexual partners among sexually active youth, and reduced the rates of unintended pregnancy and STDs.[34]

A report titled *No Easy Answers,* written by Dr. Douglas Kirby, one of the leading researchers in the field of sexuality education, also considered evaluations of HIV-prevention and sexuality education programs—both abstinence-only-until-marriage and comprehensive. It concluded that HIV-prevention and sexuality education programs that cover both abstinence *and* contraception can delay the onset of sexual intercourse, reduce the frequency of sexual intercourse, and reduce the number of sexual partners. It also found that many of these programs significantly increased the use of condoms and other forms of contraception.[35]

Critics of comprehensive sexuality education often suggest that giving youth information about sexuality and contraception will encourage them to engage in sexual activity earlier and more often. However, research has consistently found that "sexuality and HIV education programs that include the discussion of condoms and contraception do not increase sexual intercourse, either by hastening the onset of intercourse, increasing the frequency of intercourse, or increasing the number of sexual partners."[36]

The conclusion reached by these studies is echoed in a review by the World Health Organization of evaluations of 35 sexuality education programs. The review concluded that the programs that are most effective in reducing sexual risk-taking behaviors among young people are programs that provide information on abstinence, contraception, and STD prevention.[37]

According to Dr. Kirby, effective programs:

- focus narrowly on reducing one or more sexual behaviors that lead to unintended pregnancy or STDs/HIV infection
- are based on theoretical approaches that have been successful in influencing other health-related risky behaviors
- give a clear message by continually reinforcing a clear stance on particular behaviors
- provide basic, accurate information about the risks of unprotected intercourse and methods of avoiding unprotected intercourse
- include activities that address social pressures associated with sexual behavior
- provide modeling and the practice of communication, negotiation, and refusal skills
- incorporate behavioral goals, teaching methods, and material that are appropriate to the age, sexual experience, and culture of the students
- last a sufficient length of time to complete important activities adequately
- select teachers or peers who believe in the program they are implementing and then provide training for those individuals[38]

There is no credible evidence that a "just say no" attitude toward teen sexual activity will work. On the other hand, study after study clearly support an approach to sexuality education that includes teaching young people about abstinence, contraception, and disease-prevention methods.

EVALUATIONS SUPPORT COMPREHENSIVE SEXUALITY EDUCATION

Reviews of published evaluations of sexuality education, HIV-prevention, and adolescent pregnancy prevention programs have consistently found that such programs:

- do not encourage teens to start having sexual intercourse
- do not increase the frequency with which teens have intercourse
- do not increase the number of a person's sexual partners

Instead many of these programs:

- delay the onset of intercourse
- reduce the frequency of intercourse
- reduce the number of sexual partners
- increase condom or contraceptive use

References

1. R. Saul, "Whatever Happened to the Adolescent Family Life Act?," *Guttmacher Report on Public Policy,* vol. 1, no. 2, April 1998.
2. Ibid.
3. D. Daley, "Exclusive Purpose: Abstinence-Only Proponents Create Entitlement in Welfare Reform," *SIECUS Report,* April/May 1997.
4. C. Bartels, et al., *Adolescent Abstinence Promotion Programs: An Evaluation of Evaluations.* (Paper presented at the Annual Meeting of the American Public Health Association, Nov. 18, 1996, New York, NY.)
5. Daley, "Exclusive Purpose" *SIECUS Report,* April/May 1997.
6. Section 510, Title V of the Social Security Act (Public Law 104–193).
7. C. Dailard, "Fueled by Campaign Promises, Drive Intensifies to Boost Abstinence-Only Education Funds," *The Guttmacher Report on Public Policy,* vol. 3, no. 2, April 2000.
8. W. Smith, "Public Policy Update: More Federal Funds Targeted for Abstinence-Only-Until-Marriage Programs," *SIECUS Report,* June/July 2000.
9. Ibid.
10. Section 510, Title V of the Social Security Act (Public Law 104–193).
11. National Guidelines Task Force, *Guidelines for Comprehensive Sexuality Education: Kindergarten–12th Grade* (New York: SIECUS, 1991, 1996).
12. "Youth Risk Behavior Surveillance System—United States, 1999," *Morbidity and Mortality Weekly Report,* June 9, 2000, vol. 49, no. SS-5.

13. Ibid.

14. Section 510, Title V of the Social Security Act (Public Law 104–193).

15. R. Coles and F. Stokes, *Sex and the American Teenager* (New York: Harper and Row, 1985); Roper Starch Worldwide, *Teens Talk About Sex: Adolescent Sexuality in the 90s* (New York: Sexuality Information and Education Council of the United States, 1994).

16. Ibid.

17. "Youth Risk Behavior Surveillance System—United States, 1999," *Morbidity and Mortality Weekly Report,* June 9, 2000, vol. 49, no. SS-5.

18. "Youth Risk Behavior Surveillance System—National College Health Risk Behavior Survey, 1995," *Morbidity and Mortality Weekly Report,* Nov. 14, 1997, vol. 46, no. SS-6.

19. M. A. Schuster, R. M. Bell, D. E. Kanouse, "The Sexual Practices of Adolescent Virgins: Genital Sexual Activities of High School Students Who Have Never Had Vaginal Intercourse," *American Journal of Public Health,* 1996, vol. 86, pp. 1570–76.

20. National Guidelines Task Force, *Guidelines for Comprehensive Sexuality Education: Kindergarten–12th Grade* (New York: SIECUS, 1991, 1996).

21. R. F. Carey, et al., "Effectiveness of Latex Condoms As a Barrier to Human Immunodeficiency Virus-sized Particles under the Conditions of Simulated Use," *Sexually Transmitted Diseases,* vol. 19, no. 4, p. 230.

22. Centers for Disease Control and Prevention (CDC), "Questions and Answers about Male Latex Condoms to Prevent Sexual Transmission of HIV," *CDC Update* (Centers for Disease Control and Prevention: Atlanta, GA: April 1997).

23. D. Haffner, editor, *Facing Facts: Sexual Health for America's Adolescents* (New York: Sexuality Information and Education Council of the United States, 1994).

24. "Youth Risk Behavior Surveillance System—United States, 1999," *Morbidity and Mortality Weekly Report,* June 9, 2000, vol. 49, no. SS-5.

25. The Alan Guttmacher Institute, *Sex and America's Teenagers* (New York: The Alan Guttmacher Institute, 1994).

26. U.S. Bureau of the Census, Statistical Abstract of the US 1998 (118th edition), Washington, DC, 1998. p. 112.

27. E. Laumann, et al., *The Social Organization of Sexuality—Sexual Practices in the United States* (Chicago: The University of Chicago Press, 1994).

28. J. D'Emilio and E. Freedman, *Intimate Matters: A History of Sexuality in America* (New York: Harper and Row, 1988).

29. U.S. Census Bureau. Marital Status and Living Arrangements of Adults 18 Years Old and Over, March 1998.

30. D. Kirby, *No Easy Answers* (Washington, DC: National Campaign to Prevent Teen Pregnancy, 1997).

31. C. Bartels, et al., *Federally Funded Abstinence-Only Sex Education Programs: A Meta-Evaluation.* Paper presented at the Fifth Biennial Meeting of the Society for Research on Adolescence, San Diego, CA, Feb. 11, 1994; B. Wilcox, et al., *Adolescent Abstinence Promotion Programs: An Evaluation of Evaluations.* Paper presented at the Annual Meeting of the American Public Health Association, New York, NY, Nov. 18, 1996; D. Kirby, M. Korpi, et al., *Evaluation of* Education Now and Babies Later (ENABL): *Final Report* (Berkeley, CA: University of California, School of Social Welfare, Family Welfare Research Group, 1995); D. Kirby, *No Easy Answers.*

32.   Office of National AIDS Policy, The White House, *Youth and HIV/AIDS 2000: A New American Agenda* (Washington, DC: Government Printing Office, 2000), p. 14. (Individuals can download the report as a PDF file at http://www.whitehouse.gov/ONAP/youth_report1.pdf).

33.   Office of National AIDS Policy, *The White House, Youth and HIV/AIDS 2000,* p. 14.

34.   Joint United Nations Programme on HIV/AIDS, "Sexual Health Education Does Lead to Safer Sexual Behaviour," press release, Oct. 22, 1997.

35.   D. Kirby, *No Easy Answers: Research Findings on Programs to Reduce Teen Pregnancy* (Washington, DC: National Campaign to Prevent Teen Pregnancy, 1997), p. 27.

36.   D. Kirby, *No Easy Answers,* p. 31.

37.   A. Grunseit and S. Kippax, *Effects of Sex Education on Young People's Sexual Behavior* (Geneva: World Health Organization, 1993).

38.   D. Kirby, "What Does the Research Say about Sexuality Education?," *Educational Leadership,* Oct. 2000, p. 74.

POSTSCRIPT

Is Abstinence-Only Sex Education Effective?

As we look at the sex education controversy, all points of view can resonate with us in one way or another. Abstinence-only sex education can provide a solid way to encourage abstinence without sending any mixed messages. Comprehensive sex education can provide knowledge to those who choose to have sex about how to do so in a safer manner, but it may send a message to teens that it is acceptable to engage in sexual activity at their age.

So many questions are raised by this debate. Is it appropriate to make the moral judgment that teaching students abstinence-only is the best choice? Where do the individual religious and moral values of the students fit in? Will teaching about birth control methods and STD prevention give students a false assurance about their safety when engaging in sexual activity?

As a society, we need to remember that schools are not the only place where children receive sex education. All one has to do is listen to students during lunchtime at an elementary school, middle school, or high school to know that they are hearing about sex from their peers beginning at very early ages. Turn on the TV, and on nearly every show you will observe some sexual overtone. The Internet is full of false and/or graphic information about sex that is easily accessible by children. It is not enough for our sex education classes to teach about sexuality, whether through abstinence-only or comprehensive sex education programs. Schools need programs that will empower our children to be able to identify and combat the false information that they are bombarded with every day.

Suggested Readings

Kirby, D. (2000). What does the research say about sexuality education? *Educational Leadership,* 74.

National Guidelines Task Force. (1996). *Guidelines for comprehensive sexuality education: Kindergarten–12th grade.* New York: SIECUS.

The Kaiser Family Foundation. (2000). *Sex education in America: A view from inside the nation's classrooms.* Menlo Park, CA: The Kaiser Family Foundation.

ISSUE 17

Can Memories of Childhood Sexual Abuse Be Recovered?

YES: May Benatar, from "Running Away From Sexual Abuse: Denial Revisited," *Families in Society: The Journal of Contemporary Human Services* (May 1995)

NO: Susan P. Robbins, from "Wading Through the Muddy Waters of Recovered Memory," *Families in Society: The Journal of Contemporary Human Services* (October 1995)

ISSUE SUMMARY

YES: May Benatar, a clinical social worker, argues that the mass media and contemporary culture question the accuracy and truthfulness of survivors of sexual abuse. By doing this, the long-term effects of these abuses tend to be minimized.

NO: Susan P. Robbins, an associate professor of social work, contends that the reason some professionals are skeptical of recovered memories is that there is no research that supports the accuracy of recovered memory. She cautions that the indiscriminate acceptance of recovered memories can lead to a serious backlash of disbelief when legitimate cases of abuse are reported.

$\mathbf{T}$ here has been a definite shift in societal thinking about child abuse during the past 20 years. Historically, when an adult would come forth with an account of sexual abuse that was purported to have occurred decades earlier, these accounts were likely to have been considered by mental health professionals as fantasies. In the past decade or so, both the mass media and the helping professions have been much more likely to accept these allegations, which come to be known as recovered memories of past sexual abuse, as true. It is easy to imagine not only the problems for the person recalling such difficult memories but also the problems that families have had to endure as a result of these disclosures. One controversial question is how valid are allegations that are based upon repressed memories from years ago?

Few people would argue with the notion that human memory is not always accurate; our memories do indeed fail us at times. It has been documented in the literature, however, that traumatic memory is physiologically encoded differently than normal memory in one's brain. If so, should we assume that traumatic experiences are more indelibly etched and can be retrieved with greater accuracy than normal memory? Or is it possible that memories of abuse are not as easily recalled due to the trauma involved? Some mental health professionals believe that therapists can suggest memories to clients and that these memories can become integrated into the client's memory as if they actually happened when they, in fact, did not.

In the following selections, May Benatar argues that we, as a society, do not pay enough attention to these heinous past traumas. Susan P. Robbins contends that perhaps we accept these allegations as fact too readily.

May Benatar **YES**

Running Away From Sexual Abuse: Denial Revisited

After a period of increased professional and public awareness of how pervasive the sexual maltreatment of children is in our society, we appear to be in danger of vaulting away from hard-won insights into this major public health issue. Both propounding and expressing the prejudices of the culture, the press and other media have taken to indicting the veracity of traumatic memories of survivors of sexual abuse, minimizing the toxic long-term effects of the sexual maltreatment of children, and casting doubt on both the skill and good intentions of clinicians treating both child victims and adult survivors. We have seen front-page articles on the purported "false" memories of adult survivors of abuse; examples of "false" accusations of innocent parents, grandparents, or teachers; or speculations that therapists, many of whom are survivors themselves, intentionally or unintentionally suggest events to their patients that never took place.

A 1993 *Newsweek* cover photograph showed a middle-age couple convicted of molesting their grandchildren. The caption asks: "When does the fight to protect our kids go too far?" Does this strange juxtaposition of material imply that convicting child molesters is "going too far?" The article inside (Shapiro, 1993) reviews a few recent court cases and one reversal and addresses the issue of child testimony; the author asks whether we are panicking over child abuse. Is criminal prosecution tantamount to panic? And if it is, is the abuse of children not worthy of such a response?

In the *New Yorker*, Wright (1993a, 1993b) wrote a two-part article on the case of a Washington state deputy sheriff, who, after being accused of child abuse by his two daughters, confessed to sexually abusing them, prostituting them to family friends, and being part of a satanic cult. The case unraveled when it was discovered that at least some of the accusations and confessions by both parents resulted from overzealous questioning and suggestions by police interrogators on what were alleged to be highly suggestible subjects. The article clearly implies that this case represents one of many instances of modern-day witch hunts—the innocent "witches" in this case being those accused of perpetrating unthinkable crimes such as ritual sexual abuse, torture, and murder.

In *Mother Jones*, a well-regarded if somewhat off-beat publication, Watters (1993) also expressed concern about false memories and false accusations in a report of a young woman's delayed discovery of childhood abuse. The woman entered therapy following a severe depressive episode and while in therapy recovered memories of sexual abuse. Although the facts of the case neither exculpate the accused nor affirm the victim's accusations, the author uses this case to propose that "a substantial segment of the therapy community has charged ahead, creating a *growth* industry around the concept of recovered memories."

Even Carol Tavris (1993), a noted feminist author, cast a skeptical eye on what she termed the "incest-survivor machine," an umbrella term for therapists working with adult survivors, writers of self-help books for survivors, and the grass-roots recovery movement of adult survivors.

For clinicians working with patients to address the post-traumatic effects of childhood sexual abuse and for adult survivors struggling to take their own stories seriously and understand the difficulties of their adult lives as sequelae of and adaptation to violations that occurred during childhood, this emphasis on the "hype" of sexual abuse is deeply troubling.

Child Abuse: Past and Present Findings

The reality of child abuse is well established. Why then is it currently acceptable, even fashionable, to doubt the victims, those who prosecute for them, and those who treat their post-traumatic illnesses? This backlash against sexual-abuse survivors has social, cultural, political, and psychological roots. One reading is that this backlash is a response to the evolution in law regarding the issue of incest—an evolution that now allows some adult survivors to seek legal redress many years, even decades, after the commission of crimes. Another reason for this backlash may be related to the cultural mysogyny that Faludi (1991) documents in her book *Backlash*, which refers to the social forces that thwart the gains that women have achieved in society. On another level of analysis, we may understand this phenomenon of denial of social realities as "cultural dissociation." As a society we are unable to accept the reality of the cruelty, sadism, neglect, and narcissism that adults inflict upon children. In a world where some people still debate the reality of Nazi death camps, it is not surprising that we have difficulties acknowledging that 1 of every 3 girls and 1 of 7 to 10 boys are "used" by an adult in a manner that brings great harm to them for the rest of their lives.

The epidemiology of child sexual abuse has been carefully documented. Kinsey found in the early 1950s that 24% of his female sample of 4,000 women reported sexual abuse in childhood (before the age of puberty) (Brownmiller, 1975). Dozens of studies have confirmed this finding. Thirty years later, Russell (1986) carefully surveyed a nonclinical population of nearly 1,000 women. She reported that 38% of the sample reported being molested before the age of 18 and 28% before puberty. In addition, she found that most abusers are known to the child as trusted individuals who occupy a position of authority over the child.

In another significant study, Herman and Schatzow (1987) discussed recall of traumatic memories from childhood often dissociated by the child in an effort to maintain secrecy and safety. Fifty-three female patients in group psychotherapy reported delayed recall of traumatic memory; 74% of the women confirmed their memories of abuse by obtaining independent corroborating evidence—physical evidence, diaries, pictures, confirmation by perpetrators and/or corroboration by other family members who had also been victimized. This study appears to strengthen Russell's and Kinsey's data. Even those with delayed recall, when seeking confirmation of the reality of their memories many years after the fact, are able to confirm the memory. To my knowledge, no comparable study demonstrates *false* recall of childhood-abuse memories.

Interestingly, the conflict between the reality of child abuse and the voices of disbelief and disavowal is not unique to the 1990s; a century ago western psychiatry experienced a similar struggle and process. Masson (1984), in *The Assault on Truth*, presented important work done in 19th-century France regarding the criminal brutalization and sexual abuse of children. In setting the stage for his explanation of why Freud first adopted and later abandoned the "seduction theory" to explain the origins of hysterical neurosis, Masson discusses child abuse in Europe during that period. Forensic psychiatrists uncovered shocking facts about child abuse. Ambrose Tardieu, a professor and dean of forensic medicine at the University of Paris and president of the Academy of Medicine in Paris in 1860, published "A Medico-Legal Study of Cruelty and Brutal Treatment Inflicted on Children." He presented case after case of detailed medical evidence indicating severe child abuse, including the sexual abuse of children. He indicated that the phenomenon was not rare and that perpetrators were often parents and that victims were often very young and primarily girls.

Paul Brouardel, Tardieu's successor to the chair of legal medicine in Paris and also a contemporary of Freud, described perpetrators as "excellent family men" who were often the fathers of the victims. Brouardel was a collaborator of Jean-Martin Charcot, a neurologist who demonstrated the efficacy of hypnosis in the treatment of psychiatric patients, particularly female hysterics. Freud was fascinated by Charcot's work and came to Paris to study with him. Masson argues that Freud and his contemporaries were more than likely aware of the work of Tardieu, Brouardel, and other forensic psychiatrists in France through their studies with Charcot. Freud's early struggles to understand the underpinnings of neurosis suggest his awareness of the traumatic origins of psychic disturbance as well as the influence that the French pioneers had on his clinical awareness. In the late 1890s Freud (1984) wrote movingly and persuasively in *The Aetiology of Hysteria* about 18 cases of hysterical neurosis in which an early experience of sexual abuse had led to hysterical symptoms in adult life—symptoms similar to what we categorize today as post-traumatic stress disorder or dissociative disorder.

However, it was Pierre Janet, another visitor to Charcot's seminars, who developed both a complex theoretical understanding and efficacious treatment model for hysteria. Janet published many of his findings the year before

Freud's *Aetiology of Hysteria* appeared, but unlike Freud he held fast to the trauma model that Freud renounced. Janet described many cases of what we have come to understand as dissociative disorders and multiple personality disorder. Janet understood his patients' symptoms, much as trained clinicians do today, as ingenious and creative adaptations to overwhelming childhood stress such as physical and/or sexual abuse. He saw hysterical symptoms, not as compromise formations of drive derivatives or expressions of drive conflicts, but rather as fossils from the past, derivatives of traumatic memory, communications of early betrayals and overwhelming affects (van der Kolk & van der Hart, 1989).

Yet for most of the 20th century, Janet was *not* studied and *not* employed in our attempts to understand mental life. Freud's development of psychoanalysis obliterated Janet's work. To read Janet today, 100 years later, is to be struck with how little modern trauma psychology and our understandings of traumatic memory can add to his understandings, how clearly he explicated what we have come to rediscover in the past decade and a half, and how brilliantly he anticipated modern findings on the psychophysiology of memory.

Herman (1992) and others have proposed that Freud and his students moved away from trauma theory or the "seduction theory," because the zeitgeist of the time and place could not support such conclusions. Earlier in the century, in Tardieu's and Charcot's France, the political atmosphere was one of reform: challenges to the monarchy and the church enabled a movement toward understanding mental illness as a rational, not magical, pursuit. They viewed mental illness as a sequela of early experience that could be understood and addressed by science. These sociopolitical forces ushered in an era of more humane treatment of the mentally ill that approached mental illness as trauma based. Freud's science grew in different soil—Viennese soil—where trauma-based theory was unable to take root.

For a brief period in the 1800s, clinicians and students of forensic psychiatry knew that many children were severely abused by their families and that such abuse led to dramatic effects in the mental health of adults. They also understood effective treatment of these symptoms involved revisiting early memory and processing these memories in the context of a solid therapeutic alliance. By the beginning of the 20th century, after Freud had published *The Aetiology of Hysteria*, the political winds had shifted, as had the politics of psychiatry. Traumatic etiology was relegated to the background and endogenous intrapsychic conflicts moved to the foreground. We stopped looking at the environmental surround—the maltreatment of children—and turned our scientific gaze inward toward fantasy formation and the intricate topography of the mind.

Where Do We Go Today?

It has taken us nearly a century to get back to where we started—the work of Janet. Two concurrent social movements helped to reawaken our awareness of childhood trauma. In the 1970s, the returning Vietnam War veterans became quite active in seeking validation for their catastrophic experiences during the war. They organized themselves to obtain services from veterans hospitals and recognition for their suffering from their communities. Their illnesses became the focus for legal activity and psychiatric attention. Psychiatrists rediscovered "war neurosis" and learned from their patients about the aftereffects of severe, intense, and acute traumatic experience. Post-traumatic stress disorder became a diagnostic entity and was entered into the *Diagnostic and Statistical Manual of Mental Disorders* in 1980.

The other major social change that contributed to the reemergence of our awareness of childhood sexual abuse was the women's movement in the 1970s. Women meeting in consciousness-raising groups, helping one another to name their fears, their frustrations, and their hopes, began telling stories of sexual manipulation, sexual violence, and early experiences of sexual violation at the hands of family members. Women Against Rape centers sprang up across the country; from these centers rape-crisis-counseling centers were developed. Today, a strong grass-roots recovery movement exists, carrying the message about child abuse and dissociative disorders to the public. Individuals help one another in 12-step-type recovery groups, generating art, newsletters, books, workshops, and conferences to help heal themselves as well as educate clinicians and lay individuals.

As a result of these two powerful movements for social change, survivors of childhood sexual abuse found a voice and clinicians began to listen. By the 1980s we began to see new journals devoted to exploring the effects and the treatment of individuals so affected. A whole new subspecialty in psychiatry, psychology, and social work emerged: working with dissociative disorders. Today, however, troubling signs indicate that public and political retrenchment from various interconnecting and interactive factors are contributing to renewed denial and disavowal of the prevalence of child sexual abuse. Moreover, social, legal, political, and psychological pressures are undermining all that we have learned about the etiology and sequelae of this devastating societal problem.

Factor One

In many ways, the mass media have focused more attention on survivors than has the mental health establishment. Oprah, Phil, and Sally Jesse have featured shows alerting the public to the painful experiences of adult survivors, which has led to a "Geraldoizing" effect. Despite the fact that Geraldo Rivera has actually done a couple of interesting shows on multiple personality disorder and has devoted more time and attention to the consequences of severe childhood trauma than have many mental health professionals, his and other popular talk shows tend to be associated with sensationalism and exploitation. As a result, real problems are trivialized in the public mind. If Geraldo thinks it is interesting, it must be hype. The overall effect is chilling. Clients wonder whether their memories and intense psychic, even physical, pain associated with their abuse histories are merely childish bids for attention. A client who kept her childhood rape secret for 40 years spoke of her dread of being perceived as having the "designer" affliction of our time.

Factor Two

The effect on memory is one sequela of childhood trauma that muddies the water for both the layperson and professional. How reliable is memory?

Police and prosecutors of violent crime understand that survivors of psychological trauma make very poor witnesses. Janet brilliantly described the differences between what he termed "narrative memory" and "traumatic memory" (van der Kolk & van der Hart, 1989). Narrative memory is what we generally mean when we speak of memory. It involves a complex process whereby new experiences are integrated into preexisting schema or mental categories, along with the slow evolution and expansion of those schema. Traumatic memory is different. Trauma is an event or series of events that lies outside the ordinary, expectable events of life. It is overwhelming in its affective impact on the individual. It does not easily fit into preexisting schema, nor does it evolve easily with other memories. Traumatic memories are "dissociated." To use a computer analogy, narrative memory is stored on drive C, the drive that is generally available to consciousness and voluntary control processes. Although drive C may have subdirectories of unconsciousness as well, that is, memories that are repressed but can be brought into consciousness through psychoanalysis, dream work, free association, and the like, drive B, or dissociated, memories arise unexpectedly when someone or something triggers them into actualization: therapy, a child reaching a developmental milestone, a movie, a book, a television show, a death. Dissociated memories are fragmentary, illusive, uncertain, even terrifying.

If the trauma is not verifiable and if it occurred early in life and was severe, these dissociated states act as containers for memories and pain and assume the coherence of alternative selves, that is, separate personality or ego states that hold particular memories together. During the therapeutic process, the therapist and patient attempt to understand the nature of these drive B materials, retrieve them, and integrate them into drive C consciousness. In so doing, traumatic memory is integrated and assimilated into narrative memory.

For example, a 36-year-old woman who has been in therapy for three years struggling with depression and periodic panic attacks glances at her four-year-old daughter playing at the beach and suddenly remembers being raped by her father when she was four years old. In the following days, she questions her sanity and is unable to understand what is happening to her. Her therapist may also wonder about this bewildering experience. She will likely try to forget or trivialize it.

The impulse to both know the secrets of early trauma, and to tell it most typically fight with the impulse to keep the secret: what emerges is often jumbled and contradictory. That is the nature of traumatic memory! This is why victims are poor witnesses. The most common scenarios for survivors is to want to discredit their dissociated memories, not particularly to elevate them to heroic status. False memories, or memories that are iatrogenically induced during therapy, are not that common. Although some types of memories can be distorted or implanted in the minds of individuals under certain circumstances, evidence does not indicate that this occurs frequently, or even occasionally, in psychotherapeutic work with survivors of trauma.

Factor Three

Faludi (1991) states that approximately every 30 years a cultural backlash arises against nascent feminism. Even modest status gains by women are quickly followed by a cultural response indicating that these changes and gains are not good for society or women.

Sexual abuse and sexual violence are cast as women's issues, despite the fact that children of both sexes are affected by abuse. Attacks on feminism focus energy on maintaining the *status quo* in power relationships. As a result, child victims and adult survivors may be discredited under the rubric of women's issues. Faludi points to the 1980s as a decade of government retrenchment on women's issues, disproportionate cuts in funding for women's programs, and decreased commitment in government funding for battered women's programs, despite increases in domestic violence. A dramatic rise in sexual violence against women, an increase that outstrips other types of violent crimes, has been met with indifference at all levels of government.

The retreat from renewed awareness of child-abuse problems in general and sexual abuse in particular reflects this backlash. Interestingly, patients' veracity in therapy was never an issue until we began discussing issues of sexual abuse.

Factor Four

The changing legal climate regarding prosecution in civil incest suits has also affected adult-survivor issues. In the early 1980s, legal scholars began to reconsider the problem of seeking legal redress for crimes involving sexual abuse years after the commission of these crimes and after the statute of limitations had expired. In the *Harvard Women's Law Review*, Salten (1984) persuasively argued, "Given the latent nature and belated detection of many incest related injuries, the parent's special duty of care to his [sic] child, the youth of the incest victim, and the likelihood of psychological disabilities which preclude timely action, a tort suit for latent incestuous injuries is perhaps the paradigmatic example of special circumstances requiring equitable preservation of a potential remedy" (p. 220). As a result of this and other legal arguments, several U.S. state and Canadian provincial legislatures are considering changes in the law that toll the statute of limitations for both criminal prosecution of incest (incest *is* a crime) and civil incest suits from age 21 and/or from the time the facts of the crime are discovered. These changes in the law would acknowledge both the powerlessness of children to bring suit or initiate prosecution and the problem of associative memory, whereby memories of child sexual abuse may not be available to the victim until many years after the victimization.

This "delayed discovery" approach to civil litigation has precedent in cases involving injuries from asbestos and other harmful substances. Perpetrators are now within reach of the law years, even decades, after the commission of their crimes. This evolution in the law, however, has invigorated attacks against delayed memory in adult survivors. The False Memory Syndrome Foundation is dedicated to disseminating information on what its spokepersons describe as the growing threat of false accusations of incest and sexual abuse. Part of its mission is to provide financial assistance to families in need of legal services or legal counseling.

Conclusion

Freud anticipated the skepticism and criticism that would greet his views on sexual trauma as a cause of hysteria. Nevertheless, his views are as relevant today as they were 100 years ago. Freud discussed three aspects of work with traumatized patients:

- Patients reexperiencing an early life experience in a dissociative manner clearly demonstrate suffering, pain, shame, terror, and extreme helplessness. Suggested memories do not have this quality.
- Patients resist these memories both consciously and unconsciously and often disavow the memories immediately after the experience. People do not want to believe that they were betrayed by the adults whom they trusted for protection. Typically, such a belief requires a reorientation of one's frame of reference.
- Freud mentions that when he successfully suggested a scene to a patient, even the most compliant patients are unable to reproduce such scenes with the intensely appropriate affect and detail characteristic of dissociated memory. Although Freud did not speak of "dissociated memory" as such, he described it very sympathetically in *The Aetiology of Hysteria*.

Freud's critics had the final say, and Freud changed his mind about traumatic memories. The legacy of this intellectual struggle in psychiatry has affected tens of thousands of people whose early-life trauma has been ignored. For the past 15 years, we have struggled to reverse this legacy. We have made great strides in our understanding of female psychology, trauma, memory, and self-formation. Countervailing reactionary forces that are not grounded in scientific skepticism or informed by a spirit of inquiry would erase these gains. Both professionals and the lay public must meet this challenge by refusing to dishonor the struggles of those who refuse to forget.

References

Brownmiller, S. (1975). *Against our will: Men, women and rape*. New York: Simon and Schuster.

Faludi, S. (1991). *Backlash: The undeclared war against American women*. New York: Crown Publishers.

Freud, S. (1984). The aetiology of hysteria. In J. M. Masson (Ed.), *Freud: The assault on truth* (pp. 251–282). London: Faber and Faber.

Herman, J. L. (1992). *Trauma and recovery: The aftermath of violence from domestic abuse to political terror*. New York: Basic Books.

Herman, J. L., & Schatzow, E. (1987). Recovery and verification of memories of childhood sexual trauma. *Psychoanalytic Psychology, 4,* 1–14.

Masson, J. (1984). *Freud: The assault on truth*. London: Faber and Faber.

Russell, D. (1986). *The secret trauma: Incest in the lives of girls and women*. New York: Basic Books.

Salten, M. (1984). Statutes of limitations in civil incest suits: Preserving the victim's remedy. *Harvard Women's Law Journal, 7,* 189–220.

Shapiro, L. (1993, April 19). Rush to judgment. *Newsweek*, 54–60.

Tavris, C. (1993, January 3). Beware the incest-survivor machine. *New York Times*, Sect. 7, p. 1.

van der Kolk, B., & van der Hart, O. (1989). Pierre Janet and the breakdown of adaptation. *American Journal of Psychiatry, 146,* 1530–1540.

Watters, E. (1993, January–February). Doors of memory. *Mother Jones*, p. 24.

Wright, L. (1993a, May 17). Remembering Satan, part I. *New Yorker*, pp. 60–81.

Wright, L. (1993b, May 24). Remembering Satan, part II. *New Yorker*, pp. 54–76.

Susan P. Robbins

Wading Through the Muddy Waters of Recovered Memory

In her essay "Running Away from Sexual Abuse: Denial Revisited" Benatar (1995) addresses a timely and important topic—recovered memories of childhood sexual abuse. Delayed recovery of memories of traumatic events and the nature, validity, and accuracy of these memories have been at the center of a controversial and bitter debate among mental health professionals and researchers (see Berliner & Williams, 1994; Butler, 1995; Byrd, 1994; Ewen, 1994; Gleaves, 1994; Gold, Hughes, & Hohnecker, 1994; Gutheil, 1993; Lindsay & Read 1994; Loftus & Ketcham, 1994; Peterson, 1994; Pezdek 1994; Pope & Hudson, 1995; Slovenko, 1993; Wylie, 1993; Yapko, 1994a, 1994b).

Proponents of recovered memory believe that many victims of repeated childhood sexual abuse repress or dissociate all memory of their trauma as a mechanism for coping. Although conscious memory of the trauma is not available to the victim, it nonetheless is believed to affect one's social and psychological functioning in adulthood. Seeking therapy for various problems such as substance abuse, eating disorders, depression, or marital difficulties, unhappy adults (primarily white, middle- and upper-class women in their thirties and forties) report memories of abuse that usually surface during the course of therapy. Such memories may also surface while participating in recovery groups, attending self-help conferences, reading incest-recovery books, or as the result of a specific trigger event. These memories typically appear as terrifying images or flashbacks that proponents believe are genuine, if not precise, memories of earlier abuse. Professional knowledge about recovered memory is derived primarily from clinical case reports, and most proponents accept these case studies as confirming evidence.

Critics are skeptical of recovered memories because no reproducible scientific evidence supports these claims. They contend that the growing body of research on memory has consistently shown memory to be subject to inaccuracy, distortion, and fabrication. They have also raised serious questions about the therapeutic methods used to help clients "recover" memories, and some claim that the real feminist issue is the victimization of clients by their therapists who, either knowingly or unconsciously, are suggesting, implanting, and reinforcing memories of abuse that never happened. Many critics have expressed concern that indiscriminate acceptance of recovered memories will lead to a serious backlash of disbelief in authentic cases of abuse.

In the past five years, a rapidly growing body of literature has supported both sides of this contentious debate. Although social workers are often cited as central figures in this debate, leading social work journals have not previously addressed this controversy. Benatar's essay, although timely, adds little to this debate and is a prime example of practice prescriptions based on ideology and theoretical conjecture. In addition to a woefully inadequate review of the current literature in this area, the essay suffers from a lack of conceptual clarity, unwarranted assumptions, and factual inaccuracy.

At the outset, the issue of child sexual abuse is confused with that of "recovered memories" of abuse. These are, in fact, two different issues that have recently come to be associated with each other. The former deals with a well-documented phenomenon—the sexual abuse of children by parents, relatives, other adult caretakers, friends, acquaintances, and strangers. The latter involves the debate about traumatic memory, including the repression of traumatic events and delayed recovery of these memories. According to Loftus and Ketcham (1994), this is a debate about memory and not a debate about childhood sexual abuse.

Benatar expresses disdain for the popular media's skeptical stance about delayed memory, the techniques used to uncover such memories, and the growing incest-survivor industry. Casting this skepticism as an antifeminist backlash against sexual-abuse survivors, she discounts the crucial issue of "false memories" and asserts that those who even question the veracity of traumatic memories are eroding the important gains made in our recognition of childhood abuse. Throughout, she improperly equates skepticism about recovered memories with denial of child sexual abuse.

Adding to this conceptual confusion, Benatar fails to draw distinctions among children who are current victims of abuse, adults who have always remembered traumatic incidents of childhood abuse, and those who have only recently recovered previously amnesic memories. Because this important point is neither addressed nor explored, all client reports of childhood abuse (which she refers to as "their own stories") are inferentially cast as being equally valid descriptions of historical events.

Child Abuse: Past and Present Findings

Benatar correctly notes that "the reality of child abuse is well established." Given the increasing empirical evidence substantiating the reality of child abuse, it is most unfortunate that her ensuing discussion is based on specious analogies, incomplete data, and the use of unverified historical theories.

For example, labeled as "cultural dissociation," she equates the denial of the reality of Nazi death camps to what she believes is a prevalent societal denial of child abuse. In comparing the widely discredited beliefs of a relative few to a broader cultural misogyny that disavows child abuse, she engages in fallacious and distorted logic based on improper generalization and false analogy (see Fischer, 1970).

More problematic is the narrow sample of studies Benatar cites to support her discussion on the epidemiology of child sexual abuse, a problem further compounded by the lack of any critical analysis or discussion of the methodological limitations of these studies. A more thorough review of the literature reveals a broad range in the estimated prevalence of childhood sexual abuse. Although studies on child sexual abuse date back to 1929, few systematic studies utilizing careful statistical analyses were done before the late 1970s and early 1980s (see Demause, 1991). Retrospective surveys have reported base rates ranging from 6% to 62% for women (Burnam, cited in Peters, Wyatt, & Finkelhor, 1986; Wyatt, 1985) and between 3% and 31% for men (Landis, 1956; National Committee for the Prevention of Child Abuse, cited in Goldstein & Farmer, 1994). Researchers attribute the wide disparity in prevalence rates to the varying methodologies and definitions of sexual abuse used in each study. Studies that broadly define sexual abuse to include verbal propositions, for example, yield much higher estimates than do those using narrower definitions that only include forced sexual contact. Other definitions have included exposure, peeping, masturbation, unwanted kissing, and fondling (see Baker & Duncan, 1985; Finkelhor, Hotaling, Lewis, & Smith, 1990; Lindsay & Read, 1994; Russell, 1986, 1988; Williams & Finkelhor, 1992). Further complicating this problem, some studies fail to clarify the definition of sexual abuse being used (see Wassil-Grimm, 1995).

Because the primary focus of Benatar's essay is on recovered memories of abuse, the data she cites are also shaded by her failure to distinguish between incestuous and nonincestuous abuse. This is a critical point because the pathogenic and traumagenic nature of child sexual abuse has been linked in numerous studies to incest by a biological parent in general and, more specifically, to repeated molestation by fathers involving contact abuse and the use of force specifically (see Conte & Berliner, 1988; Elliott & Briere, 1992; Herman, 1981; Russell, 1986). Significantly, recovered memories typically involve repeated incest (see Bass & Davis, 1994).

It is difficult to obtain reliable data on incest because most studies do not make sufficient distinctions in their categorization of abusers. Based on a small number of retrospective studies, estimates indicate that approximately 4% to 5% of girls have reported being abused by a father, adoptive father, or stepfather before the age of 18 (Wassil-Grimm, 1995). Data from Williams and Finkelhor (1992) and Russell (1986) indicate that between 1% to 2.8% of girls are abused by a biological father. The rates are higher, of course, when abuse by other family members is included. Further, most cases of sexual abuse involve exhibition, masturbation, and both nongenital and genital touching rather than forced penetration (Lindsay & Read, 1994; Wakefield & Underwager, 1992). Russell's (1986) data showed a marked trend toward stepfathers abusing more frequently, using verbal threats, and being more severely abusive.

Two separate reviews of retrospective studies of childhood sexual abuse (Lindsay & Read, 1994; Wassil-Grimm, 1995) concluded that the preponderance of surveys indicate that the prevalence of intrafamilial incest is lower than the rates reported in the memory-recovery literature. In contrast, Demause (1991) contended that the known rates should be increased by 50% in order to correct for factors that lead to underreporting, including repression. Although the factors he cited are valid, his figures are based on pure speculation. Likewise, Bradshaw (1992) claimed that approximately 60% of all incest is repressed. To date, no replicable scientific evidence supports these claims. In a critique of what she sees as a "cycle of misinformation, faulty statistics, and unvalidated assertions" by incest-recovery authors, Tavris (1993) noted that inaccurate and sometimes concocted statistics are "traded like baseball cards, reprinted in every book and eventually enshrined as fact."

Another issue that is rarely discussed in the recovery literature is that not all children who are sexually abused experience the abuse as traumatic or develop psychological problems as an adult (Browne & Finkelhor, 1986; Kendall-Tacket, Williams, & Finkelhor, 1993; Russell, 1986). A review of recent empirical studies by Kendall-Tacket et al. (1993) found that many women are totally asymptomatic. Contradictory evidence also surrounds the relationship of sexual abuse to high levels of dissociation and multiple personality disorder (see Beitchman, Zucker, Heed, deCosta, & Cassavia, 1992; Brier & Elliott, 1993; Hacking, 1995; Kluft, 1985; Lindsay & Read, 1994; Nash, Hulsey, Sexton, Herralson, & Lambert, 1993a, 1993b). These findings should not minimize the severe trauma and psychological distress that some abuse victims experience; rather, they should alert us to the fact that the sequelae of childhood sexual abuse is not the same for all victims. Not surprisingly, those who demonstrate higher levels of traumatization and psychopathology are more often found in clinical samples than in the population in general (Russell, 1986).

It should be clear from the above discussion that *all* statistics on child sexual abuse should be interpreted very cautiously. Because of its hidden nature, child sexual abuse is seriously underreported. However, data from clinical samples, especially those samples undergoing therapy for childhood sexual abuse, are likely to overestimate its prevalence. Conversely, underestimates are likely if the data are based on retrospective surveys of adults in the general population, because some may choose not to report their abuse and some may not remember it. Despite discrepancies in the data, it is painfully clear that sexual abuse of children is a serious and pervasive problem that occurs more often than previously believed. As Pope and Hudson (1995) have astutely pointed out, even when conservative estimates of 10% for women and 5% for men are used, this means that 14,000,000 adults in the United States are former victims.

Revisiting Freud and Janet

Benatar gives a brief description of Freud and Janet's theories of repressed or dissociated trauma, supported only by historical case studies. Although case studies are an important source of information, they should not be confused with scientific findings. Despite a widespread belief in the validity of case reports that show repression or dissociation to be a common response to sexual abuse (see Blume, 1990; Chu & Dill, 1990; Courtois, 1988, 1992; Ellenson, 1989;

Erdelyi & Goldberg, 1979; Fredrickson, 1992; Kluft, 1985; Mennen & Pearlmutter, 1993), little support for this belief can be found in empirical studies. In a review of 60 years of research, Holmes (1990) could not find any controlled studies that supported the concept of repression.

The few studies that were initially thought to provide possible evidence of repression (Briere & Conte, 1993; Herman & Schatzow, 1987; Loftus, Polonsky, & Fullilove, 1994; Williams, 1994) have yielded divergent results, with rates ranging from 18% to 59%. Methodological limitations, however, restrict the ability of any of these studies to support fully the mechanism of repression or dissociation (see Lindsay & Read, 1994; Loftus, 1993; Pope & Hudson, 1995). Despite Benatar's assertion that the Herman and Schatzow study supports the claim of delayed traumatic recall, this study has received widespread criticism because of its nonrepresentative sample, lack of specification of methodology (including criteria for confirmation of abuse), the use of composites of cases, little or no amnesia in the majority of cases, and the possibility of suggestion during therapy (see Lindsay & Read, 1994; Pope & Hudson, 1995; Wassil-Grimm, 1995). In short, Herman and Schatzow's study is far from conclusive.

Studies have shown to the contrary that people typically remember their past abuse. Loftus, Polonsky, and Fullilove (1994) found that in their sample of 105 women involved in outpatient treatment for substance abuse, the majority (54%) reported a history of childhood sexual abuse; the vast majority (81%) had always remembered their abuse. In Williams's (1994) study of 100 women with documented histories of sexual abuse, the majority (62%) acknowledged their abuse when asked by the researcher. Because no follow-up interview was conducted in either of these studies, it is impossible to know whether those failing to report their past abuse did so due to repression, ordinary forgetting, normal childhood amnesia, or the desire not to disclose a painful event. Femina, Yeager, and Lewis's (1990) longitudinal study of 69 adults with documented histories of child abuse (primarily physical) found no evidence of total amnesia. The majority (62%) readily reported their abuse to the interviewer. Those who initially denied or minimized their abuse acknowledged in a follow-up "clarification" interview that they did, in fact, remember their abuse but chose to withhold the information for various reasons.

In order for us to validate the clinical impressions gained from current and historical case histories, we need carefully designed studies to test the repression/dissociation hypothesis. Pope and Hudson (1995) suggested that the design of the Williams study is a useful starting point. Strict criteria for inclusion and the use of clarification interviews, similar to those used by Femina et al. (1990) would be a necessary addition to the study design. Pope and Hudson proposed that a series of case reports could be used to present preliminary evidence if they strictly adhered to the research criteria. They noted that given the high prevalence of repression suggested by many authors, this area "begs further carefully designed studies to resolve one of its most critical questions." In sum, both the existence and prevalence of repression have yet to be scientifically validated; the same is true for the type of dissociative amnesia hypothesized in the recovery literature.

Traumatic Memory

In her discussion of traumatic memory, Benatar exhibits a seriousmisunderstanding of memory, in general, and memory organization, storage, and retrieval, in particular. Based on a narrow and inaccurate reading of van der Kolk and van der Hart's (1989) article, she presents an oversimplified typology of memory and compounds it with a misleading computer analogy.

Memory researchers widely accept that memory is *constructive* and *reconstructive*, not reproductive (Loftus, 1993; Loftus & Ketcham, 1994; Rose, 1992; Squire, 1987). Neuroscientist Steven Rose (1992) cautioned against the use of a flawed brain/computer metaphor:

> Brains do not work with information in the computer sense, but with *meaning* [which] is a historically and developmentally shaped process . . . because each time we remember, we in some senses do work on and transform our memories; they are not simply being called up from store. . . . Our memories are recreated each time we remember [emphasis added].

In their review of current research on memory processing, encoding, and state-dependent learning, van der Kolk and van der Hart (1989) reappraise Janet's early theory of psychopathological dissociation in an attempt to link it with recent findings. However, in contrast with Benatar's firm assertion that "traumatic memory is different," this is not what the authors conclude. They state that

> [Janet's notion] that traumatic memories are stored in memory in ways different from ordinary events is as challenging today as it was . . . almost 100 years ago. One century later, much remains to be learned about how memories are stored and keep on affecting emotions and behavior.

Likewise, in her ensuing discussion of trauma, dissociation, and memory, Benatar confuses theory with fact, stating that "if the trauma is verifiable and if it occurred early in life and was severe, these dissociated states act as containers for memories and pain and assume the coherence of alternate selves." Numerous studies on verifiable traumas (Leopold & Dillon, 1963; Malmquist, 1986; Pynoos & Nader, 1989; Strom et al., 1962; Terr, 1979, 1983) have shown to the contrary that vivid (although not necessarily accurate) recall of traumatic events is common. No subjects in these studies repressed the event or developed dissociative amnesia. Post-traumatic symptomatology most commonly involves intrusive images, flashbacks, nightmares, and anxiety attacks, such as those seen in Vietnam veterans.

It is also well established that adults rarely have recall of any events prior to the age of two or three and only sketchy memories up until age five (Fivush & Hudson, 1990; Loftus & Ketcham, 1994; Pendergast, 1995; Usher & Neisser, 1993). This normal "infantile amnesia" is developmentally based and is not due to trauma. Traumatic amnesia in adults is a well-documented phenomenon and involves either large portions of the memory (one's name, address, and other personal information) or circumscribed traumatic events, with good recall of everything prior to and subsequent to the event. In both cases, people are *aware* of the fact that they have amnesia (see Loftus & Ketcham, 1994).

In the last decade, with the revival of Freud's seduction theory and Janet's theory of dissociation, some clinicians and researchers have begun *theorizing* that traumatic memories of *repeated* childhood sexual abuse are encoded differently from other traumas and result in a total loss of awareness of not only the events but of the amnesia itself (see Herman, 1992; Terr, 1991, 1994). The idea that these painful memories are somehow "split off" or dissociated into compartmentalized areas of the mind remains an untested hypothesis. To date, attempts to establish a link between dissociated or repressed trauma and current findings in the neurobiology of memory have been speculative at best. Despite her personal conviction that traumatic memories and ordinary memories are qualitatively different, Herman (1992) acknowledged that "the biological factors underlying . . . traumatic dissociation remain an enigma." To paraphrase Klein (1977), we must avoid confusing what a theorist has merely claimed or believed with what she or he has actually proved or demonstrated. Even van der Kolk and van der Hart (1989) conceded that "we can neither confirm or [sic] contradict most of Janet's observations on memory disturbances following traumatization."

Veracity of Client Reports

Benatar is partly correct in her assertion that "veracity in therapy was never an issue until we began discussing issues of sexual abuse." However, this conclusion is based on the faulty premise that acceptance of a client's narrative truth is presumed to be an accurate historical account of events, which is not necessarily the case. In most cases, the veracity of a client's narrative report of life events is not an issue unless the therapist becomes aware of contradictions. It is important to note that allegations of sexual abuse, when made by children or adolescents, are now routinely subjected to extensive collateral verification by an independent investigator (Faller, 1988).

Although psychoanalysts since Freud have been trained to believe that memories of seduction and sexual abuse are incestuous wishes (Masson, 1990), the response on the part of most mental health professionals has been to ignore, minimize, or avoid the topic of sexual abuse (Craine, Henson, Colliver, & MacLean 1988; Jacobson, Koehler, & Jones-Brown, 1987; Post, Willett, Franks, House, & Weissberg, 1980; Rose, Peabody, & Stratigeas, 1991). Whether this is a result of disbelief is, according to Rose et al. (1991), a topic of endless debate. The fact that clinicians have routinely failed to inquire about or respond to reports of sexual abuse represents a serious omission, especially given the prevalence of abuse found in clinical populations.

Contrary to Masson's (1984) and Miller's (1984) assertions that Freud abandoned his theory about the primacy of incest in the etiology of hysteria, Demause (1991) argued that an unbiased reading of Freud shows that he continued to believe in his patients' spontaneous reports of *conscious* memories of abuse. Freud concluded that only *unconscious* memories of early infantile scenes of seduction were "phantasies which my patients had made up or which myself had perhaps forced on them" (cited in Demause, 1991). If Demause is correct, it would appear that even Freud came to question the veracity of *recovered* memories of sexual abuse but did not doubt those memories that were always remembered. In a similar vein, Hacking (1995) noted that Janet revised his early formulations and dropped the concept of dissociation in his later writings. He eventually came to believe that double (or multiple) personality was a special and rare case of bipolar disorder, which he termed "les circulaires." It is interesting that the proponents of recovered memory extensively cite his earlier work while ignoring his later ideas.

It is widely acknowledged that it is impossible to verify charges of sexual abuse in the absence of external corroboration. Because of its hidden nature and the tendency for perpetrators to deny their guilt, it is sometimes difficult to find the necessary corroboration, especially decades after the alleged abuse occurred. But we must be clear that clinical judgment alone is not a sufficient predictor of veracity. In his discussion of the child sexual abuse accommodation syndrome, Summit (1983, 1992) acknowledged that "there is no clinical method available to distinguish valid claims from those that should be treated as fantasy or deception." He further cautioned that "the capacity to listen and the willingness to believe … is not an admonition to interrogate or assume that every disclosure is real" (Summit, 1992). Clearly, we must be open to listening to our clients and willing to help them explore issues of past abuse. However, we must be cautious about accepting a client's narrative truth as historical fact in the absence of corroboration. This is especially true in the case of recovered memories; some memories may be fully accurate, some may be partly accurate, and some may be totally false. This does not imply that we should disbelieve our clients but rather that we maintain a neutral stance about historical accuracy. Historical accuracy becomes mandatory, however, when this debate is moved from the therapist's office into the courtroom (see Gutheil, 1993; Slovenko, 1993).

A more controversial but intricately related issue that Benatar fails to address is that of recovered memories of satanic ritual abuse, alien abductions, past lives, preverbal body memories, in *utero* trauma, and cellular memory (see Goldstein & Farmer, 1993, 1994; Mack, 1994; Mulhern, 1991; Pendergrast, 1995; Richardson, Best, & Bromley, 1991; Robbins, 1995; Smith, 1995; Victor, 1993). These memories raise interesting questions regarding both the veracity of client reports and the therapeutic methods used to retrieve or recover them: Are all such memories possible? If not, which ones are? Where do we draw the line? Based on what criteria? How can we determine their accuracy? These questions are significant because a growing number of therapists involved in memory- recovery therapy believe in the validity and accuracy of all recovered memories (Loftus, Garry, Brown, & Rader, 1994; Smith, 1995; Yapko, 1994a, 1994b). Not surprisingly, their clients come to believe in them as well.

False Memories: Fact or Fiction?

Skepticism about "false memories" is often voiced by proponents of recovered memory because it is seen as a backlash to the discovery of childhood sexual abuse and an attempt to silence the victims; as such, false memories are equated with "denial" of abuse (Bloom, 1995; Rockwell, 1995). In the past several years this has become the subject of debate in scholarly journals and professional conferences. Because these issues become tangled and confused, it is important once again to make the distinction between the debate about memory and the documented reality of abuse; the false-memory debate is not about the latter.

A growing body of research has shown that partially and wholly inaccurate memories are not an unusual phenomenon. Because memory is extremely malleable, it is influenced by various factors, and false memories can be created through exposure to misinformation (Loftus, 1993; Terr, 1994). According to Terr, a false memory can be "a strongly imagined memory, a totally distorted memory, a lie, or a misconstructed impression." Numerous studies have shown that people can be led to construct not only inaccurate and confabulated details of past events, but detailed memories of entire events that never happened (see Haugaard, Reppucci, Laurd, & Nauful, 1991; Loftus, 1993; Loftus & Ketcham, 1994; Neisser & Harsch, 1992; Pynoos & Nader, 1989; Spanos, Menary, Gabora, DuBreuil, & Dewhirst, 1991).

Evidence about erroneous memory has sparked concern that memories of abuse are being created by therapists who, through well-intentioned but misguided therapeutic methods, may directly or indirectly evoke specious memories with the use of hypnosis, guided visualization, "truth" drugs, abreactive therapy, dream and body memory interpretation, or suggestive questioning (Byrd, 1994; Gangelhoff, 1995; Gutheil, 1993; Lindsay & Read, 1994; Loftus, 1993; Ofshe & Watters, 1994; Pendergast, 1995; Yapko, 1994a). Although proponents of recovered memory therapy incorrectly believe that false or suggested memories cannot be experienced with the same emotional intensity as can recovered memories of real trauma, evidence suggests otherwise (see Loftus & Ketcham, 1994; Yapko, 1994a). As Loftus and Ketcham noted, reconstructed memories, once adopted, come to be believed in as strongly as genuine memories. Concern about false memory is bolstered by detailed accounts of coercive therapy and lawsuits filed by "retractors"—hundreds of women who have left therapy and recanted their allegations of abuse (see Goldstein & Farmer, 1993, 1994; Pendergrast, 1995).

Studies documenting distorted and confabulated memory in children and adults have been discounted by some proponents of memory recovery because they do not speak directly to the issue of false memories of childhood sexual abuse. Benatar echoes this position along with reservations similar to those noted by Berliner and Williams (1994) and Pezdek (1994) that little scientific evidence supports the claim that false memories of abuse are common or that memory-recovery therapy is widespread. Because little research has been done in this area, this is an accurate appraisal of our lack of scientific knowledge about false memories induced in therapy. However, it is noteworthy that many who accept the "truth" of recovered memories of childhood victimization are not willing to extend the same credibility to those who claim they were victimized by their therapists. Nonetheless, methodologically sound studies are necessary to validate the phenomena of false memory as well as recovered memory; we must rely on the same standard of proof for both.

Where Do We Go From Here?

Clearly, the reluctance of clinicians to address the reality of child sexual abuse poses a serious barrier to accurate and effective assessment and treatment. Rose et al. (1991) noted that "short- and long-term sequelae result not only from sexual and physical abuse, but from inappropriate treatment and nonrecognition of the abuse." Given social work's commitment to multidimensional assessment and holistic, nondichotomous thinking (see Compton & Galaway, 1989; Haynes & Holmes, 1994; Hepworth & Larsen, 1993; Morales & Sheafor, 1995), it is critical that clinical practitioners gather accurate information about their client's past and present biopsychosocial functioning, strengths and resources, developmental history, significant life events, and reactions to and feelings about these events. In this holistic context, it would be unconscionable to fail to inquire about physical and sexual abuse—past or present. We must be sensitive to the fact that clients may choose initially not to disclose their abuse until a level of trust is developed in the therapeutic relationship. Failure to disclose should not *automatically* be assumed to be due to repression or dissociation.

We must also be cautious about hastily attributing a laundry list of non-specific symptoms to prior abuse, as this defeats the purpose of a multidimensional assessment. When a previously repressed history of sexual abuse is revealed, it is especially important to consider the use of collateral sources of information because clients may themselves be confused about these memories. However, collateral sources should never be used without the client's express permission. The use of collateral sources does not imply that the social workers should take on the dual roles of investigator and therapist, because doing so represents a serious conflict of interest (Mason, 1991). Instead, collateral information should be used to help both the practitioner and the client gain a well-rounded picture of the situation. Hepworth and Larsen (1993) noted that important factors that may otherwise be overlooked can often be identified by persons close to the client. According to van der Kolk and van der Hart (1989), Janet frequently interviewed his patients' family members and acquaintances in order to get as complete a picture as possible.

Conclusion

Social workers who work with victims of childhood sexual abuse, especially those whose claim is based solely on recovered memories, should become acquainted with the full range of clinical and social scientific literature on the topic. Clinical case studies must be balanced with scientific findings; both are crucial sources of knowledge. Many clinicians receive only training or information that supports a narrow ideology and practice methodology. As I have suggested elsewhere (Robbins, 1995), social workers must be fully informed in order to "evaluate critically these disparate ideological positions and the adequacy of the research that supports them." This is especially important because a recent study by Feld (1995) found that few social workers are provided with any content about memory or memory retrieval in their academic programs.

In addition, social workers need to be fully aware of their own personal biases in order to prevent them from interfering with assessment and treatment. Preconceived beliefs about repression, dissociation, and recovered memories may lead to an ideological stance that inhibits thorough and accurate assessment. It is imperative that we recognize the serious consequences for our clients and their families when our personal biases lead us to either underdiagnose or overdiagnose childhood sexual abuse. Further, we must remember that the imposition of our personal values and beliefs is antithetical to our deeply held value of client self-determination (Hepworth & Larsen, 1993).

As a result of the lack of scientific verification and the polemical debate shaping research and practice, we must wade cautiously through the muddy waters of recovered memory. Social workers may feel caught between two conflicting sets of claims that demand allegiance to one side or the other. It is doubtful, however, that positioning ourselves at the extremes of this debate will lead to a stance that is in the best interests of our clients. Amid the black and white positions of what Loftus and Ketcham (1994) call the "true believers" and "skeptics," a middle-ground stance is often hard to find, despite the grey areas of uncertainty and ambiguity that exist. Acknowledgment of these grey areas does not mean, however, that one is in "denial" or is uncaring or negligent as a practitioner. We must be open to new findings in this area but we must also be cautious in distinguishing between conjecture and fact.

Finally, when skepticism about the ideology of the recovery movement is based on a thorough review of valid, scientific findings, it must not be cast as antifeminist backlash. As Klein (1977) aptly noted, "Scientific questions are to be settled by appeals to evidence rather than by appeals to authority—even the authority of a Freud."

POSTSCRIPT

Can Memories of Childhood Sexual Abuse Be Recovered?

The controversy surrounding the accuracy of recollections of abuse (sometimes called false memories) tends to obscure the issue regarding the susceptibility of human beings to adopt false beliefs at the suggestion of someone else. In typical cases a person establishes a belief that abuse has occurred before any memory of it has surfaced and then looks for evidence to confirm the belief. Robbins uses this explanation to reject the accuracy of these memories, whereas Benatar argues that we should accept them more readily.

Making a revelation about child abuse may leave an individual deeply depressed and even suicidal. Equally problematic is the impact on the family, who is often torn apart psychologically and forced to endure a nightmarish court battle when the alleged perpetrator of the abuse is summoned to court. The challenge is to ascertain the difference between what a person feels and believes versus the literal, physical reality upon which the memories are based. Should we, as a society, turn our backs in disbelief on all those coming forth with repressed memories? Do we continue our present trend of predominant belief and acceptance of these allegations? What about a person who cannot prove such allegations but experiences the pain of the abuses and believes they occurred? Do we merely turn our backs, or do we try to help even though the allegations may not be true? Finally, if we do choose to help, how do we go about providing such assistance?

Suggested Readings

Berliner, L., & Loftus, E. (1992). Sexual abuse accusations: Desperately seeking reconciliation. *Journal of Interpersonal Violence, 7*(4), 570–578.

Gardner, R. A. (1994). Differentiating between true and false sex abuse accusations in child custody disputes. *Journal of Divorce and Remarriage, 21*(3), 1–20.

Gellert, G. A. (1995). Sensitivity and specificity in child abuse detection. *Journal of Child Sexual Abuse, 4,* 99–104.

Ney, T. (Ed.). (1995). *True and false allegations of child sexual abuse: Assessment and case management.* New York: Brunner/Mazel.

Scotford, R. (1995). Myths, memories and reality. *Contemporary Hypnosis, 12*(2), 137–142.

Yapko, M. (1993, September/October). The seductions of memory. *The Family Therapy Networker,* 30–37.

Contributors to This Volume

EDITORS

DIANA S. DELCAMPO is the child development and family life specialist with the New Mexico Cooperative Extension Service at New Mexico State University in Las Cruces, New Mexico, and holds the rank of professor. She is a member of the National Council on Family Relations and the National Extension Family Life Specialists' Association. She received a BS from Concord College in West Virginia, an MS from Virginia Polytechnic Institute and State University, and a PhD in curriculum and instruction from the University of Michigan. She presently develops educational programs in child and family development, supervises grant projects, and coordinates projects with other state agencies in New Mexico. She has published educational guides, chapters in several books, symposium proceedings, and articles in various journals.

ROBERT L. DELCAMPO is a professor of family science at New Mexico State University in Las Cruces, New Mexico. He is a licensed marriage and family therapist, clinical member, and approved supervisor of the American Association for Marriage and Family Therapy. He also holds memberships in the International Family Therapy Association and the National Council on Family Relations, and he is a former president of the New Mexico Association for Marriage and Family Therapy. He received a BS from the State University of New York, an MS from Virginia Polytechnic Institute and State University, and a PhD in family relations and child development from Florida State University. His work has appeared in such journals as *Family Relations* and *Contemporary Family Therapy*.

STAFF

Larry Loeppke	Managing Editor
Jill Peter	Senior Developmental Editor
Nichole Altman	Developmental Editor
Beth Kundert	Production Manager
Jane Mohr	Project Manager
Tara McDermott	Design Coordinator
Bonnie Coakley	Editorial Assistant
Lori Church	Permissions

AUTHORS

ADVOCATES FOR YOUTH is an organization in Washington, D.C., that helps youths make informed and responsible decisions about their reproductive and sexual health.

RUDOLPH ALEXANDER, JR. is a professor in the department of social work at Ohio State University and is the current director of the social work program.

KERBY ANDERSON is the president of Probe Ministries International, holds an MFS from Yale and an MA from Georgetown University, and is the author of several books.

DIANA BAUMRIND is a researcher at the Institute of Human Development, University of California at Berkley and is known nationally for her publications and research on parenting and spanking.

MAY BENATAR is a clinical social worker in private practice in Montclair, New Jersey. She currently teaches and lectures to professional groups on sexual abuse and the treatment of dissociative disorders.

WILLIAM J. BENNETT is codirector of Empower America. He served as secretary of education under President Ronald Reagan and as director of the White House Office of National Drug Control Policy under President George Bush.

T. BERRY BRAZELTON is founder of the Child Development Unit at Children's Hospital Boston and has been a practicing pediatrician for 45 years. He has authored many books on children and families.

JEANNE BROOKS-GUNN is professor of child development and education at Teacher's College, Columbia University, and the author of numerous publications. Her specialty is policy-oriented research focusing on family and community influences on child and youth development.

PAUL CAMERON is the publisher of the Family Research Report, Colorado Springs, Colorado, which examines data on families, sexual social policy, drug addiction, and homosexuality.

MARK A. CARROZZA is the director of the Institute of Health Policy and Health Services Research at the University of Cincinnati. The Institute addresses local, state, and national health care issues from an interdisciplinary perspective.

THE CENTER FOR SCIENCE IN THE PUBLIC INTEREST is a consumer advocacy organization that conducts research in order to represent citizens' interests and provides information to consumers about health.

STEPHANIE COONTZ is cochair of the Council on Contemporary Families and teaches history and family studies at Evergreen State College in Olympia, Washington. She has written several books, including *The Way We Never Were: American Families and the Nostalgia Trap* (Basic Books, 1992).

PHILIP A. COWAN is a researcher at the Institute of Human Development, University of California at Berkley.

FRANCIS T. CULLEN is the Distinguished Research Professor of Criminal Justice at the University of Cincinnati and has interests in criminology and white collar crime. He has written four books in the area of crime and theory.

CARLA M. CURTIS is a professor at Ohio State University. Her areas of research interest include child and family policy, social welfare policy, and regulatory analysis.

W. J. DOHERTY is both a professor and marriage and family therapy director at the University of Minnesota in St. Paul, Minnesota.

KYLA DUNN is a former biotech researcher and is now a reporter for PBS and CBS.

MARTHA F. ERICKSON is director of the University of Minnesota's Children, Youth and Family Consortium. She developed the Steps Toward Effective, Enjoyable Parenting (STEEP) and is the author of numerous journal articles and book chapters as well as a weekly parenting column.

NANCY FOLBRE is cochair of the National Network on the Family and the Economy and is professor of economics at the University of Massachusetts. Her interests include the interface between economics and feminist theory. She has written numerous books and papers.

JIB FOWLES is a professor of communication at the University of Houston–Clear Lake. He is the author of *The Case for Television Violence* (Sage Publications, 1999).

DAVID GATELY was a graduate student of psychology at the Ohio State University in Columbus, Ohio, when he coauthored "Favorable Outcomes in Children After Parental Divorce" for the *Journal of Divorce and Remarriage.*

ELIZABETH THOMPSON GERSHOFF is a researcher with the National Center for Children in Poverty, Columbia University, Mailman School of Public Health.

STANLEY I. GREENSPAN is clinical professor of psychiatry and pediatrics at George Washington University Medical School.

WEN-JUI HAN is assistant professor of social work at the Columbia University School of Social Work. Her professional interests include effects of maternal employment and impact of welfare reform.

THE HENRY J. KAISER FAMILY FOUNDATION is a non-profit, private operating foundation that focuses on providing unbiased information on major health care issues.

LESLIE DOTY HOLLINGSWORTH is an assistant professor at the University of Michigan in Ann Arbor, Michigan. Her research focuses on the adoption of children and on children's racial identity.

WADE F. HORN is assistant secretary for children and families in the department of health and human services. He has been a clinical psychologist, president of the National Fatherhood Initiative, and a columnist for the *Washington Times.*

MERRILYN O. JOHNSON is from the Nursing Ph.D. Collaborative Program at the Medical University of South Carolina and the University of South Carolina in Columbia, South Carolina.

LISA KOLB is a public information specialist for the Missouri Department of Social Services in Jefferson City, Missouri.

EDWARD F. KOUNESKI is currently completing his doctoral dissertation in family social science, with a specialization in marriage and family therapy, at the University of Minnesota.

STEPHEN KRASHEN is currently a professor of education at the University of Southern California and is the author of more than 250 articles and books in the fields of bilingual education, neurolinguistics, second language acquisition, and literacy.

LAWRENCE A. KURDEK is a psychologist at Wright State University in Dayton, Ohio.

ROBERT E. LARZELERE is a researcher with the department of psychology's Munroe-Myer Institute, Nebraska Medical Center in Omaha, Nebraska.

LORI A. McGRAW is the 4-H program coordinator for the Oregon State University Extension Service. Her responsibilities include involvement in the school-age child care programs and the 4-H Adventures Program.

NATIONAL ADOPTION INFORMATION CLEARINGHOUSE provides accurate information related to adoption and is a federal service of the Children's Bureau, Administration for Children Youth and Families, U.S. Department of Health and Human Services.

GREG PARKS is an intern program specialist in the Research and Program Development Division at the Office of Juvenile Justice and Delinquency Prevention, which is part of the United States Department of Justice.

DAVID POPENOE is a professor of sociology and an associate dean for the social sciences at Rutgers–The State University in New Brunswick, New Jersey. He is the author of *Disturbing the Nest* (Aldine de Gruyter, 1988).

ROSALIE PEDALINO PORTER of Amherst, Massachusetts is an advisor to school districts across the United States on the education of immigrant children.

SUSAN P. ROBBINS is an associate professor in the Graduate School of Social Work at the University of Houston in Texas. She is the author of *River and Jungle* (Random House, 1993).

LISBETH B. SCHORR is director of the Harvard University Project on Effective Services in Boston.

ANDREW I. SCHWEBEL is a professor in the department of psychology at The Ohio State University in Columbus, Ohio. He is coauthor, with Mark A. Fine, of *Understanding and Helping Families: A Cognitive-Behavioral Approach* (Lawrence Erlbaum, 1994).

SEXUALITY INFORMATION AND EDUCATION COUNCIL OF THE UNITED STATES (SIECUS) is a national nonprofit organization in New York that promotes comprehensive education about sexuality and advocates individuals' rights to make responsible choices about sexual behavior.

THOMAS M. VANDER VEN is assistant professor in the department of sociology and anthropology at Ohio University in Athens, Ohio. His areas of specialization are crime and delinquency as well as linkages between work, family, and crime.

JANE WALDFOGEL is associate professor of social work and public affairs at Columbia School of Social Work. Her professional interests include social policy impact on child and family well-being as well as child protective services and child welfare policy.

ALEXIS J. WALKER is both a professor of human development and family sciences and director of the gerontology program at Oregon State University.

ROBERT A. WEINBERG is a member of the Whitehead Institute for Biomedical Research and is a biology professor at MIT.

MARY-LOU WEISMAN is a freelance writer who has written about children, ethics, and social issues for the *New York Times* and *The New Republic*.

JOHN PAUL WRIGHT is an instructor in the division of criminal justice at the University of Cincinnati.

KARL ZINSMEISTER is editor in chief of *The American Enterprise* and the author of a book on the American family to be published soon.

Index